Aryan Problem Revisited

Edited by
Devendra Swarup

Originals
Delhi

Articles first Published in the Journal '*Manthan*' in
April-Sep. 1994 & October 1994-March 1995 Issues

Published with Permission 2017

ISBN 10: 81-8454-151-1
ISBN 13: 978-81-8454-151-9

Published By
Originals
(an imprint of Low Price Publications)
A-6, Nimri Commercial Centre,
Near Ashok Vihar Phase-IV,
Delhi-110052
Phones: 011-27302453
e-mail: info@Lppindia.com
Website: www.Lppindia.com

Printed At:
D K Fine Art Press P Ltd.
Delhi-110052

PRINTED IN INDIA

Contents

Introduction

The Aryan Race and Invasion Theory is not a subject of academic interest only, rather it conditions our perception of India's historical evolution, the sources of our culture and socio-economic-political institutions. Consequently, it has a strong bearing on the contemporary Indian politics as well as the future of Indian nationalism.

The teaching of Indian history begins with the so-called Aryan invasion of India. According to this theory, a race of people called "Aryans" entered India around 1500 BC and conquered the native people, who were "Dravidians" and "Austrics", and imposed their language and religion on them, besides creating a social order which converted the natives into the "lower castes" in a hierarchical caste-structure. It is to be noted that almost all the current disintegrative and separatist movements–whether regional or casteist in character– have their intellectual roots in this Aryan Race and Invasion Theory.

The most extraordinary aspect of the theory of Aryan invasion is that it has its genesis not in any Indian records, but in European politics and in German nationalism. It has no support either in literature, tradition or science. It is essentially the creation of 18th and 19th century Europeans, especially Germans that was later adopted by the British colonial government as a convenient administrative tool to divide and control the people of India.

So the Aryan invasion has been a political creation right from the start. It was also racial in origin. It is interesting to note that several leading researchers in Europe and America are in the process of rejecting the Aryan invasion theory. But Indian history books are not yet prepared to accept the verdict.

The issue assumes importance because it is a question relating to the origins of our culture. In fact, our identity depends upon it. For thousands of years we have looked to the *Vedas* as the wellspring of our existence. None of our ancestors ever questioned it. And now, in the last century and a half, others are telling us that the *Vedas* don't really belong to us. That they are impositions by barbarians foreign invaders.

Are we to accept this without raising questions and examining the credentials of these people, who, not coincidentally were alien colonisers, and their modern Indian followers? Should we not feel suspicious about their motives–that they may be making the imposition of their own alien ideas acceptable to us by claiming all our tradition to be alien imposition?

One of the great myths perpetuated about nineteenth century European scholars is that they were somehow dedicated scholars free from human weaknesses like ambition, bias, prejudice and even dishonesty. They were products of their age and no one is free from the biases of the age. Most of them had missionary and political axes to grind. Max Muller in fact had been paid by the East Indian Company to further its colonial aims. The idea of the Aryan race and the Aryan nation has its roots in European anti-semitism and German nationalism that eventually led to Nazism in Germany. It is not a coincidence that the most articulate proponents of the Aryan invasion of India also happened to be ardent German nationalists like Max Muller, Lassen and Weber.

Even after nearly fifty years of Independence, Indian historians belonging to the mainstream continue to toe the Western line. They rarely question the idea of Indian history and culture imposed upon them by Western scholars. They seem more concerned about what westerners think about them than advancing independent views. They have taken great pains to keep abreast of Western fashions. This does not lead to originality.

Shocked by the outbreak of the First World War the Western scholars such as C.J.H. Hayes, Boyd C. Shafer and Hans Kohn etc. made a deep study of the evolution and character of nationalism in Europe. They have exposed the unscientificness of many of the social sciences which were used in the nineteenth century to create the myth of Aryan Race and Invasion.

Now, with the discovery of the lost track of the *Rigvedic* river Saraswati, the excavation of a chain of Harappan sites from Ropar in the Punjab to Lothal and Dhaulavira in Gujarat all along this lost track, the discovery of the archaeological remains of *Vedis* and *Yupas* connected with *Vedic Yajnas* at Harappan sites like *Kalibangan,* decipherment of the Harappan script by many scholars as a language of the Sanskrit family, the view of the archaeologists like Prof. Dales, Prof. Allchin etc. that the end of the Harappan civilisation came not because of the so called Aryan invasion but as a result of a flood, the discovery of the lost Dwarka city beneath the sea water near Gujarat coast and its similarity with Harappan civilization–all these new discoveries establishing full identity of the Harappan civilization with *Vedic* civilization demand a re-examination of the Aryan Race and Invasion Theory.

Interestingly, many Western scholars are also having a second look at the nature and antiquity of the *Vedic* literature in general and the *Rigveda* in particular. On the basis of new researches in linguistics and other branches of sciences such as mathematics, geometry and even astronomy etc. many scholars are inclined to place the antiquity of *Rigveda* somewhere around 5000 B.C. which, knocks down the prevalent chronological framework of Indian history.

Indian savants like Swami Vivekanand, Sri Aurobindo and Dr. B.R. Ambedkar had long back rejected this theory as unscientific and untenable.

As a result of all these researches the Aryan Race and Invasion theory is seriously questioned in the West, as is evident from a book written originally in French by a Russian scholar Leon Poliakov titled "The Aryan Myth" of which an English translation was published as far back as 1974.

It is difficult to believe that the Indian scholars who are still dinging to this outdated theory and are fighting for its retention in our history text books, are not aware of all these researches and studies. Obviously, they seem to be guided more by their ideological prejudices and political inclinations than by objective and scientific research. But now many Indian scholars such as K.D. Sethna, Dr. S.R. Rao, Dr. S.P. Gupta, B.K. Thapar, Prof. S.S. Misra, Bhagwan Singh, Shrikant Talageri, N.R. Waradpande, Dr. Subhash Kak, Dr. N.S. Rajaram etc. have brought out serious research studies demolishing this theory and exposing its political roots.

It is high time that the Indian Intelligentsia. Journalists and people come forward to expose and defeat the vested interests which are still using this outdated theory to further their disintegrating and separatist politics aimed at the weakening of Indian nation as well as falsification of history.

Almost a year ago, to be precise, on 9th December, 1993, the Deendayal Research Institute and the Voice of India, jointly organised at Delhi a symposium on the Aryan Problem in Indian History. Many eminent archaeologists and historians, such as S.R. Rao, the excavator of Lothal & Dwarka, Prof. S. S. Misra, Head of the Deptt. of Linguistics. B.H.U., Dr. N.S. Rajaram, formerly a scientist at NASA in U.S.A, Shrikant Talageri of Bombay. S.P. Gupta of Delhi participated.

On that occasion the above statement was drafted in the Institute and issued to the Press.

This statement fully delineates our view of the Aryan Problem and its bearings on the future of India as well as the world at large. The present two issues of Manthan are our humble effort towards the fulfillment of the appeal made at the end of that statement. The first volume presents some historiographical studies on the genesis and application the Aryan myth, while the second volume brings together recent archaeological, philological and even astronomical researches by very competent scholars in India and abroad. We hope these researches will go a long way in preparing the ground for exploding this myth forever.

Earlier, we had tried to present a historiographical review of the genesis of the Aryan Race Theory, the search for its original homeland anywhere outside the modern boundaries of India, and, as its corollary, of an Aryan invasion on India. This review clearly shows that this theory was born out of the European politics of the nineteenth century and was applied to Indian history only to serve the imperialist policy of the British colonialists on one hand and the religious aims of the Christian missionaries on the other. Rooted in the national rivalries of the nineteenth century Europe, this theory of the superiority of an imaginary Aryan race became the bedrock of the nascent German nationalism against French domination, leading to the French-German Wars resulting in the unification of Germany in the year 1871. The rising tide of racial nationalism with strong imperialist ambitions drowned the whole world in the blood-pools of the two World Wars, which were nothing but the outbursts of the continuing national rivalries among white peoples of European origin. These European people, belonging to the different newly emerging nation-states took their national prejudices, born out of false national identities, which, in its turn, were created by the half-baked, subjective nineteenth century theory of an organic relationship between language, blood and culture. This belief in rigid separate national identities became a major psychological obstacle to the process of welding the different linguistic groups of European migrants to the U.S.A. into an integrated homogeneous American personality.

This American problem followed by the First World War (1914-1918) made many perceptive European and American intellectuals to re-examine the nature and history of the modern nationalism of European brand, as well as to have a fresh look at its intellectual foundations built by the newly born social sciences such as philology, anthropology and archaeology etc. This disillusionment of western intellectuals may be best summed up in the following words of the great American historian Carlton J.H. Hayes written as A Personal Apology dated July 18, 1960 in his work *Nationalism : A Religion* (Macmillan 1960).

"Most of my adult life has been devoted to observation and study of nationalism. My interest in it was first aroused by the outbreak of the World War I. That event took me by surprise and shocked me out of the easy optimism about a future of uninterrupted progress and international peace which I had shared with many of my generation, and it showed me, too, that merely economic considerations did not really explain the ultra- patriotic popular acceptance of war. In the autumn of 1914, I wrote for the *Political Science Quarterly,* a first article on nationalism."

Similarly, we find another great intellectual–Sir Julian Huxley shocked by the outbreak of the World War II, declaring the Aryan race theory a myth created by the most subjective and unscientific minds. The two UNESCO statements on Race and Race-Differences published on July 18, 1950 and June of 1951 pronounced, in a way, the death-knell of the so-called scientific racism invented by the nineteenth century European patriot-scholars. Thus, Europe and America have got rid of the *frankestein* of the Aryan Myth. But it is puzzling to see that a section of Indian academicians claiming themselves to be scientific historians are still clinging to this exploded myth, to an extent that they go hysteric at the very mention in the textbooks of Indian history of this alternative view emerging out of the recent philological, anthropological, archaeological and historical studies.

On a closer examination of their writings one may discover their real motives and bias behind this stubborn unscientific attitude. In fact, the Aryan Race and Invasion theory seems to have become a powerful instrument in the hands of divisive and separatist forces in India. Born in politics, this theory continues to be a tool of party politics and ideological battle that goes on in this country. One has only to read a fortnightly called *Dalit Voice* to have a feel of these political overtones. This fortnightly professing to be the spokesmen of the Dalit Movement, relishes to paste European labels such as Aryan Nazis is Fascists etc. to those whom it considers its adversaries. Similarly, Muslim fundamentalist scholars are also trying to use this discredited theory to justify their own separatist politics and to beat the forces of nationalism. As an example of this line of thinking, we reproduce some quotes from an article published in the *Observer of Business and Politics,* dated 30 Oct., 1993, under the title "Exploding the Aryan Myth." The author claims to be a sympathiser of the Muslim cause. He sees in Hindutva movement its arch enemy and charges that "the Hindutva theory of indigenous Aryans is governed by political calculations." Elucidating these calculations, he writes: "the newly discovered historical truth" appears to be a key element in the fascist and rabidly anti-Muslim discourse of the Hindutva brigade. The obsession with Aryans and their origins reveals that the Hindutvawadis, like their Nazi counterparts, fanatically believe in the thoroughly discredited Aryan master-race theory."

He does not care to explain how removal of the Aryan race theory from the text books is compatible with the belief in the Aryan master-race theory. Admitting the vested interest in the Aryan invasion theory he says. "Radical tribal, dalit and backward caste movements have today become a force to reckon with, and they are attempting to mobilise support by projecting the "upper" caste Oppressors as the descendants of Aryan invaders who forcibly enslaved the Dravidian aborigines of this land" and therefore, "the assertion that the Aryans were not outsiders and invaders can be seen as a response to "lower" caste assertion to the contrary, and as a means to effectively silence protests against the imposed "upper" caste hegemony." At another place he writes, "If Muslims have to be projected as the sole invaders of this land, the Aryans need to be presented as natives." Perhaps, the scholars of this breed believe that there can be no research without any partisan political objectives and any attempt to update textbooks in the light of recent researches should be dubbed as politically motivated.

What is most unfortunate is that the Marxist historians, who have come to control through political machinations the History Department in many universities and the establishments like Indian History Congress and Indian Council of Historical Research, instead of exploding the myths created by the colonialists, are employing all their intellect and influence to perpetuate them. Beginning from D.D. Kosambi they readily accepted the Aryan race and invasion theory and even now, when researches in various disciplines have gone much ahead, they are steadfastly clinging to this exploded theory, which is evident from the latest writings of Prof. R.S. Sharma, who is now-a-days leading the Marxist school of historians. This is not the place to examine all his information and arguments in favour of the Aryan invasion or migration theory, but it may be mentioned that Prof. Sharma places ideology above everything and in his own words he believes in the dictum, "no ideology, no history." Although the ideology of Marxism has lost much of its ground and relevance outside India, here it seems to have become an identity-symbol for group formation in the field of academics. Hence to accept the results of recent scientific researches may mean to abandon the positions taken earlier and thus a loss of Identity. Otherwise, why should such an erudite scholarship react so strongly to any mention of the alternative views and should insist on the perpetuation of one-sided picture. Anyhow, a detailed critique of the Marxist position or Aryan Problem is very much called for.

In this book, we have tried to present some of the fruits of the recent researches by most competent scholars on this issue. They speak for themselves and do not need of any comment from us. We gratefully acknowledge and feel deeply indebted to their scholarly contributions to the cause of objective research.

1

India's Image in XVIII Century Europe

A. Leslie Willson*

German readers by 1750 had learned much about India. From the ancient writings of Greek historians something was known of the fabled land, its monsters, its strange customs, and its inexplicable philosophical and religious affinities with the Western world, but nothing was known of its literature. Fable collections and literary treatments of the epic of Alexander contributed little information about India proper. Seventeenth-century novels offered spurious or superficial India backgrounds.[1] Though there was a host of travellers after Portuguese and Dutch explorers opened wedges in India, travelers whose journeys to the East turned into tomes, the principal sources were the accounts of Baldeus, Bernier, Mandelslo, and Rogerius. From these noteworthy observers it was learned that the great subcontinent of India was peopled, not with savage aborigines, though there exited strange, even repulsive sects, but with a civilized, even a cultured race. In a pleasant countryside, so favoured by nature's abundance that it was likened to the Garden of Eden,[2] the purity of white contrasted pleasantly with the green luxuriance of vegetation. The people, whose hierarchy of priests enjoyed the exclusive privilege of being able to read the prosody of the holy books, received instruction on the origin of things; they were admonished to observe principles of right moral conduct. The rites of the *Brahmans* indicated that their system of religious worship was very old. A belief in metempsychosis, already familiar to Europeans through Pythagoras, was found to be flourishing in India, minutely defined and deeply interwoven into the canopy of religion and of great influence upon everyday living. The body of legend, the extent of which was hardly recognized by the early travelers, was a token of an ancient society. A host of new ideas began to seep into the intellect of Europe, and the tongues of Europe tasted strange and exotic words, among them: Ganges.

---

* An American researcher. This article is from his work, "*A Mythical Image: The Ideal of India in German Romanticism:*" Duke University Press, Durham N.C. 1964

1. *Les Brames sont les maitres de Pythagore, les instituteurs de la Grece, et par elle de l'Europe entiere.*

BAILLY

Although the number of volumes of travel literature concerning India was sizable before 1750, examples of this literary genre increased mightily between 1750 and 1800. They were a generally widespread and favorite reading matter in the second half of the eighteenth century. Collections of books of travel began to appear as early as 1747,[3] and by 1780 there were six multi-volumed collections available.[4] A number of periodicals of the era, too, carried either reports about or excerpts from travel books. The collections contained mainly reprint of older accounts of travels, but concurrently there appeared from the pens of contemporary travellers a multitude of journals, histories, narratives, memoirs, and communications, some not dependable and some most authoritative. It was in these books that the Romantic mythical image of India had its inception, for from them were culled the opinions and assumptions and beliefs which, when gathered and sorted and combined by theorists who were compelled by an attitude of philosophical humanism and bursting with a longing for primal verities, resulted in the development of that mythical image.

From the plethora of travel books and treatises on India which appeared in this half century, the following are representative of a host of minor works: Gerbett, Gatterer, who calls the Hindus the gentlest of people,[5] Niebuhr, who describes Indian pagodas and provides numerous pictures of Indian sculptures,[6] Rochon, Stavorinus, and Boyd.[7] Reinhold Forster (1729-1798) translated several books on India and published two collections of travel narratives, one with Matthias Sprengel (1746-1803).[8] Sprengel himself later published a selection of geographical and statistical reports about newly discovered lands and their inhabitants.[9] Jean Bernouli (1744-1807) also brought out a three-volume compilation about India.[10]

The persuasion that India was the source of all wisdom had prevailed for centuries. John Z. Holwell (1711-1798), a former governor of Bengal and a survivor of the famed Black Hole of Calcutta, gives an account of his favourable impression of the religious and moral percepts of India. Because of his acquaintance with one of the holy books of the Hindus (the Sanskrit *Satapatha-brahmana,* called the *Chartah Bhade* in Holwell's adaptation,)[11] he believed he discerned a great influence of Indic culture upon other lands in ancient times. The more familiar he became with the Sanskrit work, the more clearly he claimed to see that the mythology as well as the cosmology of the Egyptians, the Greeks, and the Romans was borrowed from the teachings of the *Brahmans* contained in the *Satapatha-brahmana*. Even the extreme rituals of Hindu worship and the classification of Indic gods found their way West, although extremely falsified and truncated.[12]

Another statement concerning India as the originator of knowledge came from Alexander Dow (d. 1779), who spent some time in military service with the East India Company as a colonel, and who translated Firishtah's history of Hindustan in 1768. He prefaces his translation of the Persian historian with a "Dissertation Concerning the Customs, Manners, Language, Religion and Philosophy of the Hindoos," in which he makes the understatement that the "*Brahmans* of the East possessed in ancient times, some reputation for knowledge."[13] The French translator of this work affirms in the preface more comprehensively the probability that the Persians, the Egyptians, the Greeks themselves, and perhaps the Chinese originally received their wisdom from Hindustan.[14] The same idea was advanced in 1775 by Voltaire (1694-1778), in a letter to the astronomer Jean Sylvain Bailly (1736-1793), in which he said that he finally was convinced that astronomy, astrology, and metempsychosis had come to the West from the Ganges.[15] Bailly himself, although he believed that the Persians, the Chinese, and the Indians had all descended from a common ancestral people, nevertheless wrote that the *Brahmans* were the masters of Pythagoras, the tutors of the Greeks and, through them, of all Europe. He called the wisdom of India *sage and sublime*.[16] William Macintosh, in 1782, adds further to this picture of the sublimity and the antiquity of Indian knowledge and its influence on the West:

> All history points to India as the mother of science and art. This country was anciently so renowned for knowledge and wisdom, that the philosophers of Greece did not disdain to travel thither for their improvement.[17]

Between 1768 and 1781 Pierre de Sonnerat (1794-1814), a learned student of the French botanist Philibert Commerson, made several trips to the East Indies and to India. In his account of these voyages he writes that many people came to the Hindus to borrow the elements of their wisdom, and that Pythagoras left Greece to study under the *Brahmans*, regarded then as the most enlightened of men. Sonnerat, too, places the inception of wisdom in India when he writes that India, in all its splendor, gave religions and laws to all other peoples, and that Egypt and Greece were indebted to India for all their fables and their sapience.[18]

The German translators of English, French, and Italian travels literature often could not refrain from either appending an investigation of their own—a miscellany of foreign lore they themselves had collected—or else commenting with approval or disapproval in footnotes upon the work at hand. Such a translator was Christian Dohm (1751-1820), who translated the narrative of Edward Ives (d. 1786) into German in 1774. Dohm was perhaps the first to think of India in terms of the cradle of humanity. In a footnote to Ives he observes that the production of coco palms and other trees and plants occurred naturally and did not have to be achieved by artifice and inventiveness. He wonders if this fact should not support the very probable hypothesis, founded on other grounds, that India was the true fatherland, the cradle of the human race.[19] Further on in the volume he elucidates in more details, saying that the requirements of life, food, shelter, and clothing were simply gifts of nature in India and did not have to be attained through labor and ingenuity as in less mild regions of the earth. He uses this reason to reinforce his thesis that India appeared to have first nourished human culture, and he finds that the historical proofs for the antiquity of the Indians and their philosophy receive new weight from this physical principle. He suggests that it is a priori, presumable that the human mind occupied itself earliest with objects of metaphysical speculation in such regions where human activities were already sustained with enough for physical needs. He asserts that this was particularly so in South Asia, especially in India, which in this respect had advantages over China.[20]

At the end of this passage Dohm apologizes for the digression and asks his readers for ideas relative to the thesis he proposes. He seems to believe that he is the first to suggest that India may be the very birthplace of civilization. Dohm states that the chief source for his supplementary remarks was Holwell, and doubtless it was from this author that he took the theory that geographical location, the whole milieu of a bountiful nature and climate, affects the way of life and the mode of thought of a people,[21] although such a theory had been implied earlier, in 1756, by Voltaire in his *Essai sur les maeurs et Tesprit des nations,* where, speaking of India, he states that mankind gathered as a matter of course in its delightful climate.[22]

Louis Marie Degrandpre (1761-1846), a French voyager with scholarly pretensions, disputed Voltaire's implication that India was the original home of humankind, and was bold enough to say in his travel narrative that he dared to presume the *Ezur Veda*, supposedly written before the conquests of Alexander, had not been written in Bengal at all. He said further that, were it not for the respect he had for the ashes of the man, he would have the audacity to oppose the opinion of a great author who had not hesitated to declare that India, toward the Ganges, was the land in which mankind first assembled in social groups.[23]

Dohm, in another footnote to Ives, conjectures that the heat of the climate dried up all violent, dissolute passions among the Indians. Nature, which gratified all his needs effortlessly, prevented the Indian from being mischievous and deceitful, and he became so only when unnatural despotism deprived him of the gifts of nature. Dohm further believes that the philosophy of India and its religion is an outgrowth of a simple culture in a state of harmony with a beneficent nature, not the result of subjective speculation. The philosophical ideas are symbols with a rich content—perhaps more original than those of any other people—inspired more by nature and self-reflection than by political priests or lawgivers.[24] Sonnerat, as well, remarks on the effect of climate upon the intellectual development of a people, saying that it is certainly true that the first sparks of reason burned brilliantly in those climes because intellectual faculties do not develop except where physical needs are quelled. Several times he points to the agreement of Indian mythology and religious dogmas with those of all the Asiatic peoples. This similarity was for him indisputable proof that all the Eastern religions had a common source in India, presumably the birthplace of all nations.[25]

Travel narrators and commentators in the latter half of the eighteenth century shared the common belief that India was very ancient. The translator of the French edition of Dow says that the philosophical wisdom one finds in the *sastras*, the purity of their dogmas concerning the unity, the attributes, and the providence of God, concerning the immateriality and immortality of the soul, the liberty of man, the punishments and requitals to come, to most important questions of theology and metaphysics which one finds discussed there, all of this spirit, and consequently a preceding antiquity of a prodigious length.[26] Dow himself says "there are many hundred volumes in prose in the Shanscrita language, which treat of the ancient Indian, [and] the author...has great reason to believe, that the Hindoos carry their authentic history farther back into antiquity, than any other nation now existing."[27] Sonnerat believes that all peoples go back to a real or a fabulous origin, but declares the origin of the Hindus was lost in the night of time, and that among the Indians could be found the vestiges of a most distant antiquity.[28]

Robertson, in his disquisition on India, predicates his own theory of the great age of their culture on the antiquity of Indian commerce, which he holds to be evidence of a highly civilized society. He finds further proof in government, citing the vast kingdoms encountered by the Greeks of Alexander's expeditionary forces.[29] The conception of India as the very source of civilization, as the nation where human culture was first bred, contributed in great measure to the formation of the Romantic mythical image of India.

The curious mixture of primitivism (for the Indians were not a mechanical society) and sublime culture (but they had developed the arts to a high degree) was in the possession of a people who were appraised differently by various observers. Holwell, representative of a minority, reveals a sharply critical opinion of the people of India. He announces that the Hindus, taken as a whole, are as spoiled, craftly, superstitious, quarrelsome, and malicious a people as any in the known world, if not worse, especially the common swarm of *Brahmans*.[30] This view might perhaps be explained in Holwell's case by his incarceration in the Black Hole and no doubt by the fact that his relations as a governor with foreign subjects were not conducive to pleasant experiences.

Guilliaume le Gentil de la Galaisiere (d. 1792), who travelled to India in 1761 to observe the transit of Venus and who stayed almost two years at Pondichery, delineates a more flattering picture of the Hindu. He describes especially the natives of the coast of Coromandel (a part of India frequented often by Europeans because of European settlements there). The Indians are quite handsome and well-formed, he reports, noticing particularly their black, lively, soulful eyes. He reiterates that India is the most accommodating and charming land under the sun, and that it is inhabited by the gentlest and most obliging of peoples.[31]

Macintosh, always favorable in his estimate of every phase of Indian life and culture, says:

> Their persons are straight and elegant, their limbs finely proportioned, their fingers long and tapering, their countenances open and pleasant, and their features exhibit the most delicate lines of beauty in the females, and in the males a kind of manly softness. Their walk and gait, as well as their whole deportment, is in the highest degree graceful.[32]

The temperament of the Indian conformed to the ease of his life in the midst of the bounteous nature which impressed most travellers. Ives says that the Indians are a very quiet and harmless kind of people who would insult no one.[33] Macintosh comments with enthusiasm: "The tranquillity of their minds, even in the most trying circumstances, is expressed by a constant smile that sits gracefully on their placid countenances," and he goes on to say that "the Hindoos are naturally the most inoffensive of all mortals." He comments at greater length on the skill of their imitative talents as artisans and their intrepidity of spirit:

> In Asia, particularly in India, both on this side and beyond the Ganges, there is a scrupulous tenacity of ancient customs and manners...In arts [of imitation] the Hindoos are so dextrous, that the original model is not

> to be distinguished from the new production...For works of imitation, their nature seems peculiarly fitted, by that patient perseverance which so eminently distinguishes them...And with all this perseverance and straining of attention, they preserve an evenness of spirit.[34]

Sonnerat, describing the inhabitants of the Coromandel coast, says that they are black, both tall and well-made, but weak, lax, and effeminate. He says their natures incline to joy and gaiety, and that they love games, dancing, spectacles, and music.[35] Pierre-Marie-Francois Pages (1748-1793), in his *Voyages autour du monde* 1767-1776 (Paris, 1782), praises the simple, innocent customs of the Indians, their orderly and quiet way of living, and is inclined to credit their abstinence from eating meat and highly spiced foods for their striking gentleness of spirit.[36]

A Carmelite monk, Paulinus a Sancto Barthologmaeo (an Austrian, born Johann Philipp Wesdin, 1748-1806), who was among the earliest to devote himself to the study of India and Sanskrit,[37] is astonished at how one people differs from another. The Indians are agile, nimble, and weak, but are polite and obliging. They act after reflection, love moderation, and lead a very decent life. The Arabians, on the other hand, are clumsy, coarse, robust, and loyal, but seldom take regard of reason and propriety.[38]

Macintosh, in his boundless ardor for the Indian, would place him above the European:

> In refinement and ease [the Hindus] are superior to any people to the westward of them. In politeness and address, in gracefulness of deportment, and speech, an Indian is as much superior to a Frenchman of fashion, as a French courtier is to a Dutch burgomaster of Dort...The *Hindoos*, especially those of the higher Castes, are in their demeanor easy and unconstrained....but their ease and freedom is reserved, modest, and respectful...An Indian [is polite] because he respects you.[39]

The moderation of the Hindus was noticed by Ives, who says that they are very temperate in eating and drinking, and seldom use strong liquor except as medication. His translator, Dohm, also has a favourable picture of the India, whom he calls good-natured, calm, moderate, and comparable to the ever-pure Indian sky. In yet another footnote to Ives, Dohm praises the moral sense of the Hindu, which is ingrained in him by the teachings of the *Vedas* through the *Brahmans*. He says that their moral teachings are immense and broad; their morality is not exactly prescribed, not hypercritical, but noble and honourable. Their morals and customs are not capricious and decisive, but conciliatory and patient.[40] Macintosh, also, has praise for Indian morality in the tradition of the *Brahmans*, saying that "their moral principles were the most sublime that could be imagined."[41]

The high code of moral conduct, however, was damaged by the influx of Europeans, who brought greed to the gentle, inoffensive Hindu. Ives says that somewhat deeper inland the people were also said to be very honorable and upright, and that on the coast they presumably knew nothing of deceit until they learned it from European traders. His translator and commentator Dohm also mentions the ruinous example of foreigners.[42] Reinhold Forster, who provides many footnotes for the German edition of Paulinus' *Reise,* also cannot refrain from mentioning the deleterious influences of the Mohammedan and the European on the Hindu. He accuses the Muslim princes of being the first to bring misery to the formerly happy lands and says that what the Mohammaedans began the Europeans finished, bringing with them as soldiers the refuse of all nations.[43]

Paulinus himself calls attention to the intelligence of the Indians exhibited in their aptitude for language. He relates that from time to time several young Indians came to him, some of them heathen, some converted to Christianity, some speaking French quiet well, others, who had received instruction from the Jesuits, knowing Latin. Thus he decided that the Indians had aptitudes for scholarly pursuits, and that their Indic dialects uncommonly facilitated their mastering of European languages.[44] Degrandpre is also cognizant of the ease with which the *Brahmans* learned languages, saying that it was marvelous, and further that they all spoke and wrote French, English, Portuguese, Arabic, the Malabar dialect, and their holy language, which no one not belonging to their caste knew.[45] Macintosh is very impressed that education does not seem limited to a select group, but that

> . . . even the inferior classes are taught reading, writing, and arithmetic: the youth are taught, not within doors, but in the open air; and it is a singular, but not unpleasing spectacle, to behold, in every village, a venerable old man, reclined on a terraced plain, teaching a number of surrounding boys, who regard him with the utmost reverence and attention, like a shepherd feeding his flock. In those simple seminaries....the gentle and tractable sons of the Hindoos are not only prepared for the business, but instructed in the duties of life; a profound veneration for the object or objects of religious worship; a reverence of their parents; respect for their seniors; justice and humanity towards all men, but a particular affection for those of their own Caste.

Concerning the language spoken by the Hindus, Macintosh is full of admiration: "The Hindoo language is beautiful, expressive, and nervous. In reading and speaking, the Hindoos are very musical...There is a dead language, understood only by...the priests, called the *Sanscrit* language, in which their sacred volumes are written."[46]

The commentators emphasize that the keepers of the holy language, in which were preserved all of India's treasures of knowledge, were most unwilling to divulge their mysteries or to instruct the Europeans in Sanskrit; not even fellow Hindus might be taught to read the holy texts, for the *Brahmans* through the centuries had reserved this privilege for themselves. Dow says: "The *Vedas* are, by the *Brahmins*, held so sacred, that they permit no other sect to read them....The *Brahmins* themselves are bound by such strong ties of religion, to confine those writings to their own tribe, that were any of them known to read them to others, he would be immediately excommunicated." He also mentions that "these books not only treat of religious and moral duties, but of every branch of philosophical science." Dow himself received instruction in Sanskrit but found it very difficult to learn, hard to pronounce, and so complex that when the time came for him to leave India he had not learned it thoroughly.[47]

Dohm, again in his appendix to Ives, remarks that the *Brahmans* accept no converts to their religion, chiefly because they do not wish to reveal Sanskrit, the vehicle of their knowledge and religion. It is well-known, he says, that the *Brahmans* accept no proselytes and hand their teachings on only to their descendants and never, except with the greatest of resistance, instruct foreigners.[48] Degrandpre writes that the *Brahmans* are little communicative. It is a tenet of their religion, he says, to withhold the knowledge of their language and their books from all the world.[49] But Robertson records that Europeans have, only after hundreds of years of direct intercourse with India, just now begun to win the confidence of *Brahmans*:

> That all the science and literature possessed by the *Brahmins*, were contained in books written in a language, understood by a few only of the most learned among them, is a fact which has long been known; and all the Europeans settled in India during three centuries, have complained that the *Brahmins* obstinately refused to instruct any person in this language. But at length, by address, mild treatment, and a persuasion, that the earnestness with which instruction was solicited, proceeded not from any intention of turning their religion into derision, but from a desire of acquiring a perfect knowledge of their sciences and literature, their scruples have been overcome. Several British gentlemen are now completely masters of the Sanskrit language. The mysterious veil, formerly deemed impenetrable, is removed.[50]

The remarkable stability of the social system in India rested on the division of the populace into castes, a segregation promulgated in the holy books. And the only interpreters of the sacred writings, the *Brahmans*, had maintained their immutable supremacy in the caste hierarchy in part because of the tenacity with which they held to their privileged position as wardens of the ancient, hallowed language. Specifically, Degrandpre says that if anything could keep the *Brahman* on his exalted pedestal it was the secrecy which they spread over their primeval tongue, their mysteries, their holy books, and over the wisdom involved. And more than anything, perhaps, was the privilege they insisted upon of attending to the altars themselves. The fact that some English scholars had succeeded in learning Sanskrit and in translating various works found in that ancient tongue seemed to indicate to Degrandpre that the *Brahmans* were now in danger of losing their high and select position, if, indeed, they had not falsified the material they supplied to translators, thereby observing the religious injunction not to reveal the mysteries of their religion or the cryptic language in which it and their other knowledge was couched.[51]

Paulinus is awed by the fact that the Sanskrit books, containing the wealth of Indian wisdom, were written in verse, and that even their astronomy, art of medicine, and history were divided into cantos.[52] This observation did not go unnoticed by Romantic theorists, who trumpeted a universal poetry, the poetic expression of all wisdom.

Macintosh lauds the ancient tradition of *Brahman* purity:

> It appears, from the concurring testimony of ancient writers, that the *Brahmins* of India, about two thousand years ago, lived innocent, pure, and austere lives, abstaining from wine and animal food; and as much as possible, from all sensual enjoyment. They...endeavoured to shelter their feeble virtue by retirement in caves and woods, where they subsisted on the spontaneous productions of the earth.

He deems it no compliment to his contemporaries that the *Brahmans* are no longer appreciated as well as they had been in the ancient past. He believes that, although the *Brahmans* as a social and ethical group may have become decadent, their philosophy has maintained its original "pure and excellent" virtues.[53] Dohm would place the burden of degeneration upon foreign depravities. He purposely says nothing regarding in the religious concepts of India because previously travelers had usually mixed up everything: the profound philosophy of the *Brahmans* with the silliest superstitions of the rabble, pure concepts which had originated in India with absurd ideas which had crept in from abroad.[54]

Dow excoriates European travelers for casting aspersions upon a religion and a philosophy they failed to investigate in an effort to understand its strange ways.[55] Macintosh stoutly defends the Hindu against charges of idolatry:

> Thus far only the Gentoos are idolators, that in worshipping the great God of the universe, they place before their bodily eyes, for the information of their minds, such representations as are calculated to recall, in a vivid manner, to the imaginations, those attributes which they believe that Almighty being only to possess.[56]

And Sonnerat, also, disavows the charge of idolatory and gives a succinct description of the Supreme Being worshipped by the Indians. He denies that the Hindu wisemen are idolators, for they only invent tales which the *Brahmans* recite to maintain the faith of the people. They worship a supreme and infinite Being, and when asked how they would depict God, they reply without hesitation that He is as difficult to depict as the voice which leaves the mouth of the sound of a bell. Such phenomena can only be heard, just as God can be felt without being defined or depicted in a perceptible form.[57]

In his translation of a *sastra* of the *Vedas*, Dow presents a dialogue in which Narud (Reason) speaks with Brihma (the Wisdom of the Divinity) and seeks to realize a conception of God:

> NARUD: What shall we think of God?
>
> BRIHMA: Being immaterial, he is above all conception; being invisible, he can have no form; but, from what we behold in his works, we may conclude that he is eternal, omnipotent, knowing all things, and present everywhere.[58]

Even Paulinus, the Carmelite monk, is aware of the essence of the Hindu deity, for he avers that the Indians believe in a single, true God who has the fundament of His existence in Himself and lives from eternity to eternity.[59]

Thus the sketchy knowledge which Europeans had before 1750 concerning India was extended and enlarged by the multitude of travel books and commentaries, printed singly or in many collections, in the last half of the eighteenth century. These accounts are chiefly subjective and written in an uncritical manner with a highly affirmative praise of India and the Hindu. A curious mixture of fact, fiction, and opinion offers the source for the development of the mythical image of India refracted by German Romanticists.

India was looked upon as the source of all human wisdom. Through long centuries the ancient culture which had developed in the very cradle of humanity, the land of the Ganges, had brought forth a great array of natural sciences and a complex system of religion whose influence was extended to all the Western world through the Greeks. The great antiquity of the *Brahmans*, whose historical beginnings were lost in the ages, attested the immemorial character of the Hindu religion and of the language which had preserved the tenets of that religion for millenia. The high development of ancient Indian culture was proved by the cryptic prosody of its religious scriptures and the hoary ruins of its pagodas and their fantastic sculptures. No other people on earth seemed so old, and certainly and no other people revealed a culture whose sublimity in arts and the sciences and philosophy was so ancient.

The contemporary Hindu was pictured as an unspoiled child of nature, whose simple and gentle spirit risked depravity by less cultivated Europeans. His moral sense, imbued into him for centuries, was broad and admirable. He was moderate in his sensual enjoyments and gifted with an inborn intelligence. These exalted people were not idolators, but worshipped a God whose essence in metaphysical terms was not unlike the familiar God of Christianity.

All these attributes of India and the Hindu needed but the stamp of authenticity to initiate the development of a mythical image, and this stamp was supplied by the first Sanskrit translators.

Notes & References

1. Immensely popular (ten editions between 1689 and 1766) because of sensational, sanguinary battles, human sacrifice, and the pomp of exotic ceremonies was the *Asiatische Banise* by Heinrich Anselm von Ziegler und Kliphausen. Heroic-galant in the tradition of the *Amadis-Roman*, Ziegler's novel was much imitated, furnishing even an opera (J. Becceau, 1710) and a dramatic tragedy (Friedrich Wilhelm Grimm, 1733). The villain Chaumigrem appears later as a figure in the puppet theater of Goethe's young Wilhelm Meister. Ziegler dealt freely with his sources; the most frequently cited is Rogerius. In the novel Bhartrihari furnishes the name of "Bartrouherri," the Moorish commander of Chaumigrem's field peices; see Henrich Anshelm von Zigler and Kliphausen (*sic*), *Asiatische Banise oder blutiges doch muthiges Pegu* (Leipzig, 1707), in *Deutsche National-Litteratur,* ed. Joseph Kurschner (Berlin, n.d.), XXXVII, 285. Another novel with a fainty India background in the flamboyant style and manner of Ziegler's *Asiatische Banise,* and provoked by its success, was *Der asiatische Onogambo* (Hamburg, 1673) by Everhard Guerner Happel. The excrescent subtitle sums up the work's grandiose ambitions and its limitations: "Darin Der jetzl-regierencde grosse Sinesische Kayser Xunchius. Als ein umbschweiffender Ritter vorgestellet, nachst dessen und anderer Asiatischer Printzen Liebes-Geschichten und ritterlichen Thaten, auch alle in Asien gelegene Königreiche, sampt deren Beschaffenheiten, Ordnung ihrer Regenten, und dren vornechmsten Thaten kurtzlich mit eingefurt werden."
2. It is doubtful whether Olearius is correct in assuming that Mandelslo speaks of Ceylon in saying that "Maffaeus wie auch Paulus Venetus (lib 3 c 22) schreiben auch. . . dass man darvor halte / es haben unsere erste Eltern

ihren Sitz allhier gehabt / und sey in dieser Gegend das Paradiss gewesen;" see Olearius, *Reisebeschreibung* (1658 ed. of Mandelslo), pp. 146. The site of the Garden of Eden in India is generally laid in Kashmir; see Francois Bernier, *Voyages* (2 vol.; Amsterdam, 1699), II, 277: "De tout ce que je viens de dire on peut assez conjecturer que je suis un peu charme de Kachemire; & que je pretens qu'il n'y a peut-etre rien au monde de pareil any de si beau pour un petit Royaume...& ce n'est pas sans quelque raison que les Mogols l'appellent le Paradis Terrestre des Indes."

3. Schwabe, *Allgemeine Historie.*
4. Grundmann, pp. 17-18, and pp. 18, n.1.
5. Johann Christoph Gatterer, *Allgemeine historische Bibliothek* (16 vols.; Halle, 1767-1771), VI, 233 f.
6. Carsten Niebuhr, *Reise nach Arabien* (3 vols. Copenhagen, 1774-1778), II, 32 ff.
7. For the works of authors not supplied in footnotes, see Bibliography.
8. Reinhold Forster and M.C. Sprengel, eds., *Beitrage zur Volker-und Landerkunde* (14 vols.; Leipzig. 1781-1784, 1786-1790). Forster was co-editor of only three volumes (to 1783); the remainder were edited by Sprengel alone. See also Reinhold Forster, trans. and ed., *Magazin von merkwurdigen neuen Reisebeschreibungen* (16 vols,; Berlin, 1790-1798).
9. M.C. Sprengel, *Auswahi der besten auslandischen geographischen und statistischen, Nachrichten zur Aufklarrung der Volker-und Landerkunde* (14 parts in 7 vols.; Halle, 1794-1800).
10. *Jean Bernoulli, ed. Description historique et gèographique de l'Inde* (3 vols; Berlin, 1786-1789). Volume 3, Part 2, dated 1789, is a translation of *Des Pater Josef Tiefenthaller's....historisch-geographische Beschreibung von Hindustan,* first published in Berlin, 1785-1788.
11. J.Z. Holwell, *Merkwurdige historische Nachrichte von Hindostan and Bengalen,* trans. J.F. Kleucker (Leitpzig, 1778), pp.266 f. Since Holwell states that he did not have time to learn Sanskrit, his *Chartah Bhade* was not taken directly from the original. Grundmann (p. 71) states that Holwell's source, the *Satapatha-brahmana,* was later lost.
12. Holwell, p. 275.
13. Alexander Dow, trans.,*The History of Hindostan* (from the Persian of Firishtah, Muhammad Kasim ibn Hindu Shah) (3rd ed.; 3 vols.; Dublin, 1792), I, xix. In the "Dissertation" Dow relates his own impressions of the customs and culture of India and gives also a partial translation of a *sastra* of the *Vedas.*
14. Alexander Dow, *Dissertation sur les maeurs, les usages, le langage, la religion et la philosophie des Hindous,* trans. M.B....(Paris, 1769). pp.xiv.
15. Jean Sylvain Bailly, *Lettres sur l'origine des sciences et sur celle des peupies de l'Aste adressèes a M. Voltaire* (Paris-London, 1777), pp. 1 ff.

16. *Ibid.*, pp. 51.

17. Macintosh, I, 310.

18. M. (Pierre de) Sonnerat, *Voyage aux Indes Orientales* (2 vols.; Paris, 1782), I, 3, 4. This author, who laced his first-hand observations with anecdotes culled from Rogerius, supplied Goethe with the sources for two Indic-colored works: "Der Gott und die Bajadere" and "Paria".

19. Edward Ives, *Reisen nach Indien und Persien,* trans. Christian Willhelm Dohm (2 vol.; Leipzig. 1774), j, 100-101. Dohm was later the author of *Geschichte det Englander und Franzosen im ostlichen Indien* (Leipzig, 1776).

20. Ives *Reisen*, I, in Dohm's "Zusatze des Ubersetzers," pp. 41-42.

21. Holwell, pp. 317.

22. Francois Voltaire, *Qeuvres completes,* ed. Louis Moland, (52 vols.; Paris, 1877-1885), XI, 49.

23. B. [*sic.* L.] *Degrandpre, Reise nach Indien und Arabien in den Jahren* 1789 *und* 1790 (Berlin, 1803), p. 196. He refers here to Voltaire's conjecture in the *Essal sur les maeurs* that the Indians in the region of the Ganges were perhaps the most ancient people assembled in tribes (*Oeuvres*, XI, 49). Actually, Degrandpre's suspicions later were confined, for the *Ezur Veda* was a fraud. Voltaire also called India the cradle of all the arts (Oeuvres, XI, 158).

24. Ives, I, 375-342.

25. Sonnerat, I, 3.

26. Dow, *Dissertation,* pp. xii-xiii.

27. Dow, *History,* I, iv.

28. Sonnerat, I, 2-3.

29. Robertson, pp. 257, 262-263.

30. Holwell, pp. 313 t.

31. Guillaume (Joseph) le Gentil (de la Galaisiere), Reisen in den indischen Meeren 1761-69, in Vols. II and IV of *Neue Sammlung von Reisebeschreibungen* (Hamburg, 1781), IV, 324, 308. The original work was *Voyage dans les mers de l'Inde* (2 vols; Paris, 1779-1781).

32. Macintosh, I, 321-322.

33. Ives, I, 86.

34. Macintosh, I, 301-302, 332.

35. Sonnerat, I, 27.

36. Grundmann, pp. 67.

37. Ernst Windisch, in his *Geschichte der Sanskrit-Philologie* (Strassburg, 1917), lists on pp. 19-20 the following Germans who were the first from that land to study Sanskrit: the Jesuits Hinrich Roth, who studied Sanskrit on his travels in India from 1650 to 1660, Athanasius Kircher, who in 1667

published Sanskrit material received from Roth, and Johannes Ernst Hanxleden (in India from 1699 until his death in 1732), who was the first European to write a Sanskrit grammar. Paulinus was in India from 1776 to 1789 and toward the end of the century published in Rome a grammar and a treatise on *Brahmanism.*

38. Paulinus a Sancto Bartholomaeo, *Reise nach Ostindien,* trans. Reinhold Forster, in *Magazin von merkwurdigen neuen Reisebeschreibungen,* XV (Berlin, 1798). pp. 133.
39. Macintosh, I, 320-321.
40. Ives, I, 86, 375-376.
41. Macintosh, I, 311.
42. Ives, I, 86, 375.
43. Paulinus, *Reise,* pp. 66, n.
44. *Ibid.*, pp. 17-18.
45. Degrandpre, pp. 70.
46. Macintosh, I, 324-325.
47. Dow, *History,* I, xxi-xxii, xxvii-xxviii.
48. Ives, I, in Dohm's "Zusatze," p. 33; Bernier also points out (in *Voyages,* II, 138) that the faith of the *Brahmans* was not universal, that God meant it only for them, and that for this reason they accepted no foreigners in their religion.
49. Degrandpre, pp. 162.
50. Robertson, pp. 287.
51. Degrandpre, pp. 70, 163-164.
52. Paulinus, *Reise*, pp. 371.
53. Macintosh, I, 311, 314, 317-318.
54. Ives, I, Dohm's "Zusatze," pp. 51-52.
55. Dow, *Hisotry,* I, xx.
56. Macintosh, I, 320.
57. Sonnerat, I, 6.
58. Dow, *History*, I, xxxvii.
59. Paulinus, *Reise,* pp. 326.

2

European Origins of Racism

Leon Poliakov*

From about 1940 to 1944, the most important differentiation between the inhabitants of Europe was that between Aryans and Semites: the former were permitted to live, the latter were condemned to die. In most cases the sentence was actually carried out during the course of those four years. The reasoning behind this had been the subject of many books. It will be enough to quote the most influential author of the period, Adolf Hitler:

> The Jew completely lacks the most essential prerequisite of a cultural people, namely the idealistic spirit...He is and remains a parasite, a sponger who, like a pernicious bacillus, spreads over wider and wider areas according as some favourable area attracts him...Wherever he establishes himself the people who grant him hospitality are bound to be bled to death sooner or later...He poisons the bold of others but preserves his own blood unadulterated....To mask his tactics and fool his victims, he talks of the equality of all men, no matter what their race or colour may be....To all external appearance, (he) strives to ameliorate the conditions under which the workers live; but in reality his aim is to enslave and thereby annihilate the non-Jewish races...The black-haired Jewish youth lies in wait for hours on end, satanically glaring at and spying on the unsuspicious girl whom he plans to seduce, adulterating her blood and removing her from the bosom of her own people. The Jew uses every possible means to undermine the racial foundations of a subjugated people...The Jews were responsible for bringing negroes into the Rhineland, with the ultimate idea of bastardizing the white race which they hate and thus lowering its cultural and political level so that the Jew might dominate.[1]

The allusion to the Negro in the Rhineland, who is only slightly less obnoxious than the Jew, may be noted. In fact, for Hitler, three major

---

* A Russian author. The above article forms Introduction to the English translation of his work "*The Aryan Myth; A History of Racist and Nationalist Ideas in Europe*", orginally published in French. Its English translation was published in 1974 by Chatto-Heinemann.

groups made up the whole of mankind, of which only the Aryan was a true representative, the real master of the Universe:

> ...(the Aryan) is the Prometheus of mankind, from whose shining brow the divine spark of genius has at all times flashed forth, always kindling a new that fire which, in the form of knowledge, illuminated the dark night...As a conqueror, he subjugated inferior races and turned their physical powers into organized channels under his own leadership, forcing them to follow his will and purpose. By imposing on them a useful, though hard, manner of employing their powers he not only spared the lives of those whom he had conquered but probably made their lives easier than these had been in the former state of so-called "freedom"...While he ruthlessly maintained his position as their master, he not only remained master but he also maintained and advanced civilization....If we divided mankind into three categories—founders of culture, bearers of culture, and destroyers of culture—the Aryan alone can be considered as representing the first category...Should he be forced to disappear, a profound darkness will descend on the earth; within a few thousand years human culture will vanish and the world will become a desert.[2]

Such was the historical philosophy of National-Socialism's leader. If it did not hinder him from becoming the master of the Third Reich—it seems on the contrary to have helped him—the reason was that similar views, sometimes with a different emphasis, had been held for two or three centuries by numerous thinkers in Germany and elsewhere.

Division of European Population

It is well known that the division of the European population into Aryans and semites was originally based on a confusion about the nature of men (races) and their culture (languages). This confusion was pushed so far that, at the end of the nineteenth century, the Aryan theory had achieved pride of place among men of learning alongside the theory of spatial ether. In its various forms, the Aryan theory nearly always involved a value-judgement in favour of the Aryans, and the ideologists of the Third Reich did no more than stress this bias out of all proportion. We are therefore dealing in the first place with an episode in the history of anthropology, badly warped by European ethnical egotism. The latter has very ancient pre-scientific origins.

There can be no doubt that if, at the beginning of this century, the West still entertained the flattering notion of its superior civilization, often thought of as an Aryan birthright, the Hitlerite catastrophe banished such ideas from political and public life so effectively that now a fresh confusion has arisen, between science and ethics. Antiracism has been promoted to the rank of a dogmatic orthodoxy which the present state of anthropological knowledge is unable to corroborate, but which will brook no criticism, and which is an impediment to sober thinking. This has produced a self-censorship, to a great extent retroactive, by authors of all kinds, but particularly historians who, often without knowing it, try to reinterpret the history of modern thought under this influence. *It begins to look as if, through shame or fear of being reacist, the West will not admit to having been so at any time,* and therefore assigns to minor characters only (like Gobineau, H.S. Chamberlain, etc.) the role of scapegoats. A vast chapter of western thought is thus made to disappear by sleight of hand, and this conjuring trick corresponds, on the psychological or psychohistorical level, to the collective suppression of troubling memories and embarassing truths. The last fanatics or instigators of Aryanism here play the part of the king's fool. Another way of making these troublesome reminders vanish from the field of consciousness is to level the accusation exclusively at Germany. Hence the problem of the "unredeemed past" of Germany, which quite rightly upsets a minority of German intellectuals and, in other countries, has provided food for thought for a number of critics, must be considered as a problem for the entire Western World, which refuses to probe deeply into this old ideologoical sore.

Such are the roots of a form of censorship which falsifies contemporary scientific thought to the point that it becomes "a weathercock shifting with ideological winds", to use the words of the American anthropologist P.L. Van den Berghe.[3] Nevertheless, these ideological winds reflect the uneasiness of a society which not so long ago, in thought if not in deed, was an accomplice of Hitler's racism: a society whose repressive taboos are therefore rooted in prohibited actions, for performing which a strong inclination exists in the unconscious.[4] One might go so far as to believe that the rioting French students, who in May 1968, when we were writing these lines, demonstrated with cries of "we are all German Jews",[5] were likewise attempting, though without realizing it, to dispose of that taboo.

The Role of the Church

Before relating out contemporary era to the pre-Christian past of our continent, it will be useful to recall the myth of origin propagated in the intervening period by the Church. Christianity taught that all men descended from a common ancestor, Adam, through the partriarch Noah and his sons, whose progeny is described at length in the Bible (Genesis, x). Even before the Christian era, Jewish exegetes were busy identifying the branches of ancient races, and they were doubtless the first enquirers who tried in this way to extend their knowledge to the whole of the known world.[6] According to a Talmudic saying, the common ancestry of mankind should edify all its members for none could say to another "My father is greater than thine."[7] The Fathers of the Church took up these genealogies again and combined them with local and regional traditions. Each people was thus endowed with a specific myth of origin, though all derived from Noah, thereby giving firm expression to the overriding concept of the universal brotherhood of man.

After Noah, the lines of descent passed through Japheth, Shem or Ham, to whom there was sometimes added a fourth brother, Jenithon or Manithon. The imagination of writers was given free rein and innumerable variants were proposed. The dominant tendency, however, which conformed to certain etymological hints contained in the Bible, was to attribute the paternity of Europeans to the children of Japheth, that of the Asians to those of Shem, and that of the Africans to those of Ham. It should be noted that the latter were the objects, according to the Bible, of a mysterious curse, for they were the condemned to serve their cousins as slaves ("And Canaan shall be his servant....", Genesis ix, 27).[8] Following this passage, a widely adopted theory established the division of the three main medieval social orders with Ham as the ancestor of the serfs, Shem as that of the clerks, and Japheth as that of the nobles. Thus from the earliest times the Hamites or Blacks were placed on the bottom rung of human hierarchy. Adopting this line of thought, an apocryphal Arab Gospel of the sixth century, in which Jesus changes some Jewish children into goats, reveals a great deal in a few words when it makes Jesus address their mothers as follows: "The children of Israel have the same rank among the peoples as the Negroes."[9]

Doubts were cast on the Biblical doctrine of a single human race well before the eighteenth century.

First Attempts at Racial Classification

Early in the sixteenth century two ideologies came into conflict for the first time. Spain was the principal centre of this debate which, in so far as concerned the American natives, set Christian anthropology at odds with the anthropology inspired by the Classics. For humanists like Juan Sepulveda, imbued with Aristotle's ideas, the Indians were barbarians and therefore born to be slaves. For the Dominican, Bartolome de Las Casas, they were a part of Adam's posterity to be evanglized and treated as free men. However, the existence of whole peoples, who had not been envisaged by the Fathers or by tradition and who had lived without baptism or hope of salvation, put a considerable strain on theological imagination. Las Casas himself compared his Indians to beings without the strain of original sin.[10] The discovery of America, therefore, raised extremely important problems of dogma.

The Holy See soon gave its authority to the views of Las Casas and, truly men, veri homines, capable of receiving the Catholic Faith and the Sacraments. The Spanish monarchy, under Philip II, supported this interpretation. But the Dominican apostle, so revered in Latin America, might be judged quite differently in Africa today since, in order to spare his well-loved Indians, he proposed importing African slave labour.

In this way, a form of discrimination became apparent which was already perceptible in the first book about the New World (De orbe Novo by Pietro d'Anghiera, 1516) where "white" Indians were contrasted with "black" Ethiopians. It can also be seen in the first attempt at "racial classification" (by Francois Bernier in 1684) when the Indians were assimilated to the white race.[11]

Black men became the butt of merciless censure by the white man, from Noah's curse on Ham, whom first rabbinic and then Protestant exegesis considered responsible for the crimes of castration and incest,[12] to the classification of Linnaeus and descriptions of several philosophers of the Enlightenment. Blackness, and with it a great range of evil associations, was contrasted with whiteness, as was innocence with crime, vice with virtue, and bestiality with humanity.

All these views and judgements, which were debated in cosmopolitan *salons* during the eighteenth century, had their origin in the Iberian peninsula. It was there too that the great key-words–mestizo, mulatto, negro, Indian and caste—originated and from there that they spread abroad, in common probably with the word "race" itself.

Again it was in the Iberian peninsula that another debate developed, after the Renaissance, which illustrated clearly how societies can in special circumstances establish their hierarchies and formulate their philosophies. The religious unification of Spain from 1492 onwards had given rise to the problem of the *conversos* or converts, either *Moriscos* (Muslim converts) or *Marranos* (Jewish converts), who had been more or less adequately baptized in the fifteenth century. Spaniards of all ranks laid claim to their authentically Christian birth, proclaimed themselves *Old Christians* and imposed on the hapless *New Christians* a discriminatory legislation-the decrees of purity of blood—which relegated the latter to the bottom of the social scale.

The New Genealogies

Contrary to what Christopher Columbus supposed, America was not the Indies. However, since the Indians had been adopted by papal decree into the human fold, through what lineage were they to be connected to the common father, Adam, and how did they come to inhabit the New World? That they were not aborgines, and descended from a "second

Adam" in America, had already been confirmed to Cortes, the conqueror of Mexico, by the Emperor Montezuma.[13] Coctes' chaplain, Lopez de Gomara, was the first to question whether these people, whose very existence contradicted the views of the Church Fathers, especially those of St. Augustine, were not members of the famous Ten Lost Tribes. The great scholar, Arias Montano, concluded that the Aztecs and Incas must be the descendants of Shem.[14] This theory later drew its most able defenders from the ranks of Spanish and Portuguese *Marranos,* because the dispersion of the Jews in all the countries of the earth was thought to foreshadow the end of Exile. The theory was propagated in the Netherlands and in Great Britain by Rabbi Manasseh been Israel,[15] and it inspired the activities of William Penn at the end of the seventeenth and those of the Mormons, Joseph Smith and Brigham Young, in the mid-nineteenth century. But it found no favour in Spain. There the Jescuits, who controlled education and research as well as the evangelization of countries overseas, preferred to link the Indians with Japheth.

This thesis was first launched by the Jesuit Jose de Acosta, the provincial of Peru, one of the great missionaries who had been instructed by Ignatius Loyola to adopt the language and customs of the local inhabitants, the better to covert them. In his *Natural and Moral History of the Indies* (1590) which was translated into all the main European languages, Acosta put the question of "how did the first men reach the Indies?" It seemed obvious to him that these men came originally from the Old World since "Sacred Scripture teaches us that all men proceeded from one single man". From this it followed "that men came hither from Europe, from Asia or from Africa."

If we have dealt at some length with these ideas of Acosta, whom his French translator described as the "Pliny and Herodotus of this newly discovered world", it is because the discovery of America would henceforth dominate the new concepts of anthropology. It is also because this provincial of Peru was the first of the great series of Jesuit missionaries who, by living on the spot in the manner of the twentieth century anthropologists, tried to identify themselves with the indigenous Americans or Asians, and who, primed with their humanist culture, already began to develop theories of comparative religion.[16] The *Relations* which members of the Society of Jesus like Ricci, Duhalde, Lecomte and Lafitau sent their Superiors proved to be the best source of information in Europe about the inhabitants of other continents.

Meanwhile, in Rome, the guardians of Catholic tradition and dogma soon began to reproach the Jesuits for latitudinarian recruiting of

Christians, and the great dispute about the Chinese Rites was the well-known result. It is true that the desire for evangelical success prompted a number of missionaries to impute to their flocks inherent virtues and graces which made it a simple task to qualify them for baptism.

It was above all in the Netherlands, among the Protestant countries, that the question of the origins of mankind and of particular peoples was raised from the end of the sixteenth century onwards. The University of Leyden was then the centre of Protestant science and exegesis. At that time the problem of the origin of the American Indians caused so much concern, we are told, that a young woman, possessed by the devil, repeated incessantly in Latin: "Quomodo insulae animalia acceperint, et eo homines post Adamum pervenerient?"[17] Hugo Grotius proposed an eclectic solution to this problem. North America, he declared, was populated by the Germans who had come from Iceland and Greenland; Central America by the Ethiopians, and South America by the Chinese and Javanese. All Noah's Descendants were thus to be found in the New World and, though Grotius did not specify their respective lineages, he too identified Japtheth with lapetus and Ham with Jupiter Ammon.[18] A decisive step forward was taken by his German disciple, Georgius Hornius, a Professor of Leyden and author of *Arca Noae, sive historia imperiorum et regnorum*....(1666). According to Horn, the posterity of Noah was divided as follows: the Japhethites became Whites, the Semites became the Yellow Reaces, and the Hamites became Negroes. History and mythology as principles of classification were now joined by a fresh criterion to which they would progressiviely succumb-the colour of the skin.[19]

It was from this angle that the French philosopher and sceptic, Francois Bernier, was soon to tackle the problem. He wrote his *Nouvelle Division de la terre par les differentes especes ou races d'hommes qui l'habitent* in 1684.[20] In it he delcared: "I have observed that there are, in the main, four or five races of men among which the difference is so conspicuous that it can properly be used to mark a division." These races were the European, with whom Bernier linked the Egyptians and the swarthy Hindus ("their colour is only accidental and is due merely to the fact that they are exposed to the sun"): the Africans ("their blackness is essential"); the Chinese and Japanese ("they have broad shoulders, flat faces, hidden noses and small, pig-like eyes") and the Laplanders ("these are vile animals"). As to the Indians, Bernier, as we have seen, aligned them with the Europeans ("I find nothing like enough difference to make them a separate race and distinct from ours"). In this classification, perhaps the first writing in which the term "race" appears in its modern sense, Bernier was not concerned with genealogies and origins, that is to say with the temporal dimension. He was a modern man, already imbued with the mechanistic thought of what was then the *avant-garde in* France, and he divided mankind both according to skin-colour and other physical traits, and according to geographical or spatial considerations.

Leibniz, with his agile mind, immediately seized upon the polygenist implication of this new approach. After summarizing Bernier's thesis he declared: "All this is not a reason for supposing that all the men who inhabit the earth do not belong to the same race, as modified by different climates...."[21]

India seen as Cradle of Mankind

In the eighteenth century, when the West was seeking to free itself from the confines of Judaeo-Christian thought, many authors recommended the ancient wisdom of China as an example for Europe. None of them, however, thought of locating the origins of mankind or of all human knowledge in the Celestial Empire. India was another matter. The special and mysterious fascination of India has continued to make itself felt right up to our own times. Many an esoteric doctrine claims to derive from India. The Middle Ages and the Renaissance did not look as far afield as this, since their knowledge of antiquity was confined to the Hebraic or Greco-Latin cultures. Nevertheless, it was the Bible itself which suggested that the origin of mankind might be discovered somewhere to the east of Judaea. A pointer in this direction was provided by the description of the Garden of Eden, bounded by four rivers, one of which was the Euphrates. The migration of Abraham from Ur of the Chaldees started in the same area. But even more indicative was the story of the Flood in which Noah's ark was grounded on the heights of Mount Ararat in the Caucasus. These mountains figured with equal prominence in Greek legends in which they were the scene of several famous myths, while some Pythogorean traditions drew attention to countries even further to the East, since Pythagoras himself was reputed to have absorbed the wisdom of both Persia and India.

The origin of *Homo sapiens* was still being sought in those regions at the time when scientific reasoning, without as yet discarding the truths which claimed to be revealed, was trying to come to terms with them. Buffon elaborated a relatively coherent theory according to which "the first people worthy to be called by that name" had emerged, when the earth cooled off sufficiently (thirty thousand years ago in his estimation), somewhere to the east of the Caspian Sea.[22] This people "merited all our respect as the creator of science, of the arts and of all useful institutions." Furthermore, "it was very happy because it was very wise". Later, other men "still ignorant, wild and barbaric" had attacked and destroyed this civilization of Eden and plunged the whole of humanity "into the night of ignorance once again." Only the *Brahmins* of India were able to preserve a flicker of the old learning. This anthropodicy, which was based on speculations by the astronomers Cassini and Bailly,[23] seemed to echo the old mythologies of the Golden Age and the Fall.

Buffon tendered to interpret Biblical data in an allegorical manner. His great rival, Linnaeus, advanced views which conformed more closely to a literal interpretation of the Bible but which, far from being coherent, seemed to defy all logic. Starting with the story of the Flood he imagined a very high mountain emerging from the deep somewhere near the Equator. The arctic animals dwelt in couples on the snowy summit of this mountain while the tropical animals, as well as the first human couple, lived round its base. With the emergence of new lands men and animals took possession of them, increased and multiplies Linnaeus, however, did not trouble to explain how reindeer and polar bear could, without dying, have crossed tropical zones in order to go and multiply in polar regions.[24]

Without furnishing such exact details as Linnaeus, the scholars of the Enlightenment, who were monogenists for the most part, generally looked to the mountains as the cradle of the human race. This was certainly true of the geographers. In their view, the presence of seashells in all latitudes confirmed the hypothesis of a universal inundation and therefore corroborated the story of the Flood. Now it was known that the highest mountains in the world towered over India and China. But the fact remains that traditions, perhaps influence by the reluctance of the Whites to admit affiliation to the Yellow races, focussed attention on the near side of the Himalayas and of Kashmir not beyond them.

Reference to Origin of Culture and Religion

Apart from the supposedly scientific theories, a totally different kind of argument was developed for polemical purposes with special reference to the origin of culture and religion. The deist school, turning the Bible against itself, tried at first to prove that Moses had filched his revelations from Egypt. "To imagine that a company of poor, contemptible, egyptianized slaves....were intended in the divine Counsel and Wisdom as a light to the Gentiles" was for Thomas Morgan the same as "supposing what we speak with scorn, that God was disappointed of his End, and took as wrong means, as Moses himself."[25] Voltaire, who was a disciple of the English deists, turned the theory in favour of India. As a polygenist, he did not place the origin of mankind there but he strove to demonstrate that Adam had taken over everything, even his name, from the Indians.[26] The *Encyclopaedia* of Diderot likewise suggested, in the article on India, that the "sciences may be more ancient in India than in Egypt." To many contemporaries, however, it seemed quite obvious that this was due to polemical bias, "a desire to discover in the ancient Orient a rival society to that of the Hebrew", as Edgar Quinet was to say later.[27] Some importance should also be attributed to the backing which the Indian theory received from the celebrated astronomer Jean Bailly who, on the strength of his mathematical calculations, situated the earliest men in the regions of Greenland or New Zemlya and transferred them at a later date to the valley of the Ganges where they founded the arts and the sciences. The arctic origins were soon forgotten and Voltaire was able to record his agreement with Bailly in the following terms:

> I wholly share your opinion when you say that it is not possible for different peoples to have shared the same methods, the same knowledge, the same legends, the same superstitions, unless all these things had been adopted by a primitive nation which taught, and led astray, the rest of the world. Now I have long since regarded the dynasty of the *Brahmins* as having been this primitive nation. You must be familiar with the books of Mr. Holwell and Mr. Dow....Finally, sir, I am convinced that everything has come down to us from the banks of the Ganges, astronomy, astrology, metempsychosis etc.....[28]

John Holwell and Alexander Dow were two English authors who in their writings on India gave prominence to the high level of culture and the ancient wisdom of the *Brahmins*. More emphatically than Dow, his French translator, M.B.***, declared in 1769 that all ancient cultures and religions were of Indian origin. Moses was an Indian renegade and Mahomet an impostor.[29] The French naturalist, Pierre de Sonnerat, also deserves a mention. For him India was "the legislator of all the peoples". He found analogies between different western mythologies and religions and deduced that they had a common source in India, the birthplace of the human race (*Voyage aux Indes orientales,* 1782).

These ideas, as they appeared in successive translations and travellers' tales, captivated the imagination of Kant, who modified the popular arctic and astronomical theory of Bailly by placing the origin of mankind in Tibet. "This is the highest country", he argued:

> No doubt it was inhabited before any other and could even have been the site of all creation and all science. The culture of the Indians, as is known, almost certainly came from Tibet, just as all our arts like agriculture, numbers, the game of chess, etc...seem to have come from India.

Here Kant expressed himself hypothetically; but he was less cautions when he allowed himself to be beguiled by etymological fancies. Then he tried to connect Manichaeism with the saying *"O mani padme hum"* and Abrahma with Brahma[30] (an etymology which had already been proposed by some Renaissance writers). But it was Johann-Gottfried Herder above all who introduced the passion for India into the Germanic lands and who prompted the imagination of the Romantics to seek affiliation with Mother India.

Herder's view about the details of this affiliation changed in the course of time, but basically he associated with the Indian birthplace a kind of "natural revelation" which was also a poetic initiation (poetry was for him the primitive language of humanity) of which the original form had been lost. Nevertheless, this Lutheran pastor did not depart from tradition since he considered the Bible as the most accurate copy of the legendary poem. "Historically, all that we have left in the whole world is the written tradition which we are wont to call Mosaic....:"[31]

Herder believed that, ethinically or racially, the Germans could be related to the Persians, which caused him to rejoice;[32] but morally it was to the Indians that he gave the palm, claiming that

> the *brahmins* have formed their people to such a degree of gentleness, courtesty, temperance, and chastity, or at least have so confirmed them in these virtues, that Europeans frequently appear, on comparison with them, as beastly, drunken or mad. In their air and language they are unconstrainedly elegant; in their behaviour, friendly; in their persons, clean; in their way of life, simple and harmless...they are not destitute of knowledge, still less of quiet industry or nicely imitative art; even the lowest castes learn reading, writing and arithmetic....[33]

Primeval Mountain Region

In his *magnum opus, the Outlines of a Philosophy of the History of Mankind*, Herder strongly opposed the Noachian or Jewish genealogy:

> The pains that have been taken, to make of all the people of the Earth, according to this geneology, descendants of the hebrews and half-brothers of the jews, are contradictory not only to chronology and universal history but to the true point of view of the narrative itself.....nations, languages and kingdoms were formed, after the deluge, without waiting for envoys from a chaldean family...Suffice it, that the firm central point of the largest quarter of the Globe, the primitive mountains of Asia, prepared the first abode of the human race....[34]

He supported this history of a primeval mountain region with every kind of argument, from the speculations of Linnaeus on the "mountain of creation" to the geographical deductions of Pallas and Zimmermann and the astronomical calculations of Bailly. He revealed the essence of his vision in a poetic flight:

> Let us abandon these regions where our predecessors, like Buet, Buxtorf or Bochart, sought the beginning of the world! These corners of Arabia and Judaea, these basins of the Nile and the Euphrates, these coasts of Phoenicia and Damascus, where the human race might have come into existence like mice or rats; all these must be left behind! Let us scale the mountain laboriously to the summit of Asia. Where will this lead us? The horizons swing back and forth. History, which has dated all things from that beginning, will have another beginning and another end. Our vision becomes clouded. Whither are we going?....Patience.[35]

Adopting Herder's style for a moment, one could say that Germany, striving to extricate herself from Judaeo-Christian fetters, soon responded to this aspiration; with Schopenhauer she longed to be the child of India and Buddhist; with Nietzsche, the child of Persia and a follower of Zarathustra. It is certainly true that Herder, with his longings for the primitive, with his exaggerations and also with his flashes of genius, seems both to have anticipated and sharpened the contradictions of romantic Germany; and not of Germany alone, for it is perhaps with good reason that the orientalist, Raymond Schwah, considered him the main instigator of those "prejudices which, even today, prompt our worship of the infantile and the primitive."[36]

Thus we see that a wide variety of authors and schools located the birthplace of the entire human race between the Indus and the Ganges. It only remained for linguistics to make its contribution, in a decisive though ambiguous manner, by dispelling with one certain truth a fog of adventurous suppositions, and at the same time advancing a new hypothesis as fragile as any of those which preceded it. According to this new theory it was not the whole human race but one particular race—a white race which subsequently became Christian—which had descended from the mountains of Asia to colonize and populate the West. It seemed as if the Europeans of the scientific age, having freed themselves from the conventional Noachian genealogy and rejected Adam as a common father, were looking around for new ancestors but were unable to break with the tradition which placed their origin in the fabulous Orient. It was the science of linguistics which was to give a name to these ancestors by opposing the Aryans to the Hamites, the Mongols-and the Jews.

Notes & References

1. *Mein Kampf*, London 1939, trans. by James Murphy, pp. 225-73.
2. *Ibid*., pp. 243-8.
3. Paul Mercier, *Histoire de l'Anthropologie,* Paris 1966, pp. 15.
4. "Delving into the mystery of our origins and the complex feelings upon which its rests, appeared no doubt with the first gleams of intelligence", Andre Leroi-Gourhan, *Le Geste et la Parole,* Paris 1964, pp. 9.
5. A. Borst, *Der Turmbau von Babel, Geschichte der Meinungen uber Ursprung and Vielfalt der Sprachen und Volker, Stuttgart* 1957-63, 6 vols. This wrok is a real encyclopaedia of the genealogical legends of western history.
6. Cf. A. Borst, *op.cit.*, vol. I, pp. 126.
7. Sanhedrin 59 b; cf Hans Kohn, *The Idea of Nationalism,* New York 1951, pp. 585.
8. According to the account in Genesis (x 6), Ham had four sons, only one of whom, Cannan, was cursed by Noah. However, it was customary to regard all Ham's descendants as being burdened with the consequences of Ham's affront to Noah.
9. "Evangile arabe de l'enfance", *Evangiles apocryphes,* trans.by Peeters, Paris 1914, Vol. II; cf. F. Lovsky, *L'antisemitisme chretien, Textes choisis et presentes....*Paris 1970, pp. 351.
10. Cf. Marcel Bataillon, *L'unite du genre humain...*op. cit., pp. 93.
11. Bernier's classification about races.
12. It should be remembered that the curse on Ham in the ninth chapter of Genesis, verse 25, is directed against his fourth son, Canaan. In the Jewish exegesis of Rachi this verse is interpreted as follows: *Cursed be Canaan...*"Because of you I shall not have a fourth son to serve men. Cursed be your fourth son therefore, he shall be enslaved to the descendants of his elder brothers on whom falls the duty of serving me." And what was Ham's reason for making him an enunch? He said to his brothers: "Adam had two sons and one killed the other to inherit the earth, and our father has three sons and desires a fourth!" For Protestant exegesis, see Don Cameron Allen, *The Legend of Noah, op.cit.*, pp. 77-8.
13. Borst III/I, pp. I, 145.
14. *Ibid*., pp. I, 145 and pp. I, 152.
15. Rabbi Manasseh ben Isreal of Amsterdam put forward the theory in his book *The Hope of Israel* (1650) which he translated into Latin and dedicated to the English Parliament. He later went to England and negotiated with Cromwell for the return of the Jews to that country.
16. Cf. M. Harris, *op.cit.*, pp. 16-18 and W.H. Muhlmann, *Geschichte der anthropologie,* pp. 44-6.

17. Don Cameron Allen, *The Legend of Noah op.cit.*, pp. 55.
18. Borst III/I, pp. I, 298-I, 300.
19. Borst III/I, pp. I, 305-I, 307; and Adalbert Kelmm, *Die Sakularisierung der universal-historian Auffassung; Zum Wandel des Geschtschtsdenkens...*,Gottingen 1960, pp. 113.
20. *Journal des Scavans,* Paris, 24 April 1684, pp. 85-9.
21. *Ottum Hanoveriana sive Miscellanea,* Leipzig 1718, pp. 37 (quoted by Ashley Montagu in Edward Tyson, M.D., F.R.S., Philadelphia 1943, pp. 397.)
22. *Des epoques de la nature,* "septieme epoque".Cf. *CEuvres philosophiques de Buffon,* Ed. by J. Piveteau, Paris, 1954.
23. On the authority of a certain passage in Josephus, Cassini and Bailly assumed that the Ancients could calculate with precision the movement of the stars. Cf: the notes in Piveteau's edition of Buffon's works.
24. Cf. E.A. W. zimmermann, *Geographische Geschichte des Menschen und der allgemein verbreiteten vierfussigen Thiere,* Vol. III, Leipzig 1783, pp. 192-5.
25. T. Morgan, *A brief examination of the Rev. Mr. Warburton's Divine Legation of Moses,* London 1791. Cf. *Histoire de l'antisemitisme,* Vol. III, pp. 80-81.
26. See the articles "Adam" and "Genese" in *the Doctionnaire philosophique* by Voltaire as well as Chap. CXLIII ("De l'Inde") in the *Essai sur les moeurs et l'esprit des nations.*
27. Cf. Raymond Schewab, *La Renaissance orientale,* Paris 1950, pp. 26.
28. *Lettres sur l'origine des sciences et sur celle des peuples de l'Asie adressees a M. de Voltaire par M. Bailly et precedees de quelques lettres de M. de Voltarie a l'auteur,* Paris 1777, pp. 3 (letter from Voltaire of 15 December 1775).
29. *Dissertation sur les moeurs et les usages de l'Inde,* translated by M.B.***, pp. xiii-xiv.
30. Cf. Helmuth v. Glasenapp, *Das Indienbild deutscher Denker,* Stuttgart 1960, pp. 11-12.
31. Cf. Rene Gerard, *L'Orient et la pensee romatique alelmande,* Paris 1963, pp. 40.
32. *Ibid.*, pp. 22.
33. J.G. Herder, *Outlines of a Philosophy of the History of Man*, trans. by T. Churchill, London 1803, Vol. II, pp. 34.
34. *Ibid.*, Vol. I, pp. 517, 518.
35. The conclusion of "*Alteste Urkunde des Menschengeschiechts*" (*Sammiliche Werke,* Vol. VI,) Berlin 1883, pp. 500.
36. *La Renaissance orientale, op.cit.*, pp. 225.

3

An Intense Competition for Being Aryans

Paramesh Choudhury*

There was a competition as to who was the real Aryan and was a superior race among the different European nations.

"These Aryans rivalries were necessary. Nations can not prosper and flourish except by intense competition or Drawin's struggle for existence.-Triestchke."

This chapter tells the story of these rivalries.

In 1987 the first volume of 'Black Athena' was published. In this book Martin Bernal stated that his first objective was to dethrone the Aryan model which was constructed at the time of western hegemony on the rest of the world.

According to this author, most of the scholars who established the Aryan model were racist and antisemitic. So many evidences has he presented to show how the Aryan model was set up to supplant the more historically true ancient model.

The Aryan model was constructed at a time when Western scholars were endeavouring to become scientific. 'Scientific' as a historian, they had to ignore ancient references and mythical creatures like centaurs and sirens. The view of Greece being civilised by Egyptians and Phoenicians would have gone against laws of 'racial science' and the 'ethnic principle of history' which was the new contribution of historiography. In the pursuit of an apparent 'scientific' position, a ethnic principle of history which was the new contribution of historiography. In the pursuit of an apparent 'scientific' position, a narrower perspective limiting their geographical and historical scope was adopted. Thus, these 'scientific' scholars invited a conflict with the new archaeological discoveries.[1]

---

* A Calcutta based scholar, author of "*The Indian origin of the Chinese Nation*" A portion of his book "*The Aryans : A Modern Myth*" (Delhi,1993) is reproduced here for the benefit of scholars.

In 12 long chapters, he has tried to prove how Cretan history was distorted, downplaying Egyptian influences which 19th and 20th century scholars interpreted Cretan religious beliefs to fit into the Aryan model's assumptions. 'Extreme' Aryanists even denied any Egyptian and Phoenician influences on Greece. The 'Ultra Europeanists' went still further to deny any outside influences on pre-Hellenic Greece.

Mr. Bernel has also shown that the Western scholars have been used to use conventional chronologies giving dates younger than those given by carbon 14 tests. Because, the new C 14 dates and archaeological findings supported the things opposed by the Aryanists.[2]

Let us now enter into the story of the competition of being Aryans among the European nations.

The chief scientific sponsor of the Aryan myth in France was Ernest Renan, a man who, by becoming the channel for all the main intellectual currents of his time and by seeking to please everyone, ended up as the almost official ideologist of the Third Republic.

Renan deserves the same rank with his friend Max Muller as a propagandist for Aryan Myth. Renan was regarded as an authority by the whole of international learned society. Both the them issued warnings after 1870-71 against seeking political advantage from the confusion between languages and races. But this self-criticism had little effect. Their writings before the Franco-Prussain war continued to make headway in one encyclopaedia after another. A series of text books spread their influence as racists.

Love of Germany went deep in the young Renan. "Germany, which had been mistress for several years," moulded him too closely in her image. In a letter of 1856 to Gobineau he justified this passion:

> "Your book is most remarkable full of vigour and originality of mind. But is misunderstood in France. The French intelligence does not adapt itself easily to ethnographic considerations. France has little belief in race. The fact of race has been practically erased from her consciousness. The same difficulty is with linguistics. French language is no more than detritus of the fourth or fifth zone, certainly the cause why the French mind accepts with difficulty, the true principles of comparative philology. A people like the Germans, who still cling to their primordial roots and speak a language which has its origin in itself."[3]

Renan's approval of Gobineau is as self-evident as is Tocqueville's disapproval. There is a remarkable affinity between the idea of a language which has "its origin in itself", and the idea of "creation of the self by itself" which the German humanists had put around in their attempt to glorify Germany. Renan's contempt for the coloured or "savage" people was common in France at that time.[4] But it was certainly from Germany thinkers that he drew the substance of his Aryan doctrine. He never really freed himself from theological ideal. This might have coloured his doctrine of the Aryans.

This led him to assign a common birthplace to the two "great and noble races, the Aryan and the Semitic",[5] while differentiating sharply between the two as to their periods of influence:

> The Semites are incapable of doing that is essential. Let us remain Germans and Celts; let us keep our 'eternal gospel', Christianity. Only Christianity has a future....[6] Once this monotheism was accomplished, the Semitic race rapidly declined. The Aryan race alone was left to lead the march of human destiny.

Renan compared the Semites as a decadent people with the Aryans as the newly chosen race, and revealed the confusions which had arisen between race, language and religion, between a "new Israel" for Christian and the fantasm of "Arya". Renan proposed the following anthro-pogeny as he contemplated "mount Imaus" (the Himalaya), the imagined birthplace of white humanity:

> Salute those sacred summits, there the great races carried the future of humanity in their hearts, contemplated infinity for the first time and introduced two categories which changed the face of the world, morality and reason. When the Aryan race, after thousands of years of striving, shall have become the masters of the planet, their first duty will be to explore that mysterious region. No place in the world has had a comparable role to that of the nameless mountain or valley where mankind first attained self-consciousness. Let us be proud of the old patriarchs. They at the foot of Imaus, laid the foundations of what we are and of what we shall become.[7]

There was a patriarchal genealogy to supplant that of the Chaldeans. The Aryan race became "Masters of the planet", thanks to reason and science, thanks to

> a search, thoughtful, independent, strict, courageous and philosophical, a search for the truth, which seems to have been the characteristic of this race.[8]

Renan contrasted these qualities of the Aryans with the fearful shallowness of the Semitic spirit, narrowing the human mind and closing it to all subtle ideas.[9]

The Aryan Bible

Renan was already a famous scientific authority. In 1863 he became an internationally famous author with the publication of his *Life of Jesus*. That was translated into ten languages. In this book Semitic race became the *Jewish people*. He described them in the traditional manner that Jewish unbelievers joined orthodox Catholics in their protests: "(Renan) asks the Catholics to excuse him for diminishing Jesus, whom he makes out to be a man, by insulting the Jews, who made Him a martyr" (Adolphe Cremieux).[10] In other works, too, Renan used terms, using Semitic race or Jewish race on the one hand, and Indo-Germanic race, Indo-European or Aryan race on the other, though his preference was for the latter term.

The Life of Jesus was sold over the 1,00,000 copies in a few months followed by 321 critical pamphlets or refutations produced a number of imitations. The following year, the aged Michelet joined the ranks with his *Bible de l'humanite*:

> In the full light of the sun among our forefathers, the sons of light—Aryans, Indians Persians and Greeks my book is born but met with opposition from Memphis, Carthage. Tyre and Judaca. Egypt in her monuments, Judaca with her scriptures, established their Bibles, gloomy but of lasting influence. Our parent Bibles have come to light and it is more apparent that the Jewish Bible belongs to another race. No doubt a great book, and always will be. But very gloomy and full of gross equivocation—beautiful but full of doubt like death.[11]

Soon, other Aryan Bibles appeared. Of these Jacolliot's (Louis) the Bible dans l'Inde (1868) is most noteworthy. Jacolliot, after saluting "India, the birthplace of the human race and ageless mother with bountiful breasts" put forward another version of the universal Indo-Aryan religion. Moses became Manu (Manu→Manes→Minos→Moses). Jesus was derived from Zeus (Zeus→lezeus→lsis→Jesus). These daring etymologies, which he claimed to have discovered was based on the apocryphal laws of Manu. Jocollio was able "to ascribe the origins of the Bible to the highlands of Asia. He regarded the Old Testament as no more than a collection of superstitions, the Jews as a degraded and stupid people and moses as a fanatical slave charitably educated at the court of Pharaohs."[12]

A soothsayer had foretold. Only linguistic proof was a scientifically valid test of the origins of nations. This confusion between race and language was more prominent in Hegel in that, according to his *Philosophy of History,* India was a prehistoric country. Moreover, Hegel had nothing but contempt for the philosophy, character and customs of the Indians.[13] He wrote ironically of the view current during the period of Bailly. Schelling and Schlegel. According to this view, a primitive Indian people could have been the creators of all wisdom and the arts, "This picture", he observed, "revives that of the earliest state of Man in Paradise. Theologians earlier on elaborated this, saying, that God had spoken to Adam in Hebrew, but adapts it to other needs."[14]

Some of the scholars of that time perfected the pseudo-scientific form of the Aryan myth. It was at that time when the German devil himself undertook the study of Sanskrit and of Hegel.[15]

In 1820 Karl Ritter described[16] vividly how Indian armies led by Buddhist priests and missionaries burst into the West, Johann Gottfried Rhode, asserted the superiority and priority of Zoroaster's teaching over that of Moses.[17] Christian Lassen, the pupil of the Schelegel brothers wrote that the Indo-Germans were the foremost among the Caucasian peoples. That was a question of belief of the Schlegel brothers who wrote about 1845:

> We do not believe that this is due to chance. It flows from their superior, more widespread talents. History teaches us that the Semites did not lose the harmonious balance of all those forces of the spirit characterizing the Indo-Germans.
>
> The Semites can not claim credit for their philosophy they borrowed from the Indo-Germans. Their outlook and notions rendered them unable to rise with serenity to the contemplation of pure ideas. The Semites are egotistical and exclusive in their religion.[18]

Lassen also contrasted the *Aryans* of India with the people of Deccan. He compared the Dravidians with the natives of Australia and America who had been conquered by the Europeans. At the same time he did not forget to assert that the highest castes in India were also the whitest. He concluded:

> The Aryans were the most highly organized, the most enterprising and the most creative among the people. Also the youngest, because the earth only produced the most perfect species of plants and animals at a late date. This relationship will ultimately reveal itself in a similar way in the political field.[19]

That was the basic element of the myth: *triumph of the strongest, the pre-eminence of youth, the superiority of the Whites.*

August-Friedrich Pott. *proved* the Asiatic origin of the Europeans on linguistic grounds. He used poetic images such as the course of the sun or the maternal breast of Asia, in support of his views:

> The march of culture, in its general lines, has always followed the sun's course. The people of Europe at first nurtured in the cradle of Asia. Like small children they played around this mother. The factual proof is provided by European and Asiatic languages. There, and nowhere else, were situated the playground and school of the earliest material and spiritual energies of the human race.[20]

The grammarian K.F.O. Westphal burst in with more resounding effect while dealing with modes of speech:

> Our Indo-German ancestors learned with the same artlessness as when they seized their first food for sustenance, or when for the first time, the Indo-German man took the Indo-German woman into his arms to give birth to a being of his own image.[21]

Hippolyte Taine glorified the ancient Aryan people:

> In its languages, religions, literatures and philosophies, shows that a common blood and spirit linked all its offshoots.[22]

From the very year of its foundation the Anthropological Society of London show that the term Aryam was in general use. In 1871 Darwin in his *Descent of Man* accepted the classification. Nietsche in Germany, in his earliest work the *Birth of Tragedy,* (1871) distinguished between an Aryan and a Semitic essence symbolized by the Promethean Myth and by Adam's Fall respectively or by the ideas of sacrilege and of sin. In Germany, the words Germanic or Indo-Germanic were often used. Antisemitic propaganda, when using scientific arguments, liked to contrast the "Indo-Germanic" race with the Semitic to the advantage of the former. The big popular encyclopaedias of Brockhaus and Meyer from 1864 and 1867 respectively included Articles under the heading Arier, defined from the start as Indo-Germanic. But, the 14th edition of same states specifically that its is better to apply the term *Arier* only to "Asian Aryans" and to use the term Indo-Germanic or Indo-European to describe the "European Aryans."

In its original form the belief in Aryan origins presupposed a twofold article of faith: (1) Europeans are members of the Aryan race, (ii) this race is derived from the high plateau of Asia. An origin distinct from the Jews, proved to be far more tenacious. An Asiatic origin was questioned by the majority of scientists from the end of the century. One of these, the English philologist Isaac Taylor, in his book on *The Origin of the Aryans,* rejoiced in the overthrow of the "ancient tyranny of the Sanskritists".[23] The next scene is that of a tyrannical influence of lingusistics on anthropology. It was, in the era of structural anthropology, even throughout the nineteenth century, that linguistics imposed its methods and authority on the other sciences of man. Anthropologists were well aware of this.

Language and Anthropology

In 1862, Paul Broca, the leading anthropologist of the "physical" school in France remarked that the linguistic specialists had one big advantage over them. They could do without the anthropologists, but the anthropologists could not do without them. They were thus the vassals of linguistics and grateful vassals. But he emphasized, they must not be, they could not be its slaves.

Broca could not accept the certainty of the Aryan theory. He told that the philologists in seeking to establish the origins of their races and languages, have discovered probabilities but nothing definite. In the present state of their knowledge he was afraid, the names advanced as a substitute for that of Indo-Europeans are statements of theory rather than of fact.

But, he regarded the use of the terms *Aryans races* as "perfectly scientific" while describing its counterpart—*the Semitic races—as a* "gross error."

We come across similar suspicion with regard to the decisions of the philologists in the works of a great pioneer of cultural anthropology Edward B. Tylor (1832-1917). "A man's language is no full and certain proof of his parentage," he wrote, "Much bad anthropology has been made by thus carelessly taking language and race as though they went always and exactly together." Even then Tylor described the Gypsiesas "our Aryan forefathers".[24] We get the same impression from a manual by Paul Topinard (1830-1911), called *'Anthropologie'*. He was the first influential writer to suggest that the French were not "Aryans by blood, but a mixture of races superimposed on one another."

The influence of linguistics on anthropology are best described by the German Theodor Waitz (1821-1864), in his book *Anthropologie der Naturvolker* which claimed originality in its day. Without using the expression "Aryan race", he raised a question whether Europeans were in any way superior to primitive peoples. He thought influence of linguistics justified on two grounds: (1) The characteristics of language are more stable than racial or ethno-racial qualities and thus provided a more reliable guide to historical continuity. (2) Methods of comparative philology had reached a higher degree of exactitude than those of physical anthropology, especially craniology, Proof of this superiority can be found in the relative agreement among the students of linguistics as to the main results of their science, while the physical anthropologists, when dealing with the human races, seemed engaged in a general affray. In a word, the strength of the philologers was in their unity.[25]

Adolf Bastian (1826-1905) a German anthropologist looked with favour on the "tyranny of the Sanskritists":

> ....civilized peoples were in the course of developing spiritually towards an unquantifiable end, and all classifications depending on the corporeal were bound to be sterile and contradictory. Philology, with its subsidiary branches replaces craniology.[26]

He widely dealt with the nomadic Aryans, as ancestors of the "civilized peoples", though the quest for their "cradle of origin" seemed to him to be derived from a mythology which was in no way superior to that of the Zulus, who have the belief that the nomads of South Africa came out one after another from a cave".

Rudolf Virchow, stressed the usefulness of craniology and the study of other physical characteristics. Without such data, he wrote, in the eighteen seventies, "decisions on the ethnical situation of people will be placed unquestionally in the hands of the linguists". The latter in their purism had originally postulated "pure" races, which was indefensible in anthropology, they were also introducing politics into the debate by relating both Aryans (like the Celts) and non-Aryans (like the Sardinians and Iberians) to the same Latin race. Thus they confused races, nations and languages. "Language may nationalize and de-nationalize", he concluded, "but it can not be an indication of blood-relationship."[27]

A host of minor writers who followed Max Muller and Ernest Renan displayed their linguistic imperialism even more crudely. F.G. Bergmann (1812-1895), for whom the origins of "the primitive peoples of Japheth's race" should be investigated by "sciences which are part physical and part philosophical"—obviously the sciences of language.[28] Honore Chavce (1815-1877), who thought he had scientifically demonstrated "by the facts of the natural history of language, the essential differences in mental constitution and therefore in cerebral organization" between Aryans and Semities.[29] The philologist A-F Pott, was prompted by his reading of Gobineau, a German anthropologist and wrote an essay on the *Inequality of human races,* based mainly on *philological science, or the work of Count Gobinent which bears the same title.* He thus contributed to the posthumous fame of the latter.[30]

Other scientists with no interest in the question of human origins revealed their uncritical acceptance of the Aryan myth. The great linguist August Scheleicher (1821-1868), for example, after summarizing J. Grimm's thesis about "successive waves of immigrants", concluded: "We must, therefore, look to the highlands of central Asia to find the homeland of the original Indo-Germanic people."[31] This 'phrase' was itself part and parcel of those "assertions of the linguistic experts (who), on this as on other subjects, have influenced the judgements of anthropologists."[32]

PICTET: Linguistic Palaeontology

The Genevan philologer, Adolphe Pictet, influenced by Renan and who, in turn, influenced Max Muller emphasized in his volumionous *Essai de paleontologie linguistique* published in 1859, that the *primitive Aryas* thrived in Iran:[33]

> Before history began, a whole race was destined by Providence to reign one day supreme over the entire earth. It grew up slowly in the primitive cradle, preparing for a brilliant future. Nobility of blood and the gift of intelligence, was won over natural setting, beautiful but harsh. This race created by its labours the basis of a lasting industrial organization. Thus rising above the elementary necessities of life, they brought about an early development of thought...

Then a hundred pages of philological speculation was carried on at the end. Pictet summarized his ideas:

> They were a race of the Aryans, endowed from the beginning with the very qualities which the Hebrews lacked. They were destined to become the civilizers of the world. A providential plan does nowhere emerge more clearly than in the parallel courses of these two contrasting streams. The former was destined to absorb the other. The religion of Christ became the torch of humanity. The genius of Greece adopted it. The power of Rome propagated it. Germanic energy gave it new strength. The whole race of European Aryas, under its beneficent influence, and by means of endless conflict, raised itself gradually to the level of modern civilization. Thus the race of the Aryans, more favoured than any other, came to be the main instrument of God's plan for the destiny of mankind.[34]

Aryanism: Vehicle of Christianity

He thus confuses the Aryan race, in its capacity as an instrument of God's plan, with the Christian people. In 1882, Renan gave it his support to the view that "Christianity is the most genuine form of the Aryan religion is to a great extent true", And he added: "St Bernard Francis of Assisi St Teresa, Francis of Sales, Vincent de Paul, Fenelon. Channing...are people of our race; they feel with our hearts and think with our brains."[35] This idea was developed more directly in 1867 by the treasurer of the Anthropological Society of London, the Rev. Dunbar Heath in his book '*On the Great Race-elements in Christianity.* He showed that "all Aryan mythologies delight in depicting the descent of gods upon earth to combat evil... The Aryan spirit considers law to be evil and supports the rights of conscience." The contemporary Semitic race and proclaimed that Jesus was the Devil while the Aryan race continued to revere him as God. This race had elaborated the doctrine of the Trinity—a concept far removed from "all the instincts of the Semites". In conclusion, Heath declared that "Christianity is a religion derived principally from Aryan sources... being professed by Aryans now and not being professed by semites now" and being "in a fair and full sence of the word a truly Aryan religion".[36]

Franco-Prussain War (1871)

In the meantime there occurred Franco Prussian war.

Arnand de Quaterfages, the head of the French school of anthropology, shared the general agreement about the Aryan origins of the Europeans. Witnessing the Prussian army's[37] bombardment of the civil population and scientific institutions, he at once tried to explain this conduct as unworthy of a civilized people, in terms of anthropology. Such barbarity, he wrote could only be attributed to the existence[38] of the primitive inhabitants in north-eastern Europe who had preceded the Aryans. The Prussians were not real Germans. From the anthropological point of view, *Finns* or *Slavo-Finns*, that is to say "men who preceded all history" and contemporaries of the period when "there lived in Europe the rhinoceros and the elephant, the reindeer and musk-ox". They had retained "a truly national imprint" of their past:

> The Finns will never consume an insult, real or imagined. Whenever he finds an opportunity, he will avenge himself by any means without showing any scruple. This can only explain the numerous murders which take place among the peasnats belonging to this race.

This made everything clear. "Not relishing the subjecting of the Germans to the Slavo-Finns, Germany adopted the hatreds and furthered the instincts of those whom she has appointed her leaders." That explained well the bombardment of the Museum of Paris and the burning of the Strasbourg Library in particular. The black hatred of the Finns, the jealous hatred of the semi-barbarian for a superior civilization, was nowhere more clearly displayed. After this Europe must expect some dark days in the future. Would the Slavo-Finns then want to dominate the Latins as well as the Germans? And would the world submit in silence to being divided in this way?

German Superiority

Quatrefages's theory met with a certain success in France. In 1872 an illustrated textbook by Louis Figuier called *Les Races Humanies* contained his views. This writer continued to place the "Teutonic family" at the head of the human race. He was of the opinion that Quatrefages had 'proved scientifically' that the Prussians were not members of this family. "These Finns, the primitive inhabitants along the shores of the Baltic, were characterized by trickery and violence combined with remarkable tenacity. Modern Prussians rivie all these vices of their ancestors."[39] In Germany this "Finnish theory" naturally aroused indignation. The main newspapers took a hand in the affair and the *kolnische Zeitung* accused Quatrefages of being an "ignorant naturalist" and a "learned liar".

International scientific opinion was divided into two camps. Italian and English scientists disagreed with Quatrefages who was supported only by Hamy and Broca, his colleagues. The latter paid the Germans back in their own coin, stating that it was they who were the first "to excite racial patriotism, which was certainly more vigorous than ordinary patriotism, among the German nations."[40] Quatrefages was obliged to make a partial retreat. In his lecturers in 1872, he declared that his objective had been a purely scientific one.

> No doubt I was not loath to remind the Germans that the Prussians are not their brothers...But if Prussia had been as devoted a friend of France as she has shown herself to be an implacable enemy I should have acted in the same way.[41]

Later, in his classic *Histoire generale des races humaines* Quatrefages was eager enough to rehabilitate the *Finnish Race* as special and ancient branch of the white race:

> There is something special about the Finnish races from several points of view. They have got a past far more remote than that of the Aryans and the Semites, properly so called. They are probably contemporaries of the pre-Semites, their blood must have mingled with that of many other races junior to them. In any case, if only because they are the first-born, one cannot refuse them a place alongside their fellow races, whatever a greater history the latter may have.[42]

This was in reply to the scientific counter-attack organized by Adolf Bastian and Rudolf Virchow, the two outstanding figures in German anthropology. The Former came to the defence of the Finns, those "poor orphans of anthropology" who had already been roughly handled Gobineau in his *Essai*. There were no longer, Finns or Slavs in Prussia, absorbed or destroyed as they were by the advance of Germanism. "In the same way as the Indians, they have disappeared, like snow, beneath the rising sun of history....", Bastian relied much on the great Darwinian argument: "The flood of Germans advancing towards the East and implacably rolled back the weaker race following the law of victory to the strongest, the law of the *struggle for existence.*" It was no use being befogged by "Celto-Latin verbiage", especially in the nineteenth century when the Germanic people had become the standard-bearers of scientific culture in Europe. Bastian concluded that the Germans had built themselves a new dwelling in the eastern marches, and what their fathers had conquered the sons would be able to keep.

> Prussia is a country of warriors: so it was and so it will remain as long as it is necessary to protect the marches of the East, but above all those of the West, against the trouble-makers.[43]

This militant tone mirrored the nationalist excitement which got hold of Germany immediately after its reunification. The old tendency to Germanomania was to add to new patriotic responsibilities, a combination that gave birth to certain obligations considered imperative. Max Muller so warned in Strasbourg in 1872.[44] The disavowal by the Jewish historian, Heinrich Gratz was even more significant. In 1868 he described the German people as "the German Michael" i.e. a simple and harmless figure of German folklore. But in 1879 he revised this opinion in the following terms:

> Glorious victories, the unification and the success of Germany under brilliant leaders took place later. Earlier on, the German people in general had the reputation of being like the German Michael...Though true before 1870, this judgement is now false.[45]

A deeper symptom of the change of mental climate may be discovered in the cult of "blond virility", a phenomenon which invaded Germany only after 1870-1871.[46]

Enters the Science of Craniology

The second critic of Quatrefages was Rudolf Virchow (1821-1902), scholar of the widest learning and a deputy in the Reichstag. An anatomist and craniologist, his approach to the dispute was much more serious than Bastian's.

This science of "craniology" in the nineteenth century is worth dilating. It looks like an offshoot of the "phrenology" of Lavater and Gall. It was when criticizing their views around 1845 that the Swedish scientist, Andreas Retzius, introduced the idea of a *cephalic index.* It was the dolichocephalic peoples such as the Scandinavians, the Germans, the English and the French, which were "endowed with the highest faculties of the mind". "Brachycephaly" was an indication of a different origin which was described as Turanian, as distinguished from Iranian or Aryan, and which was typical of retarded peoples such as the Lapps, the Finns or Finno-slavs and the Bretons.[47] The theory of craniology, got sophisticated by the Paris school. The concept of the cephalic index and other indices were gradually added to it. Extraordinary measuring instruments, which mostly sprang from Broca's ingenious mind, came into use in ever incsreasing numbers. All manner of special characteristics, like the "complexity of cranial dentures" were put forward as proof of the superiority of European skulls over those of *inferior races*, and it was the common opinion that the wizards in Paris could distinguish at a glance between a Roman, a Frankish and a Saracenic skull.[48] Within a short time, European science was convinced that skulls would yield the information necessary to define human races, with their respective qualities, more accurately than languages.

Virchow must have felt himself especially concerned as a native of Pomerania, germanized only in the twelfth and thirteenth centuries, he reproached Quatrefages for exclusivism and Prussophobia. He criticized him more in form than in substance and seemed not to find his "Finnish hypothesis" in the least extravagant.[49] But he wanted to make quite sure. Immediately after the Treaty of Frankfurt before this scholar called his colleagues together to form a commission "to establish a statistical record of the shapes of skulls throughout Germany following a method to be formulated by the commission".[50] They were to measure the skull of all soldiers. But, the army chiefs refused collaboration with Virchow and his friends. So, they were only to consider "associated" characteristics such as colour of hair, eyes and complexion. This new approach, was assisted by the German educational authorities and also by those of Austria, Switzerland and Belgium.[51]

Questionnaries were sent to all the teachers in these countries. It was specified therein that the theory that European peoples came from a common Asiatic country of origin was open to doubt. The Indo-Germanic or Aryan immigration had got mixed up with an aboriginal population in Europe. The Aryans were blond and dolichocephalic, the natives dark and brachycephalic. Statistics about the distribution of the colour of eyes and hair in Europe would show if the assumption was true or not. Scientific accuracy required a careful examination of all children with the exception of Jews and foreigners. The questionnaire ended thus:

> Teachers will not hesitate to make their contribution to a scientific enterprise whose purpose, like that of schools, is the gaining of self-knowledge; for the knowledge of our origins is an essential part of the study of our own human nature.[52]

The investigation involving fifteen million school-children lasted more than ten years. Virchow had gone to Finland to establish that, contrary to the prevalent belief, the overwhelming majority of the Finns was blond and in 1885, communicated the general result of the enquiry to the Prussain Academy of Sciences.[53] These results were "as decisive as they were surprising." The so-called French theory was demolished. Northern Germany including the territory East of the Elbe showed that the people there were of essentially Germanic stock as blond hair and blue eyes predominated there. Germanic migrations to the West and South—of Goths, Franks and Burgundians were finally overwhelmed by the native populations. But those in the East had resulted in a definitive Germanization, "the formation of a new, purely German, *Volkstum*. The fact that the dynasties of both the Hapsburgs and the Hohen-zollerns should have had their real origins in that region is certainly not without significance.[54] The Germano-Aryan honour of Prussia was saved: The patriots, concerned by the threat of the "Slav invasion", were satisfied.

Virchow, however, as a political man fought against the rising tide of pan-Germanism and anti-semitism; as a scientist he deplored the misuse of science for political agitation and warned his colleagues: "The questions which we are dealing with, when taken over by the people, soon become national questions."[55] He restrained the racist enthusiasm of his friends often. Virchow seems also to have been the first great scientist to suspect that "dolichocephaly", the new totem of the Germanomaniacs, was a malleable and mutable standard and therefore lacked all historic-anthropological value.[56] His faith in craniolgoy was shaken, though he did not completely abandon it: In 1891, he expressed an opinion on some skulls which were dug up in Hungary—"similar to Aryan skulls. There is nothing to prove that they do not belong to an Aryan people but, in any case, they are not Mongolian and not Australian. I can be sure of that."[57]

French-German Debate

Thus on the Finnish-Slav front, French science had suffered a setback. The battle continued to rage in other spheres as the English philologist, Issac Taylor, described in 1890:

> The question has been debated with needless acrimony. German scholars, notably Posche, Penka, Hehn, and Lindenschmidt, have contended that the physical type of primitive Aryans was that of the North Germans—a tall, fair, blue-eyed dolichocephalic race. French writers, on the other hand, such as chavee. De Mortillet, and Ujvalfy, have maintained that the Aryans were brachycephalic, and that the true Aryan type is represented by the Gauls.
>
> The Germans claim the primitive Aryans as typical Germans who Aryanized the French, while the French claim them as typical Frenchman who Aryanized the Germans. Both parties maintain that their own ancestors were the pure noble race of Aryan conquerors, and that their hereditary foes belonged to a conquered and enslaved race of aboriginal savages, who received the germs of civilization from their hereditary superiors. Each party accuses the other of subordinating the results of science to Chauvinistic sentiment.
>
> Thus Posche, in somewhat inflated language, writes: "The true scientific theory, which uplifts itself calm and clear, like the summit of Olympus, over the passing storm-clouds of the moment, is that a noble race of fair-haired, blue-eyed people vanquished and subjugated an earlier race of short stature and dark hair. In opposition to this is the new French

> theory, without scientific foundation, originating in political hatred, which asserts that the primitive Aryans were a short and dark people who Aryanized the tall fair race."
>
> M.Chavee, on the other hand, contends that the intellectual superiority lies with the other race, Look, he says, at the beautifully formed head of the Iranians and Hindus, so intelligent and so well developed. Look at the perfection of those admirable languages, the Sanskrit and the Zend. The Germans have merely defaced and spoilt the beautiful structure of the primitive Aryan speech.
>
> Ujvalfy says, "if superiority consists merely in physical energy, enterprise, invasion, conquest, then the fair dolichocephalic race may claim to be the leading race in the world; but if we consider mental qualities, the artistic and the intellectual faculties then the superiority lies with the brachycephalic race."
>
> De Mortillet also is strong to the same effect. The civilization of Europe is due, he contends, to the brachycephalic race.[58]

Taylor himself called the "Ural-Altai Brachycephalics" as primitive Aryans to whom, he related the Finns and the Celts.

Thus the Aryan myth, just like the Trojan, became an apple of discord between France and Germany, the main development in Germany or in Scandinavia. This was carried out under the cover of science, and was favoured by the natural prudence of real scientists like Virchow, Kollmann, LonLuschan and others by the end of the century. They agreed that they were more ignorant than what they had been twenty years earlier. The hopes of finding the ancestors of European peoples in India had banished: Even that, in fact, the Aryan race no longer existed.[59]

But authors as Posche, Penka and Kossina came forward to drown all the doubts and scruples, as Virchow observed sarcastically, "derived all civilized peoples, the Greeks, the Italians etc. and, how could it be otherwise, the ancient Trojans too—from the prehistoric Germans".[60] This school of thought came to be dominant in Germany in the twentieth century and which, in Hitlerism, abandoned any pretence at scientific impartiality. The most famous spokesman of this school, the anthropologist George Heberer, declared about a prehistoric site in Thuringia:

> It is linked with one of the most significant phenomena of history, the birth of Indo-Germanism! That this German territory, this Germany should have been the homeland of the race which is said to have achieved the highest cultural ahievements can not leave us, who are its heirs, indifferent. We cultivate a heritage which is indeed our own, which did not reach us from elsewhere, and did not come to us from the Orient. It was here that it was founded and here that it developed throughout the

millennia. This truth faces us with obligations. Once more, a new humanity is being established today, in the course of a titanic struggle in the heart of Europe....[61]

This is the way the old Germanic tradition of "the creation of the self out of itself" perpetuated or renewed. It is worth noting that under the Third Reich it was the idea of Nordic man which commanded agreement rather than that of *Aryan man or Germanic man.* The over-estimation of dolichocephalic blonds reached such a pitch that the Party authorities issued a circular ordering that the susceptibilities of swarthy Germans, or of those with round heads, should be spared.[62]

An anthropological debate ensued in France at the end of the nineteenth century. That was a continuation of the controversy about the Two Races. The Third Republic chose to be Gallic. It looked as though the rejected Germans were retreating to the charge disguised as "dolicho-blonds". Broca's successor Paul Topinard was a staunch supporter of the peaceful bourgeois Republic:

> The Gauls, according to history, were a people formed of two elements: the leaders or conquerors, blond, tall dolichocephalci, leptoprosopes, etc. But the mass of the people, were small, relatively brachycephalic, chamaeoprosopes. The brachycephalic were always oppressed. They were the victims of the dolichocephalics, who carried them off from their fields and forced them to follow their invasions, as at Delphi. The least unfortunate sought refuge, as poor and obscure people in the mountains. In time their fate changed. The blond people changed from warriors into merchants or industrial workers. The brachycephalics breathed again. Being naturally prolific, their numbers increased while the dolichocephalics naturally diminished. Today, in France, among other countries, in Southern Germany, etc. they constitute the laborious, sober, farsighted, peace-loving and patriotic population. Does not the future belong to them?[63]

The views of Georges Vacher dee Lapouge (1854-1936), the main champion of the dolicho-blond Franks, was most eloquent and hopeful of the future of his country:

> The confusion of ideas runs deep. The failure of the Revolution is obvious. This means above all a replacement of the dolicho-blonds by the brachycephalics as the holders of power. The brachycephalics gained power by the Revolution and, as a result of democratic development, this power tends to be concentrated in the lower classes, those which are most brachycephalic. The Aryan, as defined, is something quite different. He is the *Homo Europeans,* a race which made France great, the members of which are, indeed almost extinct.[64]

Lapouge ascribed all the misfortunes of France to the extinction of the Aryans. With the passing of time his craniology, which he called anthroposociology, became more spiteful:

> It was a serious matter that the curse of the cephalic index should make the brachycephalics born slaves having lost their own, they had constantly to seek out new masters. That was an instinct common only to brachycephalics and to dogs. Wherever they were they had to live under the domination of the dolicho-blonds. In the absence of Aryans, under that of the Chinese and the Jews....[65] That was indeed a serious matter.

Lapouge endeavoured to point out that: "the ancestors of the Aryans cultivated wheat when those of the brachycephalics were probably still living like monkeys."[66] It sounds delirious. But his delirium fostered in him a presentiment of other kinds of madness. That had a world-wide effect. He forecast:

> The conflict of races was about to start openly within nations and between nations. One could only ask oneself if the ideas of the fraternity and equality of man were not against nature. I am convinced that in the next century people would slaughter each other by the million because of a difference of a degree or two in the cephalic index. It was by that sign, that replaced that Biblical shibboleth and linguistic affinities, that men will be identified. The last sentimentalists would be able to witness the most massive extermination of peoples.[67]

Lapouge was certainly revered in Germany where William II considered him to be "the only great Fenchman"[68] who had followers in other European countries. His scientific method was mainly to prepare tables comparing the cephalic index, religious beliefs, the extent of urbanization and tax receipts from one region to another.[69] Some of these correlations were preoccupying Max Weber at about that time. But from skull alone Lapouge sought to wrest the secrets of ethics and conduct. In France, Celestin Blugle, impressed though he was by Lapouge's work, attacked him only on ground of principles and not of scientific truth.[70] The influential French philosopher Alfred Fouillee, was rather suspicious of the future of France and of Europe because of the "retreat of the dolichoblonds":

> He expressed the view that they were becoming more and more Celto-Slav and "Turanian" once again, as they were before the arrival of the Gauls. But the so-called Aryan element in their midst was losing importance and influence. That was the phenomenon causing anxiety to some anthropologists. It was happening though less rapidly, to all other European peoples. There was so to speak, a slow and general russification of Europe, including Germany itself, a spontaneous pan-Celtism or pan-Slavism. It was not yet possible to foresee the fortunate or unfortunate results of this change. Only it could be said that balance of their three constituent races had been compromised.[71]

It was in a harmonious proportion of German, Celtic and Latin blood that Fouillee propagated, the special genius of France lay. The romantic historians embezzled this idea during the restoration. They had a firm hold on the Dreyfus affair. This provoked this party, emerged as the result of the Dreyfus affair, at par with German national-socialism. Both shared an idealization of an archaic past, and appeal to "instincts" and cult of hartred and violence.[72] Its ancestor-cult was so all-embracing that it was at war with the Jewish race, while the Action Francaise welcomed Celts, Ligurians, Galatians, greeks, Germans and Romans to its pantheon. But it suffered from political powerlessness because of its failure to formulate a monolith elementary myth of origin. They only owed unquestionable allegiance to the French Kings. But, that was not enough. Moreover, one notes again in this instance the contrast, between an authentically western tradition in France, and the Germanic or Slav claims to "autochthony". Charles Maurras propagated the "Latinity" of the English. This racialist glorified the lineage of the Roi Soleil:

> The Spanish and Italian ancestries must neither be exaggerated nor belittled. They exist. Perhaps they were less a hindrance than a help to some of the more marked and constant features of a very pure Celto-Galatian. Louis Bertrand says "of a Latin". But could one go further back, to that Gallic pre-Latinism? Yes, one easily can and thus can explain our most ancient ties with Greece and Rome.[73]

Maurras was also the person to gloss over the traditionally and officially *Frankish* lineage of the king. Contradictions or paradoxes as those of the *Action francaise* may be found in the opening lines of Jacques Bainville's *History of France* which reads that the ligurians and the lberians, who were dark and of medium height still provide the basis for the French population. The tradition of the Druids tells us that the Gauls were in part indigenous, in part immigrants from the North and from beyond the Rhine. Thus there had been a fusion of races in prehistoric times. The French people is an amalgam, better than a race, a nation. It may be said that France began at that time. Her civilization was too strong to survive the fresh influx of the Franks, while leaving material power in the hands of these barbarians. And she required Frankish power. She could assimilate men, and refine them. Her civilization, her religion is Roman.[74]

Hence there is nothing surprising that in 1940-1944 the pro-Hitler anthropologists of Paris dubbed the *Action francaise* "Action Marrance"—Marrano, or crypto-Jewish. Maurras himself was descsribed by the anthropologist Montandon a Nazi sympathizer, as the prototype of the Latino-Semite.[75]

Notes & References

1. Martin Bernal—Black Athena Vol I-IV. Free Association L. Books, London 1991.
2. *Ibid.*
3. Letter from Renan to Gobineau, 26/6/1856, Czuvres, Vol X pp. 203-5.
4. Historic Generale et systeme compare deslangues semitiques (1847-55). Czuvres Vol VIII pp. 580-9.
5. Hestoure des langues semitiques. Czuvures, Vol VIII pp. 585.
6. L'Avenir religieux des societes modernes (1860) Ceuvres I, 239, 242, 243.
7. Histoire des langues semitiques ibid.
8. De l'ongine du language (1848-1858) Ccurves, VIII, 98.
9. Discours des langues Semitiques.
10. S. Posener, Adolphe Cremeux, Paris 1933, Vol II, pp. 157.
11. Raymond Schwab, La Renaissance Orientale, Paris 1950 pp. 417.
12. L. Jacolliot, La Bible Dans' Inde, Vie de lezeus Christna, Paris 1873.
13. H. von Glasenapp, Das Indeienbild deutscher Denekr, op. cit., pp. 38-60.
14. Die Vernunft in der Geschichte, pp. 158.
15. See the cycle "Heimekehr" (1823-1824): "I called up the Devil and he appeared...He is an able diplomat and speaks eloquentaly of Church and State. He is somewhat pale but small's the wonder, for he is now studying Sanskrit and Hegel..."
16. Die Vorhalle des Europaischen Volkergeschichte...by Carl Ritter, 1820 (in R. Gerard, op.cit., pp. 192-4).
17. CF Historic de l'antisemitisme, Vol. III, pp. 325-6.
18. Christian Lassen, Indische Altertumskunde, Vol. I, Bonn 1847, pp. 4141.
19. *Ibid.*, pp. 513.
20. Etymologische Forschungen (1833-1836), Vol. I, pp. XXI.
21. S. Reionach, "Le mirage de la litterature anglaise", Paris 1905, Introduction, pp. XXII.
22. H. Taine, Histoire de al litterature angalise, Paris 1905, Introduction, pp. XXII.
23. I. Taylor, The Origin of the Aryans, An account of Prehistoric ethnology and civilization of Europe, London 1890, pp. 332.
24. E.B. Tylor, An introduction to the study of man...London, 1881, pp. 152, 112.
25. T. Waitz, Anthropoligie der Naturvaolker, Leipzig 1859, Vo. I, pp. 281-3.
26. A Bastian, 'Das Bestandige in den Menschenrassen und die Spielweite ihrer Veranderlichkit', Berlin 1868, pp. 23-4 and 156.

27. R. Virchow, Die Urbervolkerung Europa's, Berlin 1874, pp. 35-6.
28. F.G. Bergmann, Les peuples primitifs de la race de Japhete, Colmar 1853, pp. 6.
29. Honore Chavee, Les langues et les races, Paris 1862, pp. 60.
30. "Lettres do cosima Wagner a Gobineau. Revue hebdomadaire", 23 July 1938, pp. 287.
31. A Schleicher, Compendium der vergleichenden Grammatik... (1861), pp. 7-8.
32. "Le mirage oriental", in L'Anthropologie, Vol. IV (1893), pp.553.
33. M. Muller, Lectures on the Science of Language, London 1862, pp. 240 et seq., especially pp. 249.
34. A. Pictet, Les origines indo-Europeennes ou les Aryas primitifs, Essai de paleontologie linguistique, Paris 1859, pp. I, pp. 753-4.
35. Marc Aurele, et la fin due monde antique, Euvres completes, 1947-1961 ed., pp. I, 142.
36. On the Great Race-Elements in Christianity by the Rev. Dunbar I. Heath, in "Journal of the Anthropological Society of London", V (1867), pp. XIXXXVIII.
37. Revue des cours scientifiques de la France et de l'etranger, V, (1868), pp. 727.
38. Reveue des Deux Mondes of February 1871, pp. 687 et seq.
39. L. Figuier, Tableau de al nature; Les races humaines, Paris 1872 (4th ed., 1885), pp. 59.
40. Revue d'anthropologie, I (1872), pp. 163-4 (La race prussienne et M. Mantegazza).
41. A. de Quatrefages, "Les origines europeennes", Revue scientifique de la France et de l'etranger, 1872, 2nd semester, pp. 28.
42. A de Quatrefages, Histoire, generale des race humaines, Paris 1889, pp. 454-5.
43. Zeitschrift fur Ethnologie, IV (1872), pp. 45-64 (a review of La race prussienne by Quatrefages. It is signed B.)
44. *Ibid.*
45. Der Berliner Antisemitismusstreit, published by W. Bochlich, Frankfurt a/ M 1965, pp. 52.
46. Erich Bierhahn, "Blondheit and Blondheitskult in der deutschen Literatur". Archiv fur Kulturgeschichte, XLVI (1964), pp. 309-33.
47. A Retzius, Ethnologische Schriften, Stockholm 1864.
48. "In the course of digging,the archaeologist must collect the maximum number of samples and not content himself with sending a few skulls to the laborätory of the Etudes with the question: tell me, are they Franks, Burgundians, Saraccens or Romans?" P. Topinard. L'Anthropologie, Paris 1876, pp. 235; cf. also pp. 229.

49. R. Virchow, "Ueber die Methode der wissenschaftlichen Anthropologie, Eine Antwort an Herrn de Quatrefages", Zeitschrift fur Ethnologie, IV, 1872, pp. 300-302. Also Die Urbevolkerung Europa's, Berlin 1874, especially pp. 31.
50. Correspondenzblatt der deutschen Gesellschaft fur Anthropologie, Ethnolgoie and Urgeschichte, June-October 1871, pp. 53.
51. Virchow, Archiv fur Anthropologie, XVI (1886), pp. 275-475, and especially pp. 284-5.
52. *Ibid.*, pp. 282.
53. R. Virchow, "Vortrag uber die physische Anthropolgoie der Finnen", zeitschrift fur Ethnologie, VI (1874), pp. 169-89.
54. R. Virchow, Die Verbreitung des blonden und des brunetten Typus in Mitteleuropa, "Sitzungsberichte der komiglich preussischen Akademic der wissenschaften". 1885, Vol. I, pp. 39-47.
55. R. Virchow, "Die Anthropologie in den letzten 20 Jahren", correspondenzblatt der deutschen Gesellschaft fur Anthjropolgoie...January 1889, pp. 91.
56. R. Virchow, Crania Ethnica Americana, Berlin 1894, especially pp. 32.
57. Correspondenzblatt der deutschen Gesellschaft fur Anthropologie... September 1891, pp. 79.
58. I. Taylor, The Origin of the Aryans, London 1890, pp. 226, et seq.
59. R. Virchow, "Die Anthropologie in den letzten 20 Jahren", Correspondenzblattt...., 1889, pp. 99;
60. R. Virchow, Correspondenzblatt.., 1891, pp. 77.
61. Karl Saller, Die Rassenlhre des Nationalsozialismus, Darmstadt 1961, pp. 57-9.
62. L. Poliakov J. Wulf, Das Dritte Reich und seine Denker, Berlin 1959, pp. 411-13.
63. P. Topinard in L'Anthropologie, IV (1893), pp. 505.
64. G. Vacher de Lapouge, L'Aryen, son role social, Paris 1899, p. VII, pp. 22 and 464.
65. *Ibid.*, pp. 238.
66. *Ibid.*, pp. 372-3.
67. *Ibid.*, pp. VII and "I" Anthropolgoie et la science politique", Revue d' anthropologie, 15 May 1887, pp. 15.
68. G. Montandon, "Gerorges Vacher de Lapouge", L'Ethnie francaise, May-June 1941, pp. 5.
69. L'Aryen, son role social, especially pp. 413-61.
70. C. Bougle, "Anthropolgie et democratie", Revue de metaphisique et de morale, V (1897).

71. A Fouillee, "Degenerescence? Le passe et le present de notre race", Revue des Deux-Mondes, 1895 (5), pp. 815.
72. The thesis of Mme Capitan-Peter, Une pensee de droite: l'Action francaise, Paris 1970.
73. *Ibid.*
74. J. Bainville, Historie de France, "Livre de Poche" ed. 1964, pp. 7 and 18.
75. The Huxley, Emancipation-black and white, "Lay sermons...", London 1887, pp. 18, et seq.

4

Sudden Shift to European Home

O. Schrader*

A host of ethnographical, historical, and linguistic arguments seemed to constitute a crushing mass of evidence in its favour. This was the state of things, when suddenly in England, the first doubt was cast on the Asiatic origin of the Indo-Europeans—on this hypothesis which had almost attained to historical certainty. R.G. Latham was the man who, is a work abounding in heterordox views (*Elements of Comparative Philology*, London, 1862), repeated and supported with further arguments a view which he had indeed enunciated before (cf. *The Native Races of the Russain Empire,* London, 1854; and still earlier, Latham's edition of *Germania*, 1851, lxvii, p. cxxxvii.), "that the original abode of the Indo-Europeans is rather to be looked for in Europe" (cf., *loc. cit.*, 611, *f.*).

Latham starts from the assumption that Sanskrit is closely connected with the Lithu-Slavonic languages, an assumption which he considers proved, as regards sound-lore in particular, by the facts, which we have already given, with respect to the Indo-Germanic gutturals. Consequently the original position of Sanskrit must have been in contact with that of the Slavo-Lithuanians, and either Sanskrit must have reached India from Europe, or else Lithuanian, Slavonic, Latin, Greek, and German must have reached Europe from Asia. For a decision between these two possibilities, both equally probable in themselves, there is not the least shred of evidence forthcoming. "What I have found in this stead is a tacit assumption that as the east is the probable quarter in which either the human species, or the greater part of our civilization, originated, everything came from it. But surely in this there is a confusion between the primary diffusion of mankind over the world at large, and those secondary movements by which according to even the ordinary hypothesis, the Lithuanic, &c., came from Asia into Europe" (p. 612).

---

* A XIX Century German Scholar. The above extract is taken from the English translation of the second and enlarged edition of his original German book "*Sprachvergleichung und Urgeschichte,*" The translation was published from London in 1890 under the title, "*Prehistoric Antiquities of the Aryan Peoples: A Manual of Comparative Philology and the Earliest Culture.*"

The matter reduces itself therefore to a consideration of general probabilities. Now, since Latham proceeds to argue, a *priori* it is probable that the smaller class proceeds from the area of distribution of the greater, and since in natural science it is usual to derive the species from the area of the genus and not the genus from the area of the species, and further, since Teutonic is not derived from English, not Finnic from Magyar, but the reverse, therefore the starting-point of Sanskrit also must be sought in Europe and on the eastern or south-eastern borders of Lithuanian. Or, as it is put in the edition of *Germania* mentioned above:

> When we have two branches, which belong to the same family and are separated from each other, one of which covers a larger area and shows the greater number of varieties, while the other possesses a narrower range and greater homogeneity, it is to be assumed that the latter is derived from the former and not the reverse. To derive the Indo-Europeans of Europe from the Indo-Europeans of Asia is the same thing in ethnology as if in herpetology one were to derive the reptiles of Great Britain from those of Ireland.

Equally serious doubts as to the force of the arguments put forward in favour of the Asiatic origin of the Indo-Europeans were expressed in the year 1867 by W.D. Whitney (*Language and the Study of Language,* p. 20, *f. cf.,* p. 203). He is of opinion that neither myth, history, nor language, warrant any conclusions whatever as to the situation of the original Indo-Germanic home. Specially incomprehensible is it to him, how anybody could have regarded the geographical reminiscences of the Zend Avesta (cf. above, p. 85) as indicating the direction of the Indo-Germanic migrations.[1]

The ranks of the doubters were joined in the following year by Th. Benfey, who, however, does not share Whitney's sceptical point of view, but takes his stand with decision in favour of deriving the Indo-Europeans from Europe, (Cf. Preface to the *Worterb, der indog, Grundsprache,* by A. Fick, 1868, p. viii., and *Geschichte der Sprachwissenschaft,* 1869, pp. 597-600). "Since geological investigations," he says, on p. ix. of the Preface, "have made it certain that Europe has been the abode of man for inconceivable ages, all the reasons which have hitherto been regarded as proving that the Indo-Europeans came from Asia, and which really have their basis in the prejudices instilled into us with our earliest education, fall to the ground." A decisive argument against Asia and for Europe, however, is afforded by certain facts of language: names for the great Asiatic beasts of prey, the lion and tiger, are as conspicuous by their absence from the original Indo-Germanic fauna as is that of the Asiatic beast of transport, the camel. "From the fact," it is added in the *History of the Science of*

Language (Geschichte der sprachwissenschaft, p. 600, note), that the Hindus designate the lion by a word which (*simhá*) is not formed from an Indo-Germanic root,[2] and the Greeks by an undoubted loan-word (λîs, λεων from Hebr. *laish*, &c.), it may be inferred that in the original language the lion was known to neither, but that both nations made their acquaintance with it after their separation, and in all probability continued to use the name which had been given to it by the non-Indo-Germanic peoples amongst whom they first became acquainted with it. Benfey holds out the promise of a thorough investigation of the question as to the original home of the Indo-Europeans, but has not yet accomplished it. All that we can learn more precisely from later indications is that (cf. *Allgemeine Zeitung,* 1875, p. 3270) Benfey lays the scene of Indo-Germanic evolution close to the boundaries of Asia, in the country north of the Black Sea, from the mouths of the Danube to the Caspian. In this way the "swamps rich in salt," which occur on the shores of the Aral and the Caspian, would just explain the acquaintance with salt which Benfey ascribes to the original people (cf. above, p. 40, f.).

Latham's and Benfey's polemic against the assumption that the home of the Indo-Europeans is to be sought in Asia, found as eloquent advocate in L. Geiger, who, in an essay written in 1869-70, *On the Original Abode of the Indo-Europeans* (*Uber die Ursitze der Indogermanen,* published in *Zur Entwicklungsgeshichte der Menschheit,* 1871, p. 113, f.) endeavours to show that Germany, in particular Central and Western Germany, must be regarded as the original home of the Indo-Europeans. Amongst the arguments which Geiger produces for his hypothesis, a prominent position is taken by the character of the vegetation[3] in the way of trees, which the original land of the Indo-Europeans is shown to have had. Besides firs, willows, ashes, alders, hazel-shrubs, there are, according to Geiger, three forest-trees especially in the names of which the languages show remarkable agreement: the birch (Sans. *bhurja.* Lith. *berzas,* Russ. *bereza,* Germ. *birke*), the beech (Lat. *fagus,* G. "oak", Germ Buche), and the Oak (Sans. dru, Goth. *trui*, "tree, timber, G "oak," O. I. *daur*, ditto). Now, of these trees the beech is to be regarded as peculiarly adapted to determine the original Indo-Germanic home. Since the home of this tree is to be looked for in the west of the Prussian Baltaic provinces, while on the other hand, "at the beginning of the Christian era, the beech had not yet reached Holland (*cf.* Geiger, *op.cit.*, p. 136) nor England (Caesar, B.G., v. 12), and in the primeval Indo-Germanic period had not got anything like so far north, we must go south to the region in which this tree can be certainly supposed to have flourished in ancient times, which as regards Germany will take us to about the Thuringerwald." Geiger altogether leaves out of consideration in this conclusion the fact that the name of the beech does not occur amongst the Asiatic Indo-Europeans. The same argument, therefore, is obviously more correctly employed by Fick merely to determine the home of the European members of the Indo-Germanic family (cf. *Worterbuch,* p. 1047, *f.*)

Another fact which is to bear out Geiger's hypothesis in that the only two kinds of grain which were cultivated in the primeval period were barley and rye. This view is based, as far as rye is concerned, on the O.H.G. *rocco*, Pr. *rugis*, Lith. *rugiei* Russ. *roz*, &c., which in accordance with Grimm and Pictet is compared with Sans. *vrihi*, "rice." That the original meaning, however, of this series of words was "rye," follows from the fact that the North European languages agree as to the meaning both with each other and with the Thracian *βριεα* (*Galenus de alim, facult., i.* 13). "A soil on which rye and barley flourish but not wheat can only be looked for in the north of Europe; but for a very early age a more southern zone also must undoubtedly be excluded from the cultivation of wheat." (p. 140).

Highly prized, too, in the original Indo-Germanic period, according to Geiger, was "the genuinely European colouring plant," woad (G., Lat. *vitrum,* Teut. *waid*, from *waisd*), which the Indo-Europeans used for tattooing the body, an idea to which Geiger is led by Caesar's notice (B.G., v. 14) of the ancient Britons: *se vitro inficiunt, quod, caeruleum efficit colorem.*[4]

A further argument in favour of Germany, in our author's eyes, is what Pictet had already pointed out, viz., that the Indo-Germanic languages possess identical names only for spring, summer, and winter, but not for antumn. Now since, according to Tacitus, Germ. *hiems et ver et aestas intellectum ac vocabula habent, auctumni-perinde nomen ac bona ignorantur*, the following inference is drawn: "On the strength of this noteworthy passage, we will venture to say: if the abode of the original Indo-Germanic people was not Germany, then at any rate as regards temperature and the effect produced by the seasons, it must have been exactly like the Germany of Tacitus" (p. 146).

The fauna of the primeval period, too, was of a northern character. The sea was perhaps known to the Indo-Euroepans only by hearsay, and Geiger does not make them dwell in its neighbourhood. Their want of familiarity with it is shown by the absence of a common name for salt, for mussel, oysters, sails, varieties of fish (except the names for the eel), &c.

Finally, let us mention that the light-complexioned type of man, which is claimed as the original Indo-Germanic type, and which is seen most clearly amongst the Teutons, is supposed to point to Germany as the original home of the Indo-Europeans.

In the same year in which Geiger's work appeared, J.G. Cuno also offered his opposition (*Forschungen im Gebiete der alten Volker-kunde, I. Teil: Die Scythen*) to the dominant theory of the Central Asiatic origin of the Indo-Europeans. Cuno starts from the assumption that the original Indo-Germanic people must have numbered many millions, a view to which he is led by his absolutely unique interpretation of the kinship of the Indo-Germanic languages and its causes. He does not explain it by the assumption of a common derivation of the Indo-Germanic languages from one and the same original language. His view is that over the whole extent of a great and homegeneous area idioms different from each other from the very beginning grew up, having more or less likeness to each other. Consequently he sees in "the more deep-seated differences between the individual members of the Indo-Germanic family," not "modifications of what was once identical," but "independent species of the same genus" (p. 67). Under these circumstances the question for him is "to find an extensive area, habitable throughout, as homogeneous as possible as regards geography and climate, containing no "people-sheds" within its limits, and such, therefore, that in it a homogeneous people could take its rise and have an organic growth" (p. 31). Such an area in Cuno's opinion occurs but in one place on our planet, and it includes the east of Europe, Northern Germany and the north and west of France, i.e., the whole enormous tract of land between lat. 45 and 60, extending from the Ural to the Atlantic Ocean. If the Lithuanians, Slavs, Teutons, and Celts, in this way, are the original inhabitants of the lands they now occupy, the original home of the Greeks no less, as their myths and language indicate, must be looked for in the north and in the neighbourhood of the Lithuanians. This follows, not only from what is said by Herodotus (iv. 108), who knows of a town of the Geloni in the land of the Budini[5] possessing a Greek cult and language, but especially from the close affinity which Cuno asserts exists between Greek and Lithuanian (pp. 42-45).[6]

In favour of his hypothesis of the origin of the Indo-Europeans, Cuno has another argument, which the science of language seems him to offer of itself. "If the original home of the people and language of the Indo-Europeans is the lowland and mountain spurs of Central and Eastern Europe, if language and people had their origin there then there must be numerous points of contact between the Indo-Germanic family of languages and its immediate neighbour, the Finnic family" (p. 50). And as a matter of fact, Cuno contrives to collect, in the way of numerals, pronouns, and names of kin, a whole heap of Finno-Indo-Germanic equivalents, which, according to him, cannot be due to borrowing, but must have been the common property of the two languages at the time of their origin. As, now, it follows that the Finnic and Indo-Germanic families of language were neighbours from the beginning, and as, on the other hand, it would be absurd to assume that the Finns and Indo-Europeans, for instance, undertook a joint emigration from Asia, the certain inference is "that the primeval Indo-Europeans lived then, where the main body of them are to be found at the present day, and that the movements which took place were from South-East Russia through the Turanian steppes to Persia, and not, reversely, to South-East Russia."

Whatever may be our opinion about the arguments alleged in support of deriving the Indo-Europeans from Europe, the fact is to be noted that the demurrers of the scholars mentioned gave the most violent shock to the sway of the dominant hypothesis of the Asia origin of the Indo-Europeans. The last twenty years, therefore, may be justly termed a period of struggle, as between the two conflicting views.

Notes & References

1. The translator and editor, J. Jolly (874), on the other hand, expresses himself decidely in favour of the East as the original home of the Indo-Europeans, especially because of "the ever increasing probability of an original connection between the Indo Europeans and the Semites" (cf. pp. 304, f., of the German edition).
2. Cf. Part iv, ch. ii.
3. Cf. Part iv, ch. iv.
4. The subject of the tattooing of the body by the Indo-Europeans is discussed at greater length, both as regards the process itself and the evidence of language for it, by Geiger in Zur Entwicklungs yeschichtz der Menschhcit, pp. 71, f.
5. Cf. Kiepert, Lehrbuch d. alten Geographie, pp. 342.
6. As we shall not return to this subject, we may as well say here that the arguments brought forward by Cuno to show the close kinship of Lithuanian and Greek, from their very nature can prove absolutely nothing. The grammatical points of agreement between Greek and Lithuanian, which Cuno produces, either are to be found in, or may with certainty be inferred of, other languages also (Lith, witkun= λυκων , but also Slav *vluku* and Goth. *vulfe=vluk-am* and *vulf-am*; Lith. *du-siu*= δωσω but also Irish *fortias, tiasu*: *fortiagaim*, &c.). Nowhere is an attempt made to discover any new formations peculiar to the two languages. As for what Herodotus says, the historian himself explains the Geloni as descendants of Greek refugees from the Pontic emporia.

5

The Myth of an 'Aryan Race'

Sir Julian Huxley*

Apart from these general considerations, certain fallacies of unscientific 'racial' conceptions, and in particular the myth of an 'Aryan race', call for separate discussion.

In 1848 the young German scholar Friedrich Max Muller (1823-1900) settled in Oxford, where he reminded for the rest of his life. The high character and great literary and philological gifts of Max Muller are well known. About 1853 he introduced into English usage the unlucky term *Aryan*,[1] as applied to a large group of languages. His use of this Sanskrit word contains in itself two assumptions—one lingustic, that the Indo-Persian sub-group of language is older or more primitive than any of its relatives; the other geographical, that the cradle of the common ancestor of these languages was the Ariana of the ancients in Central Asia. Of these the first is now known to be certainly erroneous and the second now regarded as probably erroneous. Nevertheless, around each of these two assumptions a whole library of literature has arisen.

Moreover, Max Muller threw another apple of discord. He introduced a proposition which is demonstrably false. He spoke not only of a definite Aryan language and its descendants, but also of a corresponding 'Aryan race'. The idea was rapidly taken up both in Germany and in England. It affected to some extent a certain number of the nationalist historical and romantic writers, none of whom had any ethnological training. It was given especial currency by the French author Count Joseph de Gobineau (1816-82). Of the English group it will be enough to recall some of the ablest, Thomas Carlyle (1795-1881), J.A. Froude (1818-94). Charles Kingsley (1819-75), and J.R. Green (1837-83). What these men have written on the subject has been cast by historians into the limbo of discarded and discredited theories.

---

* Renowned British scientist and thinker. Joint author with A.C. Haddon of "We Europeans".

The above extract is taken from his "Race in Europe" published in 1939 as no. 5 of the series "Oxford Pamphlets on World Affairs" (OUP, London) (pp. 19-23).

In England and America the phrase 'Aryan race' has quite ceased to be used by writers with scientific knowledge, though it appears occasionally in political and propagandist literature. A foreign secretary recently blundered into using it. In Germany the idea of an 'Aryan' race received no more scientific support than in England. Nevertheless, it found able and very persistent literary advocates who made it appear very flattering to local vanity. It therefore steadily spread, fostered by special conditions.

Max Muller himself was later convinced by scientific friends of the enormity of his error and he did his very best to make amends. Thus in 1888 he wrote:

> I have declared again and again that if I say Aryas, I mean neither blood nor bones, nor hair, nor skull; I mean simply those who speak an Aryan language....When I speak of them I commit myself to no anatomical characteristics. The blue-eyed and fair-haired Scandinavians may have been conquerors or conquered. They may have adopted the language of their darker lords or vice-versa....To me an ethnologist who speaks of Aryan race, Aryan blood, Aryan eyes and hair, is as great a sinner as a linguist who speaks of a dolichocephalic dictionary or a brachycephalic grammar.[2]

Max Muller frequently repeated his protest, but alas! 'the evil that men do lives after them, the good is oft interred with their bones'! Who does not wish to have had noble ancestors? The belief in an 'Aryan' race had become accepted by philologists, who knew nothing of science—and the word was freely used by writers who claimed to treat of science though they had no technical training and no clear idea of the biological meaning to attached to the word 'race'. The influence of the untenable idea of an 'Aryan race' vitiates all German writings on anthropology which are now allowed to appear. If the term 'Aryan' is given a racial meaning at all, it should be applied to that tribal unit, whatever it was, that first spoke a language distinguishable as Aryan. Of the physical characters of that hypothetical unit it is the simple truth to say that we know nothing whatever. As regards the locality where this language was first spoken, the only tolerably certain statement that can be made is that it was somewhere in Asia and was not in Europe. It is thus absurd to distinguish between 'non-Aryans' and 'Europeans'.

There is no need to trace in detail the history of the Aryan controversy. it will be enough to say that while the Germans claimed that these mythical Aryans were tall, fair, and long-headed—the hypothetical ancestors of hypothetical early Teutons, the French claimed that the Aryan language and the Aryan civilization came into Europe with the Alpines

(Eurasiatics), who are of medium build, rather dark, and broad-headed. The decipherment of the language of the very 'Jewish'-looking Hittites—which was certainly Aryan—and the discovery of certain Aryan languages in North-West India throws a new complexion on the whole question of the origin of the Aryan languages.

Both the German and the French views cannot be entirely true, but both may be partially or entirely erroneous. In so far as the cultural origns of our civilization can be associated with any particular physical type, it must be linked neither with the Nordic nor the Eurasiatic, but rather with the Mediterranean. As regards the general physical measurements of the existing population of central Europe, the prevailing physical type is Eurasiatic rather than either Nordic or Mediterranean.

Notes & References

1. The word Aryan was first used quite correctly by Sir William Jones (1746-94) as a name for the speakers of a group of Indian languages.
2. Max Muller, Biographies of Words and the Home of the Aryans, London, 1888, pp. 120.

6

The Rise and Fall of Scientific Racism

S.K. Mahajan*

Beginning with the 15th century, white Europeans came in contact with more and more people around the globe most of whom looked physically different. Thanks to their superior military technology, the Europeans soon found themselves exterminating, enslaving or subjugating many of these peoples. All this was highly profitable although difficult morally to justify.

A morally defensible rationale for slavery and colonialism would have been highly useful. It would suppress any feelings of guilt within the community, silence any internal conscientious rebels and keep the less privileged groups demoralised with a nagging feeling of their possible inferiority. Initially, therefore, religion was tried. Colonalism and slavery were seen not as immoral means of economic exploitation but as means to civilize the barbarians and save their heathen souls by bringing them into the Christian fold.

This worked for some time but not very long. When the African slaves in American colonies had been converted to Christianity it was argued by some that they were now the equals of whites and should be freed. This meant reduction in profits, making it imperative to think up a better argument in support of the natural right of the whites to rule over other people. If it could be shown that the white man was endowed with superior mental and moral attributes which were necessary for humanity's progress but were missing in non-whites, then the European domination could be rationalised as the "white man's burden". And what better way was there to prove this than the method of science? Science enjoyed enormous prestige and authority in the resurgent West during the 18th and 19th centuries. No one could raise moral objections against a scientifically proven idea.

---

* A scientist with the Genetic section, Biology and Agriculture Division, BARC, Bombay. His review article on Nancy Stepan: *The Idea of Race in Science: Great Britain 1800-1960* (Macmillan Press and St. Antory's College Oxford, 1982) is being reproduced here from *SCIENCE TODAY*, December, 1982.

Such were the social imperatives that led to the genesis, around the year 1800, of what Nancy Stepan calls the "Race Science" in her book. Throughout the 19th century and for the first half of the 20th, race-science remained a major obsession with western biologists, anthropologists and psychologists. The basic hypothesis of this science was something like this:

Based on their biological constitution human beings can be classified into a small number of well-defined racial types. These racial types are fixed and can be arranged in a hierarchy in which the European whites are at the top and the African blacks at the bottom with others coming in between. The physical, mental and moral worth of any individual is determined by the hierarchical status of the racial type to which he belongs.

The primary goal of the race-scientists was to generate empirical data as well as a theoretical framework in support of the above hypothesis. This they did with remarkable zeal, diligence and persistence for well over a century in the face of formidable practical as well as theoretical set-backs. The heads and limbs of millions of people were measured. Some experts carried out hundreds of measurements on single skull, others introduced fancy biological measures of racial types such as the *index of negritude* (an algebraically defined precise measure of the darkness of skin!) the *facial angle* and the *cephalic index.* The most famous example, perhaps, was that of Samuel George Morton, one of the most influential and respected American scientists of the 19th century. Morton had collected over one thousand human skulls, including those of 600 Red Indians and 17 Hindus. He measured the cranial capacity of these skulls by filling them with mustard seeds or lead shots and used this data to produce tables which were repeatedly reproduced in textbooks for nearly a century.

It has been demonstrated by Stephen Jay Gould that Morton's raw data gave no significant difference between the mean cranial capacities of the Caucasian (Europeans, Jews and Hindus) and the Negro skulls. Morton had himself used the same data to classify mankind into a hierarchy of races in which the Caucasians and the Negros occupied the top and the bottom respectively. For doing this Morton had to resort (perhaps unconsciously) to selective use as well as misrepresentation of his data. There were others too who were busy inventing seemingly objective tests of mental ability and measuring IQs of thousands of subjects. Unfortunately, one of the most important proponents of the IQ tests, Sir Cyril Burt, has been shown to have invented a fictitious collaborator and many fictitious identical twins to buttress his views.

In spite of the great labours of the race scientists, their work has now been mostly forgotten. Apart from the profound changes in the global socio-political scene two factors internal to science have contributed to this—the inability of the race scientists to find universally acceptable criteria for racial classification, and the difficulties in reconciling the racial hypothesis with two of the most important developments in the biological theory, namely Darwinian evolution and Mendelian genetics.

According to Darwin's theory of evolution, all species are gradually changing due to accumulation of variations under natural selection. This conflicted with the hypothesis of fixed differences between different human races. However, so deep was the biologists' commitment to the racialist hypothesis that to accommodate it, it was proposed that after the development of the human brain, natural selection had ceased to operate on man who was now supposed to be experiencing only social evolution. Similarly, Mendelian genes were initially interpreted as stable hereditary determinants which would serve the purpose of transmitting fixed racial traits from one generation to another. However, between 1900 and 1920, evidence steadily accumulated to show that the genes were mutable and were the substrates on which natural selection operated. This led to the development of population genetics (as a synthesis between Mendelian genetics and natural selection) between 1920 and 1940, followed by the emergence of molecular biology of the gene.

These developments changed the basic 'paradigm of biology'. In the new framework, the innate differences between races, if real, had to be reflected in the racial genotypes. All attempts to define racial genotypes or correlate well-defined Mendelian genes with commonly accepted racial phenotypes have been unsuccessful making the race hypothesis difficult to reconcile with modern biology. The idea of race has not of course died out. The IQ-measures and the sociobiologists are keeping it alive. They aspire to trace the genetic determinants of mental ability (IQ) and morality (social behaviour) in the (secret) hope that the results will somehow support the race hypothesis and give racism the scientific legitimacy it has all along sought.

After an exhaustive, and at times repetitive, survey of the history of scientific racism, Stepan concludes that its most significant feature is the persistence of the scientist's commitment to the race hypothesis through so many ups and downs. This, she feels, has implications about the nature of biology and that of scientific inquiry itself. What are these implications? Stepan is not explicit on that.

One implication, of course, is that all scientific hypotheses and theories, especially those in sciences related to human beings, are coloured by the predilections of the scientists behind them and the predilections by their environment. Throughout the last two centuries, the West has dominated the world. It is hardly surprising that the western scientists have persistently stuck to a hypothesis that could explain this phenomenon scientifically. Initially, when biology sought to explain the diversity and history of all living beings by observing their phenotypes and classifying them into outwardly related groups, biologists sought to do the same with human beings. As biology matured and discovered genes, which were somewhat mysterious and less commonsensical entities, but nevertheless better representations of the biological reality, they are trying to discover genetic bases for mental and moral differences between individuals with the hope of extending them to traditional, physically different racial groups.

The second and more important lesson of the race science, however, is that 'science' is a difficult goddess to please. It is to the credit of the method of science that successfully foiled for two centuries the white man's efforts to create a grandiose international caste system. But for its commitment to the method of science, the West might even have succeeded. After all, there was some sanction of commonsense in the idea. Imagine what would have happened if the superiority of the white races had to be established by criteria other than scientific, say, by incorporating into the Bible a paragraph giving the whites the status of a chosen people or by incorporating a law of *karma* with the provision that good deeds in the past birth result in a European birth. How could such ideas be disproved or dislodged?

7

The Origin and Development of the Aryan Myth

Louis B. Synder*

Doctrine of Aryanism

Racialists, not satisfied with merely proclaiming the superiority of the white over the coloured race, also felt it necessary to erect a hierarchy within the white race itself. To meet this need they developed the myth of Aryan, or Nordic, superiority. The Aryan myth in turn became the source of other secondary myths such as Teutonism (Germany), Anglo-Saxonism (England and the United States), and Celticism (France). These myths have been exploded, but they, nevertheless, have had considerable influence on the course of recent history, affecting the actions of individuals as well as nations.

Role of Linguistic Paleontology

In 1786, the British Orientalist, Sir William Jones (1746-1794), settled the foundations of modern comparative philology when he observed that similarities between the Greek, Sanskrit, Latin, Persian, Celtic, and German languages could be explained only by the existence of a common ancestral tongue. "There is a reason...for supposing that both the Gothick and the Celtick, though blended with a very different idiom, had the same origin with the Sanskrit." This pioneer observation on the similarities between languages led Thomas Young (1773-1829), a British physician, who was the first to decipher the Rosetta Stone, to use the term "Indo-European" to designate the common root of this family of languages.

From this time on, a group of philologists who called themselves linguistic paleontologists (paleontologists deal with the life of past

---

* Was Professor of History of the City College of New York; author of several books on History of Nationalism. General editor of the Anvil Books. The above article froms part of his book "*The Idea of Nationalism: Its meaning and History*" Van Nostrand, USA 1962.

geological periods based on the study of fossils) began to identify language with race. Soon there emerged the Aryan myth—the idea that the Indo-European group of languages was exactly the same as the Indo-European race. This identity of language and race was assumed even though there was not the slightest proof for the identification.

Then the term Indo-European was replaced by Indo-Germanic, a designation made general in the works of James Cowles Prichard (1786-1848), a British philologist and ethnologist, and Franz Bopp (1791-1867), a German linguist. Bopp, who is credited with initiating the era of modern linguistics, also helped confuse the issues. In his major work, *Comparative Grammar,* which appeared in six parts from 1833 to 1852, Bopp painstakingly compared significant words in various languages as he sought to find original grammatical constructions and phonetics laws. He concluded that the great Indo-European linguistic family included seven branches—Greek, Italian, Teutonic, Slavonic, Lithuanic, and Albanian. There were other closely related Asiatic groups, he said, notably the Iranic (especially Zend and Persian), Indic (a series of modern Indian tongues), and Armenian (a combination of Greek and Iranian). With zealous national pride, Bopp named his family of languages, *Indo-Germanic,* thereby alienating Frenchmen and Englishmen, who preferred the term Indo-European.

Rise of German Nationalism

At this point the stream of racialism merged with the currents of romanticism and nationalism. Romanticism, reasserting imagination and sentiment and emphasizing individualism in thought and expression, was a reaction against eighteenth-century rationalism. It was a potent factor in the rise of nationalism, especially German nationalism. Bopp's laudation of the great Indo-Germanic family was but one expression of a rising German nationalism. There were many others who worked along the same lines, notably Johann Gottlieb Fichte (1762-1814), who tried to prove the existence of a tri-logic of race, language, and nation; Georg Wilhelm Friedrich Hegel (1770-1831), who praised the Prussian monarchy as representing civilization at its zenith; the brothers Grimm, Jakob Ludwig Karl (1785-1863) and Wilhelm Karl (1786-1859), who stimulated German national pride by philological studies and fairly tales; Karl Lachmann (1793-1851), disciple of the Grimms, who sought diligently for primitive racial kinships; the brothers von Schlegel, Karl Wilhelm Friedrich (1772-1829) and August Wilhelm (1767-1845), specialists in Oriental studies; Johann Gottfried von Herder (1744-1803), who emphasized the uniqueness and coherence of German national culture; and others. There emerged the theme of the German as an ideal racial type, as the apotheosis of all that was noble and great. This persistent Aryan myth culminated finally in Hitler's pronunciamento that "true intellectual achievements have never been made by racial aliens, but always by strictly German spiritual forces."

Max Muller's Charisma

The Aryan was the creation of Friedrich Max Muller (1823-1900), Anglo-German philologist and Orientalist. In the years 1859-1861, fashionable carriages rattled up Albemarle Street in London to the Royal Institute and discharged aristocratic passengers who had come to listen to the lectures of the distinguished German scholar at Oxford. The professor dominated his audiences. The good ladies of London were thrilled by the eloquence of Professor Muller, who held them spellbound with tales about their Aryan ancestry. Not only the ladies of London, but also scholars throughout the world, were impressed by the erudite German professor. Muller repeatedly hammered away at the idea that the terms Indo-European and Indo-Germanic must be replaced by Aryan, because the people who invaded India and who spoke Sanskrit called themselves Arya. This primitive Aryan language indicated that there was an *Aryan race,* the common ancestor of German, Celts, Romans, Slavs, Greeks, Persians, and Hindus.

Starting with an acquired theory of "irresistible impulse," Muller described the migrations of the early Aryans, who, like a swarm from a central beehive, surged into northwestern Europe. "The main stream of the Aryan nations," he wrote in his *History of Ancient Sanskrit Literature* (1859), "has always flowed toward the northwest. No historian can tell us by what impulse those adventurous nomads were driven on through Asia toward the isles and shores of Europe...It requires a strong will, or a great amount of alertness, to be able to withstand such national or rather ethnical movements."

Muller presented no proof for his identification of the Aryans as a race, nor did any other scholars. Eventually, Muller himself recognized his error. In 1888, with rare scholarly courage and integrity, he repudiated his earlier view: "To me an ethnologist who speaks of Aryan race, Aryan blood, Aryan eyes and hair, is as great a sinner as a linguist who speaks of a dolichocephalic dictionary or a brachycephalic grammar." He now insisted that Aryan in scientific language was utterly inapplicable to race. It meant language and nothing but language, he said, and if one were to speak of an Aryan race at all, it should be nothing more than Aryan speech.

But the damage was already done. By this time the Aryan myth had been appropriated by the racialist. It was to become the main weapon in their arsenal of ideas.

Search for the Elusive Aryan

Long and fruitless was the search for the original homeland of the Aryans. There is no such thing as an Aryan race, yet energetic attempts were made to trace its place of origin. The home of the parent Aryan group was placed in three widely separated areas—Asia, Europe, and North Africa.

This unrewarding search for the original homeland of the Aryan occupied the time of many scholars, especially philologists and anthropologists. For the racialist, the search itself was unimportant. He liked the word Aryan because it was taken from and old Sanskrit legend and meant "noble" or "pure". For him Aryan meant nobility of blood, incomparable beauty of form and mind, a superior breed. Every worthwhile achievement in history, he assumed, has been made by the Aryan race, and all civilization is a struggle to the death between creative Aryan and disintegrative Jew.

This view of Aryan nobility persists even though there is no Aryan race. Cyril Bibby put it this way: "to speak of an 'Aryan race' is as great abuse of words as to speak of a 'black-skinned language'." All attempts to correlate the Aryan language with the Aryan race are not only unsuccessful, but absurd. Undoubtedly, there existed a parent tongue, whether it be called Aryan, Indo-European, or Indo-European, or Indo-Germanic. Search for this original language has been complicated by the fact that the early peoples who spoke it have disappeared and have left few or no written records of their speech. There is neither ethnic nor cultural uniformity among so—called Aryan peoples. Ethnic stocks have become lost in chaotic confusion. Aryan racialism has been described as sociopolitical rationalization with no scientific support. This is, perhaps, a fancy way of indicating that it is nonsense. This conclusion was stated by Frank H. Hankins:

> The obvious impossibility of ever locating the Aryan homeland; the increasing complexity of the problem....;the even more remote possibility of ever learning anything conclusive regarding the traits of the mythical 'Aryan'....;the ridiculous and humiliating spectacle of eminent scholars subordinating their interest in truth to the inflation of racial and national pride—all these and many other reasons led scholars of the first rank even before 1890 to declare that the Aryan doctrine was a figment of the professional imagination or that it was incapable of classification because the crucial evidence was last, apparently forever.

Arthur de Gobineau, Apostle of Aryanism

The doctrine of Aryanism received its most potent stimulus through the work of Joseph Arthur, Comte de Gobineau (1816-1882), a French diplomatist, publicist, and founder of the cult of Gobinism. Descendant of a burgher family traced to the seventeenth century, Gobineau sought at first to prove the nobility of his family's origin (he was altogether fascinated and intrigued by his own blond beauty) and ended by elevating budding racialism into an important historical movement.

Between 1853 and 1855 Gobineau published a four-volume work, *Essai sur l'inegalite des races humaines,* which became the bible of racialist literature. His thesis was simple; all human races are anatomically, physically, and psychologically unequal. Why do civilizations degenerate and fall? Not through fanaticism, luxury, corruption of morals, irreligion or bad government—these are unmeaning accidents. A civilization will certainly die, Gobineau maintained, when the primordial race-unit is so broken up and swamped by the influx of foreign elements that its effective qualities are destroyed. So long as the blood and institutions of a nation keep to a sufficient degree the impress of the original nation, that nation will continue to exist.

As soon as isolated groups grow great and civilized, Gobineau continued, when the majority of their people have mixed blood flowing in their veins, only then do they assert that all men are equal. But all men are not equal. If they were, why is it that every nations adds to the names of others epithets that suggest unlikeness (for example, the Romans ridiculed "cowardly Graeco-Romans, irreligious Carthaginians, and seditious Alexandrians")?

Christianity, Gobineau said, neither created nor changed the capacity for civilization. All human races can recognize the truths of Christianity, but this must not be confused with the "very different faculty" which leads one race, and not another, to rise higher on the ladder of civilization.

Gobineau further believed that every human activity, whether moral or intellectual, has its original source in one or the other of two currents, the "male materialistc current" and the "female intellectual current." Only the races which have one of these elements in abundance, without, of course, lacking altogether the other, can reach a high state of civilization. This argument was of extraordinary appeal to German racialists. Our present civilization "has been created by the mingling of the Germanic tribes with the races of the ancient world." And further: "The richness, variety, and fertility of invention of which we honour our modern societies, are the natural, and more or less, successful result of the maimed and disparate elements which our Germanic ancestors instinctively knew how to use, temper, and disguise."

Gobineau announced himself as categorically opposed to the notion of a multiplicity of origins of the human species. Racial differences, he said, are permanent. Races are unequal in strength or beauty. There are only three races: the white (Caucasian, Semitic or Japhetic); the black (Hamitic); and the yellow (Altaic, Mongol, Finnish, and Tatar). He rejected Blumenbach's five varieties and many sub-varieties and Parichard's seven on the ground that they included "notorious hybrids."

The white race, said Gobineaun was the superior race. All civilization derive from the white race, and none can exist without its help. "A society is great and brilliant only so far as it preserves the blood of the noble group that created it." And again: "there is no true civilization, among for European peoples, where the Aryan branch is not prominent." And finally: "European peoples degenerate only in consequence of the various admixtures of blood which they undergo; their degeneration corresponds exactly to the quantity and quality of the new blood."

Gobineau's *Essay* is an imposing and passionately earnest work. But the tone of earnest conviction is not enough to mask the fact that this is a notoriously bad book. It is filled with paradoxes, contradictions, and inconsistencies. The historical construction, in both general features and details, is weak. Not one single important observation, even when in itself seemingly true, may be taken as proved on the authority of the author. Objections arise at every turn. The reader will always want proofs—but they are not forthcoming.

Gobineau's contention that racial types are permanent does not bear close scrutiny. He described "the strict and unassailable permanence" of form and feature of the ancient peoples, "to which the earliest documents bear witness," but he produced no early documents to prove his point. The racial type, he argued, is never affected by climate, region, or lapse of time. But he gave no proofs, nor did he provide an explanation for the existence of black Jews in Abyssinia.

Examples of Gobineau's many contradictions: "By *black* men I mean Hamites." But in a preceding chapter: "The Hamites are unreasonably considered to be of Negro origin." The white race is superior in beauty and physical strength, but the "happiest" blend from the viewpoint of beauty is made by the marriage of white and black!

In the final pages of the first volume appears Gobineau's theme and his most gloring inconsistency. The noble Aryan race, he says, is degenerating because of the primary error of race intermixture. At the same time, the great Aryan race is the savior of mankind and is leading it to a higher and more civilized plane. Gobineau seemed to be constitutionally incapable of making up his mind. Nor was he aware of his own inconsistencies and contradictions.

Gobineau's racialism was distinctly a class concept. Always the uncompromising aristocract, he lived in a France moving away from his ideas of aristocracy and absolutism. Frenchmen were not impressed by his theories. Tocqueville, who was attracted by Gobineau's ingenuity, nevertheless rejected his racial ideology as false. "A best," Tocqueville said, "your fame will be an echo from across the Rhine."

Tocqueville was precisely right. After the Franco-Prussian War of 1870-71, Aryanism became a nationalist dogma in the newly unified German state. German intellectuals were intrigued by Gobineau's insistence that one race and one alone was capable of creating a true civilization. Here was pleasant, even if unscientific, verification of Germany's right to world leadership. Gobineau's exaggerated praise for the early Germanic tribes was taken to mean laudation for the contemporary German citizen, though this was far removed from Gobineau's original idea. A gullible and credulous German public readily swallowed the thesis of Teutonic racial supremacy.

Gobineau was introduced to the German public by the composer Richard Wagner, who believed Aryanism to be the perfect explanation for the superiority of the German spirit. Professor Ludwig Schemann, impressed by Gobineau's "all-conquering strength," founded the Gobineau Vereinigung in 1894 at Freiburg. "All good Germans," said Schemann, "regard Gobineau as one of the most extraordinary men of the nineteenth century, one of the greatest God-inspired heroes, saviours and liberators sent by Him across the ages." Gobineau societies appeared all over Germany. Gobineau's works were published in classic editions. In Nazi Germany he was revered as a prophet and as the great forerunner of the truths of racialism.

From Aryan to Nordic

Under the influence of the new racialism, German philologists, ethnologists, and anthropologists, although entranced by Gobineau's Aryanism, began to use the term Nordic instead of Aryan. The Nordic type was said to be one of the main divisions of the Causcasian race (Mediterranean, Alpine, and Nordic). The early conception of the Nordic included Scandinavians, Northwest Germans, Dutch, Flemings, most English, Scots, some Irish, Anglo-Americans, Anglo-Australians, English and Dutch of South Africa, Thrako-Hellences, "true" Kurds, most West Persians, Afghans, and Kafirs. Later, the term Nordic was restricted to Germans and Scandinavians.

The Nordic thesis, as propounded by the German racialist, Hans F.K. Gunther, held that the original Nordics were a Neolithic people who eventually settled in Central and Southern Germany, wandered to the Balkans, into Italy, and then into France and Spain. This thesis followed the main outlines of the Indo-Europeanization of the continent, but according to the Nordic school, the "original Nordi blood" of these people disappered. Nordic blood of the ruling class (nobles and freemen), it was said, still flows in its purest form in the veins of Germans (Chamberlain and Gunther) or of Frenchmen (Gobineau). "The Nordic race stands at the head of the whole human genus" (Lothrop Stoddard). "All blue, gray or green eyes in the world today came originally from the same source, namely the Nordic race of Northern Europe...Blond hair also comes everywhere from the Nordic subspecies and from nowhere else...the Nordic race is nearly everywhere distinguished by great stature" (Madison Grant). "The Nordic entered history to rescue agonizing humanity from the clutches of the bestial" (Chamberlain). "The Nordic man is distinugished by a highly developed sense of reality, which, in combination with an energy that may rise to boldness, urges him on to far-reaching undertakings" (Günther). To prevent *denordicization,* or disappearance of Nordic blood, became the great historical mission of the present descendants of the Nordic *Urmensch.*

Nordic Teutonism

Gobineau gave the Aryan myth form and content, but it remained for an Englishman, son of a British admiral, to take over the Aryan race doctrine and fashion it into a battle hymn of Nordic-Teutonic racial supremacy. Houston Stewart Chamberlain (1855-1927), born at Southsea, published (1896) a biography of Richard Wagner, whose daughter he had married. Eventually, he became a naturalized German. His admiration of all things German was coupled with an equally intense hatred for anything concerned with England. During World War I, he wrote propaganda pieces directed at his native land.

In 1899, Chamberlain published the first edition of his *Foundations of the Nineteenth century,* which was immediately hailed in Germany as a historical masterpiece. Although it was an expensive volume, more than 60,000 copies were sold as soon as Kaiser Wilhelm II discovered it to be "a work of the highest importance." Within three years three editions were exhausted. Before its appearance in an English translation in 1909, it went through eight editions.

Chamberlain's aim was to reveal the bases on which nineteenth century, "an inexhaustible theme," rested. In the first part, he discussed in detail the events previous to the year 1200: the legacy of the old world, with chapters on Hellenic art and philosophy, Roman law, and the revelation of Christ; the heirs of the old world, with chapters on racial chaos, the entrance of the Jews into Western history, and the Germanic invasions; and the struggle of the heirs to maintain their inheritance, with chapters on religion and the state. In the second part, dealing with events from 1200 to 1800, Chamberlain described the Teutons as the creators of a new culture.

According to Chamberlain, the entrance of the Teutonic race into the history of the world formed an opposing positive force to the spread of the diminutive but influential race of Jews. "To this day these two powers—Jews and Teutonic races—stand, wherever the recent spread of the Chaos had not blurred their features, now as friendly, now as hostile, but always as alien forces face to face."

In his second volume, Chamberlain analyzed the rise of the Teutonic world and the struggle of the great powers for supremacy and possession. The work of Teutonism is "beyond question the greatest that has hitherto been achieved by man." "What is not Teutonic consists either of alien elements not yet exorcised, which were formerly forcibly introduced and still, like baneful germs, circulate in our blood, or of alien wares sailing, to the disadvantage of our work and further development, under the Teutonic protection and privilege, and they will continue to sail thus, until we send these pirate ships to the bottom." Chamberlain argued that all achievements in science, industry, political economy, and art were stimulated and propelled by the Teutonic race. The nineteenth century, in his view, rested upon a secure Teutonic foundation.

8

Homelands in Question

Collin Renfrew*

The time has now come to question more seriously whether the various attempts hitherto undertaken to locate some original 'homeland' for the Proto-Indo-Europeans have had any very sound basis. I have already indicated that in my view they have not. Although there are many good ideas and many relevant comments in what has been written on this subject, I believe that no coherent and plausible theory has yet been advanced. I shall argue in this chapter that most writers have fallen into what can now be recognized as dangerous traps. They have placed too much faith in the idea of some reconstructed Proto-Indo-European vocabulary, from which some kind of word-picture of the original homeland might be put together. They have too readily assumed that a given pottery form, or an assemblage of items of material equipment, can be equated directly with a group of people and hence supposedly with a particular language or language group. And they have not adequately explained *why* all these languages, or the speakers of all these languages, should be wandering around Europe and western Asia so tirelessly, in a series of migrations, thus setting up the pattern of different languages which we see today. Later I shall make some suggestions which I believe overcome these particular difficulties: they will be found controversial by most authorities on the subject for the very good reason that in several respects they disagree with most existing views on it.

First it is worth re-stating some general and important points. In the first place, as the great linguist, Max Muller, said in 1888,[1] the term 'Indo-European' refers to language, not to people or groups of people. Of course the languages were spoken by people, but that does not justify our speaking of 'Indo-Europeans' or 'Aryans' in nay other sense than

---

* Head of the Department of Archaeology in the University of Cambridge, Author of more than half-a-dozen books on European archaeology. The above article is from his magnum opus "*Archaeology and language. The Puzzle of Indo European Origins*", Cambridge University Press, New York, 1990.

of those persons who spoke the languages in question. That implies that if I am brought up speaking only one language, for example a Semitic language, and then I learn an Indo-European language, in a very real sense, I have *become* an Indo-European. And my children, especially if this language which I have learnt becomes their first language, will be Indo-Europeans too, even if both their parents originally spoke a Semitic language and came from a different cultural background.

In this sense, then, it is not correct to speak of an Indo-European culture. Nor, if the term Celtic and Germanic and Italic are similarly defined in terms of language, is it correct to speak of a Celtic or a Germanic or an Italic culture. Tremendous confusion about linguistic and cultural origins has come about because language and culture have not been properly distinguished. Of course language and culture often go together. In a modern European nation-state, very often as you cross the frontier, the language changes, and sometimes so does the whole way of life, and with it the system of beliefs and religion. But this is not necessarily so. Groups of people with very different cultures can speak the same language, and conversely, within an area where the way of life is essentially the same, different languages may be spoken.

Above all its is a serious mistake to equate race and language. The term 'race' has of course been seriously abused in the past, and very often it is not clear at all exactly what it means. Of course if one asks a Chinaman, a Frenchman and a Nigerian to stand in line, they may look decidedly different from each other (even there one has to be careful over definitions: there are plenty of black Frenchmen, and there are white Nigerians). But when we consider Europe and western Asia, it is not at all clear in terms of physical anthropology that there are different races at all. Yet it is true that there can be physical features which correlate at a statistically significant level with country of origin or with descent: a higher proportion of Swedes have fair hair and blue eyes than Italians. Today blood groups can be studied as well as external physical characteristics, but the notion of 'race' is extremely difficult to define with precision.[2]

The difficulties become overwhelming when one is dealing only with skeletal material, as is the archaeologist's usual lot in life. There is at the moment no scientifically acceptable way of taking a set of skeletal measurements and saying that a body or a skull which shows them must be assigned to a particular 'race'. The metric characteristics of different populations can be compared, and it may be possible to make inferences on that basis, but they will probably not be racial ones in any meaningful sense. If there were significant, recurrent patterns in the skeletal material which allowed us to distinguish between different groups of people in a meaningful and valid way, then we would have to develop a study of prehistoric races. The reason for discounting this approach is not so much that we dislike the consequences of 'racism', but that it does not accord with the data.

If we agree to try to separate language, race and culture in a clear way, the starting point for a consideration of Indo-European problems must always be the study of language. Indo-European studies represent a very considerable field of scholarship, and the techniques of comparative linguistics are sophisticated and well developed. There is not much point in an archaeologist who is not properly trained in the linguistics field setting out to make new or challenging statements of a linguistic nature; but when we begin to speak about the groups of people who spoke these languages, and about the historical circumstances which brought about their distribution, then we are fairly and squarely within the field of archaeology. These are the issues which I propose to follow up here.

1. The Lure of the Portolexicon

Much of the confusion which surrounds the question of the origins of the Indo-European languages comes from the notion that the languages themselves contain all the evidence that is necessary to permit an accurate historical reconstruction and an identification of the location of an original homeland. Early enthusiasm for the 'comparative method' of linguistic reconstruction led to the application of the view that when related (cognate) words were discovered in two different Indo-European languages, the original word in the proto-language notionally parental to both of them could be found. In this way, Proto-Indo-European was constructed the original language (*Ursprache*) of the original people (*Urvolk*) in their homeland (*Urheimat*). This was the method of linguistic palaeontology, as it was grandiosely termed, and with its aid the actual vocabulary of words, the protolexicon, of the *Urvolk* could be established.

There remains much of value in the comparative method, and the approach is indeed one of the most useful ways to study the relationship between the Indo-European languages, but as we shall see in the next chapter the 'family tree' model of language change, on which the initial ideas of linguistic palaentology depended, is now thought to be too simple an idea. Loan-words (words borrowed from a neighbouring language) are acquired by languages and they are not always easy to recognize. Yet obviously, when several common loan-words were acquired by two languages in, say, the first century AD, they can give no insight into the vocabulary of the notional parental language spoken centuries or millennia earlier. The wave model for linguistic change leads to a different picture.

If the languages with related words are geographically far apart, the linguistic palaeontologist can argue that borrowing from one by the other is unlikely. So he will argue that because the Irish *ri*, 'king', and the Latin *rex* along with the Sanskrit *raja* are cognate and geographically remote, then a word for 'king' formed part of the protolexicon.

The basic principle of linguistic palaeontology is that if the Indo-Europeans can be shown by linguistic analysis to have had the name of a specific thing within their protolexicon, then they can be assumed to have been acquainted with the thing itself.

Thus the best modern survey of historical linguistics, by Winfred Lehmann, can say:[3]

> Proceeding to the everyday life of the Indo-European community we find terms for 'herd, cow, sheep, goat, pig, dog, horse, wolf, bear, goose, duck, bee, oak, beech, willow, grain'. The lack of specific terms for grains or vegetables indicates a heavy reliance on animals for food.

This argument, and really very little else, has led to the notion that the Proto-Indo-Europeans were nomads. The method can even be used to make chronological inferences. To quote Lehmann again:[4]

> The time during which the Indo-European community flourished has been subject to less dispute. When we attempt to reconstruct words for metals, we can ascribe to the Indo-Europeans vocabulary no words even for 'silver' or 'gold', let alone 'iron' and scarcely even a general term for 'metal, bronze, copper,' Latin *aes* 'copper, bronze.' Old English *ar* 'brass, copper' leads to New English *ore*, Sanskrit *ayas* 'bronze', later 'copper'. On the basis of such vocabulary we characterize the Indo-European community as late neolithic. Fortunately archaeological discoveries have led to the identification of this community with a culture located north of the Black Sea from the fifth millennium BC...

The method is applied to the localization of the homeland by focusing on features of the natural environment. The protolexicon contains the names of certain animals and trees. It follows from the application of the general principle that the Indo-Europeans must have been acquainted with these things. If, then, we can point to some region in Europe or Asia where it can be demonstrated that these species were living a frw thousand years ago, and if that is the only area where they could all be found, then that must be the homeland, so it is argued, and the problem is solved.

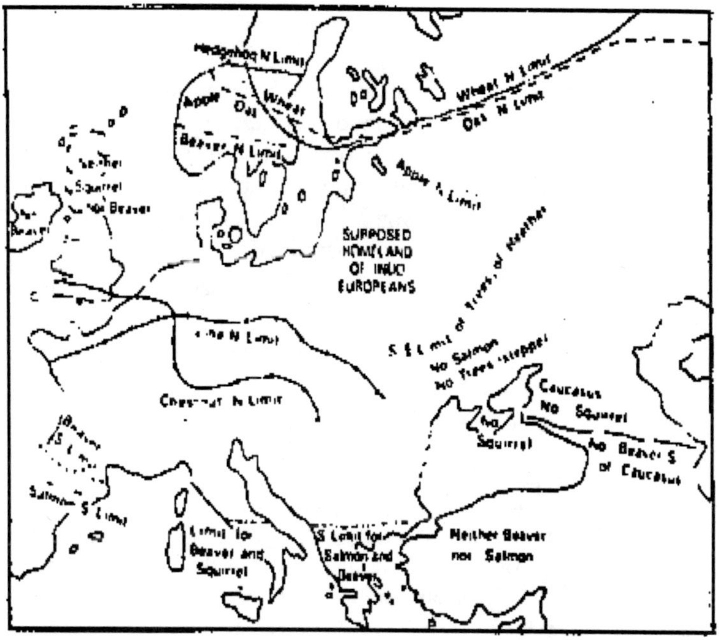

FIG. 1 The limits of the distribution of various plant and animal species in Europe: the evidence of linguistic palaeontology for the homeland of the Indo-Europeans (*after Mann and Kilian*).

Alas, matters are not so easy, and the method has many objections. In the first place, any innovation, any discovery which results in a new product, will often carry the name of that product with it. So to find a word for 'wheel' or 'cart' or 'copper' or 'bronze' in several languages does not necessarily tell us very much about the origins of those languages, although it is of interest for the words themselves. Loan words are to be expected in such circumstances.

Secondly, it is well known that the meanings of words change. Often an old word is retained and used with quite a different meaning when some innovation has occurred. A good example is the English 'car' (carriage) which a couple of centuries ago had an entirely different meaning. Or as J. Fraser pointed out nearly sixty years ago in a very well-argued paper,[5] 'it is not necessary to assume, as some have done, that the Indo-Europeans were acquainted with an intoxicating drink because they had a word corresponding to our mead', and because Sanskrit and Greek have verbal forms from the same root with the sense of 'to be intoxicated'. As Fraser points out, the transference of a name meaning 'drink' to any kind of alcoholic drink is common. The Slavonic *pivo* is cognate with the Latin *bibere* and originally meant simple a drink, but now means 'beer' in Slavonic languages.

Similar problems apply to institutions. Some writers have tried to suggest that the terms for 'father, mother, brother, sister, son, daughter, daughter-in-law' indicate a common Indo-European kinship system, with a close relationship with the son's wife but not between a man and his in-laws. But the British social anthroplogist, Jack Goody, has cogently argued that such inferences are not warranted.[6]

Again, some writers have taken the presence in several Indo-European languages of a cognate term for 'king' as an indication of the institution of kingship in the 'homeland'. But the opposite conclusion is also advanced. To quote Lehmann again:[7]

> But the absence of general terms for leaders of larger social groups requires us to conclude that social organizations in the Indo-European community were restricted in size. A word for 'ruler' related to the Latin regere 'guide' is found in Latin rex, Irish *ri*, Sanskrit *raj*—but other dialects have different terms, such as Greek *basileus* and Old English *cyning*. Accordingly we may posit for the Indo-European community a well developed family system but not higher social or political organization.

This, however, looks like very dangerous special pleading, for there are very few words indeed which are represented by cognate forms in *all* Indo-European languages. As Stuart Piggott has very pertinently remarked, quoting A.B. Keith:[8] 'taking the linguistic evidence too literally, one could conclude that the original Indo-European speakers knew butter but not milk, snow and feet but not rain and hands'.

The argument about the distribution of living species is put most vigorously, but it too has its pitfalls. Simply to draw on a map the boundary of the occurrence of the various species of trees which have cognate names in the Indo-European languages does not establish for us the boundaries of Proto-Indo-European, as some have argued.[9] For the existence of cognate, or even identical words in various dialects and regions does not indicate that they all refer to the same things. It has often been pointed out that a robin in England is not the same bird at all as a robin in America. So that when we find words related to 'birch' and 'beech' in several Indo-European languages it does not follow that the common word in Proto-Indo-European from which they were descended had the same specific meaning.

Indeed if we look at the modern boundaries for a particular species of tree on a vegetation map, it will not surprise us that the various languages within the boundary have terms designating that tree, and presumably the languages which lie entirely outside the boundary will not have a name for a tree they do not know exists. If the Proto-Indo-Europeans did indeed originate within the area, they may well have had in their protolexicon terms ancestral to the modern ones, as the linguistic palaeontologists would suggest. But if we imagine that there was an original homeland *outside* the boundary, and that the territories within it came to speak Indo-European languages through the processes of linguistic displacement, then they would need to develop an appropriate vocabulary after their arrival. They might well then draw upon pre-existing terms in their own vocabulary which had previously held a rather different meaning (like the immigrants to the New World with their 'robin'). Or entirely new words might be developed and be adopted, following the wave model for language change, throughout the territory to which they were appropriate. Either way, the territory through which the term for the species in question is found will not extend far beyond the natural habitat of the species, and there may be a good deal of uniformity in terms used within that boundary.

These points were well stated by Fraser in his articles, which it is worth quoting at length:[10]

> I have already pointed out that the significance attached to the fact that the Indo-Germans were acquainted with the horse and the cow may have been exaggerated. We do not really know the precise meaning of the Indo-Germanic words in question; we do not know whether they mean the domesticated or the wild animals; and for that reason it is difficult to see how these names can safely be used for the purpose of determining the original home of the Indo-Germans. The same difficulty arises in the case of other etymological data used by the Linguistic Palaeontologist. We are constantly told that the Indo-Germans knew the beech and the birch trees, and this had counted for a great deal in the attempts that have been made to fix their home. But strictly speaking, we do not know that they were acquinted with those trees; all we know is that their vocabulary contained two words the later form of which in the historical Indo-Germanic languages are, generally, the name of the beech and the birch respectively. But it must be noticed that in Greek the word cognate with the English 'beech' is the name of the oak; and we must assume that this is not the only case in which either word has undergone a change of meaning. And if the speakers of a language when they change their homes and move into new surrounding, give the names of things familiar in their old homes to things in the new that resemble them or take their place, it may appear that in arguing from the beech and birch to the original home of the Indo-Germans we are arguing in a vicious circle.

It is the case that the words which are repeatedly used in trying to establish a homeland are rather few. The names for trees have indeed been argued with comprehensive scholarship by Paul Friedrich in his book *Proto-Indo-European Trees.*[11] The animal species were briefly quoted above. Childe, in *The Aryans*, gave a considerable list, derived from the work of Otto Schrader. To avoid seeming selective, I quote below the words which Childe listed:[12] he went on to give their equivalent form (where it exists) in Sanskrit, Greek, Latin, Celtic, Teutonic, Lithuanian, Tocharian and Armenian.

> god, father, mother, son, daughter, brother, sister, father's brother, grandson or nephew, son-in-law, daughter-in-law, father-in-law, mother-in-law, husband's brother, husband's brother's wives, husband, woman, widow, house-father, clan, village headman,? sib.? tribe or clan, king, dog, ox, sheep, goat, horse, pig, steer, cow, gelding, cattle, cheese, fat, butter, grain, bread, furrow, plough, mead, copper, gold, silver, razor, awl, sling-stone, bow-string, javelin, spear, sword, axe, carpenter, chariot or wheel, axle, nave, yoke, ship, oar, house, door-frame, door, pillar earth-walls.

The argument most frequently put forward from this list of words is that it includes more names of animal species than of plants, and that the subsistence of the Proto-Indo-Europeans was therefore that of a pastoralist economy. But this view is, unfortunately, based upon a very simplistic view of pastoralism. It is now well-established that a pastoral economy, with emphasis upon domestic animal species, can only arise following the emergence of agriculture. The old idea that pastoralism could represent some intermediate stage between the hunting and gathering of the palaeolithic and mesolithic period and the agriculture of the neolithic, has now been thoroughly discredited. Everywhere pastoralists are dependent upon their co-existence with farmers, and much of their diet is formed by agricultural produce. Writing of the Basseri in his *Nomads of South Persia,* the social anthropologist, Frederik Barth, points out:[13]

> The normal diet of the Basseri includes a great bulk of agricultural produce, of which some tribesmen produce at least a part themselves. Cereal crops, particularly wheat, are planted on first arrival in the summer camp areas and yield their produce before the time of departure; or locally resident villagers are paid to plant a crop before the nomads arrive, to be harvested by the latter....A great number of the necessities of life are thus obtained by trade and flour is the most important foodstuff, consumed as unleavened bread with every meal; and sugar, tea, dates and fruits and vegetables are also important. In the case of most Basseri, such products are entirely or predominantly obtained by trade....

Of course it is not to be argued that all nomad groups have a subsistence economy like that of the Basseri. Some may place more emphasis on milk products than they do, others also drink the blood of their cattle. But the underlying point remains, that all pastoral nomads are also dependent on the domesticated plants produced by agriculture.

It thus seems entirely naive to use the argument that because several animals species have cognate names in the Indo-European languages, animals were originally more important in the economy than plants. If the Proto-Indo-Europeans were familiar with domesticated sheep, goats or cattle, then they must certainly also have been acquainted with wheat, barley and peas and also a range of other animal species. If there are no common words today among the Indo-European languages for these species, then other explanations must be found. Once this point is accepted, the preponderance of animals amongst the cognate names must be seen as the result of essentially linguistic factors, rather than as a feature of the presence and absence of the relevant species in the natural environment of the original *Urvolk*. The whole argument collapses, and the myth of the pastoralist Indo-Europeans loses all substance.

Many of the arguments bearing upon the natural environment are equally weak. Much is made of absence of words for Mediterranean species, such as the vine and the olive, from the supposed protolexicon. But if these words were present in some protolexicon, they could scarcely be expected to have continued in use in areas where these species are no longer encountered. We know that the domesticated vine is a relatively recent species in central and northern Europe: the absence of a relevant term in the early languages of those areas need thus occasion no surprise.

In all of these discussions, it may further be argued, there has been a tendency to forget that we are not dealing with a single time period, but over a vast time depth. To reconstruct, from the existing languages, a proto-language at a particular point in time is thus an over-ambitious task. The linguist, Ernst Pulgram, caricatured this tendency, and following Fraser, offered a splendid *reductio ad absurdum*:[14]

> If we reconstructed Latin on the evidence of the Romanic languages alone, ignoring and neglecting the existence of Greek, Keltic, Germanic and the other ancient Indo-European dialects, and if thereupon we derived from the state of the common Romanic vocabulary conclusions on the culture of the speakers of Latin (whom then we should call Latins, I suppose, and ascribe to one race or another, depending on our patriotic or political leanings), we might well arrive at the following results: Proto-Romanic *regem* and *imperatorem* show us that the Latins

> lived in a monarchy under kings or emperors (but what shall we make of *rem publicam* which could presuppose a Latin republic?); since all Romanic languages contain words cognate with French *pretre* and *eveque* 'priest' and 'bishop', the Latins were Christians; also words cognate with French *biere*, *tabac*, *cafe* are common Romanic, evoking a picture of Caesar's soldiers guzzling beer and smoking cigars in sidewalk cafes; and since all Romanic languages name a certain animal *cheval, caballo, cal*, etc., and have words for 'war' like *guerre, querra*, the Latins called the horse *caballum* and the war *guerram* and were no doubt warlike people with a strong cavalry.

In reality, of course, the Roman words for 'horse' and 'war' are *equus* and *bellum*, and this marvellous piece of nonsense reconstruction brilliantly exemplifies the dangers of linguistic palaentology.

Now these arguments are not intended as an attack upon the comparative method, as used by competent linguists to examine the histories of particular, words, and to study by this means the relationships between specific languages. I hope that I am aware to the very considerable erudition which underlies many of the linguistic arguments which are put forward. My criticism is of the simplistic use of such data to reach supposedly historical conclusions. Certainly the circumstance that the Sanskrit word for 'chariot', *ratha*, is agreed by competent linguists to be cognate with the Latin for 'wheel', *rota*, is interesting, and merits historical explanation. But that is a far cry from saying that the two cognate words tell us that some hypothetical Proto-Indo-Europeans used chariots with wheels (or indeed carts with wheels) in their original homeland.

There may be good arguments for placing the Indo-Europeans in an original homeland in South Russia, but in my view the findings of linguistic palaeontology are not among their number. They could probably be accomodated to almost any homeland theory, just as they have already been made to fit a good many very differrnt ones. The present distribution of the Indo-European languages has to be seen not as simply the dispersal of an *Urvolk* from an *Urheimat*, speaking an *Ursprache*, but rather as the end product of a whole series of *processes*. The methods of comparative linguistics have much to offer in the study of these processes, but the construction of a protolexicon may not be their most useful contribution.

2. The Formation of New Groupings: Corded Ware and Bell Beakers

If the first error of the champions of an Indo-European 'homeland' was to base their thinking upon the shifting sands of linguistic palaeontology, their second was archaeological. It is one which has bedevilled much of European prehistory, indeed world prehistory in general; to conclude that the emergence of a new pottery style or a new complex of finds in an area indicated the development—or even the arrival—of a new group of people. Modern archaeology is shifting completely away from that kind of 'migrationist' thinking. Probably the most graphic examples are offered by the interesting cases of the Corded Ware people and of the Beaker Folk. Both form an essential link in the chain of argument of those claiming a south Russian homeland and of those pressing for central or northern Europe.

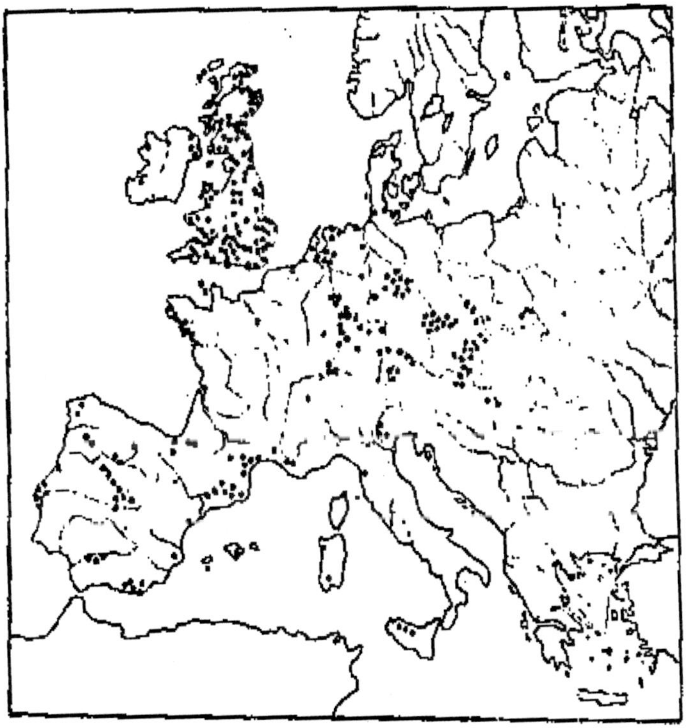

FIG. 2 The distribution of Bell Beakers in Europe (after childe).

There is absolutely no disagreement about the reality and the widerspread nature of the Beaker phenomenon. A Beaker is a drinking vessel, with incised decoration, falling into one of a number of characteristic forms, of which the most famous is the Bell Beaker, so-called after its shape, which the French call 'campaniforme'. Towards the end of the late neolithic period, around 2300 BC following calibrated radiocarbon dates, burials are found in many parts of western Europe containing the skeleton of a single individual accompanied by the characteristic drinking vessel and by other items which form a recognizable 'kit'. These do indeed often include stone arrowheads and sometimes a perforated stone object often interpreted as an archer's wristguard, so that the proposal that these people were archers seems well-substantiated. Sometimes there is a copper dagger and on occasions other objects of metal, such as gold earrings. These are among the earliest finds of metal objects in the areas in question. There is, however, no convincing evidence that they rode horses, but there are at least some indications that in western Europe the first appearance of horses' bones is associated with Bell Beakers.[15] Many archaeological studies contain maps of the finds of Beaker burials: Gordon Childe's map of 1949 is shown in FIG. 2.[16]

There have been many theories about the origin of the Beaker assemblages. Although there is a fashion today among archaeological theorists for seeing independent origins of innovations, it is difficult to avoid the conclusion that there was a connection of some kind amongst these various finds. In the 1920s, when most changes were accepted as resulting from movements of people, all these things were hailed as the work of a 'Beaker Folk', who, it was claimed, were racially distinct that is to say that their skull measurements showed them to be distinctly brachycephalic (round-headed). Argument has raged ever since as to whether the origin of this 'folk' was in the west, in Iberia, or in the east, perhaps in Hungary or Yugoslavia, or again in the north in Scandinavia. Indeed very elaborate theories have been produced to account for the variations in the evidence in even greater detail. The German archaeologist, Edward Sangmeister, developed a theory of a 'Reflux', a *Ruckstrom,* whereby Beakers and their accompanying assemblages were developed first in Spain and moved gradually across Europe, to be followed by the Reflux[16] which carried various central-European features back to Iberia.

Even so harsh a critic as Professor Grahame Clark, who in 1966 published an influential paper entitled. 'The invasion hypothesis in British prehistory', could not escape the notion of a migration to Britain from continental Europe of people bringing with them the customs of Beaker burial.[17] In 1977, however, the British archaeologist, stephen Shennan, in his doctoral dissertation entitled 'Bell beakers and their context in central Europe: a new approach',[18] came up with a new set of ideas. He suggested that we should view the Beaker assemblages as 'status kits'—collections of objects possessed by individuals of rather high status in the community, which were used by those persons to assert and display that status, and hence to enhance it. The importance of material goods in the assertion and maintenance of the ranking of prominent individuals within their communities has been increasingly recognized by archaeologists over the past fifteen years. Indeed the basic idea goes back to the very earliest days of archaeology, when excavators recognized the skeletons they were uncovering as 'chiefs' or 'princes' if these were accompanied by rich gravegoods such as gold and amber objects. The gravegoods accompanying Beaker burials are never as rich and impressive as those of the succeeding early bronze, age, but they do represent, in most areas where they are found, a new tendency to emphasize the individual during burial by means of accompanying gravegoods of special value.

This approach by Shennan emphasizes an increasing tendency among archaeologists to think in social terms. In Britain the Beaker burials follow a period where there was already much ritual activity documented by the large 'henge' monuments of the later neolithic period. Stonehenge is the most famous of these (although the great stone circle was erected later), but there are other, larger onces, such as Avebury. I suggested in 1974 that one might think of these late neolithic societies as 'group-oriented chiefdoms',[19] where the central power within the societies of the time was expressed in these massive communal works. These could be contrasted with the 'individualizing chiefdoms' of the succeeding early bronze age where rich gravegoods accompanied specially favoured individuals. Shennan suggested that the emergence of Beaker burials, with their accompanying prestige goods, could be seen as part of this process, and as part of the transformation in British society between the neolithic and the early bronze age. He also suggested that the idea of Beakers and the accompanying 'kit' spread rapidly through north and central Europe (and so to Britain) as local leaders copied their neighbours, vying with each other in the dispaly of these fashionable goods:[20]

> We have, then, in the Bell Beaker phase, at the very beginning of the Bronze Age a highly significant pattern of contact linking virtually the whole of central and western Europe in what is essentially a time of innovation, diffusion and adoption in various spheres, including ritual and ideology, in a number of very different local situations.

Instead of the old explanation in terms of migration and diffusion it is possible in many cases to recognize a process of what has been termed 'peer polity interaction', where a number of local communities, none more prominent than the next, interact together. In this way a new 'nuclear area', a new 'style zone' comes about, and new things are created and diffused. This is what seems to have happened in the case of the Bell Beakers.[21] What we see emerging in north-central Europe, and soon after in Britain, is a new system. As the British archaeologist, Alasdair Whittle, writes (with particular reference to Britian):[22]

1. There were important changes in environment and resource by the mid-third millennium B.C. which are likely to have affected sub-sequent economy, settlement and society, providing a situation in which competition for basic resources is plausible particularly in southern England.

2. The Beaker phenomenon was not ethnic, nor was it in essence novel. Attention must be paid to its details, particularly the settlement evidence, to provide an empirical demonstration of this view but the main aim should then be to interpret the phenomenon in other ways.

3. Here it was seen as part of wider and longer-lasting processes of social change in which communal needs for cohesion were increasingly replaced by more individual acquisition of status in response to competition for scarce resources. Many other features of the period may illustrate these processes too. In this sense the specific content to the Beaker phenomenon is of no concern, only its wider function.

These ideas are now at the centre of a whole phase of new research in Britain, where economy, social organization and ideology are taken into account together with their interactions. Of course it soon be comes very detailed. The Swiss archaeologist, Alain Gallay,[23] has given a most plausible review. The overall result of these studies is to admit the significance of the Beaker phenomenon, and to see it as a symptom of very significant changes taking place in European society at that time. These changes were, in part, related to the impact of the new technology of metallurgy, and also to developments in subsistence practice.

All of this means that there were indeed new exchange networks being built up in Europe, and new ideas (and new kinds of competition and emulation) developing because of them. It is perfectly correct to talk of processes of diffusion, but there is no longer a unique centre of diffusion. The interactions are taking place between equals, between peer polities. The old ideas of ethnic influence are thus rejected, and there is no suggestion that there were necessarily significant movements of peoples at that time. Nor is it argued that the elite individuals which we see in the Beaker burials, often under burial mounds or barrows, were incomers. There is no need to argue any widespread occurrence of elite displacement. These were probably local elites, coming into greater prominence partly through their manipulation of the exchange networks, and adopting the paraphernalia of elite display that their neighbours were in some cases already using. In adopting them they sometimes added to them, and these ideas may have been taken up by *their* neighbours. There was a whole network of interactions, and no single point of innovation can be identified.[24]

In these circumstances there is no special argument here in favour of language displacement. The demographic composition in each area was largely unchanged, and in most cases the local elite had local origins. There was plenty of opportunity for the adoption of local-words: the acquisition of new objects and new techniques offers plenty of scope for that. And the more intensive networks of communication which arose at that time would certainly make easier the spread of linguistic innovations. In these circumstances we can see that this would not have been a time when a new language, even an Indo European language, would have been dispersed from its 'homeland'. There was nothing particularly 'vagabondic' about the populations involved, and no argument for seeing the Beaker elite as footloose wanderers.

These arguments seems to me totally destructive of the suggestion that there were Kurgan invasions at this time, or that a new Kurgan language spread throughout the regions in question. It is certainly true that the Beaker elite were sometimes buried under a mound, a barrow, which in Russian might very properly be referred to by the term 'kurgan'. But so what? Even if this particular feature had indeed been learnt from south Russia, it scarcely carries with it linguistic implications, other than the possibility of an interesting loan-word. In fact collective burial under burial mounds had been carried out for two thousands years in the west, and the Beaker burials are not the first in these areas to employ single burial.

Very comparable arguments can be applied to the Corded Ware culture of north Europe. Again it is not in doubt that there is a large area in which burials occur, usually single buraials, under burial mounds, with the deceased accompanied by cord-decorated pottery, sometimes with a 'battle-axe' (i.e. perforated stone axe). In 1969 the Czech archaeologist, Evzen Neustupny, wrote an influential and persuasive article on 'The Economy of the Corded Ware Culture'[25] in which he showed that there was no good argument for the widely-held notion that these were nomad pastoralists with an economy different from that of other farming communities of neolithic Europe. And in 1981 the East German specialist, Alexander Hausler, examined in detail the arguments for an eastern origin of the Corded Ware cultures, and argued firmly for a local origin, dealing also with the implications for the Indo-European problem.[26]

The socio-ideological approach has recently been applied by the British arhaeologist, Christopher Tilley, to the origin of the Corded Ware/ Battle Axe cultures of Scandinavia. There the transition is between the middle neolithic TRB (i.e. Trichterbecher=Funnel Beaker) culture and the succeeding BAC (Battle Axe/Corded Ware) groups. As Tilley emphasizes:[27]

> Both the TRB and BAC appear to have been characterized by cereal-based economies, supplemented by hunting, fishing, gathering and livestock...In phase IV of the TRB all aspects of ceramic design are simplified and at some stage the tombs ceased to be centres of ritual activity and the change to BAC occurred. The individual is asserted for the first time in burial practices and there is little evidence of elaborate ritual surrounding the funerary activities. A small range of grave goods accompany the dead, but no hierarchical distinctions are apparent.

Tilley's approach to the Corded Ware is in some ways very different from Shennan's view of the Beakers, but they see no fundamental change in farming practice, and no incursion by incoming groups: in both cases the explanation is framed primarily in social terms.

It should be noted that none of these studies excluded the possibility that local groups might well be biologically distinctive. The Swiss physical anthropologist, R. Menk, has indeed suggested that the Beaker-using population of Switzerland was different physically from contemporaries of other cultures. But he points out that:[28]

> The Corded Ware complex is biologically heterogeneous. the local groups of the core area (Central Germany, Czechoslovakia, Poland) form a very homogeneous bloc...This bloc shows no biological affinities to the Ukrainian Kurgan populations.

It would in my view be wrong to place much weight upon conclusions drawn from physical anthropology until the methodology is better developed. At any time the existence of local populations who are to some extent biologically distinguishable should cause little surprise.

The overall implications of these conclusions about the Beaker and Corded Ware cultures are considerable. We have seen how major culture complexes may emerge through the operation of local factors. Through networks of interaction they can be influential over wide areas, leading to the widespread adoption of new ideologies and new ways of expressing them. Nothing in what we have seen suggests that this was a period when language replacement was a particularly active process. These conclusions are also important for the later bronze age and iron age, when other very wide-ranging culture complexes are seen (the so-called Urnfields). They are also relevant to our understanding of the Celts and Germans.

3. The Dynamics of Population Change

The existing homeland theories, as we have seen, make the fundamental mistake of equalting the emergence of a new culture complex with the intrusion of a new linguistic group, and they rely unwisely upon the resources of linguistic palaeontology for a physical description of the homeland. Unfortunately they also suffer from a third, equally damaging deficiency: they give absolutely no clear and adequate indication as to *why* there should have been a spread at all.

In the old days of Kossinna it might be possible to suggest that the innate racial superiority of the Proto-Indo-Europeans allowed them to expand their territories at a certain point in time and conquer most of Europe and northern India. That was always naive as well as arrogant, and such ideas of racial superiority are happily less prevalent today. But even accepting that unpersuasive premise, the theories had internal inadequacies. They rarely explained why the Indo-Europeans should choose that particular moment to break out, as it were. Or to put the matter another way, they did not explain why these Indo-Europeans had hidden their light under a bushel, for so long upon the steppes of south Russia, before setting out to fulfil their fateful destiny.

No post-war writer had adopted such arguments, and there seems no need to take them seriously today. Why then should there have been a dispersal from the supposed homeland at all?

Two possible mechanisms for languages displacement can be proposed. The first is the demographic one: that there were massive transfers of population or significant technical advances allowing a significant increase of population. That view was adopted rather unthinkingly by earlier writers, who liked to use the metaphor of a swarm of bees: the Indo-Europeans *swarmed* from their northern *hive*. But it is not at all clear why the population density should be greater in the 'homeland' than in neighbouring areas. That explanation simply does not apply.

The other main theory is elite dominance. In some cases an incoming minority can indeed take control of an existing system, and the takeover can sometimes result in language replacement. However, for a really effective takeover there needs to be some pre-existing hierarchical structure to be taken over. And while in Britain it could be argued that the late neolithic monuments imply the existence of chiefdoms, the evidence from continental Europe does not always lead to the same conclusion. Even more essential is the existence of some hierarchical social structure within the invading group who will form the new elite. It is difficult to see the necessary conquest, and the new elite administration, being brought about by immigrant groups whose social structure is essentially egalitarian. Yet the case for an effective ranked society, for the existence of chiefdom, amongst the 'Kurgan' groups in their south Russian homeland has never been effectively argued. Professor Gimbutus has given the best account,[29] and she lists several village settlements within what is sometimes termed the Srednij Stog II culture, at Dereivka in the lower Dnieper region, for instance. There are also various hill-fort sites, including Mikhajlovka. She looks primarily to the Maikop tomb away to the east in the Kuban region of the north Caucasus for rich graves as documenting the Kurgan immigrants, it is not clear that they are of particularly high status.

Nor is it entirely clear what made the Kurgan people efficient as warriors. The appeals of older generations to the 'warlike spirit' of the Proto-Indo-Europeans are entirely unsubstantiated: the suggestion that they were mounted warriors does not carry conviction. There is indeed the strong likelihood that the horse was intensively exploited in the steppes of south Russia at about this time and there is some evidence that it was used for riding. The story of the use of the horse is indeed a crucial one for the steppelands, but there is little evidence for westward incursions by mounted warriors at this time: that case cannot really be made before the late bronze age.

The central idea underlying much that is written is that the people of the homeland were pastroal nomads, and that this somehow gave them some adaptive advantage in their move westwards. This idea, however, quite wrongly implies that a pastoralist society is particularly suited to the economic exploitation of central and western Europe, as indeed it is for the steppe lands of eastern Europe and of central Asia. We have already seen that recent work on the Beaker and Corded Ware peoples suggests that they were as much settled farmer as their predecessors.

Around this time, late in the European neolithic, there was a move towards a more intensive subsistence economy in many areas, involving the increasing use of milk and cheese, of animal traction for the plough, and perhaps of wool and hides. This 'secondary products revolution', as Andrew Sherratt[30] has termed it, probably did allow the more intensive exploitation of areas that were not used before, and may well have led to more widespread grazing of livestock, perhaps in uplands which were not previously used. Transhumance, with the moving of cattle away from the village and up to summer pastures may have developed at this time. But central and western Europe is not really suited to nomad pastoralism, with the implication that the whole community leaves its winter base during the summer months and moves over great distances. Of course the reason that Europe is not effectively used in this way is that it gets by very well, with a higher density of exploitation, with mixed farming. Nomad pastoralist economies generally operate either where farming economies are not very successful, or (more often) on the margins of such economies. The development of a greater degree of pastoralism during the later neolithic, in the regions where it did occur, may have filled an ecological niche that was not previously well used. It no doubt supplemented the existing pattern: it did not replace it.

There is, moreover, no reason to think that any move towards the greater use of domestic animals resources was prompted from outside each individual area. The domestic animals were already available in each. Such developments as did take place may be seen as part of a locally-occurring process of intensification: they need not indicate the arrival of new groups of people. Thus while it is perfectly possible that a nomad pastoralist society did develop in the south Russian steppes at about the time suggested, this development in itself is not likely to have influenced central or western Europe very much, either directly or indirectly.

It is interesting, also, to enquire more closely into the origins of this nomadic way of life in the steppes. How did the steppe pastoralist economy originate? As indicated earlier, nomad pastoralism is always dependent in part on the existence of agriculturists. It is clear that nomad pastorlism normally develops out of mixed farming and herding, where a pattern of transhumance can be adapted to one of true nomadism appropriate to the more difficult steppe environment. If the problem is put in these terms, it is clear that the Kurgan pastoralists must in some senses be a secondary growth following upon a primary mixed farmers? The most obvious candidates are those on the western fringes of the south Russia steppe lands: the Cucuteni culture of Romania and the Tripolye culture of the Ukraine.

Ward Goodenough, of the University of Pennsylvania, has persuasively argued this case:[31]

> Once the steppe was conquered it inevitably became a source of out migration. Until it was conquered it was a waste, waiting for people on its periphery to evolve a technology that would allow them to begin to move in and exploit it...
>
> What I have been saying obviously leads to a conclusion that the Battle Axe or Kurgan cultures originated about 3500 BC in an area bordering on the region occupied by Cucuteni and Tripolye peoples, who themselves practised a mixed farming and herding economy.

Goodenough rightly sees here the 'evolutionary background of pastoral nomadism as an adaptation of an older European transumance to the more difficult steppe environment'. This view has, of course, revolutionary consequences for the 'homeland' theory. For it means that the initial colonization of the western part of the steppes took place from the west. The first language of the western steppes must, on this basis, have been the language spoken by the farmers of the neighbouring lands to the west.

4. Conclusion

Three lines of argument thus lead us to reject the notion of a south Russian homeland for the Proto-Indo-Europeans. The main reason for the failure to locate such a homeland arises, I think, first from as unwise reliance on linguistic palaeontology in a rather uncritical way. Secondly it is a migrationist view. And thirdly it springs from a tendency not to consider with sufficient care the processes at work. It is all too easy to equate a pottery style with a linguistic group and to proceed upon that rather simplistic basis.

These critical comments do not imply that the works under review have not come up with many relevant observations, and with points which need explanation. Professor Gimbutas, for instance, and archaeologist colleagues in Romania and the Ukraine, have rightly shown that after the early Cucuteni and Tripolye cultures in those areas, there follow pottery styles which have much more in common with those of the steppes. It is possible that once the new pastorlist economy of the steppes was established, the arable steppe boundary may have shifted some way westward. What may have been in reality an evolution from mixed farming to pastoralism in that area could thus appear in the archaeological record as a westward movement. Nor need one doubt that several of the characteristics of steppe culture which did then develop were indeed taken up in neighbouring lands to the west. These 'Kurgan' influences may in some cases have involved some movement of people. In others they may simply reflect the adoption of some practices derived from the steppes by the populations on their western margins. At a detailed level there is much work to be done in following up these ideas, but from the standpoint of Europe as a whole, it is difficult to believe that there was any significant and sustained movement of population from eastern to central Europe at this time around 3500 to 3000 B.C. This is not the solution to the Indo-European problem, although it may well be relevant to it.

Notes & References

1. Muller F.M., 1888, *Biographies of words and the Home of the Aryas,* London, Longmans Green.
2. Montagu M.F.A., 1964, *The concept of Race,* New York, Free Press.
3. Lehmann W.P., 1973, *Historical Linguistics, an Introduction*, New York, Holt, Rinehart and Winston, 232.
4. *Ibid.,* 233.
5. Fraser J., 1926, 'Linguistic evidence and archeological and ethnological facts', *Proceedings of the British Academy* 266-67.

6. Goody, J., 1959, 'Indo-European Society', *Past and Present* 16, 88-92.

7. See 3.

8. Piggot S., 1950, *Ancient India,* Harmondsworth, Penguin, 246.

9. (a) Friedrich 1970(a), 'Proto-Indo-European trees', in G. Cardona, H.M. Koenigswald and A. Seen (eds.), *Indo-European and Indo-Europeans,* Philadelphia, University of Pennsylvania Press, 11-34.

   (b) Friedrich 1970, *Proto-Indo-European Trees,* Chicago, Chicago University Press.

10. See 5.

11. See 9 (b).

12. Childe V.G., 1926, *The Aryans, a Study of Indo-European Origins,* London, Kegan Paul, Trench and Trubner, 91-93.

13. Barth F., 1961, *Nomads of South Persia,* Oslo University Press, 9.10.

14. Pulgram E., 1958, *The Tongues of Italy,* Cambridge, Mass Harvard University Press, 146-7.

15. Wijngaarden-Bakker L.H. van, 1974, The animals remains from the Beaker settlement at Newgrange, Co. Meath, first report, *Proceedings of the Royal Irish Academy* 74c, 313-83.

    Chapion T., Gamble C., Shennan S., and Whittle A., 1984, *Prehistoric Europe,* London Academic Press.

    Bokonyi S., 1979, 'Copper age vertebrata fauna from Ketegyhaza', in I. Ecsedy (ed.), *The people of the Pit-Grave Kurgan in Eastern Hungary,* Budapest, Akademial Kiado, 101-18.

16. Sangmeister E., 1963, 'La civilization du Vase Campaniforme', in *Les Civilizations Atlantiques: Actes du Premier Congres Atlantique, Brest* 1961.

17. Clark J.G.D., 1966, 'The invasion hypothesis in British Prehistory', *Antiquity* 40, 172-89.

18. Shennan S.J., 1977, *Bell Beakers and their context in Central Europe*: a New Approach (Unpublished Ph.D. dissertation, University of Cambridge.)

19. (a) Renfrew C., 1974(a), 'Beyond subsistence and economy: the evolution of social organisation in prehistoric Europe', in C.B. Moore (ed.) *Reconstructing Complex Societies*, (Supplement to the *Bulletin of the American School of Oriental Research* 20) 74.

    (b) Renfrew C., 1974b, 'British prehistory, changing configurations', in C. Renfrew (ed.), *British Prehistory, A New Outline,* London Duckworth.

20. (a) Shenann S.J., 1982, 'Ideology, change and the European early bornze age', in I Hodder (ed.) *Symbolic and Structural Archeology,* Cambridge, Cambridge University Press, 159.

    (b) Shennan S., 1986, 'Central Europe in the third millennium B.C.: an evolutionary trajectory for the beginning of the European bronze age', *Journal of Anthropological Archaeology* 5, 115-46.

21. Burgess, C. and Shennan S., 1976,. 'the beaker phenomenon, some suggestions', in C. Burgess and R. Miket (eds.), *Settlement and Economy in the Third and Second Millennia B.C.* (B.A.R. 33), Oxford, British Archaeological Reports, 309-26.

22. Whittle A., 1981, 'Later neolithic society in Britain, a realignment', in C.L.N. ruggles and A.W.R. Whittle (eds), *Astronomy and Society in Britain during the period 4000-1500 B.C.* (B.A.R. 88), Oxford, British Archaeological Reports, 335.

23. Gallay A., 1981, 'The western Alps from 2500 to 1500 BC (3400 to 2500 BC), tradition and cultural changes'; *Journal of Indo-European Studies* 9, 33-35.

24. See 20 (b).

25. Neustupny E, 1969, 'Economy of the corded ware cultures', *Archeolgicke Rozhledy* 21, I, 43-68.

26. Hausler, A., 1981, 'Zu den Beziehungen zwischen dem nordpontischen Gebiet Sudost-und Mitteleuropas im Neolithikum und in deu Fruhen Bronzezeit und ihre Bedeutung fur den Indo-europaische Problem', *Prezgled Archeologiczny* 29, 101-49.

27. Tilley C., 1984, 'Ideology and power in the middle neolithic of southern Sweden', in D. Miller and C. Tilley (eds), *Ideology, Power and Prehistory,* Cambridge, Cambridge University Press, 121 and 142.

28. Menk R., 1980, 'A synopsis of the physical anthropology of the Corded Ware Complex on the background of the expansion of the Kurgan cultures', *Journal of Indo-European Studies,* 361.

29. Gimbutas M., 1970, 'Proto-Indo-European Culture: the Kurgan culture during the 5th to the 3rd millennia B.C.', in G, Cardona, H.M. Koenigswald and A. Senn (eds.), *Indo-European and Indo-Europeans,* Philadelphia, University of Pennsylvania Press, 155-98.

30. Sherratt A., 1981, 'Plough and Pastoralism: aspect of the secondary products revolution', in I. Hodder, G. Isaac and N. Hammand (eds.), *Pattern of the Past: Studies in Honour of David Clarke,* Cambridge, Cambridge University Press, 261-305.

31. Goodenough W., 1970, 'The evolution of pastoralism and Indo-European Origins', in G. Cardona, H.M. Koenigswald and A. Senn (eds.), *Indo-European and Indo Europeans,* Philadelphia, University of Pennsylvania Press, 258 and 262.
    Anthony D.W., 1986, "The Kurgan culture, Indo-European origins and the domestication of the horse: a reconsideration", *Current Anthropology,* 27, 291-314. That there was some westward transmission of the Pontic form of Kurgan burial does seem documented by the Hungarian evidence: (Ecsedy I, 1979, *The People of the Pit-Grave Kurgans in Eastern Hungary* (Fontes Archaeologici Hungarie, Budapest, Akademial Kiado).

9

Genesis of the Aryan Race Theory and its Application to Indian History

Devendra Swarup*

> ...it is to be regretted, that notwithstanding the Boden Sanskrit Professorship at Oxford, so little attention is paid there to Sanskrit. Both Professor Lee at Cambridge and Dr. H.H. Wilson at Oxford complain of the little encourgement given to Oriental studies in their respective universities.

This remark came from a missionary scholar Rev. J. Long in 1849, three years after his arrival in Calcutta from England. He lamented:

> Even the best philological works published in England itself are generally mere translations from the German. Since closer attention has been directed, of late, to the literary treasures confined in the German language, philological science has become increasingly popular in England; but the Bopps, Adelungs, Grimms, Burnoufs and Humboldts of Germany led the way, while Oxford and Cambridge lagged far behind, content to be humble imitators.

Rev. Long admitted that "Etymology has risen, through the exertions of philosophical minds of Germany, to the rank of a Science".

Long's article, which carried these remarks stood in support of his statement, because it happened to be a review of the German scholar Frank Bopp's classic. "*A Comparative Grammar of the Sanskrit, Zend, Greek, Latin, Lithuanian, Gothic, German and Slavonic languages,*"— a work which was originally published in German in the year 1833, but was translated into English twelve years after in the year 1845 and was reviewed by Rev. Long four years later in the year 1849.

It is really puzzling to find that Great Britain which boasted to have offered the literary treasures of India to the European scholarship by having established the Asiatic Society of Bengal in the year 1785—only

---

* Retired as Reader in History, Delhi University. The above paper was presented to a seminar on the Aryan Problem held at the Mythic Society, Bangalore in July, 1991.

a few years after the conquest of Bengal, should have waited till 1832 to found the first Professorship in Sanskrit at Oxford, while France had led the way in the year 1816 and Germany in the year 1818. It is interesting to know that while Sir William Jones, the founder of the Asiatic Society of Bengal, is being credited to have made the beginning of the science of comparative philology in his famous discourse presented to the Society in the year 1786. England founded its first Philological Society of London in the year 1842, long after these sciences had grown into maturity in Germany and France.

Why was Great Britain so indifferent to these newly born sciences for such a long period and what made her suddenly to realise their utility and importance? The answer to these questions may, perhaps, be found in a deeper study of the aspirations of nascent German nationalism, struggling to emerge as a united state on the European map and thus leading to the emergence of German-French rivalry, role of Indology and Sanskrit studies in the strengthening of German nationalism, Anglo-French rivalry led to Anglo-German collaboration in the field of policies as well as indology. But Britain's imperialist interests in India resulted in a wide divergence in the attitudes of these two European nations towards Indian history and culture.

British Imperialist Aims

Lord Wellesley's military successes in India, particularly against Tipu Sultan and the Marathas during 1798-1804, mark a decisive shift in the British attitude towards India. Hence after, no serious rival was left to challenge their ultimate supremacy over India, and now Britain's main concern was how to instill a sense of superiority complex in her young administrators going to India, how to give permanency to her Indian empire and how to convert India into a market for her goods produced by the newly born machine-based Industrial Revolution. This was a concern shared equally by all the sections of opinion builders—be they the Evangelicals led by Wilber force and Charles Grant, or the Utilitarians led by Benthem and James Mill or liberal imperialists led by Henry Dundas or Lord Minto or Lord Hastings. Though they differed in their respective solutions of the imperialist problems, they all seemed to agree on one point that glorification of India's past was not in their national interest, as it would strengthen Indians' consciousness of their cultural superiority and would instill a sense of inferiority in the young British administrators who, in the words of James Mackintosh, were getting '*Brahminised*' under the spell of a superior literary and cultural tradition still surviving in India. The Evangelicals felt that Christianisation of India was the only divine mission behind the establishment of British rule over India, it alone could lead to the permanence of British rule over India, and creating an Indian market for British goods. It was their considered view that for the conversion of Indians to Christianity, it was necessary to denigrate their customs, manners, religious beliefs and cultural traits. Similarly the newly born Utilitarian school felt that now when Europe had given birth to a unique scientific and industrial revolution, and religion had lost its appeal, the recent military and political set-backs suffered by India at the hands of the Britishers, ought to be projected as a consequence of the failure of its decadent culture and morality against a superior civilization and thus Indians should be made to realise the inferiority and hollowness of all their own philosophy, civilization and tradition. The cumulative effect of this thinking led to the demise of the era of admiration for Indian history and culture represented by Charles Wilkins, Nathaniel Halhed, William Robertson, Thomas Maurice and Sir William Jones and others, and to the beginning of a new era of a wholesale denigration of everything in Hindu history and culture as well as in the contemporary Hindus manners and customs.

Pamphlet War in England

This new trend was reflected in a long and vigorous pamphlet war which was waged in England between the Hindu-baiter-missionaries, utilitarians and imperialists on one side and Hindu-admirer-Englishmen, who had spent many decades of their life in Indian civil or military service or as businessmen and who had seen the Hindu reality from close quarters, on the other. The central question in this pamphlet-war was whether introduction of Christianity in India was necessary for the salvation of decadent Hindus or whether in the field of culture, morality and manners, England, instead of teaching the Hindus, could itself learn a lot from them. This public debate came to an end with the inclusion of a pamphlet, written by the Evangelical leader Charles Grant under the title, *Some Observations on the Manners and Morals of Hindus* (said to have been originally written in 1792 and circulated to the members of the Council of Directors and Proprietors in the year 1798, but which came to the public knowledge in 1812 only) in the Parliamentary papers published by the House of Commons in the year 1812, on the eve of the impending debate on the East India Company's Charter Renewal Bill of 1813.

This shift in the official attitude towards India was also evident in the decision of the Court of Directors to place all the official secret records at the disposal of James Mill, who, as a Utilitarian, was a powerful exponent of the European superiority over the decadent Hindu India. James Mill, who had never visited India and did not know any of the Indian languages, sat to write a History of British India in the year 1806 and after labouring for twelve years published in 1818 a bulky *History of British India* in six volumes. A few years later, Macaulay referred to it in the House of Commons as "on the whole the greatest historical work which had appeared in our language since that of Gibbon." Mill's *History of British India* was immediately introduced as a textbook in the Hileybury College, which used to train and mould the future British administrators of India. It held the field unchallenged for twenty five years, being reprinted in 1820, 1826 and 1840, and again in 1848 and 1859.

It is a puzzle that while Mill had ostensibly set out to deal with the history of British India only, why did he dwell in such detail on ancient Hindu civilization and how did he choose to make such a sweeping condemnation of that civilization? In his view, "to ascertain the true state of the Hindus in the scale of civilization is an object of the highest *practical* importance to the people of Britain", and the test he applied was "exactly in proportion as utility is the object of every pursuit, may we regard a nation as civilized."

Quite obviously, the image of India, which was emerging out of the Indological researches being pursued by the German and the French scholars went quite contrary to the official British view of India in general and Hindus in particular which was projected by Charles Grant and James Mill. This led in England to a calculated indifference to Sanskrit studies and to the new comparative sciences born out of them. But, gradually a section of Christian missionaries and British scholars was veering round to the view that Sanskrit could also be made an effective vehicle of evangelization of Hindu upper classes. This was very effectively presented in the 1822 issue of the quarterly series of the *Friend of India,* edited by Drs. Carey and Marshman of the Serampore Mission and was reiterated by H.H. Wilson also. It was this quest for evangelisation of India which led to the establishment of the Boden Chair of Sanskrit at Oxford in the year 1832, of which H.H. Wilson was the first occupant. Through their long experience in India, missionaries had discovered that the intellectual and moral superiority of the *Brahmins*, their moral authority over the Hindus all over India, irrespective of caste, creed, language and regional differences among them, and the firm grip of caste organization over Hindus were the major obstacles in the way of evangelization of India. How to overcome these obstacles was their main concern in those days. Some perceptive minds saw that instead of wasting efforts on the conversion of the higher castes, it would be more fruitful to concentrate their efforts on the lower sections of the Hindu society and especially on the tribal population living in forests and jungles. As far back as 1835, a Scottish missionary, Dr. John Wilson, who had arrived in India in the year 1828, in his presidential address to the Bombay Literary Society, emphasised that the tribals should be the main object of their study and research. Missionaries like Hislop in Central Provinces, Stevenson and Wilson in Bombay, Caldwell in Madras Presidency, J.C. Marshmar, J.Long and Alexander Duff in Bengal etc., started working in this direction and tried to utilise the philological studies, made in Germany and France, to serve their own mission of evangelisation.

German scholars had an attraction for Sanskrit studies for two reasons. First, they were entirely dependent upon British friendship for their access to India's literary treasures, and secondly their common enmity towards France provided an emotional bond between the rising German nationalism and British imperialism. It could lead to Anglo-German collaboration on intellectual as well as political level. German savant, Franz Bopp, who is celebrated as the founder of the Science of Comparative Philology, had to spend about eighteen months in England for his studies of Sanskrit literature. Britain was trying to utilise all these contacts with German scholars in a very subtle manner to further her imperial interests in India. Probably, it was a part of calculated efforts that in the year 1816 Thomas Young (1773-1829), a British physician, who is said to have been the first to decipher the Rosetta Stone, suggested the term "Indo-European" to designate the common root of the family of languages which was till then identified as Sanskritic or "Indo-Iranian",— both pointing to the antiquity and superiority of the Sanskritic tradition. But Julius Klaproth in order to boost German national pride coined the word "Indo-Germanic" in the year 1823, which was immediately picked up and popularised by German philologists, generating heart-burning among French scholars. Britain very subtly persuaded a grateful Franz Bopp to add the weight of his scholarship and influence to the use of the term 'Indo-European' which he out of a sense of gratitude to the British 'patronage' did in his *magnum opus "Comparative Philology"*, mentioned above.

The coming of a German scholar Chevalier Bunsen, as ambassador of Prussia to England in the year 1841, marks the beginning of the Anglo-German collaboration on political as well as intellectual planes. Bunsen read a Discourse before the Ethnological Section of the British Association for the Advancement of Science, emphasising the usefulness and importance of the Science of Philology and Ethnology. Next year, the Philological Society came into existence in London, and in 1843 the Ethnological Society took birth in England. Bunsen became instrumental in bringing Frederick Max Muller to England who played such an important role in the evolution and popularization of the 'Aryan Race Theory' and its application to the interpretation of India's past and present.

It seems that much before Max Muller had entered the field, some missionary scholars in India had already perceived the potential of the science of comparative philology in uprooting the hold of the *Brahmins*, Sanskrit language and the *Vedic* tradition over the minds of Indian masses. A history text book prepared by an anonymous missionary scholar, whose Hindi translation was prepared and published with the help of Rev. John James Muir in the year 1846, asserted that the *Brahmins* had entered India from across the Indus river, had brought Sanskrit language and the *Vedas* with them, and had foisted them on the aboriginal people of India. This text-book highlighted the view that the forest and jungle people had not adopted the Brahmanical culture and were outside the pale of Hinduism. Rev. John Stevenson had published a translation of the *Samveda* in the year 1842 and suggested that this *Veda* was brought into India from outside.

Elphinstone's History of India (1841)

This biased view of the missionaries was not shared by sober scholars. Mount Stuart Elphinstone, who had entered India as a sixteen year old lad in the year 1795 and having served as a writer for many years had risen to be the first Governor of Bombay Presidency in the year 1819 and after retirement from this position in the year 1827, had returned to England, began to work on the history of ancient India, published the first serious research work in the year 1841. In his *'History of India'* Elphinstone instead of presenting a dynastic and political history of ancient India, concentrated on the evolution of Hindu philosophy, religion, social and political institutions, language and literature, sciences, crafts and arts etc. In one of the chapter of this book he discussed the origin of the Hindus and formation of their society in the light of ms study of *Manusmriti*. He concluded,

> It is opposed to their foreign origin, that neither in the Code (of Manu) nor, I believe, in the *Vedas*, nor in any book that is certainly older than the code, is there any allusion to a prior residence or to a knowledge of more than the name of any country out of India. Even mythology goes no further than the Himalayan chain, in which is fixed the habitation of the gods.

After discussing the question of the "common origin of Sanskrit language with those of the west" and the original home of the common ancestors of these linguistic groups, Elphinstone opined.

> To say that it spread from a central point is a gratuitous assumption, and even contrary to analogy; for, emigration and civilization have not spread in a circle, but from east to west. Where, also, could the central point be, from which a language could spread over India, Greece, and Italy and yet leave Chaldea, Syria and Arabia untouched? The question, therefore, is still open.

Elphistone's final verdict was:

> There is no reason whatever for thinking that the Hindus ever inhabited any country but their present one, and as little for denying that they may have done so before the earliest trace of their records or tradition.

Used the term 'Arya'

Obviously, such opinions were not palatable to the missionaries and administrators and, therefore, we find in the 1840s systematic scholarly efforts to give a racial interpretation to India's diversity and to use the new sciences of philology and ethnology for reconciling the Indian upper classes to the British rule. We find scholar missionaries like Long, George Smith, and John Wilson suggesting that philological studies would help in creating sympathy between the European rulers and the native ruled. They felt that if it could be proved that Europeans and Hindus belonged to the same race, and that if the Hindus could be made to believe, to quote the words of Rev. John Wilson, that "the Hindus and ourselves are cousins in the family", and "now it [India] has become partly by its own consent, and partly by provoked conquest with the most enlightened and philanthropic nation in the world. Little more than a year ago, I noticed in a public discourse the palpable benefits of this connexion".

It is out of this quest for searching out a uniting bond between the British conquerors and the conquered Hindus, the use of the word "*Arya*" for the common family of languages, as well as, the common ancestors speaking the mother language, might have occurred to some creative mind. Although the use of the word *Arya* seems to have begun since the days of Frederick Schlegel, in the year 1808 that was only in a qualitative sense and not in a linguistic or racial sense. In the latter sense we find its conscious and systematic use in the writings of two German scholars, Burnouf and Lassen and perhaps British ethnologist James Cowles Pritchard (1786-1848). Pritchard included a section on Arian Race in *Natural History of Man* published in the year 1845. Pritchard tried to show in his book that:

> nations who speak languages of cognate origin and who are proved by that connecting bond to be the descendants of one original stock, are spread from the mouth of the Ganges to the British Islands and the

> northern extremities of Scandinavia. These are collectively called Indo-European nations. Pointing to Indo-Iranian branch. Pritchard says, that "the great branch of this stock is divided into two principal stems. Tradition falls short of the era of separation, and we can not trace them to one centre; and we find them both arising, from two principal foci, at not great distance from each other, and situated to the eastward and westward of the river Indus.

Pritchard draws attention to the fact that these two stems have one common name—Arians or Aryas, which is the ancient national designation for both of the Persian and Indian branches. On the authority of Greek writers as Herodotus, Strabo and others, he says that the ancient Medas called themselves Ari, a name which survived in the Aria or Ariane of the Greek geographers. Further he says that Aryavarta was the holy land of the *Brahmins*, the country lying between the Himalayas and the Vindhya mountains, which was the ancient abode of the Hindus. Then he goes on to show that to the westward of the Indus, not far from Bamian or from Balkh, was the country which the earliest traditions of the Persians point out as the primeval seat and paradise of their race, *Eeriene Veedgo,* or the pure Iran. Pritchard concludes that the most accurate analysis of ancient historical documents thus coincides with the result of the philological research.

German scholar Christian Lassen published the first volume of his gigantic *magnum opus* on the history of ancient India entitled "*Indische Alterthumskunde"* in the year 1847. This volume contains an exhaustive story of Indian Geography (IA, I, 1-416) and a lengthy section on Indian ethnology (ibid, 421-567). When this volume was published little was known of *Vedic* literature and therefore we hardly find any mention of it. Here we find the Aryan race theory with all its characteristics. He contrasts the Aryans of north India with the people of the Deccan. He asserts that the highest castes in India were also the whitest. Propounding the principle of superiority of the Aryan race Lassen writes:

> the Aryans are the most highly organised, the most enterprising and the most creative among the peoples; they are also the youngest because the earth only produced the most perfect species of plants and animals at a later date. This relationship will utlimately reveal itself in a similar way in the political field.

He endeavoured to show that the way indeed, the which India is distributed between the different peoples that inhabit it, indicates that the "Aryans" whose complexion distinguishes them from the original inhabitants, must have come into the land from the north-west. Lassen's writings are full of the spirit of anti-Semitism and Christian evangelism. He sees in Christianity the fulfilment of mankind. Commenting on Lassen's Aryan Racism, Poliakov says:

> Here are basic elements of the Aryan myth, the emphasis on biology, the deserved triumph of the strongest, the preeminence of youth, superiority of the whites. Here we find the seeds of Darwin's theory of evolution as well.

In the same year, 1847, the Transaction volume of the British Association for the Advancement of Science carried an article by F. Max Muller under the title "*On the Relation of the Bengali to the Arian and Aboriginal Languages of India*". This seems to have been the first article written by Max Muller after his arrival in England in the year 1846, and it shows that by then Max Muller had started dividing Indian languages into two distinct families–one, Arian and the other Aboriginal. Thus we see that by the year 1847 the term 'Arya' had begun to be used as a synonym of Indo-Germanic and Indo-European in linguistic as well as in racial sense.

Intellectually alert missionaries like John Wilson were not only keenly watching all these scholarly developments but were in close touch with the leading European Indologists. John Wilson, while on his way to India from England after his second marriage in the year 1846, had made it a point to meet Christian Lassen at Bonn and had received some printed forms of his forthcoming book, "*History of Ancient India.*"

It was a continental scholar Rasmas Rask, who had, following the authority of Strabo, for the first time, vaguely suggested that the South Indian languages were probably "Scythian". Pritchard in his writings tried to examine this suggestion of the Scythian relationship of the Dravidian languages, and gave a few grammatical illustrations also, but was not sure about this relationship and wished to see the problem, not merely stated, but solved!

It is important to note that a vague suggestion coming from scholars like Rask, Pritchard and later Lassen was developed into a full-fledged invasion theory by Rev. John Wilson in his missionary zeal. In a letter dated 25 July 1859, ostensibly addressed to his parents, but really meant for the friends of missions at home, Wilson wrote:

> I must make a general remark not unworthy of the friends of missions at home. The first race who entered India were 'undoubtedly' from Turania, or the eastern Scythia. They are primarily represented at present by different nations and tribes in India located to the south of the river Krishna and speaking the Canarese, Tooloo, Telugu, Malayalam and Tamil languages, which have still a great affinity with the Tartar dialects. The distinctive peculiarity of the religion of these races is the worship of ghosts and demons whom they seek to conciliate by offering blood.

Further, elaborating the Aryan Invasion Theory, Wilson said, "The races which in the second instance, entered India were from Ariana, the eastern part of Iran or Persia, probably the original seat of the Indo-Teutonic family of nations. They are located in India to the north of the Krishna, and their languages are all derivatives from the Sanskrit".

These Aryan invaders, in Dr. Wilson's view, brought the *Brahmanas* and the *Vedas* with them and, to quote his own words:

> The Aryan tribes in conquering India, urged by the *Brahmanas*, made war against the Turanian demon worship, but not always with complete success.

Here Wilson is trying to use the Aryan Race and Invasion Theory to sow the seeds of north-south conflict in India.

Further in the same letter he turns his attention to the mountain and forest aboriginal tribes, which, in his view, "are still, as far as *Brahminism* is concerned, sturdy non-conformists".

Hinting at how such comparative studies may be helpful in the missionary efforts in India, Wilson says:

> "It is among the Turanian races, and the devil worshippers, as in Tinnevelly and other places in the south of India, which have no organized priest-hood and bewitching literature, that the coverts to Christianity are most numerous". He notes with satisfaction that "The day of their merciful visitation seems to be at hand" while "that of the Brahminical Aryan tribes with all their pride of caste and systematic creed, seems to be more distant". At the end he emphasises that, "No equitable comparison of the results of Christian missions in India can be made with the forgetful of this fact.

In a letter dated 2 December 1850, addressed to Alexander Duff, the noted missionary at Calcutta, Wilson informs:

> For four nights I discoursed on the Religious History of Western India as illustrated by the ancient remains, for four nights on the introduction and diffusion of the Turanian and Iranian races in India, principally with a view to the illustrations of the origin and progress of *Brahminism*; for thirteen, on Natural theology, and desiredness and necessity of a Divine Revelation.

Further he informs Duff:

> I am at present discussing the question, where is the Divine Revelation to be found, and in connection with this I am reviewing the sacred writings of the Hindus, according to their classes. I have directed a good deal of attention lately to the *Vedas*.

According to this letter, Wilson was holding a geological class once a week on Friday mornings which was attended regularly by the son of a prominent philanthropist of Bombay, Juggernath Shunkur Set.

Later on, in January 1858, Wilson delivered a lecture before the Mechanics' Institution at Bombay, which was published in October 1858, under the title *India Three Thousand Years Ago.* In this book, we find the early history of India in general, and *Brahmanism* in particular, begin presented in terms of Aryan Invasion Theory. Wilson utilises the Invasion Theory, on one hand, to highlight Aryan-Dravidian conflict and the non-Aryan origins of the tribal population of India and on the other, to create a sentiment of sympathy between Indians and their British ruler. He says,

> The Aryans and ourselves, it is hence obvious, are cousins in the human family. A body of the same people travelling to the south, came to India by the mountain passes leading to the Indus; and acquired dominion over the Turanian peoples, the Dasyus, that had got to the climes of the sun before them and had become in consequence somewhat darkened in their skin. Another body of the same people wandered to the far west, and, after becoming domiciled and blessed there, have come to India, with their ships, and with their goods, three thousand years later, and acquired dominion over the representatives of both Aryans and Dasyus.

Wilson wants us to believe that "what has taken place since the commencement of the British rule in India is only a reunion, to a certain extent, of the members of the same great family".

All these facts are important to understand the limited role which Max Muller had really played in the circulation and propagation of the Aryan Race and Invasion Theory. As stated earlier, the term "Arya" had already been adopted by many continental and English scholars before Max Muller had migrated to England in the year 1846 and wrote in the year 1847, his first article on comparison of the Bengali language with the Arian and aboriginal languages as well as the famous article "On the *Vedas*" which he how contributed to the Prussian ambassador Bunsen's great work in the year 1851. But his correspondence with Bunsen shows that Max Muller consciously decided to use and popularise the term "Arya" in place of the old terms "Indo-Iranian", "Indo-Germanic" or "Indo-European" for two reasons:

Firstly, he felt that these terms were artificially created among the educated, were of recent origin, and had no roots in the ancient languages and therefore would not get any support.

Secondly, the word "Arya" was an ancient term used in Sanskrit and old Iranian literature profusely and therefore would be readily acceptable to the upper classes of India, who would easily swallow the theory of Aryan greatness and their kinship with their European masters.

It is important to know, that Bunsen had come to England as Prussia's ambassador to create bridges of Anglo-German collaboration in political and intellectual fields. He had brought Max Muller to help him with his great intellectual capacity and powerful expression in English language for the fulfilment of this political mission. Max Muller served his friend very faithfully and effectively. Besides this, Max Muller was an enthusiast in the cause of conversion of Hindus to Christianity as any Christian Missionary could claim to be, as is evident from his published correspondence as well as his pamphlet war with his competitor Monier William for the Boden Professorship in the year 1862. Therefore, in a calculated manner, he tried to popularise the use of the term "Aryan" in place of the old terms and tried to persuade all his contacts in France and Germany also to adopt it.

The term "Arya" was now gaining wide currency in Europe. Between 1854 and 1855 a French scholar Joseph Arthur Comte de Gobineau published a four-volume work "*Essai sur l'inegalit des races humanines*" (Inequality of Human Races) in which he classified mankind into three races and established the superiority of the white, that is of the "Aryan race". Gobineau asserted that "There is no true civilization, among the European peoples, where the Aryan branch is not prominent". He sincerely believe that the great Aryan race is the saviour of mankind and is leading it to higher and more civilised planes, but feared that the noble Aryan race is degenerating because of the primary error of race intermixture.

These racist ideas were immediately grasped and applied to Indian history by the missionaries and their friends in bureaucracy in India.

As early as the year 1856 we come across a very long article written by a Calcutta-based British physician Dr. Norman Chevers, a servant of the East India Company, but a very close friend of the missionaries like Rev. Long and Alexander Duff and carried immense influence upon young bureaucrats like W.W. Hunter and others. The article entitled "*Aryan Race*" contained an up-to-date survey of the philological and ethonological studies going on in Europe. Applying the Aryan Race Theory to Indian situation Dr. Chevers emphasized the racial affinity between the English masters and their Indian subjects. He wrote:

> Alexander then, and Dalhousie now, at an interval of twenty-one centuries, who carried their power across the land of the five rivers, did no more than to assert the claim of the youngest sons to share with their elder brothers in the division of their common motherland. While highlighting the racial unity between Indian and European Aryans, Chevers was equally keen to project the racial difference between Indian Aryans and Tribal peoples. He says:

Tribal people are the representatives of the nations which inhabited India previously to the "Hindu invasion" and suggested systematic studies of hill races from this angle. He lamented that "little or nothing has been done hitherto to distinguish the Aryan from the lamurian" and suggested the use of the newly born science of Craniology in this direction. Interestingly, Dr. Chevers suggested also the use of photography of the skulls for comparing the forms and dimensions of the various crania. The suggestion was picked up by the British government and put into practices about 1860.

The same year (1856), Father Rev. Robert Caldwell fulfilled the wishes of Dr. Chevers with the publication of his pioneer work, *A Comparative Grammer of the Dravidian or South Indian Family of Languages,* which put the stamp of scholarship on the theory of separate racial origins of north and south Indians.

The Great Revolt of 1857 marks a watershed in the evolution of the British imperialist policy in India. The sudden and unexpected rebellion by the Bengal Native Infantry, the most trusted instrument of British expansion in India, shook the British administrators out of their slumber. A deeper analysis of the causes which led to this sudden catastrophe revealed to them that it was the factor of rigid caste organization and the *Brahmin* preponderance in the Bengal Native Infantry which lay at the root of this sudden outburst. It could not be just coincidence that in the year 1858, almost simultaneously, four separate write-ups on caste system of the Hindus appeared in England, India and America, applying the Aryan race theory to the institution of caste. In England Max Muller wrote his long article on Caste and John Muir published his first volume of *Original Sanskrit Texts* carrying a compilation of references from Sanskrit sources on Caste.

In India, Rev. Wilson published his two-volume work on Caste, and surprisingly in far-off U.S.A., W.D. Whitney also chose to write an article on *Caste in India*. Wilson, Max Muller and Whitney all tried to trace the origin of the caste system in the Aryan Invasion Theory and thus declaring the *Brahmins* as the pure descendents of the Aryan invaders who invented the caste system for perpetuation of their supremacy over the conquered people.

The main objects of the British imperialist policy after the 1857 Revolt were to reconcile the upper classes to the British rule, to implement a policy of "Divide and Rule" by giving Indian diversity and institutions a racial interpretation and to uproot all the bonds of unity that had evolved through a very long historical journey.

By now the British policy-makers had come to realise that Aryan Race and Invasion Theory could be very effectively used to lay down intellectual foundations of their new Imperialist policy. Perhaps, as a part of this policy, we find John Muir publishing in 1860, the second volume of his *Original Sanskrit Texts*, incorporating the recent debate about the original home of the Aryas, as well as bringing together stray references from the Sanskrit literature which could throw some light on this point.

As stated earlier, since 1860, repeated instructions started coming from the Secretary of State in London for collecting detailed information about the forest and jungle tribes scattered all over India along with photographs of their representative specimens.

In 1862, Sir Samuel Laing, the Finance Member in Governor General's Council, delivered a lecture before the Dalhousie Institute at Simla, wherein he endeavoured, with the help of recent philological researches, to present the thesis on common Aryan parentage of the European rulers and the Indian natives and thereby concluding, that the Indians were to be treated as equals by the Englishmen. This lecture coming from a top member of the Government of India, thrilled the hearts of educated Indians.

Alluding to the Indian aspiration for equality with their English masters, Sir Henry Maine, the Law Member of the Viceroy's Executive Council and Vice-Chancellor of the Calcutta University, said in his Convocation Address delivered in March 1864:

> Probably, if we could search into the hearts of the more refined portions of the native community, we should find that their highest aspiratuion was to be placed on a footing of real and genuine equality with their European fellow citizens.

and in this connection referring to Sir Laing's Dalhousie Institute lecture, Sir Maine remarked:

> Most of you have heard of one remarkable effort which was made to establish this portion. The effect produced by Laing's lecture on the Aryan race must have been prodigious, for, I am sure, I scarcely see a single native book or newspaper which does not contain some allusion to Laing's argument.

It is important to note that the failure of 1857 Revolt was immediately followed by Charles Darwin's Theory of Evolution, which was based on the twin principles of "struggle for existence" and "survival of the fittest". It goes to the credit of Sir Henry Maine that in his book, *Ancient Law* published in 1861, he perhaps for the first time effectively introduced the comparative historical method into English thought. After his stint as Legal Member in India from 1862 to 1869, he utilized the philological theory of treating Sanskrit as a member of the Aryan family of languages and also used the German scholar Von Maurer's work on the "*Aryan Institution: the German Mark*". He argued that the Indian village community was also an Aryan institution, surviving in full vigour. In Henry Maine's opinion:

> India was the great repository of verificable phenomena of ancient usage and ancient juridical thought and thus, the existing society in India could throw light in Europe's distant past.

Although Sir Maine believed that the government of India by the English has been rendered appreciably easier by the discoveries which have brought home to the educated of both the races the common parentage of the Englishmen and the Hindu, he did not mean that India was in an advanced state of civilization, rather her state was that of "the infancy of the human mind prolonged". His view was that:

> "The primitive Aryan groups, the primitive Aryan institutions, the primitive Aryan ideas have been arrested in India at an early stage of development". (*Rede Lectures, 1875).*

Here, we find a very subtle attempt of applying the theory of evolution to Indian institutions and of emphasizing India's backwardness compared to their progressive European brothers.

At this stage we suddenly find important Government officials like James Talboys Wheeler, W.W. Hunter, John Beames, E.T. Dalton and others, producing book after book on Indian history, philology and ethnology. In 1867 James Talboys Wheeler, who was acting as an Assistant Secretary to the Government of India in the Foreign Department, started publishing his five-volume *History of India from the earliest times* interpreting it in the light of the Aryan Invasion Theory, W.W. Hunter in 1865 started writing his famous "*Annals of Rural Bengal*" in which he tried to apply the Aryan race theory at micro-level on a district called Beerbhoom, which he described as "the outpost of the Sanskrit race on the west of Lower Bengal and which had to bear the sharp collisions of Aryan civilization with ruder types prevailing among the aborigines". The publication of this book in 1868 in England earned much appreciation and many rewards for Hunter. He was requested by his friends in the Royal Asiatic Society such as John Muir and Edward Thomas to stay back in England for some more months and to prepare a *Comparative Dictionary of the Non-Aryan Languages of India and High Asia.* Two boxes containing the data about the hill tribes residing in the Himalayan region and collected by Brian Hodgson during his long stay in India and Nepal as a civil servant, were placed at his disposal for preparing this work. His furlough was extended as a very special case by the Secretary of State and surprisingly Hunter, without knowing much of the tribal dialects, was able to publish this work under the above title within a small period of five months in November 1868.

A thirty two pages long Introduction at the beginning of this *Comparative Dictionary* spells out in most clear words, the imperialist motives underlying the work. He says:

> Although the pre-historic aborigines living on the plains of Hindustan succumbed so completely beneath the Aryan invaders, as to 'lose' all remembrance of their separate ethnical existence, but "among the mountains and lofty plateau, they have preserved their nationality intact, and are engaged in an incessant warfare against plain aggressors".
>
> The principal end of my researches has been purely a practical one, because the English are now trying to reclaim them. But in order to civilise them, it is necessary first to understand them, and this book, for the first time in the history of India, places the governing race (i.e., the English) in direct communication with eighty millions of its non-Aryan subjects and neighbours.

Further, he says:

that these races are capable of being politically utilized, and by proper measures may be converted from a source of weakness to a source of strength.

He specially mentions that the book has been written "for the convenience of European students and of missionaries".

Expressing his gratitude to the missionaries for "the zealous cooperation which I have received throughout from missionaries of all denominations, both in India and at home", he admits:

> It was to these noble and devoted men that I owed my first materials, and from them I learned that missionary enterprise means not only the propagation of the Christian faith, but also the civilization of whole races and the winning back of long lapsed peoples to a new life.

After paying these tributes to the missionaries, "where scholarship is warmed with the holy flame of Christian zeal". Hunter asserts that "no history of the British occupation of India will be complete without their mention."

Spelling out his imperialist objectives, Hunter says:

> The Hindus are an increasing and consequently an encroaching people. Their advances have to be made at the expense of the hill and forest tribes. Our difficulty is a military one. A vast native army had to be maintained, and this army must be watched by another army with different interests and of a different race. The whole burden of supplying the surveillance at present rests upon the population of the British Islands—a population scarcely one-eighth of the Indian people, separated from India by the width of the globe, and by the repugnance which a northern nation has to exile in the tropics; above all, a population who have so much assured comfort, and so many avenues to distinction in civil life, as to render military service distasteful. The difficulty will increase to a yet unsuspected intensity, as the effects to co-operation among the lower classes and of the present tendency of public opinion to a more democratic tone of Government begins to tell.

He further explains:

> From this difficulty, the aboriginal tribes of India hold out a means of relief, in interest, in race, in religion, in habits of life, they are cut off from the Hindus and Musalmans by a gulf....and their ethnical refulgence is kept in a constant glow by the remembrance of ancient wars and recent wrongs....of the valour of many of these tribes and that unquestionable fidelity and capacity for discipline, which are the raw materials of soldier stuff, there is no question...the part played by the aboriginal troops during the mutiny is fresh in every Indian stateman's memory, and therefore, by extensively employing these tribes as military police and as soldiers we should not only relieve the English population of a burden greater than it can permanentely bear, but we should offer a livelihood to brave predatory peoples...the aboriginals will supply them the labour, and would be a good target group for conversion to Christianity.

He concludes:

> They have yet to start on the path of progress. It remains for us to decide whether that path is to lead them to Hinduism, or to the purer faith and civilization which we represent.

This introduction penned down by W.W. Hunter clearly shows how scholars, administrators and missionaries were working hand in hand to achieve the common goal of the British imperialism in India by manipulating and distorting her history in the light of the newly created subjective theory of Aryan Race and Invasion on India.

10

Invasion Theory and Indian Nationalism

Srikant G. Talageri*

A race of people, called the "Aryans", is supposed to have invaded India somewhere around 2000-1500 BC from the north-west. These Aryans, after centuries of warfare and bloodshed, are supposed to have destroyed, or driven southwards, or subjugated and absorbed (as lower castes) most of the natives in the north of the "subcontinent", and then themselves occupied the northern areas.

Originally formulated by European scholars, mainly for imperialistic reasons, this theory has been perfected by Indian Leftists into a powerful weapon to be used against Indian nationalism.

Two aspects of this theory must be noted. The first is that this theory is widely accepted by almost everyone, and those who do not accept it can indeed be accused of being those who do not want to accept it. The second is that this theory had the potential to undermine the rationale of Indian nationalism, at least in the minds of those who are ever-willing to rest their thinking processes, and accept whatever half-witted formulations are placed before them in a cut-and-dried manner.

General Acceptance of the Theory

The theory is taught, as fact, to all Indian children in their school textbooks. Most educated Indians, long after they have left school and forgotten most of what they had studied there, continue to retain the memory that "Aryans" were some people who invaded India in ancient times, even if they do not realize the exact implications of this theory.

The theory has been accepted on such a scale that any textbook or scholarly book the world over, which deals with, or refers to, India's early history, mentions the Aryan invasion of India in the second millenium BC, as if it were a natural and indisputable part of proven history.

---

* A Bombay based young reasearcher. The present article has been culled from the Introductions of his two books recently published under the titles "*The Aryan Invasion Theory : A Reappraisal*" (Aditya Prakashan, N.Delhi, 1993) and "*Aryan Invasion Theory and Indian Nationalism*" (Voice of India, N. Delhi, 1993).

And, so far as the common man is concerned, that is what it appears to be-a natural and indisputable part of proven history.

Corollaries of the Theory

To the Leftist propagandists, however, the theory means much more.

It means that just as the British and the Muslim invaders came from outside, so also the Aryan invaders came from outside. Hence, Christianity, Islam and Hinduism are all equally foreign to India; or, conversely, all three are equally Indian.

Further, it means that just as Christianity and Islam were imposed on Indians by foreign invaders, so was Hinduism imposed on native Indians (Dravidians) by foreign invaders (Aryans).

For the Leftist, of course, the matter does not end there. He goes further and propounds that while the Aryans conquered India and reduced its natives to the level of lower castes within their social structure and hierarchy, in the name of Hinduism, the other invaders sought to liberate the natives from this bondage, in the name of Islam and Christianity. Hence these original natives, the "Dravidians", must reject Hinduism and align with Islam and Christianity!

In India today, the languages spoken by Indians belong to six language families:

1. ***Indo-European (Aryan)***: This includes Sanskrit, Hindi, Punjabi, Kashmiri, Sindhi, Marathi, Gujarati, Bengali, Assamese, Oriya etc.
2. ***Dravidian***: This includes Tamil, Malayalam, Telugu, Kannada, etc.
3. ***Austric***: This includes the Kol-Munda languages (Santali Savara, Gadba, etc.), the Khasi languages of Meghalaya, and the Nicobarese languages.
4. ***Sino-Tibetan***: This includes most of the languages in the Himalayas and the north east: Ladakhi, Lepcha, Bhotia, and the languages of Arunachal Pradesh, the Naga languages, Bodo, Ahom, Lushai, Meithei (Manipuri), Garo, etc.
5. ***Andamanese***: This includes the languages of the Andaman Islands.
6. ***Burushaski***: This consists of the Burrushaski language spoken in Pak-occupied Kashmir (in Hunza, Gilgit and Nagar).

All the official languages of India belong to the first two language-families: and the four southern states have Dravidian languages as their state languages. From this, it is obvious that any attempt to strike at the unity of Indian nationalism must aim at creating an "Aryan-Dravidian" divine.

Hence the "natives" who are supposed to have borne the brunt of the "Aryan" invasion have been branded as "Dravidians".

Hence, also, the Indus Valley Civilization (IVC) sites, which were discovered in this century, were immediately branded as Dravidian sites.

And an extremely venomous political movement, ostensibly a Dravidian movement, was launched, in the extreme south to throw off the shackles of Aryan Imperialism!

V. P. Singh, the mercifully short-termed Prime Minister of India, while launching his Mandal-astra to destroy Hindu Society from within by creating caste-wars, declared in Parliament that the Aryans had kept the Dravidians in subjugation for thousands of years!

Behind the Curtain

Incidentally, the Aryan invasion theory is just one part of a larger scheme which seeks to brand India as a kind Imperialists, paradise, into which people of different races and cultures poured in at various points of time; and area, therefore, with no native people of its own, to which no people can lay claim, and which belongs to anyone who has the power to acquire overlordship over it.

Suniti Kumar Chatterji, the eminent linguist, summarizes this view in the following words:

> We have the advent of the following peoples in India from the outside (no kind of man originated on the soil of India, all her human inhabitants having arrived originally from other lands...)

He then proceeds to list these immigrants, into an originally empty India, in chronological order:

1. Negritos, "from Africa".
2. Proto-Australoids, "from the east Mediterranean area (Palestine)".
3. Early Meditterraneans (Austrics).
4. Advanced Mediterraneans (Dravidians).
5. Armenoids (Dravidians).
6. Alpines (Aryans).
7. Nordics (Vedic Aryans).
8. Mongoloids.

The sheer insolence of this detailed and specific timetable of foreign immigrations into India, can be appreciated when we consider that at the very beginning of the chapter, he admits:

> ...Lack of material has not allowed us to postulate with certainty about racial movements in ancient times, and any appraisement or

reconstruction of movements of peoples in India, some four or three, or even two thousand years ago is bound to remain largely hypothetical and based on or inferred from the present situation only.

From all these picturesque accounts of various races making a beeline towards India from different parts of the world at different points of time, the only conclusion that can be drawn is, of course, that there is no such thing as "Indian" and "Foreign" in the Indian context: either everything, and everyone is Indian (or can become Indian by merely stepping within India's borders) or else nothing and no one can really be described by this term!

Needless to say, while the theory of an Aryan invasion (or immigration) is itself the result only of a long and determined effort by Western and West-oriented scholars, the other invasions (or immigrations) have not even a shred of evidence or scholarship to support them. Yet all these theories are firmly maintained as a sort of license to justify past, present and future imperialistic forays into India.

But again, while these theories are being firmly maintained, they are being maintained only behind the curtain. It is only the theory of an Aryan invasion of a Dravidian India which has been, and remains, most profitable for Hindus-baiters. Hence, it is required that the Aryan invasion be played up, and a discreet veil be dropped on the earlier invasions!

Indian Historians Divided

If Indian historians and scholars are divided, as is usually done, into "leftist" and "rightist" historians, we find that the leftist historians (including some who may not identify with the term) are unanimous not only in advocating the concept of an Aryan invasion of a Dravidian India, but also in insisting on applying their concept to present-day national politics. In at least one southern state of India, the predominant political movement is based on this concept of Aryan-Dravidian conflict.

When we come to those branded (by the leftists) as "rightist", we find a number of different opinions.

1. Some academic historians (such as R.C. Majumdar) have no objection to the invasion theory, although they would not subscribe to the political corollaries of the theory.

2. Another set of "rightist" historians, the earliest example being Lokmanya Tilak, go off at a tangent. They do not deny the concept of an Aryan invasion; they seek to compensate for it by an over-glorification of *Vedic* culture, which they see as the Aryan culture. They take *Vedic* culture back by tens of thousands of years, and find *Vedic* culture to be the first World Culture of civilized man. Tilak postulated an "*Arctic Home in the*

Vedas" (in his book of the same name). Some others see the *Rigvedic* culture in Turkish archaeological remains of the 10th millennium BC.

3. A third set of "rightist" historians, exemplified by K.D. Sethna (in his book, *The Problem of Aryan Origins*), choose to effect a compromise. Sethna advocates an amazing concept of a "belt of Ancient Aryanism" (i.e. an Original Homeland) stretching out from western India to eastern Europe.

4. A fourth set of "rightist" historians, exemplified by Swatantryaveer Savarkar, do not deny the influx of Aryans into India from outside, but they strongly oppose the political corollaries of the theory. Savarkar, while rejecting the concept of a gradual, non-conflictive immigration of civilized Aryans into India in prehistoric times. His modern followers insist, with perfect sense, that the concept of an Aryan invasion is superfluous in modern times, and that political corollaries derived from the concept are untenable.

5. A fifth set of "rightist" historians reject the concept of an external homeland of the Aryans. They advocate, instead, an Original Aryan Homeland in the northwest of India (taking the geography of the *Rigveda* as the basis for this theory), and an invasion of the rest of northern India from this area.

Two typical scholars of this opinion are A.C. Das (*Rigveda India*) and P.L. Bhargava (*India in the Vedic Age*). To them, the *Vedic* civilization of the Saptasindhu is the original civilization of the Aryans, and the "conquest" of the rest of the northern India by the *Vedic* people is a glorious affair.

Thus, P.L. Bhargava refers to it as follows:

> "The foundation of the civilization of India was truly laid in the glorious epoch when the people who called themselves Aryas colonised one district after another of the country, turning forests infested by wild beasts into merry villages, converting tracts laden with thorny bushes and shrubs into green fields, and sanctifying the atmosphere with the music of their inspired hymns." Further, "when the Aryan began to push further and further to the east and the south of India, they normally came into contact with many aboriginal tribes. These of the Dasas who led a predatory life were called Dasyus. One of the proudest tasks of Aryan kings was to eradicate these predatory Dasyus".

A.C. Das goes even further. He takes the date of the *Rigveda* back by tens of thousands of years, covering a period supposedly encompassing cataclysmic geological changes in the structure of the subcontinent. According to him:

> A large part of northern India, east of the Saptasindhu, was covered by a sea at the time of the composition of the hymns. From this Original Homeland in the Saptasindhu, he sees the Aryans later spreading out over northern India. He glorifies the alleged massacres of the Dasas and Dasyus by the Aryans, arguing that they were carried out "with the object of creating and altogether new and peaceful atmosphere in the country, conducive to their mental, moral and spiritual growth and development according to their own standard of excellence. In this, they were eminently successful in the long run, the discordant elements having been purged out of the country.

6. Finally, we have the sixth set of "rightist" historians, who absolutely reject any theory of invasion (whether from outside or the north-west of India itself) or immigration. To them, the falsity of the invasion theory is so self-evident that they do not find it necessary either to examine the theory with much seriousness, or to the consider the implications of the theory in their chronology of Indian history and civilization.

Thus, we have P.N. Oak who goes around getting "evidence" showing each and every culture and civilization in the world to be derived from the culture and civilization of Hindu India. That this claim, apart from anything else, clashes with the chronology of the alleged invasion and the alleged subsequent development of Hinduism is a matter of no correspondence to him: the theory is wrong, therefore he does not find it necessary to even consider it.

Leftist Propaganda in Media

There are three factors which are keeping the Aryan invasion theory alive in India history books:

1. The weight of scholarly world opinion.
2. Intellectual lethargy on the part of the average Indian scholar.
3. The awesome propaganda power of the Left in India.

Doordarshan is today the most powerful medium in India. Millions and millions of people in remote villages, most of them unable to read the Leftist propaganda material, are able to watch the TV sets which have been set up in every corner of India. And as a result the Leftists have acquired a captive audience of many millions.

One serial, *Amir Khusro,* devoted one entire part exclusively to the task of painstakingly explaining how the Aryans invaded India, and how this made Hinduism as foreign a religion as Islam.

Another serial, *Bharat Ek Khoj,* in its second part, graphically depicted scenes of life in a Harappan town at the time of the "Aryan invasion". The highlights were: The Harappans were firmly identified as

Dravidians; the Aryans were firmly identified as uncouth, barbaric nomads, attired in outlandish costumes, and indulging in acts of hooliganism and vandalism; and the Harappans were shown referring to them, in disgust, as "lowdown foreign dogs".

Incidentally, while the "Aryans" were so graphically depicted as barbarians, foreigners and invaders, another and a later part of the serial had Jawaharlal Nehru informing the viewers that there never was such a thing as a Muslim invasion of India!

In the face of such highly motivated propaganda, aimed at destroying the very roots of Indian nationalism, there is obviously a need to tell the truth about the Aryan invasion theory.

11

The Dravidian Theories

R. Swaminatha Aiyar*

Bishop Caldwell's Dravidian Theory

The originator of the current Dravidian theory was the late Bishop Caldwell who followed the Danish philologist Rask in classifying Dravidian as a member of the so-called Scythic family. He probably began his *Comparative Grammar of the Dravidian Languages* (1856, Second edition 1875) with the object of combating the theory then held by some scholars that these languages were directly descended from Sanskrit, but he went much further than this. Having disposed of this theory in the Introduction (pages 45 to 56) to his *Grammar* he devoted the main body of the work to comparing the Dravidian languages with one another and determining their affinities with the other language-groups of the world—Indo-European, Semitic and Scythic—the last including the languages of the Finns, the Mgyars, the Tartars, the Turks, and the Chinese and all the other languages included in the term Turanian in the terminilogy of later years. In conclusion, while acknowledging the existence of a very large percentage of Sanskrit and Indo-Aryan words in the Dravidian vocabularies, he maintained that the Dravidian languages had no structural relationship with Sanskrit and attempted to prove that the grammatical affinities of these languages were mainly Scythic-Turanian in the nomenclature of later years, occasionally Semitic, and that, where the affinities were Indo-European, these did not come into existence on Indian soil, but belonged mostly to the pre-Aryan period of pre-historic past when the Aryans and the Turanians were living as one undivided race. The book is a store-house of information on everything Dravidian, and bears evidence on every page of it to the immense learning of the author, his indefatigable research, his genius for analysis, and his familiarity with the grammars of almost all the

---

* Distinguished Tamil scholar and adminisrator born in 19th century; a linguist, grammarian, even a mathematician. Delivered special lectures at the Calcutta University on the Philology of the Dravidian languages. His magnum opus "*Dravidian* Theories" (574 pages) was published postumously, Madras, 1975.

languages of the world. Further the conclusions arrived at by the eminent author were expressed in no halting or faltering tone, many of the discussions on controvertible points being wound up with some such phrases as, '*I have no doubt', I have little doubt, It cannot be doubted'*, *'We can scarcely err in supposing'* etc. It is no wonder, therefore, that the work produced an immense sensation at the time, the views expressed therein being accepted by almost every scholar of note, and that the theories propounded therein have continued to dominate the Dravidian field for nearly seventy years. Among those, who accepted these theories in their entirety, special mention must be made of Dr. H. Gundert and Dr. F. Kittel, two missionary names, which Dravidian scholars should always hold in grateful remembrance for the Dictionaries and Grammars bearing these names.

The theory of direct descent from Sanskrit was based wholly on the extraordinary proportion of words of Sanskritic origin in the Dravidian vocabularies and took no note of the dissimilarity of the Dravidian grammatical forms to the Sanskrit forms. Bishop Caldwell had no difficulty in demolishing that theory, but he installed in its stead the equally untenable Scythic theory which it took many years of discussion to dislodge from its position. It is no disparagement to a pioneer worker, however eminent, to have it said that subsequent workers discovered serious errors in his work. The materials necessary for a historical treatment of the Dravidian question were not available in Bishop Caldwell's time and generalising on the imperfect and incomplete materials then to hand, he had sown the Dravidian field with a large number of questionable etymologies and equations which now impede progress at every step.

The Views of Gundert, Kittel And Pope

Dr. Kittel was a profound scholar of the Kanarese language and literature, and his *Kannada-English Dictionary* published in 1894 is the best that has appeared of any Dravidian language; his Grammar of the Kannada language published in 1903 deals exhaustively with the grammatical forms of the ancient, the mediaeval, and the modern Kanarese and embodies the results of the labours of a life-time.

Dr. H. Gundert, a profound scholar of the Malayalam language and literature belonged to an earlier generation, and his *Malayalam-English Dictionary* (1872) in which, in addition to his own life-work, he has utilised the materials collected in the sixteenth and seventeenth centuries by the Portuguese and Italian missionaries of Verapoli, is a monument of research; his *Malayalam Grammar* (2nd edition 1868) appears to have been the first grammar that has been published in that language.

These scholars accepted Bishop Caldwell's theories in their entirety and supplemented his work by doing for the Dravidian vocabularies what Bishop Caldwell had done for the common grammatical framework of the languages. Gundert's Dictionary furnishes under each Malayalam word information as to whether the word is to be found in other cultivated Dravidian languages also and, if so, in what other languages, and in cases where the word is common to all the five cultivated languages being given in great detail. The vast heap of materials brought together in the works of these authors is of great help of the Dravidian student in constructing proto-Dravidian vocabulary, but the want of familiarity of these scholars with the *Vedic* dialects and with the Prakrts (secondary and tertiary) arising out of these dialects detracts much from the value of the theories propounded in their works. This is specially the case with the long list of roots given in the Introduction to *Kittel's Dictionary* which Sanskrit is supposed to have borrowed from the Dravidian; the list includes a selection from the lists previously published by Bishop Caldwell and Gundert.

Pope Refutes Caldwell

G.U. Pope was a distinguished missionary, well versed in Tamil language and literature, but he did not accept Bishop Caldwell's theories; and in a series of articles in the *Indian Antiquary* he suggested enquiry as to whether in these theories "certain things have not been taken for granted rather too suddenly in regard to the Dravidian dialects". He was the first to point out that the law of the harmonic sequence of vowels did not obtain in most of these dialects. He was further of opinion,

> [1]that between the languages of southern India and those of the Aryan family there are many deeply seated and radical affinities;[2] that the differences between the Dravidian tongues and the Aryan are not so great as between the Celtic (for instance) and the Sanskrit; and[3], that, by consequence, the doctrine that the place of the Dravidian dialects is rather with the Aryan than with the Turanian family of languages is still capable of defence.

He illustrated these positions by means of copious illustrations and pointed out that "the resemblances (appeared) most frequently in the more uncultivated Dravidian dialects" and that "the identity (was) most striking in the names of instruments, places, and the acts connected with a simple life". He also promised "to consider derivative words" in a future paper "and to show that the prefixes and affixes (were) Aryan"; but no such paper appears to have been published.

Linguistic Survey of India (1906)

The next great landmark in the history of Dravidian philology was the publication in 1906 of volume IV of the *Linguistic Survey of India* which gives specimens of the chief Dravidian languages and of their dialective varieties. The preparation of this volume was entrusted to Sten Know of Christiana and Sir G.A. Grierson, the Editor of the series, is jointly responsible with him for the theories put forth in the volume. Unfortunately the area for which the Government of India ordered a linguistic survey in connection with the Census of 1901 did not include Southern India where the cultivated Dravidian languages are spoken and where the vast majority of the Dravidian speakers live. The Editors have, however, thought it advisable to give a short sketch of the principal Dravidian languages without reference to habitat, in order to make it easier to compare and classify the North Indian members of the family included within the scope of the Survey. Hence only short accounts are given to Tamil, Malayalam, Kanarese and Telugu while the minor Dravidian dialects of the South, viz., Kodagu, Tulu, Toda and Kota are not described at all.

These scholars give a summary of the results of the fifty years discussion since the first publication of Bishop Caldwell's book. It is impossible to explain in detail here how most of the Turanian affinities elaborated by the latter have had to be given up, but the net result will be clear from the following extract (page 282):

> The denomination 'Scythian' is a very unhappy one. The Scythian words which have been handed down by Greek writers are distinctly Iranian, i.e., they belong to the Indo-European family. But nevertheless the name has been used as a common designation of all those languages of Asia and Europe which do not belong to the Indo-European or Semitic families. Moreover, those languages, cannot, by any means, be brought together into one linguistic family. The monosyllabic languages of China and neighbouring countries are just as different from the dialects spoken in Caucasus or from the speech of the Finns and Magyars, as is the Indo-European family. The points in which they agree are such features as recur in almost all languages, and they are by no means sufficient to outweight the great and fundamental characteristics in which they differ from each other. In regard to the Dravidian languages the attempt to connect then, with other linguistic families outside India is now generally recognized as a failure and we must still consider them as an isolated family.

It is but natural, that such attempts should fail, for the *Vedic* Aryans probably entered India about 4,000 years ago, and if, as is held by many, the Dravidian languages were spoken not only in the South but also in the West and the North-West of India formerly, these languages must have been in contact with the Aryan dialects now for forty centuries. However, this may be confining attention to the Dravidian languages spoken now in the Deccan and Southern India and to the historic period in which large Hindu, Jain, and Buddhist colonies are known to have been established in the South. We may confidently say that the Dravidian languages have been in close contact with the Aryan dialects certainly for the last 2,000 years, and probably for 2,500 years. We also know that several aboriginal races have abandoned their mother tongues and are now speaking Aryan languages, and many indigenous dialects are now speaking Aryan languages, and many indigenous dialects are now being rapidly Aryanised under our very eyes. In regard to the cultivated languages-Tamil, Malayalam, Kanarese and Telgu-which have a literature and a grammatical standard and which have remained practically unchanged for a considerable period, it must be remembered that the *Brahmans*, Jains and Buddhists who first cultivated these languages were full of northern learning and would have greatly Aryanised their structure. In these circumstances it was illogical, to say the least, to minimise, ignore, and reject as Bishop Caldwell did, Sanskritic and Aryan analogies, and to take a jump over the Himalayas and the Hindukush in search of analogies in distant Finland, Hungary, Lapland, Caucasus, Japan etc., on the basis of an unproved assumption that the Dravidians came from the West and must have been speaking a Tauranian language originally.

In regard to the question whether or not the Dravidians are autochthonous to India, the Editors of the Survey remark:

> "With regard to the Dravidas, some authorities believe that they arrived in India from the South, while others suppose them to have entered it from the North West where a Dravidian language is still spoken by the Brahuis of Baluchistan. The Brahuis do not belong to the Dravidian race but are anthropologically Iranians, i.e., they have merged into the race of their neighbours. it is possible that the same is the case with the Dravidian tribes of the South wherever they came from, but anthropology only tells us that the Dravidian race comprises Mundas and Dravidas, and we have no information to show that the Dravidas are not the original inhabitants of the South" (L.S., Vol. IV, page 5).

The alleged relationship of the Dravidian languages with the Munda is examined at pages 2-5 of the volume and the conclusion arrived at is that the two families only agree in such points as are common to most agglutinative languages, that there is no philological reason for deriving them from the same original and that they form two quite independent families.

The Editors express an equally emphatic opinion that all "attempts to show a closer connection with the Indo-German family have proved just as futile." (Vol IV, page 282).

The Aryan Element in Dravidian Vocabularies

The conclusion (of) the present writer is to the effect that most of the Dravidian grammatical forms have arisen from suffixal elements borrowed from Indo-Aryan and that the non-Aryan element even in the basic portions of the Dravidian vocabularies is not considerable. This position is utterly at variance not only with the views of European scholars but also with those of Indian scholars generally; for though there may be many Indians who hold the opinion that there is a much larger admixture of the Aryan element in the Dravidian vocabularies than that allowed by Bishop Caldwell and Prof. Sten Konow, there are perhaps few or none who think that the Dravidian grammatical elements are derived from Aryan sources. The reason for this appears to lie in the circumstance that the Aryan elements compared with the Dravidian languages have till now been taken mostly from classical Sanskrit. For instance, at page 48 of the Introduction of Bishop Caldwell's *Comparative Grammar* some sixty words of primary importance (not including pronous and numerals) in Tamil are contrasted with their equivalents in Sanskrit and the conclusion arrived at is that the two languages have no common basis. The Sanskrit words chosen are from classical Sanskrit and not from the *Vedic* idioms or from the spoken Prakrits.

Though classical Sanskrit had its roots in a dialect similar to the *Vedic* idioms, it laterly became, owing to various causes, an artificial, literary language confined almost wholly to books and ceased to be the home speech even of the learned. Similarly, Maharastri, Pali and other literary Prakrits, though originally they were popular idioms, became highly artificial in course of time. Words relating to philosophy and the sciences are no doubt often borrowed from books, but wherever there is a large infusion of foreign words and idioms in the spoken language of a people, we have to look for their source in the spoken speech—the colloquial and vulgar idioms—not in literary works. These idioms and elements adopted at first in the popular speech ultimately find their way into literature and into books.

To ascertain to what extent Dravidian language and grammer have been affected by Aryan forms of speech we must compare the former with the popular Aryan idioms prevailing at the time when the Aryans and the Dravidians first came in contact, and not with an artificial language confined only to books. For a similar reason it will be seen that as much importance, if not more, is attached to colloquial, vulgar and dialectic Dravidian idioms as to standard and grammatical forms.

What is then the explanation of the theory now almost universally accepted that the Dravidian languages have no radical and deep seated affinities with Sanskrit, a theory which has behind it the support of a continuous tradition of over eighteen centuries? The original stock of Indo-Aryan words which the pre-historic immigrants from the North-West must have brought with them appears to have undergone a process of gradual deterioration in South Indian mouths. The causes that tended to this deterioration was the extremely limited number of consonantal sounds to be found in South Indian speeches which were even fewer than the sounds to be found in the rudest of Aryans dialects like the *Chulika Paisachika* mentioned by Prakrit Grammarians. The second was the change from the Indo-Aryan system of varied accents to the South Indian monotony under which the highest stress was on the first syllable of each word and the pitch gradually decreased in the succeeding syllables; this naturally led to the loss or deterioration of all syllables in a word except the first or the first two, and also to a change in the first vowel except the first vowel of each word. A third was the entire absence of sibilants in South Indian speeches, and the consequent deterioration and final omission of all sibilants from Indo-Aryan words. A fourth was the South Indian habit of pronouncing non-initial single *k* and *p*, and initial and non initial single *ch*, as spirants. This has led to the complete loss of non-initial *k* and *ch* in a very large number of words and to the conversion of non-initial *p* into *v* in almost all words. Another cause was the inability of South Indians to pronounce and initial *r, l, y* which has led to the insertion of an initial on-glide or the substitution of other letters in the place of the first two and the entire omission or nasalistation of the last. A similar inability to pronounce a final *t*, *r*, and *t*, has led to the conversion of these sounds into *I, n, I, I.* Owing to the steady operation of these causes, it must in course of time have become impossible to see any connection between these altered words and the speech of the northern Aryans. More important than all these was the difference in grammatical structure and syntax; while the Aryan speeches were highly synthetic, the Southern idioms arising out of their *debris* were mainly analytical, with a tendency to become agglutinative again.

Agastya was Forgotten

All but the memory of the pre-historic Aryan immigration under the leadership of Agastya had been lost by the beginning of the Christian era, and the original stock of Indo-Aryan words brought by the immigrants having been altered beyond all recognition in the speech of the South Indians it came to be tacitly assumed when attention was first directed to the materials and structure of South Indian idioms-that this altered vocabulary was part of the indigenous speech of the land except in regard to recent obvious borrowings from Sanskrit, and that the immigrants had forgotten their mother tongue and had adopted the language of the land in its stead. Kumarila Bhatta (7th Century A.D.) refers, in his *Tantravartika,* to the South Indian languages as *Dramida Bhasha* evidently under the impression that these languages were foreign to Sanskrit, and he had no idea that the basic portion of the vocabularies of these languages and the suffixial elements entering into the composition of their verb-forms had been borrowed form the *Vedic* idioms, or from Sanskrit. In fact he mentions with disapproval the attempts of certain contemporary writers to adopt words from these non-Aryan languages into Sanskrit after giving them an Aryan shape by means of suitable affixes.

Earlier than this (during the Sangam period which was a time of great literary activity in the Tamil land) nobody appears to have thought that Tamil language was in any way indebted to Sanskrit except of course in regard to obvious loan words and easily recognisable Sanskrit derivatives. These words and derivatives were placed in a special class as of Sanskrit origin, and as time passed, the theory that Tamil was a distinct language gained further strength, and was incorporated in the *Puranas* and other sacred writings.

From the very beginning, owing to the increasing needs of a progressive civilization and to the requirements of a rapidly developing philosophy and religious system, the *tatsama* and the semi-*tatsama* Sanskrit element in the South Indian vocabularies has been steadily increasing, and it now occupies considerably more than their volume. During the middle of the last century, certain orientalists perceiving the very large number of obvious Sanskrit derivatives in these vocabularies, started a theory that the Dravidian languages were descended from Sanskrit like the Aryan vernaculars of northern India, but the theory was very short-lived, and was abandoned after the publication of Bishop Caldwell's *Dravidian Grammar.*

The Current Dravidian Theory Requires Reconsideration

The aim here is to secure a reconsideration of the current theory of Dravidian Languages on the ground that the theory is based on a mis-apprehension of the real facts of the situation, and is supported by assumptions some of which can be easily disproved. A complete treatment of the question requires an investigation of the subject under the three heads, vocabulary, nominal declension, and verbal inflexions. The vocabulary of the Tamil language alone consists of about fifty or sixty thousand words. Omitting obvious Sanskrit derivatives, the ultimate roots to which the remainder can be reduced must be at least a thousand, and having regard to the fact that a very large number of roots will require detailed individual investigation, it will be impossible to investigate the affinities of all the Dravidians roots within the limits of a single volume, or even of two. It was in consequence of this that the scope of the present work was limited to the consideration of tense and mood signs which are limited in number and belong to the fundamental structure of the languages. If these signs could be proved to be of Aryan origin, it would necessarily follow that the original languages of South India must have been under the influence of Aryan languages from very early times. The present State of the Dravidian question is such that we are unable to discuss the origin of these tense and mood signs without previously disposing of a large number of misconceptions and untenable theories about Dravidian languages and Dravidian culture, which have come into existence since the publication of Bishop Calwell's *Dravidian Grammar* in 1856.

12

An Imagined Aryan-Dravidian Dichotomy

K.C. Verma*

The Aryans were present in India, at least from the beginning of the phase of full-bloom of the Harappan civilization, which according to Allchins, is to be dated 2550 B.C. (instead of his earlier date 2150 B.C., or D.P. Agrawal's 2350 B.C. or Wheeler's 2500 B.C.), and the early Harappan phase may go back to 3000 B.C., if not earlier, K.N. Sastri had assigned, on stratigraphic grounds, the lowest level of construction (as excavated) at Harappa, on mound 'F' to at least 3500 B.C. It seems that archaeologists are progressing towards this date.

The hypothesis that the Harappan civilization was the creation of Dravidians, despite all the efforts of Russian and Finn scholars and recently of Iravattha Mahadevan, has collapsed.

The vehemently held view that Dravidians were the predecessors of Aryans, as "cerebrals" have been found in the *Rigveda* has also been refuted by R. Swaminath Aiyar, P.L. Bhragava, K.D. Sethna and others.

I. From the linguistic point of view also the theory of Dravidian influence on the *Vedic* Sanskrit has been given up even by its most ardent supporters like T. Burrow.[1] There had been a prolonged controversy between Aryendra Sharma and Burrow in this matter and ultimately Burrow was constrained to concede the point.[2] Dr. Chandrashekhar also considered this problem and observed.[3]

> At this point I may touch upon the efforts going on in India and abroad to decipher the Harappan writing. The researchers of a Finnish team and a Russian team deserve special attention in this connection as they have been most systematic, using computers and statistical methods. Although no spectacular results have been achieved so far by these researches, it seems to me that the researches are vitiated by the assumption that the language of the inscription is Tamil. The tacit assumption here is that the Tamil language has not changed for a period

* Published many research articles on the history of Indology. This extract is taken from his "*The Aryans, The Veda and the Kaliyug Era of 3100 B.C.*" published by the Deptt. of Ancient Indian History, Culture and Archaeology B.H.U. Varanasi, 1984.

of nearly three millennia, which is indeed fantastic to say the least. That the Dravidian speakers once lived in the Indus valley and other parts of India is itself an unproven assumption.

The complete failure of the computer aided efforts of the Russian and Finn scholars had led Fairservis to dismiss the whole thing and insist on "the decipherment of the Harappan script in the context of the Harappan civilisation itself", even though he made futile efforts to show that the language was 'Dravidian'.[4] B.B. Lal while dealing with Mahadevan's thesis lays:

> "It is now well established that the Dravidians were present in north-west India when the Aryans entered the country most probably around the middle of the second millennium B.C. The survival of Brahui, a Dravidian language, and the presence of the words of Dravidian origin in the *Rigveda* provide irrefutable evidence for the fact." He further states: "One really wonders how the term "well established" can be used in this context when the very statement has to be substantiated by facts and figures. Brahui may be akin to the Dravidian group of languages but then it is spoken in a very small pocket of Baluchistan. To say on this meagre basis that the inhabitants of Baluchistan and of the entire North-west India" (under which term Mr. Mahadevan evidently includes Pakistan) were speaking a Dravidian language would be an unwarranted assumption. On has to bridge a gap of nearly two thousand years between Harappan inscriptions and the earliest Dravidian inscriptions, before the term "well established" can ever be thought of. Again, the region of Brahui is thousands of kilometres away from the present-day core of the Dravidian speaking area. How does one account for this? As regards some words in the *Rigveda* which appear to be of non-Indo-European origin one has to take into consideration a host of other linguistic factors before the seal can be set on their Dravidian origin. And even if some words ultimately found to have a Dravidian affinity, how does that 'establish' that the Indus civilisation was Dravidian?

The supporters of the "Dravidian hypothesis" also fail to explain how and by what means the "Dravidian speakers" were driven from north India and came under such tremendous 'Aryan pressure' that if the "*Vedic*, *Puranic* and *Sastraic* elements are excluded in the extant Sangam literature, only primitive tribal cultural element are left."[5]

II. The findings of scholars like Aryendra Sharma, B.B. Lal and K.D. Sethna and the admissions of Burrow, Mayer Hofer and others are more than confirmed by the monumental work of an illustrious Tamil scholar R.S. Aiyar. After examining the relationship between Sanskrit (*Vedic* and Classical), and the Dravidian languages, he concludes:[6]

"The conclusions which I have arrived at after a detailed examination of the question extending over several years are entirely at variance with the current theory:

(i) There are about one hundred suffixes employed in the cultivated Dravidian languages for the purpose of indicating tenses and modes of verb-forms. I find that most of these suffixes are of Indo-Aryan origin.

(ii) The personal terminations of Dravidian verbs and the pronouns of which these terminations are in many cases early forms are also most of them of Aryan origin.

(iii) The basic portion of Dravidian vocabularies consists largely of words of Indo-Aryan origin though, owing to the extremely limited character of Tamil and other early Dravidian alphabets, these words have been greatly corrupted and are very difficult of recognition.

These conclusions clearly indicate that what are known as Dravidian languages are in all their present essential features a creation of Aryan and Aryanised immigrants from the North. Further, the existence in the Tamil language of words and forms which are met with in the *Vedas* and in the Avestic language, but have disappeared from the post-*Vedic* Indo-Aryan tongues, would seem to show that these immigrants must have separated from the main body of the Indo-Aryans in the North-West in prehistoric, *Vedic* or pre-*Vedic* times. It also follows from the above that the tradition about Agastya's immigration to the South is not a mere myth and that what is known as the Dravidian civilization of the South is merely the civilization of these Aryan and Aryanised immigrants. The above conclusions are tantamount to a total negation of the current Dravidian theory in all its details and will have no chance of being listened to by the literary world unless they are presented with all the arguments which I have to urge in their support. A piecemeal treatment of the question in a number of small papers is therefore out of the question. In other words, the views propagated by Caldwell, Bittel, George Grierson, Kuiper, Burrow, etc. have been shown to be baseless.

III. The findings of scholars like Swaminath Aiyar, B.N.K. Sarma and Sri Ramadesikan appear to be confirmed by the myths, legends and traditions preserved in the Tamil Sangam literature.[7] According to this source:

(i) The Cola kings claimed descent from Rama of Ayodhya;[8]

(ii) The Cera kings claimed descent from the 'Lunar Kings' of the north;[9]

(iii) The *Vedic Rishi* Agastya was *kulaguru* of the Pandyan dynasty and was the inventor of the Tamil language and author of the earliest Tamil grammar;[10]

(iv) A Sangam poet is supposed to tell a king of Veli clan (i.e. Yadava) that his progenitors migrated to South India, from Dwaraka after the Bharata war, some 49 generations earlier;

(v) Scholars like K. Srinivasa Raghavan and V.G. Ramachandran who claim extreme antiquity for Dravidian civilisation can cite the names of north Indian kings like Manu Vaivaswata and Rama, Chandragupta Maurya and Asoka, but not of any king of a southern dynasty;[11]

(vi) The kings of the Cola, Cera and Pandya dynasties practised *Vedic* religion and performed Asvamedha sacrifice;[12]

(vii) K.A. Nilakantha Sastri says,[13] "In the Sangam anthologies, the Tamil language has reached maturity and begun to serve as a powerful and eloquent medium of literary expression, and has already received and assimilated many words and ideas from Sanskrit sources;"

(viii) "The monarchies of the Cera, Cola and Pandya were believed, at least in subsequent ages, to be of immemorial antiquity; and the poems of the Sangam attest the anxiety of all of them to connect themselves with the events of the Great War between the Kauravas and Pandavas. The first Cera monarch we hear of Udiyandjeral (c. 130 A.D., or perhaps 60 years earlier), is said to have fed sumptonously the armies of Kurukshetra and thereby earned for himself the title "Udiyanjeral of the Great Feeding". Perhaps it is best to look upon it as a conventional attribution to him of an achievement of some remote ancestor. The same honour is also claimed in other poems for the Pandyas and Colas";

(ix) The Sangam poet Mamûlnâr refers to the great wealth of the Nandas of the fifth and fourth centuries B.C.[14] In contrast to these traditions, no ruler of a dynasty recorded in the *Puranas* has claimed such descent from a South Indian royal line. It is also doubtful whether the extant Sangam literature mentions any king or other notable who could be assigned to a period earlier than the first century A.D. Swaminath Aiyar has drawn attention to the fact that the words of command to trained elephants were not in Tamil or some other Dravidian language.[15] It may also be mentioned that M.G.S. Narayanan advanced arguments, by no means negligible, to assign a higher antiquity to the Sangam literature and to place the poet Mamûlnâr contemporary with the Mauryan emperor Bindusara.[16]

Notes and References

1. Presi. Add. Ling. Sec., *PAIOC,* Delhi, 1959, pp. 195-96.
2. *Bull. of the School of Oriental and African Stduies,* Vol. XXXIII, 1971, pp. 538-59. Also Mayer Hofer, *Ranou Comm.* Vol., 1968, pp. 509-517; R.L. Turner, BSOAS, Vol. XXXIII, 1970, pp. 171-178.
3. *Excavations at Allahadino,* III, 1977, Preface, pp. II; also cited by Sethna, *Karpasa,* pp. 106.
4. "Study of the Indus Script through Bi-lingual parallels", All India *Comference of Dravidian Languages,* 2nd Session, Sri Venkateswara Uni., 1972, pp.1.
5. M.G.S. Narayanan, "The Vedic-Puranic-Sastraic Element in Tamil Sangam Society and Culture, *PIHC,* XXXVIth Session, 1975, Aligarh, pp. 76-91; K.A.N. Sastri, A *History of South India, 4th ed.,* 1976, pp. 12. B.N.K. Sarma, "Review of *Dravidian Theories* (R. Swaminath Aiyar), *Bhavan's Jour,* April 16, 1982. Also review by S.N. Sri Ramadesikan, *The Hindu,* Aug. 17, 1975. "Doubts on Caldwell", *Indian Express,* Sep. 13, 1975.
6. R. Swaminath Aiyar, *Dravidian Theories,* (Madras Law Jour, Press, Mylapur, Madras, 1975) pp. 574; pp. 551-552. S.N. Sri Ramdesikan observes, in *The Hindu,* Aug. 17, 1975. "About 50 years ago, Sri R. Swamintha Aiyar, a linguist, grammarian, scholar and in fact a versatile genius...point out that much material was not available to him (Caldwell) and that he had not considered *Vedic* idioms or the spoken Prakrta apart from the later classical Sanskrit. The author has dealt with the conjugation of verbs in extenso—particularly tense and mood sings—leaving basic vocubulary and nominal declension for seperate treatment. More than 100 Dravidian verbal forms of oridinary occurrence are shown to be derived from Indo-Aryan roots. The evidence for the great antiguity of Tamil is slender. *Tolkapiam* and the Sangam Literature may be much later than generally claimed." B.N.K. Sarma (*Bhavan's Journal,* April 16, 1982) says, "This learned work packed with solid linguistic data bearing on the inter-relation of the Dravidian family of languages with the *Vedic* dialects and their developments in classical Sanskrit and the spoken and literary Prakrts, in respect of their phonology, pronominal formations, morphology, the verbal formations, infinitieves and suffixes and, lastly, vocabulary....exposed many a self complacent theory on the subject paraded in the 'thirties of half-baked' "Dravidian philologists" misled by the baseless theories of Caldwell. Also see Swaminath Aiyar's Readership Lectures, Calcutta University. "The Aryan Affinites of Dravidian Pronouns" *PAIOC,* Madras and "Dravidian Tenses and Suffixes", *PAIOC,* Poona, 1919, Vol. I, pp. lxxi-lxxvii. *See also* the controversy between C.S. Mahadevan, *The Hindu,* June 4, 1979; K. Srinivasa Raghavan, (*Ibid.*) 28 June; V.G. Ramachandran, *Ibid,* 5th July; K.D. Swaminathan *Ibid,* 6th July, V. Balasubrahmaniam and S. Kasipandian, *Ibid,* 6th July, M.S. Mani, *Ibid,* 29th June, 1979; K.D. Sethna, *Ibid,* 25th and 28th June.

7. Sangam Literature is usually dated 100-250 A.D. see K.A.N. Sastri, *Hist. of South India,* 1955, pp. 112, *A Comp. Hist. of India,* Vol. II. pp. 514-18; S.K. Aiyangar, *Ancient India,* 1911, pp. 330-384; *Some Contri. of S. Ind. to Ind. Cul.* (Calcutta University), Preface, xvi-xxxv; Vaiyyapuri Pillai, *History of Tamil Lang. and Literature,* pp. 8-19; E.B. Emeneau, *Enc. Brit,* 1968, Vol. VII, p. 655; and T. Burrow, *Chamber's Enc.,* Vol. VII, pp. 480-81. But Burnell, *Elements of South Indian Palaeography,* 1878, pp. 47-53, Reinhold Rost, Enc. Bri., XI ed., Vol. XXVIII, pp. 389 and L.C. Innes, *Asiatic Quarterly Review,* April 1902, Vol.I, pp. 593, give much later dates. K.C. Sankar, "Date of 11th Paripadal" *JRAS,* 1932, pp. 541-45 and *Ibid*, 1924, pp. 667; L.D. Swamikannu Pillai, *Ind.* Ephemeris I, I, pp. 100-109 and L.D. Barnet, *JRAS*, 1929, pp. 137-140 assign dates after 600 A.D. and D.C. Sircar agrees with this.
8. V. Natesan, "Tamil Kings; A Paradox", *PAIOC*, Ujjain, 1972, 315-320.
9. *Ibid.*
10. *Ibid.*
11. Srinivasa Raghavan, *Chronology of Ancient Bharata,* V.G. Ramachandran, "The Real Date of Emperor Asoka" *JIH* Trivandrum, LVII, 1979, pp. 213-224.
12. V. Natesan *PAIOC*, 1972, pp. 315-320.
13. K.A.N. Sastri, *History of South India,* pp. 113-114. He admits (p. 64) that South Indian History begins with the advent of the Aryans. The third cent. B.C. date (pp. 86), of the Short Brahmi inscriptions is disputed. B.C. Chabra, N.P. Chakkravarti and K.V. Subrahmanya, *Ancient India,* No. 2, 1946, pp. 109-110, assign them to 1st cent. A.D. See my paper, "Antiquity of Dravidian Lang. & Lit." *JAHR,* Hyderabad, Vol. XXXIII, pp. 9.36.
14. *A Comprehensive History of India,* II, pp. 502-503.
15. R. Swaminath Aiyar, *Dravadian Theories*, pp. 61. "It may be mentioned that there was another art, that of training and teaching elephants, which the Dravadians did not know till the Indo-Aryans came and settled among them. For, an old Tamil work says that the language in which the elephants were given direction was *Vatamoli* Northern language" (i.e.) Sanskrit.
16. "The Maurayan problem in Sangam Works in Historical perspective," JIH, Vol. LIII 1975, pp. 243-54.

13

The Aryan Hypothesis In Indian Archaeology

Dilip K. Chakrabarti*

The Context

In 1968 the present author systematically reviewed the various attempts made till then to identify the Aryans or Indo-Iranian language-speakers in the Indian protohistoric archaeological data. Two clear conclusions emerged. First, the hypothesis were mutually contradictory, and secondly, none of them quite satisfied the minimum demands of archaeological reasoning. It became clear to the present author that the Aryan hypothesis was an intergral part of a widely held and deep-noted diffusionist approach to Indian history and archaeology.[1] The historical roots of this diffusionist approach merited analysis. In a note published in 1976 the present author demonstrated that the idea of India being invariably at the receiving end of various cultural and population movements was essentially a 'post-Mutiny' phenonmenon. The earlier attitude to India held it as a centre of civilization and culture which could send civilized *Brahmins* and Buddhist monks as far west as Scotland.[2]

It was also found that Sir William Jones' original idea of similarity between Sanskrit, Latin, Greek, etc., was a part of the pre-Evolutionary conceptual framework which accepted the biblical theory of creation and in which the common origin of various human families was an axiom. It was argued that Sir William Jones wanted to explain the ancient Indian civilization in terms of its original links with the other known old civilized human groups.[3] On the basis of the different ramifications of the Aryan hypothesis, which were discussed in detail in the singularly perceptive work entitled *The Aryan Myth* by Leon Poliakov it was realized that many of the comparatively modern Indian versions of the hypothesis

* Taught archaeology at the universities of Calcutta and Delhi in India, Dhaka in Bangladesh and recently at the Cambridge University, U.K. Author of several books and research papers on Indian Archaeology, Specialises on the Indus-Saraswati civilisation.

such as B.G. Tilak's Arctic home theory, etc. were rooted in some widely prevalent eighteenth and early nineteenth century ideas.[4] The attempted correlations between the literary logical and the Vedic literary data fall in the general range of problems of correlation between the literary evidence and the archaeological data in the Indian context, and as argued by the present author in a more recent publication, that the attempts to relate the *Vedic* literature to archaeology must take the entire basic framework of the Aryan model into consideration. It should not be a question of underlining a particular set of archaeological data and arguing that these data conform to a particular section of the *Vedic* literary corpus without at all trying to determine how this hypothesis will affect that other sets of the contemporary archaeological data and the other sections of the *Vedic* literary corpos.[5]

As far as the general diffusionist approach in India archaeology is concerned it was argued in 1977 that the historical roots of this diffusionism were related to certain basic assumptions of Indian historical studies. The first of these assumptions is the idea of the Aryan penetration of India in which the Aryans no doubt interact with autochthones but they also impose their "superior" Aryan way of life on them. *The dichotomy between the Aryan and pre-Aryan inhabitants of India is a basic premise of Indian historical studies.*

"The other assumptions relate to Indian racial and linguistic history. Though there are differences of nomenclature between the various systems of racial classification proposed, they all agree that despite subsequent intermixture the history of Indian population is essentially a series of racial migration from outside the country. What is also significant is that each of the proposed major racial stocks has been given a specific linguistic association. For instance, the proto-Australoids are supposed to have brought in a Austric language family and the Mediterraneans are said to be responsible for the introduction of the Dravidian language group. Learned attempts have been made to assess the individual contributions made by these and other language groups to the formation of Indian culture and to determine when and from where they migrated to India. The relationship of these historical, racial and linguistic models with the current predominantly diffusionist approach in Indian archaeology is obvious."[6]

The purpose of the present paper is to find answer to a straight-forward question: if there was really a widespread dissemination of the Indo-Iranian language-speakers to India in the protohistoric period, and when precisely could this archaeologically happen? Which archaeological model will best explain the total situation?

The Suggested Model

The underlying assumption is a set of three interconnected geographical premises. According to the first of these premises the entire region between the Oxus and the Indus, comprising the southern part of Central Asia, Eastern Iran, Afghanistan and the Indus system with its adjacent highlands constitutes an interaction zone. Its natural corollary is that any important political, cultural and economic happening or innovation in any one of these areas is likely to have an impact in the other relevant areas as well. Secondly, "inner India" lies to the east of Delhi-Aravalli-Cambay axis, and thirdly, the area between the Indus and the Delhi-Aravalli-Cambay line is subject to influences from both the postulated interaction zone and "inner India".[7]

The protohistoric period in this context is visualized in three stages. The cultures which are antecedent to the Indus civilization and distributed between Baluchistan, the *Derajat*, Bannu, the Potwar Plateau and Swat on the one hand and Rajasthan and Haryana on the other belong to the first stage. The sequence begins in the seventh millennium B.C. at Mehergarh in the Bolan valley in Baluchistan and continues upto the beginning of the Indus civilization in the first quarter of the third millennium B.C.[8] The second stage is comprised by the mature phase of the Indus civilization which continued perhaps till 2000 B.C. and got transformed after that into its late phase which constitutes our third stage and continued surely upto the middle of the second millennium B.C.

Oxus Indus System

There is ample archaeological proof that the cultures belonging to our first stage were closely interacting right from their beginning with the various areas of the interaction zone between the Oxus and the Indus. This has been well discussed in many publications and here we may only underline the fact in bare detail.[9] Right in its early phase Mehergarh shows lapis lazuli from northeastern Afghanistan, turquoise from the Nishapur mines of northeastern Iran and microlithic hump back trapezes characteristic of the Djeitun culture of Soviet Turkmenia. The date-range is the seventh-sixth millennia B.C. In the middle of the fifth millennium B.C. the ceramic analogies between Rana Ghundai in northeastern Baluchistan and the Iranian sites of Sialk (western Iran) and Hissar (south of the Elburz, northern Iran) are striking. Although the Iranian ibex motif has been transformed into the Iranian bull motif at Rana Ghundai, the overall similarity in pot forms and design composition is so impressive that one cannot help admitting the actual migration of potters from northern Iran to north-eastern Baluchistan in that period.

The distinctive "Quetta Ware" of the third millennium B.C. and its roots in the Namazga III level of Turkmenia are well-known alongwith the distribution of an equally distinctive terracotta type of this period from Turkmenia to Baluchistan, the *Derajat* and the Indus valley. Equally well-known are the analogues of different protohistoric Baluchistan cultures in such south Afghanistan and Seistan sites as Mundigak (south Afghanistan) and Shahr-i-Sokhta (Seistan).

Saraswati-Drishadvati System

A fact of startling significance which has become clear only in recent years is that the epi-centre of the Indus civilization lay not in the valley of the Indus but in the Saraswati-Drishadvati system to its cast. On the basis of the available data on the settlement sizes of the Indus civilization, this was tentatively suggested by the present author in 1979,[10] but in recent years M.R. Mughal's explorations in Bhawalpur along the Hakra and J.P. Joshi's explorations in the Ghaggar system in east Punjab and Haryana have put this beyond dispute. Out of 414 protohistoric sites of Mughal in Cholistan, 174 are mature Harappan.[11] In J.P. Joshi's catalogue there are 138 mature Harappan sites in Rajasthan, U.P., Punjab and Haryana. The concentration of mature Harappan sites in this region is remarkable and so also is its number of large Harappan settlements.

The interaction between the Indus-civilization and the cultural elements from "inner India" is perhaps clear in the new crop situation in Gujarat and U.P. in the late Harappan period. Millet was a new crop in Gujarat in this period and at Hulas, the late Harappan stage included, apart from wheat and barley, rice, horse gram, peas, *moong*, *urd*, finger millet, grass pea and beans. On the whole the late Harappan crop situation at Hulas is remarkably reminiscent of the central Indian and Deccanese chacolithic crop situation.

Although put very briefly the above-mentioned archaeological evidence is highly suggestive as far as the Aryan hypothesis in Indian archaeology is concerned. We feel that only in the phase of the cultures antecedent to the Indus civilization there could be a significant sharing of the Indo-Iranian language in the subcontinent. The location of the epi-centre of the Indus civilization in the Saraswati-Drishadvati system is, according to us, almost a definite indication that this civilization was speaking an early form of Sanskrit. Thirdly, that there was an interaction between the Indus civilization and the neolitic-chalcolithic cultures of "inner India" in the late Harappan phase is beyond doubt, as the crop situation in the late Harappan phase amply indicates.

Some Recent Developments

We are aware that the situation hypothesized by us in the preceding section will upset some of our cherished chronological and cultural premises. All that we can say is that most of these chronological and cultural beliefs are based on worse suppositions and logic. For instance, the *Rigvedic* society is supposed to be pastoral simply because it has frequent references to cattle. The inconvenient references to agriculture in the *Rigveda* are treated as later additions. The scholars who do this forget that effective agriculture is very old in the subcontinent, and surely no text supposedly dating from 1500 B.C. could depict predominantly pastoral society anywhere in the subcontinent. Something must be wrong with the general understanding of this text.

Another instance which comes readily to mind is the reference in the *Satapatha Brahmana* to the spread of agriculture in the Sadanira or Gandak river valley. The occurrence of wheat and barley among other crops at Chirand in the third millennium B.C. suggests a western contact, but the point is that agriculture was well established in the Gandak Valley as early as the third millennium B.C. The SB tradition apparently contains a dim protohistoric memory. To fix this text within the straightjacket of a late date (c. 700 B.C.) is surely not a logical exercise.

It is also important to move that in physical anthropology the old idea of one racial group supplanting another had become obsolete and been given up by scholars like D.Sen and K.A.R. Kennedy.[12] In archaeology diffusionist approaches are being discarded even in the Indian context.

It is also worthwhile to note that the earlier schematic model of dichotomy between the *Vedic* and pre-*Vedic* India has been given up in a recent publication of F.R. Allchin[13] who now believes in a pre-*Vedic* contact situation between and earlier group of Indo-Iranians and the Indus civilization. J.G. Shaffer has recently argued that "current archaeological data do not support the existence of an Indo-Aryan or European invasion into South Asia at any time in the pre-or protohistoric periods. Instead, it is possible to document archaeologically series of cultural changes reflecting indigenous cultural development from prehistoric to historic periods."[14]

Notes and References

1. Dilip K. Chakrabarty, *The Aryan Hypothesis in Indian Archaeology, Indian Studies: Past and Present* 9 (1968): 343-58.
2. Dilip K. Chakrabarty, India and the Druids, *Antiquity* 50 (1976): 66-67.
3. Dilip K. Chakrabarty, The Development of Archaeology in the Indian Sub-continent, *World Archaaeology* 13 (1987) 326-44.
4. L. Poliakov, *The Aryan Myth,* New York, 1974.
5. Dilip K. Chakrabarty, Archaeology and the Literary Tradition: An Examination of the Indian Context, *Archaeological Review from Cambridge* 3 (1984): 29-36.
6. Dilip K. Chakrabarty, India and West Asia: An Alternative Approach, *Man and Environment* 1 (1977): 25-38.
7. *Ibid.*
8. This early chronology of the Indus civilization is based both on calibrated radiocarbon dates and the archaeological evidence of the pre-Sargonic contact of the Indus civilization. See Dilip K. Chakrabarty, The Nippur Indus seal and Indus chronology, *Man and Environment* 2 (1978) 90-91.
9. Cf. B. and F.R. Allachin, *The Rise of Civilization in India and Pakistan,* Cambridge 1982.
10. Dilip K. Chakrabarty, Size of Harappan Settlements, *Essays in Indian Protohistory* (ed D.P. Agarwal, D.K. Chakrabarty), Delhi 1979, pp. 205-15.
11. M.R. Mughal, New archaeological evidence from Bahawalpur, *Indus Civilization: New Perspectives* (ed. A.H. Dani). Islamabad, 1980, pp. 33-41; J.P. Joshi et al, The Indus civilization: a reconsideration on the basis of distribution map. *Frontiers of the Indus Civilization* (ed. B.B. Lal, S.P. Gupta), Delhi 1984, pp. 511-30.
12. D.K. Sen, Ancient Races of India and Pakistan-A Study of Methods, *Ancient India* (1967): 178-205; Cf. K.A.R. Kennedy, Palaeodemography of India and Ceylon since B.C., *American Journal of Physical Anthropology* 31 (1969) 315-20.
13. Allchin, *op.cit.* pp. 301 ff.
14. J.G. Shaffer, The Indo-Aryan Inventions; Cultural Myth and Archaeological Reality, *The People of South Asia* (ed. J.R. Lukacs), New York 1984, 77-90.

14

How Wheeler Invented the Invasion Myth

K.M. Srivastava*

After completing the excavations at Brahmagiri in Chitradurg District of Karnataka, Sir Mortimer Wheeler turned his attention to Harappa in District Montgomery, now in Pakistan. In one of his visits to this site, Wheeler observed the remains of formidable "defences". In order to verify the nature of these defences he started fresh excavations in the citadel of the township. Here he discovered the remains of a huge mud-brick structure which he thought belonged to the fortifications, primarily aimed at defending the township against military incursions. He repeatedly brought in the Sumerian analogies of Lagash and Ur to fortify his arguments (Wheeler 1947:76). As the next logical step in the reconstruction of the history of these defences, he found as it were ready references in the *Rigveda*.[1] Picking up these references of warfare (1947:83) he made them speak in the light of his archaeological discoveries. To him (1968:132):

> It seems better, as the evidence stands, to accept the identification and to suppose that the Harappans of the Indus Valley in their decadence, in or about seventeenth century B.C., fell before the advancing Aryans in such fashion as the *Vedic* hymns proclaim.

The Myth of Conquered Forts

Curiously enough, while propounding the theory of destruction of the Harappan towns as well as the Harappan culture by the invasion of the Aryans. Wheeler combined the evidence picked up selectively from different sites. Thus, he combined the evidence of skeletons found in a disorderly manner in the streets and houses of Mohenjo-daro with the so-called mudbrick defences of Harappa. Besides the fact that this is faulty methodology, the theory of the defence and Aryan invasion could be conceived only in war-like activities and the use of military weapons by the Harappans. And this had been highly questionable right

* Former Director, Archaeological survey of India. Excavated famous sites of Sravasti, Lothal and Kalibangan. The above article was contributed to *The Frontiers of Harappan Civilization*. Ed. by Prof. B.B. Lal, S.P. Gupta & Shashi Asthana.

from the time of Marshall (1931) who first proposed the invasion theory though the invasion he had in mind was made by the Baluchi nomads and not by the Aryans. Wheeler himself has candidly admitted the absence of military outfit in Harappan towns (Wheeler 1968:73). Still he suggested that small domed pieces of copper, each perforated with two holes, were sewn on to a garment and used as an equivalent to mail (Wheeler 1968:73), but there is no supporting evidence and neither body-armour nor helmets (well known in Early Dynastic Sumer), not indeed shields, can at present be attributed to the Harappans.

He further states (Wheeler 1968:72) that it is "true, the military element does not look large amongst the extant remains, but it must be remembered that at present we know almost nothing of the civilisation." In fact the implements of copper found so far in the Harappan towns are, by and large, domestic in nature. Moreover, where are the remnants of the weapons of war supposed to have been used by the invading Aryans? Can their absence be justified in the case of the invaders as well? Similarly, if the invasion by the Aryans was the cause of the destruction of the Harappa culture, where are the remains of the Aryans at the Harappan sites? The Aryans can not be said to have destroyed the Harappan simply in a fit of temper or for the sake of pleasure. The onslaught must have had a certain aim behind it and the principal aim of an invader is generally the occupation of the site, at least temporarily. The Aryans cannot be believed to have been interested only in collecting booty from various places and abandoning the site when it is clear from the Early *Vedic* literature that the *Saptasindhu* or the Punjab-Haryana region was their homeland. Indications of people, other than the Harappans, occupying the same site immediately after its destruction, in an almost overlapping manner, are not available from the sites representing the mature Harappa culture; even the Cemetery 'H' complex at Harappa was separated from the Harappan levels by more than a metre and a half of deposit of debris (Wheeler: 1947:84).

In his usual dramatic manner, Wheeler (1969:131) wrote:

> In the *Rigveda*, the invasion constantly assumes the form also of an onslaught upon the walled cities of the aborigines. For these cites, the term used is pur, meaning a "rampart" "fort", "stronghold": one is called "broad" (*Prithvi*) and "wide" (*urivi*). Sometimes strongholds are referred to metaphorically as "of metal" (*yasi*) "autumnal" (*saradi*)— forts are also named: "this may refer to the forts in that season being occupied against Aryan attacks or against inundations caused by overflowing rivers". Forts "with a hundred walls, (*satabhuji*) are mentioned. The citadel may be of stone (*asmamayi*): alternatively, the use of mud-brick is perhaps alluded to by the epithet *ama* ("raw",

> "unbaked"). Indra, the Aryan war-god, is *purandara,* "fort destroyer". He shatters ninety forts for his Aryan protege, Divodasa. The same forts are doubtless referred to when in other hymns he demolishes variously ninety-nine and a hundred "ancient castles" of the aboriginal leader Sambara. In brief, he "rends forts as age consumes a garment".

While giving overdue emphasis to the above-mentioned statements, right from the time he undertook the excavations of the fortifications at Harappa, till late in his life, Wheeler never tried to present scholars with factual evidence of their wanton destruction. In other words, Wheeler has never proclaimed anywhere, either in his excavation reports on Harappa or in general and specific publications, that the defences at the Indus sites were, in fact, pulled down and we have their debris in a particular layer. In these circumstances, there seems no justification in the further quote form the *Rigveda* that, 'the same forts are doubtless referred to wherein other hymns he demolishes variously, ninety-nine and a hundred "ancient castles" of the aboriginal leader Sambar'. Obviously, here imagination has ridden over fact. We really wonder whether it is for this kind of historical license that throughout his life he fought the scientists who came to turn archaeology into a science.

Significantly, the literary evidence from the *Rigveda* as quoted by Wheeler in support of his theory still has one more dimension. In this context M.C. Joshi (1978:99) has made a very pertinent remark:

> There is no relevance of *ayasipuras* (forts of metal or iron) or *satabhuji-puras* or forts with hundred walls in the Harappan context. None of the Harappan fortifications knows to us bear any trace of metallic appearance or multiple walls to justify the appelations *ayasi* and *satabhuji*. Even if the latter is supposed to refer to a defence-wall with hundred angles we cannot apply the term in question to any of the fortified Harappan settlements.

To Wheeler (1968: 132) the Aryan invasion was an obsession:

> The discovery of fortified citadeis at Harappa and Mohenjo-daro, supplemented by the defences of the Harappan sites of Sutkagendor in Makran. All Murad in Sind, Kalibangan in Rajasthan, and others have changed the picture. Here we have a highly evolved civilization of essentially non-Aryan type, now known to have employed massive fortification, and known also to have dominated the river system of north-western India at a time not distant from the likely period of the earlier Aryan invasion of that region.

The picture of defences of fortifications has, on every occasion, been presented by exhibiting a section cut across the platform-like, mud-brick structure at Harappa. The author can clearly recollect his discussion with A. Ghosh, during the course of one of his visits to Lothal. The excavations were in progress and a few platforms made of mud-bricks were exposed. The platform could have easily been explained as a fortification or a defense wall but Ghosh was convinced by our explanation that they were only safeguards from the regular floods in the area. In the initial stages of occupation when the inhabitants of Lothal were confronted with the scourge of flood, they raised an embankment with the help of hard black cotton soil. When this course did not prove successful they decided to erect mud-brick platforms for occupation. The question now was if a section across this mud-brick platform were cut, would a similar section-picture be not revealed as that exhibited by Wheeler at Harappa to establish the existence of the defences? Ghosh did not lose any time in supporting our views. A close observation of Wheeler's section of fortification at Harappa would clearly show that he did not cut through the entire thickness of the "platform", only a part of it was dug. Thus none knows how exactly this structure behaved inside. To our mind, it could as well be a platform of a kind we see at Kalibangan at lest six of them, with fire altars.

The picture of the so-called defences at Harappa, Mohenjo-daro and Kalibangan as presented by Wheeler and others is not very different from that at Lothal. The so-called defences have enclosed certain areas in the same fashion as at Lothal. As a matter of fact they were never erected as a defence agianst attack or invasion but, simply as a measure against flood and also social status.

In one of his essays on society and settlement patterns, Bruce Trigger (1978:1973) has rightly pointed out:

> In the societies where authority or class divisions are more pronounced, the houses of the elite become larger and more elaborate. In such places as the Marquesas, for example, the elaborateness of the platform on which a house was built reflected the importance of its owner.

So far as the class divisions at the sites of Lothal, Kalibangan, Harappa, Mohenjo-daro etc. are concerned there is no ambiguity. Society was divided into definite classes on the basis of occupation and profession. Each one of them, it is believed, had a separate area of occupation in the city complex. The elite class which held authority over the settlements had its houses and or religious establishments on the highest point, created artificially by raising the working level with the help of high platforms. Thus, it was the class division, functional division and the distinction of the elite group from the rest which brought into existence the settlements of a so-called citadel; area completely segregated from the main city complex. In this context, another observation of Bruce Trigger (1978: 191) is also pertinent:

> A fort may become the residence of a chief and his retainers: as immovable property accumulates, the well-to-do may move into the fort, so that a town begins to develop; and artisans may settle in the town in order to sell their wares to the townsfolk and farmers who come to trade and to worship at local shrines. In other cultures, a cult centre also may serve as a fort or market place and in this way become the nucleus of city.

The growth of Harappa metropolises may have been of the same kind.

Bruce Trigger (1978: 193) further commented:

> The presence or absence of fortifications, cannot be considered as direct evidence of the prevalence of warfare, since the effectiveness of such means of defence depends in part on either offensive or defensive warfare is in the ascendant.

Dales (1964:38) is, therefore, right in raising some of the following most pertinent questions:

> Where are the burned fortresses, the arrow heads, weapons, pieces of armour, the smashed chariots and bodies of the invaders and defenders? Despite the extensive excavations at the largest Harappan sites, there is not a single bit of evidence that can be brought forth as unconditional proof of an armed conquest and the destruction on the supposed scale of the Aryan invasion.

The explanation of any citadel or fortification must, therefore, be worked out in the light of the above mentioned observations.

The Myth of Massacre

This brings us to the "massacre" of people at Mohenjo-daro, since, as said at the outset, Wheeler combined the supposed evidence of the destruction of fortifications with the skeletons found in a helter-skelter condition at this site. Wheeler (1968-129) himself was not sure if the evidence was sound since he clearly states, "unfortunately, the older excavations did not record stratification with any regard to precision, and in the absence of precise record it cannot be affirmed without shadow of doubt that the skeletal remains were not contemporary," That all the skeletal remains were not contemporary to each other as the product of a single tragedy had been conclusively proved by Dales (1964), at least four years before Wheeler reluctantly accepted the position. Moreover, it is now well known that the excavator of Mohenjo-daro and the "massacre" remains Marshall (1931), had himself separated the end of the Harappa Culture from the Aryan invasion by two centuries. He, in fact, attributed the massacre to bandits from the hills west of the Indus, who carried out sporadic raids on an already tired, decaying and defenceless civilization.

Below we quote Dales (1964) who made a thorough study of the so-called wanton killing of the masses at Mohenjo-daro since that would show in clear terms the obsession Wheeler had with his "massacred men, women and children" who were long dead.

> What of these skeletal remains that have taken on such undeserved importance? Nine years of extensive excavations at Mohjeno-daro (1921-31)—a city about three miles in circuit—yielded the total of some 37 skeletons, or parts thereof, that can be attributed with some certainty to the period of the Indus civilizations. Some of these were found in contorted positions and groupings that suggest anything but orderly burials. Many are either disarticulated or incomplete. They were all found in the area of the Lower Town—probably the residential district. *Not a single body was found within the area of the fortified citadel where one could reasonably expect the final defence of this thiriving capital city to have been made*.

It would be foolish to assert that scattered skeletal remains represent an orderly state of affairs, since there is no conclusive proof that they all even belong to the same period of a single tragedy.

Possehl (1979:287-8) also rightly points out that, in case the Aryan hypothesis is accepted, "many problems emerge":

> First, the chronology of the Indus Civilization, at least the Urban Phase during which the cities were fully occupied, cannot be projected to have a terminal date beyond 1800 B.C. It is widely agreed that the *Vedic* literature from which the hypothesis is drawn was compiled sometimes between 1200 and 800 B.C. This leaves us with a chronological gap of between 600 and 1000 years, and it hardly seems reasonable to postulate that this discrepancy can be filled by the period between the historical destruction of the cities and the compilation of the *Vedas*.

Moreover, the end of the Harappan cities, it is now widely recognized, was not the end of the Harappa culture. It was in fact succeeded by what is now called the Late Harappa culture, particularly in Gujarat, Haryana, Rajasthan and Uttar Pradesh. In other words, observes Possehl (1979:287):

> If the cities were abandoned then it must have been caused by something characteristically urban. This brings to mind institutions such as kingship and the differentiated nature of city-based political institutions; economic factors such as craft and productive specialization, including the relationships necessary to unite them with a large organic whole, systems of trade and tribute which are necessary for urban eleites and their particular style of life; and the differentiated social structure which has been presumed to characterized urbanization.

Indra, therefore, stands completely exonerated.

The End of the Harappa Culture

This leads us to the last question associated with the entire problem of mythical invasion; if not the invasion what then was the cause of the end of the Harappan towns of Harappa and Mohenjo-daro in particular and other towns in the Punjab, Haryana and Rajasthan in general where the early Aryans seem to have had their abode? As a corollary, we will also examine the roots of the Wheelerian version of the invasion theory, which, to us appears to lie in the directional changes through which Wheeler's archaeological career passed.

The end of Harappa culture may not have had a single cause. The decline in foreign trade was certainly quite important. The literary sources from Mesopotamia yield yet another kind of evidence which contributed to the decline of urban economy of the Harappans—the Mesopotamian trade with the Indus sharply declined at the end of the Third Dynasty of Ur in 18th century B.C. since from then onwards, the items which were impoted from India were procured from southern Arabia, Ethiopia and Egypt (Asthana 1979:43).

For the decline of Mohenjo-daro, however, natural causes are listed. The one now generally agreed upon is the "Floods in the Indus" a fairly detailed study of which was made by Raikes (1965: 202).

However, what applies to Mohenjo-daro may not apply to other Harappan settlements—there is no archaeological proof that Harappa was destroyed because of floods in the Ravi or Kalibangan was destroyed by the floods in the Ghaggar. For their end, the old theory of climatic changes and desiccation of land from about 1800 B.C. has been revised on the basis of fresh studies made by Gurdip Singh (1971).

There have been a few other studies (Fairservis 1967), some concerning the social break-up of the Harappans, some concerning demographic changes, and some concerning the general principles governing the rise and fall of city civilizations. However, it should be clearly understood that the end of the Harappan towns and Indus Valley Civilization was a very complex affair in which many socio-economic and environmental factors contributed and certainly not the mythical invasion by the Aryan and the mythical massacre of the Harappans. The end of the Indus Valley Civilization was a slow process and not catastrophic.

Why Did Wheeler Blow Up The Invasion Theory?

In retrospect, when we look at Wheeler's career as an archaeologist in England and India and we see him as a Brigadier in the British army during World War II, we feel he could not interpret the dubious evidence of Mohenjo-daro and Harappa in any other manner. He started his real archaeological career from Maiden Castle excavations and soon emerged as an authority on Roman archaeology. His *Rome Beyond the Imperial Frontiers* clearly shows how deeply involved he was in the Roman art and architecture, Roman concepts of town-planning-citadels, lower towns, assembly-halls, etc. Thus when he was confronted with the twin-mound towns of the Harappans and their huge fortification walls and mud-brick platforms as well as the photographs of the so-called 'massacre' at Mohenjo-daro he was at once reminded of Roman history and archaeology. Marshall's (1931) and Vats' (1940) reports of Mohenjo-daro and Harappa, respectively, as well as Piggott's *Prehistoric India* (1950- 244-248) provided him sufficient speculations on Aryan warfare and Indra's attack on Harappan towns. The common text-books on Indian history adorned his personal library. For the former army man and the Director General of Archaeology in India, as Wheeler was, the Aryan invasion of Indus towns (1961:249) was as simple as the Roman invasion of Britian and Turkey, Wheeler's successors in England, it is significant to note, were no better appreciators of archaeological evidence: Allchin and Allchin (1968: 144-56) reiterated the same. Wheeler's interpretations were somewhat lop-sided if not biased but his techniques of excavations have been model for all subsequent generations of archaeologists in India. B.B. Lal (1980), one of his foremost disciples in India, has now conclusively proved that the 'citadel' of Kalibangan, another Harappa, was the seat of religious establishments. A beginning in the right direction has been made.

Notes and References

In fact it was V.S. Agarwal who provided these references to Dr. Wheeler when the latter requested Prof Agarwal, then an officer in the Archaeological Survey of India, on tour at Harappa, although Dr. Wheeler never acknowledged it in any of his writings.

Agarwal, *et at*, 1964, Radiocarbon Dates of Archaeological Samples, *Current Science,* Vol. 39 (B).

Allchin, B, and Allchin, F.R., *The Birth of Indian Civilization* (London: Pelican, 1968).

Asthana, Shashi "Indus-Mesopotamia Trade: Nature of Trade and Structural Analysis of Operative System." D.P. Agarwal and Dilip K. Chakrabarti ed. In *Essays in Indian Protohistory:* 1977.

Dales, G.F. The Mythical Massacre at Mohenjo-daro, *Expedition,* Vol. VI, 3; 1964, 36-43.

Fairservis, W.A., "The Origin, Character and Decline of an Early Civilization." *Novitates,* No. 2302, 1967. New York: American Museum of Natural History.

Joshi, M.C., Archaeology and Ancient Tradition-Some Observations, *Puratattva,* No. 8, 1978.

Lal, B.B., Some reflections on Structural Remains at Kalibangan, Cyclostyled paper circulated by the Indian Institute of Advanced Studies, Simla, 1980.

Marshall, John, *Mohenjo-daro and the Indus Civilization,* London, 1931.

Raikes, R. L. *The Mohenjo-daro Floods,* Antiquity. Vol. XXXIX: 1965, 165-203.

Singh Gurdip. The Indus Valley Culture Seen in the Context of Post-Glacial Climate and Ecological Studies in North-West India. Reprinted in *Puratattva.* No. 6; 68-76, 1971.

Trigger, Bruce, Time and Traditions. In *Essays in Archaeological Interpretations.* Edinburgh.

Vats, M.S., *Excavations at Harappan,* New Delhi, 1940.

Wheeler, R.E.M., Ancient India: The Civilization of a Subcontinent. In *The Dawn of Civilization.* Stuart Piggott ed. London, 1961.

15

Harappan Culture is Vedic

K.D. Sethna*

Domesticated Horse

Once a strong argument for considering the Harappa Culture anterior to the *Rigveda* was the alleged lack of evidence in it for the domesticated horse which is a marked feature of the *Rigvedic* civilization no less than of all ancient Aryan communities. In 1963 the present writer publicly opposed it at some length on various grounds a number of them in addition to those already set forth by several scholars.[1] His data left him in no doubt at all. Now he had been completely justified by the excavations of J.P. Joshi. In a review of the recent publication of the full report on Surkotada, F. Chakravarty puts the situation succinctly:

> One of the startling discoveries at Surkotada has been horse bones which have refuted the earlier belief that the use of the horse was unknown to the Harappans.[2]

Absence of Iron

A still persisting plea for greater antiquity is the absence of iron. R.C. Majumdar, taking cognizance of it, pronounces judgment thus:

> The reference to iron in the *Rig-Veda* would have indeed been a very strong argument for relegating the *Vedic* civilization to a later period, but this is at best doubtful.[3]

Even Macdonell who was pledged to dating the *Rigveda* to c. 1200 B.C. and therefore well within the world's Iron Age was yet compelled to write on the *Rigveda's* use of the crucial word ayas which, in one of the later phases of Sanskrit, defintiely means "iron".

> In most passages where it occurs the word appears to mean simply 'metal'. In the few cases where it designates a particular metal, the

* Octagerianian scholar and writer; since 1949 editor of Mother India published by Sri Aurobindo Ashram, Pondicherry; author of large number of books on Indian history and culture. This article has been taken from his recent work *The problem of Aryan Origins : From an Indian Point of View* (Aditya Prakashan, New Delhi, 1922).

> evidence is not very conclusive; but the inference which may be drawn from its colour is decidedly in favour of its having been reddish, which points to bronze and not iron.[4]

Wheeler opts for "copper" as the particular sense of ayas.[5] There is also the fact that, although iron was known in Western Asia by Macdonell's date for the *Rigveda*, no Indian site has yielded this metal in that period, Sankalia, summing up available data, concludes:

> provisionally, we may fix the 6th-8th century B.C. as the date when iron was first introduced in some parts (northern) of India.[6]

Worship of the Mother Goddess

Shifting our focus from physical to psychological and cultural factors, we encounter Sir John Marshall's famous dubbing of the Harappān religion fundamentally non-Aryan.[7] Wheeler and most other scholars have accepted Marshall's verdict, but a close scrutiny to it reveals its ultimate inadequacy. There are three constituents of the Indus Valley religion which are supposed to mark the opposite pole to the religion of the *Rigveda*: (1) the worship of the Mother Goddess. (2) the worship of icons, (3) the worship of the Bull instead of the Cow.

Doubtless, the *Rigvedic Rishis* throw a host of male deities into relief. But the female onces are not only present; they are also much more than mere shadows. As Sri Aurobindo tells us, we have those five goddesses who, in his interpretation, are:

> five powers of the Truth-consciousness.–Mehi or Bharati, the vast Word which brings all things out of the divine source: Ila, the strong primal word of the Truth who gives us its active vision; Saraswati, its streaming current and the word of its inspiration; Sarama, the intuition, hound of heaven who descends into the cavern of the subconscient and finds there the concealed illuminations; Dakshina, whose function is to discern rightly, dispose the action and the offering and distribute in the sacrifice to each godhead its portion.[8]

Then there is Usha, the Dawn-Goddess who has hymn after hymn addressed to her—she is called "daughter of heaven" and "queen of plenty" (V. 792, 6), she is the luminous precursor who makes possible the advent of Surya and the other divinities. Prithivi is there too, the Earth-Goddess, co-parent with Dyau, Heaven, of everything. Goddesses also are the Rivers who are sisters of Saraswati, making with here a divine septet. Says Sri Aurobindo:

> They are figured, "as fostering cows (*dhenavah*), mares (*asvah*), they are called *sapta vānīh*, the seven Words of the creative Vak—Speech, the expressive power of Aditi...."[9]

And when we come to Aditi we reach one of the greatest conceptions of the *Vedic* religion. For, above all goddesses and above all gods stands Aditi, the infinite Consciousness and Force, Mother of every god whom the *Rigveda* throws into relief and who even in that relief points back to here by begin called Aditya, Aditi"s son. Surely, the prominent worship of the Mother Goddess could very well develop from the *Rigveda*.

Iconography in Vedism

As for the worship of icons, we may affirm that although it may not have been a practice particularly prevalent in *Vedic* times it is nothing essentially at variance with the *Vedic* spirit. The gods and goddesses of the *Rigveda* are not abstract entities; they are vividly described, splendidly imaged, brought intimately home to the devoted mind. To make icons of them would hardly been a alien movement. We can go even further and see how image-worship could most naturally arise from the kind of *Yoga* pursued by the *Rigveda*. Sri Aurobindo here has some extremely pertinent remark while commenting on a hymn to Agni, the Fire-God (I, 77), the first two stanzas of which run:

> How shall we give to Agni? For him what Word accepted by the Gods be spoken, for the lord of the brilliant flame? For him who in mortals, immortal, possessed of the Truth, priest of the oblation, strongest for sacrifice, creates the gods?
>
> He who in the sacrifice is the priest of the offering, full of peace, full of the Truth, him verily form in you by your surrenderings: when Agni manifests for the mortals the gods, he also has perception of them and by the mind offers to them the sacrifice.[10]

Sri Aurobindo explains how Agni's luminous work of creating the forms of the Immmortals in us is accomplished:

> This work he does as a cosmic Power labouring upon the rebellious human material even when in our ignorance we resist the heavenward impulse and, accustomed to offer our actions to the egoistic life, cannot yet or as yet will not make the divine surrender. But it is in proportion as we learn to subjugate the ego and compel it to bow down in every act to the Universal Being and to serve consciously in its least movement and supreme Will, that Agni himself takes form in us. The Divine Will becomes present and conscient in a human mind and enlightens it with the divine Knowledge. Thus it is that man can be said to form by his toil the great Gods.
>
> The Sanskrit expression is here a *krnudhvam.* The preposition gives the idea of a drawing upon oneself of something outside and the working or shaping it out in our own consciousness. Ā *kr* corresponds to the converse expression, *ā bhû*, used of the gods when they approach the mortal with the contact of Immortality and, divine form of godhead

> falling on form of humanity, 'become', take shape, as it were, in him. The cosmic Powers act and exist in the universe; man takes them upon himself, makes an image of them in his own consciousness and endows that image with the life and power that the Supreme Being has breathed into His own divine forms and world-energies.[11]

To the last sentence Sri Aurobindo gives the footnote:

> This is the true sense and theory of Hindu image-worship, which is thus a material rendering of the great *Vedic* symbols.

S.K. Venkateswara suggests that "the transition from verbography to iconography in Vedism may be observed in various hymns even of the *Rig-Veda Samhitā*". We may note his remark: "..in R.-V.I. 21.2 we have *Indrāgni sumbhata narah,* which Prof. Wilson translates into Decorate Indra and Agni with ornaments". In R.-V.III. 4.4 *nripesas* is explained by Prof. Roth as 'adorned by men' and by Prof. Wilson as 'of sensible shapes'. R.-V.II. 33.8 speaks of Rudra as white-complexioned (*svitīcha*), which, along with *pipise hiranyaih* (R.-V.II. 33.9) might suggest *pripesas* as 'having the form of men". Dr. Bollenson discovered a reference to images of Maruts in R.-V.V. 52.15: *nu manvāna esham devān achchha*—'to the gods of these (images) (Maruts)' *Eshām* in the passage seems to refer to something concrete which could be pointed to on the spot. Again in R.-V.IV.24 we have reference to an image of Indra which was to be hired out for a rent of ten cows and which was to be returned after use. This is the earliest passage which definitely suggests the first idea of an Indra festival. It is apparently referred to in R.-V.I. 10.1: *Brahmanas tvā satakrata udvamsam iva yemire*—'Worshippers held thee aloft as it were (on) a pole."[12]

V.M. Apte strikes a neutral note:

> Whether fetishism is to be read into a reference to an image of Indra and whether the worship of idols or images of gods was known to the *Rigveda*, are points on which no certain conclusions can be reached.[13]

Thus, at the worst, there is indecision, but the *Rigveda's* door can never be closed on any account against the Harappā Culture's iconism.

Worship of the Bull

Now for the worship of the Bull. Cows are indeed in the forefront in the *Vedic* hymns. Also, as Apte tells us:

> the name *Aghnyā* ('not to be killed'), applied several times to the cow shows that the cow was coming to be regarded as a sacred animal.[14]

But it would be well to remember Sri Aurobindo's words to the effect that just as Aditi, the supreme *Prakriti* or Nature-force, is spoken of as the Cow, the Deva or Purusha, the supreme Being or Soul, is described as Vrishabha or Vrishn, the Bull.[15] Apte too notes that Indra is sometimes conceived as a bull.[16] A hymn to Agni (I.27.1) names one Tryaruna "son of the triple Bull" (*trivrsna*)-the triple Bull being, according to Sri Aurobindo, "Indra, lord of the three luminous realms of *Swar*, the Divine Mind..."[17] *Rishi* Vamadeva, in the last hymn of the fourth Mandala, not only speaks of the four-horned Bull, the divine Purusha, whose horns may be interpreted as infinite Existence. Consciousness, Bliss and Truth, but has in addition the energetic phrase:

> Triply bound the Bull roars aloud: great is the Divinity that has entered into mortals.[18]

In view of all this, might we not say that Bull-worship could grow from the *Rigvedic* religion?

In connection with Bull-worship, we may glance at the Harappan figure wearing a three-pointed (*trisula*) horned head-dress and attended by animals. He seems to have been an important male deity and has been identified with the Shiva of Hindu tradition who too is "lord of animals" (*pasupati*) and of whom the bull is the vehicle (*vāhana*). Now, Shiva can be traced in the *Rigveda*. Hymn I, 43 1, 5, 6 addresses Rudra—the terrible and destructive aspect of the traditional Shiva—as "most bounteous", "the good, the best among the Gods", granting "health unto our steeds, well-being to our rams and ewes, to men and women, and to kine".[19] Here Rudra is, as Ralph T.H. Griffith notes, "a gentle and beneficent deity",[20] the typical Shiva. Hymn II.33.8 calls Rudra "fair-complexioned".[21] Griffith annotates:

> the while complexion of Siva, the later representative of Rudra, has, therefore, as Wilson observes, its origin in the *Rigveda*.[22]

Lastly, hymn X. 92.9 has Rudra actually described as "shiva," a word which Griffith translates "auspicious".[23]

Siva–a Vedic God

Here we may touch on a point of considerable religion philological interest. Sten Konow voices a very current notion when he writes:

"It has been asserted that...the word *Siva* must be explained from a Dravidian *Siva* 'red'. Now the word Rudra in the *Rig Veda* often seems to mean 'red', and it seems probable that the conception of the god Rudra-Siva has a tinge of Dravidian ideas. I have mentioned this word because it shows how fundamental the Dravidian influence on the Aryans can have been, not only philologically, but also on the whole method of thought."[24]

R. Swaminatha Aiyar, in the illuminating collection of papers to which we have already referred, has a critical comment on Konow:

> ...it is no doubt true that the deity Rudra is regarded as *red* or tawny in colour and that the word *siva* is used in the *Vedas* as an epithet of this deity. For *tamra* 'coppery' red and *aruna* 'red, ruddy, of the colour of the morning sky', *babhru* 'deep brown, tawny', *sumangala* 'yellow coloured', 'very auspicious' are some of his epithets, as also *Siva* and *Sivatara.* These last two words, however, do not mean 'red' but 'propitious' and 'highly propitious': this will be apparent from the other epithets along with which these two words occur, viz., *sambhu*, *sankara*, 'causing happiness', *mayobhu, mayaskara,* 'causing pleasure, satisfaction'...Of these *siva sambhu* and *sankara* have now become Rudra's names. It is the merest accident that the Sanskrit *siva* 'beneficent' has the same sound as the Dravidian *siva* (=*civa*) 'red'. Have those that assert the etymological connextion between the two words been able to quote a single passage from the *Vedas* in which *siva* the epithet of Rudra means 'red'?[25]

Aiyar has kept in view not only the *Rigveda* but also the *Taittiriya Samhita* (I. 5-7; IV, 5-8) and the *Kaushītakī Brāhmana* (XIX, 1-3) as well as the Parisistha of the *Rigveda* (X, *Anuvāka*).[26] So the conclusion and question of the above passage are wide-based and strike us as legitimate.

We may support them by a further observation. As we have been told by both Venkateswara and Griffith, the *Rigvedic* Rudra has on occasion a white or faire complexion and, as Griffith informs us, it is by this colour that the *Rigvedic* Rudra exhibits one of the origins of later Hinduism's Shiva. Not by being red but by being white in hue does the traditional Shiva distinguish himself. How, then, can the Dravidian term *siva*, signifying 'red', be at all relevant as the original name of this deity?

A long time back Sri Aurobindo returned a negative answer to the problem of relevance on the basis of his own study of the *Rigveda*. In commenting on hymn I. 154, he wrote.

> The deity of this hymn is Vishnu the all-pervading, who in the *Rigveda* has a close but covert connection and almost an identity with the other deity exalted in the later religion, Rudra...Vishnu's constant friendliness to man and his helping gods is shadowed by an aspect of formidable violence,-'like a terrible lion ranging in evil and difficult places' (I. 154.2),- which is spoken of in terms more ordinarily appropriate to Rudra. Rudra is the father of the vehemently-battling Maruts; Vishnu is hymned in the last *Sukta* of the fifth Mandala under the name of Evaya Marut as the source from which they sprang, that which they become, and himself identical with the unity and totality of their embattled forces.[27]

Obviously, if Vishnu has an *alter ego* in Rudra, one can say of the latter, as Sri Aurobindo does:

> Rudra is a fierce and violent godhead with a beneficent aspect which approaches the supreme blissful reality of Vishnu.[28]

And Sri Aurobindo is aware of the *Rigveda's* own direct picturing of Rudra in tones anticipating the character of the post-*Rigvedic* Shiva. He refers to "a current opinion among many scholars that Shiva was a later conception borrowed from the Dravidians and represents a partial conquest of the *Vedic* religion by the indigenous culture it had invaded".[29] After labelling this conception as an error, he tells us of Rudra:

> He is named the Mighty one of Heaven, but....this violent and mighty Rudra who breaks down all defective formations and groupings of outward and inward life, has also a benigner aspect. He is the supreme healer. Opposed, he destroys; called on for aid and propitiated he heals all wounds and all evil and all suffering. The force that battles is his gift, but also the final peace and joy. In these aspects of the *Vedic* god are all the primitive materials necessary for the evolution of the *Puranic* Shiva-Rudra.[30]

In the light of what we have observed from various angles, the Harappan male god whose three-pointed horned head-dress and attendance by animals lead us to recognize in him the Shiva of Hindu tradition is not in the least likely to be non-Aryan, non-*Vedic*. Quite the contrary should be the case.

Wust Supports Vedism in Indus Valley Civilisation

And in additional general support of Vedism for the Indus Valley Civilization we may refer to a fact brought home by W. Wüst.[31] The Harappan male god has three heads, just as the traditional Hindu Shiva is at times described (*trimūkha*). It has been thought that the latter's three-headedness is derived from a Harappan prototype rather than from any known Aryan model. But Wüst makes out that the three-headed diety is essentially of Indo-European origin.

We should really be not much surprised. Does not the *Rigveda* tend to help Wust out? There is not only an enemy of Indra, called Visvarupa, who is described as *trisīrsan,* "three-headed" (X. 8.8). There is also the god Agni about whom Apte informs us:

> The three-fold nature of Agni is a favourite topic with RV poets: his heads, bodies, stations, splendours and births are each three-fold. He is the earliest representative of the famous Indian trinity...[32]

Fire-Altars

To complete our picture of the element of Aryanism in the Indus Valley Civilization, there is a recent discovery which countervails an old argument of some force. We were told that in the *Rigveda* "*Agni,* or the Fire-God, received special homage" but he is a deity "of whose worship no traces are found in the early ruins of Mohenjo-Daro", and in the Harappa Culture "fire-pits were conspicuous by their basence".[33]

In 1974, however, Sankalia could write that at both the Harappān sites of Lothal and Kalibangan:

> small shallow enclosures have been found with a vertical brick, terracotta cakes and a few bones of animals, so that the pits are regarded as 'fire-altars'.[34]

"Such a fire-altars has also been noticed by Casal at (Harappān) Amri....Perhaps such 'fire-altars' also existed at Harappa and Mohenjo-Daro, but were missed in mass digging."[35]

These structures Sankalia, in agreement with the excavators, feels to be "truly religious", and their discovery "seems to clarify and amplify our knowledge of the Indus Civilization".[36] The clarification and amplification can be fully realized only when we note that fire-altars where offerings were burnt were special to the "Indo-Germanic" culture in antiquity.[37] They transmit to the Harappa Culture a distinctly "Aryan" colour.

Notes and References

1. "The Aryans, the Domesticated Horse and the Spoked Chariot-wheel", *Journal of the Asiatic Society of Bombay.* Bhau Daji Special Volume, Vol.. 38. pp. 44-68.
2. "New Light on Harappans", *The Sunday Standard* (Madras), August 25, 1974, Magazine Section, pp. 1, col. 2.
3. "The Pre-historic Period", *An Advanced History of India,* edited by R.C. Majumdar, H.C. Raychaudhuri and Kalikinkar Datta (Macmillan and Co., London, 1953) pp. 22.
4. *A History of Sanskrit Literature* (William Heinemann Ltd., London, 1928), pp. 151.
5. *Op. cit.,* pp. 132, fn. 1.
6. *Op. cit.*, pp. 15, col. 1.
7. *Mohenjo-daro and the Indus Civilisation* (London, 1967), I, pp. 110 ff.
8. *On the Veda* (Sri Aurobindo Ashram, Pondicherry, 1956), pp. 436-37.
9. *The secret of the Veda,* pp. 112.
10. *Ibid.*, pp. 263.
11. *Ibid.*, pp. 268-69.
12. "Proto-Indian Culture", *The Cultural Heritage of India* (The Ramakrishna Mission. Old Edition, Calcutta 1937), III, pp. 57-8.
13. "Religion and Philosophy", *The Vedic Age*, pp. 376.
14. *Ibid.*, pp. 395.
15. *Op. cit.*, pp. 112-13.

16. *Op.cit.*, pp. 376.
17. *Op. cit.*,pp. 414, with fn. 2.
18. *Ibid.*, pp. 296-97.
19. *The Hymns of the Rigveda,* translated with a Popular Commentary by Ralph T.H. Griffith (the Chowkhamba Sanskrit Series Office. Varanasi, 1971), vol. 1. pp. 59-60.
20. *Ibid.*, pp. 59 fn. to verse 1.
21. *Ibid.*, pp. 300.
22. *Ibid.*, fn. to verse 8.
23. *Ibid.*, Vol. II. pp. 523.
24. *The Linguistic Survey of India,* Vol. IV, pp. 279.
25. *Dravidian Theories,* pp. 137-38, 139.
26. *Ibid.*, pp. 138-40.
27. *Op. cit.,* pp. 333.
28. *Ibid.*
29. *Ibid.*
30. *Ibid.*, pp. 334.
31. "Germanien", *Monatshefte fur Germannenkunde,* 1940, pp. 212f.
32. "Religion and Philosophy", *The Vedic Age,* pp. 373.
33. H.C. Raychaudhuri, "The Early Vedic Age", *An Advanced History of India,* pp. 39, 27, 24.
34. *Op. cit.*, pp. 376, col. 2.
35. *Ibid.*, pp. 350, col. 2.
36. *Ibid.*, pp. 351, col. 1.
37. *Encyclopaedia of Religion and Ethics,* edited by James Hastings (T. & T. Clark, Edinburgh, 1925), Vol. 1, "Altars", pp. 333-34.

16

The Aryan Problem : A Linguistic Reappraisal

Dr. Satya Swarup Mishra*

The Date of Rgveda (RV)**

The evidences, both linguistic and archaeological, propose a very early date of RV than accepted at present.

Since the borrowed elements in the Uralic languages show borrowed *Rgvedic* forms in 5000 BC, the date of RV must be beyond 5000 BC. The other evidences also indirectly help for the same. The archaeological evidence analysed by Ghirshman, also speaks of the presence of Indo-Aryans much before that in their own area, i.e., India. The linguistic evidence in Anatolian borrowings shows that the Indo Aryan forms attested in them are much later than Vedic. They are Middle Indo-Aryan forms or the forms belong to a language transitional between OIA and MIA. Thus they are also helpful evidences to assert the chronology suggested by Uralic borrowings. The borrowings in other areas, in Chinese, in Korean, in Pamir, in Caucasian etc. also help us in understanding that the Aryans were going out of India again and again in different periods to different areas. The language of Indo-Aryan was definitely *Rgvedic* type by 5000 BC.

If the language of the Indus seals was Indo-Aryan as the decipherment of S.R. Rao claims, our analysis of the Indo-Aryan language presented by S.R. Rao shows that this language was also of a transitional stage between OIA and MIA and partly akin to the language of Indo-Aryan borrowings to the Anatolian. Thus, the language of *Rgvedic* Sanskrit belongs to a much earlier date than those of Anatolian borrowings.

---

* Professor and Head, Deptt. of Linguistics, Benaras Hindu University Varanasi. Author of many books including "*New light on Indo-European Comparative Grammar*": *The above taken from his "The Aryan Problem: A Linguistic Approach*" (N. Delhi, 1992).

** See all Abbreviations at the end of the article.

It may further be noted that mere calculation helps us to fix the linguistic chronology of Epic Sanskrit, since this from the point of view of the development of language must belong to date which is almost a midpoint between the date of RV and the date of MIA. Therefore, Epic Sanskrit may be placed accordingly in 3500 BC. The language of the *Ramayana* and the *Mahabharata* do not differ much from the linguistic point of view. Since traditionally *Ramayana* belongs to an earlier date, we may tentatively put *Ramayana* in 3500 BC or a bit earlier and *Mahabharata* in 3000 BC or a bit earlier say 3100 BC, which would agree with the date of *Kali* era.

The PGW culture belongs to a much later date although it is found in *Mahabharata* sites. It presents no evidence of *Mahabharata* war or any other cultural item of the *Mahabharata* period, which we know from the literature. Therefore, the chronology presented by PGW culture need not necessarily be accepted as the chronology of *Mahabharata.* Our chronology of course deals with the language of *Mahabharata.* It has no direct relation with the *Mahabharata* war.

Therefore, the date of RV as suggested above is to be taken as earlier than 5000 BC. The consideration of a common origin of Dravidians and Indo-Aryans, if acceptable, may take Indo-Aryan (which in fact will be Proto-Dravido-Indo-European or Proto-Dravido-Indo-Aryan) to a few millennia back say 8th or 9th millennium BC.

The generally accepted chronology of 1500 BC or 2000 BC for RV is now to be dispensed with in favour of the new linguistic evidence presented above.

Original Home of Aryans

Discovery of Sanskrit led to the discovery of the Indo-European language family. Soon after the question of original home of the Indo-European speech community came in. First of all scholars thought of India. But soon the place was shifted to Pamir. Still later the northern shore of Caspian Sea, as suggested by Schrader, was more or less widely accepted. This is bit central to the modern Indo-European speech community and it contains the linguistic characteristic of an original home for the Indo-European speech community. But it seems that this is widely accepted mainly because of the second point, i.e., it is centrally located and scholars prefer it for a sort of common emotional prejudice. The common linguistic characteristics are also applicable to India to a great extent. But India was not preferred, perhaps on two main grounds: India was a good place to settle down. Why should people leave it and go out to places like Europe which are inferior for habitation. Secondly,

India was not liked as original home of Indo-Europeans by many European scholars, purely on emotional grounds.

The characteristic of an original home of Indo-European speech community, as determined on linguistic evidence is almost fully present in India, as shown below.

Comparative linguistic evidence shows that people at the original home knew the following items.

1. They knew snow, compare Sanskrit *hima,* Av *zima*, Gk *kheima,* Lat *Hiems,* Lith *Ziema,* OCs *zima*, Arm *jiwn.*

2. They knew the following trees.

Birch: compare Sanskrit *bhûrja,* Ossetic barz, NE birch, Dacian place name bersovia, Latin fraxinus 'ash', OHG bircha, NHG birke, OE birce, Lith berzas, Russ bereza, Willow: Av vaetay, Gk itea, Lat Vitis vine, OHG wida, Lith vytis.

Pine: compare Sanskrit *pÏta-daru,* Gk pitus, Alb pishe, Lat pinus.

3. They knew the following animals.

Horse: compare Sanskrit *asva*, Av *aspa*, Tokh *yakwe*, yuk, Gk *hippos*, Venetic *ecu-peoaris*, 'charioteer', Lat quus, O Irish *ech*, OE *ech*, Lith *asva* mare.

Bear: compare Sanskrit *rksa*, Av *aresa*, Arm *arj*, Gk *arktos*, Alb *ari*, Lat *urus*. Mid Irish art.

Hare: compare Sanskrit *sasa*, Afgan *soya*, *soe*, Welsh *ceinach*, OHG *haso*, NE *hare*, O Pruss *sasins*.

Wolf: compare Sanskrit *vrka*, Av *vehrka*, Arm *gayl*, Gk *lukos*, Lat *lupus*, Goth *wulfs*, NE *wolf*, Lith *vikas*, OCS *vluku.*

4. They knew the following metals.

Gold : compare Sanskrit *hataka, hiranya,* Av *zaranya*, NE gold.

Silver : compare Sanskrit *rajata* Av *r zata*, Gk *arguros*.

Iron : compare Sanskrit *ayas*, Av *ayah*, Lat aes, copper, Gaulish *Isarno*, OHG *isarn,* NHG *eisen, iren* NE *iron.*

Copper : Sanskrit *lauha* (later iron), Middle Persian *rod*, Lat *raudus.*

Copper and iron are often confused and they overlap.

Therefore, from this point of view India cannot be ruled out as an original homes of Aryans or of the Indo-European speech community. But the area near Caspian Sea seems to have been chosen chiefly on the basis of the place being a bit central to the modern Indo-European speech communities, as stated above.

The theory that the Aryans came from outside to India at about 1500 BC and were responsible for destruction of the Indus valley civilization, is now no longer accepted. This theory is not only a child's dream, but it is a good example to show how, many scholars in the West have, without sufficient study, posed to make such monstrous remarks on Indian civilization. The epithet of Indra, the *Purandara*, is the basis for such conclusion. It is, however, a good sign that no one accepts it. The fire-altars in other sites of Indus civilization, now show it to be Indo-Aryan. Thus, now there is no point to think that the Aryans destroyed the Indus civilization. It was their own civilization and much later than the *Vedic* type. Since the date of RV is now accepted to 5000 BC at least, if not earlier and we have sufficient evidence of borrowings of Indo-Aryan forms and cultures outside India in different periods including 5000 BC and later, we have to admit that Indo-Aryans were going outside in the *Rgveda* stage and later stages again and again, may be through the Himalayan passes or sea routes etc.

I have already shown that, it would be a highly farfetched approach to think that the borrowed elements of Indo-Aryan found outside India, in various parts of Asia and Europe viz., in the Uralic languages, in Antolian records, in Pamiri, in Chinese and in Korean etc. were taken from the Indo-Aryan people while they were moving from Caspian area to India. It is a normal and sane way of thinking, that there was a contact with Indian Indo-Aryan people and the people of these places, as the Indo-Aryan were coming to these places from India, in different periods. There are borrowed elements from *Rgvedic*, later *Vedic*, Classical Sanskrit and Middle Indo-Aryan. Thus, there was Indo-Aryan contact with the outside world again and again.

I have also shown that a concrete evidence of the movement of Indo-Aryan outside India can be cited with a new Indo-Aryan speaking group, the Gypsies, who left India a few centuries before the Christian era, before Asoka's[1] time in 3rd or 4th century BC. Variations of the Gypsy languages are attested in different parts of Europe and Asia which shows that after migrating from India, they spread to different parts of Asia and Europe just like their forefathers who were going to different parts of the world in Middle Indo-Aryan period, in Classical Sanskrit period, in various states of the *Vedic* period, in the Indo Iranian period and perhaps also in the Indo-European period. The dialectal distributions of the Gypsy languages show that they spread to these places and settled there. Since migration of the Indo-Aryans from India was possible in the NIA stage, it may be inferred that it was equally possible in early stages. At this stage there may be a question that what is the evidence for actual migration from India to the out side world except the linguistic borrowings. Again the answer is the lingustic position of Romani. Now on linguist doubts that the Gypsis migrated from India. There is no recorded history for their migration. The linguistic analysis only sheds light on their Indo-Aryan origin. Similarly, for the earlier stages also linguistic evidence should be our guide. When we have MIA borrowings in a language outside India, we have to assume that the MIA speakers came to this place from India. When we have OIA borrowings in a language outside India, we have to assume that the OIA speakers came to this place from India.

Similarly, it may be assumed that in the Indo-Iranian stage also the Aryans had India as their original home, *airyanm vaejo,* i.e., India. As shown above the Iranians speak of movements form one to another area, and thereby produce evidence for their migration from another place to Iran. On the otherhand, Indo-Aryans never produce evidence for migration from another place to India.

To review the evidences presented above it may be summarised that Gypsies left India in 3rd or 4th century BC, which opens the possibility of the assumption that the Aryans were going outside India. Since we have linguistic evidence for presence of Indo-Aryans outside India in different periods including the earliest linguistic evidence of their presence outside India in 5000 BC, it may be assumed that they were going outside India again and again. Before this Indo-Aryan period, the Aryans migrated to Iran as inferred from the evidence of a literary analysis of the Iranian literature.

Although, evidences lead us to assume migration in the Indo-Aryan stage and the Indo-Iranian stage, it indirectly leads us to assume migrations of Aryans from India to the outside world in the Indo European stage in several waves. This assumption is based on the following analysis.

It is well-known that the discovery of Sanskrit finally led to the discovery of Indo-European language family. Indo-European comparative grammar was worked out keeping Sanskrit as the living model no. 1 which Bloomfield has clearly pointed out.[2] The Western scholars, in the beginning reconstructed Indo-European almost with slight, modification of Sanskrit. To illustrate we may quote here reconstructions from Schleicher who reconstructed only one primary vowel, i.e., *a* as against the later reconstruction of *a, e, o* as by Brugmann etc. He also reconstructed only one series of gutturals as against the three series of gutturals reconstructed later on by Brugmann etc. A few examples may be cited with reconstructions of Schleicher and Brugmann contrasted: e.g., *kas:* q^{w} *os,* 'who' (compare Sanskrit *kah*), ka: q^{w}e, 'and' (compare Sanskrit *ca*), katvāras: q^{w}etweres, 'four' (compare Sanskrit *catvārah*) kankan: penq^{w}e, 'five' (compare Sanskrit *paṇca*), kard: kerd, 'heart' (compare Sanskrit srad) etc.[3] Thus, originally the starting point for Indo-European comparative grammar was Sanskrit. Naturally first of all scholars might have thought the original place for Indo-European to be India. Somehow a complex might have not allowed them to express the fact which is clear when we analyse the following statement of Gray.[4]

> The original home of Proto-Indo-European is a problem on which no agreement has yet been reached. The earliest investigators were quite certain that it was in Asia, the continent which was the source of oldest civilization, the traditional site of the garden of Eden, and where Sanskrit was spoken. Later the concensus opinion shifted to Europe. The home has been in a narrow strip from France across Central Europe and the Kirghiz Steppes to the Iranian plateau; in the wide steppes of South Russia north of Black Sea between the Volga and the mouth of the Danube; along the Baltic, in Lower Saxony, i.e., the area between the frontier of Holland and the Oder, and between southern Scandinavia and Thuringia and on the northern slopes of the Caucasus.

Thus, Gray also has fully realised that first of all India was staken to be the original home of the Proto-Indo-European speech community. But he has avoided the word India. He prefers the word 'Asia', 'the place where Sanskrit was spoken', etc. This clearly shows although India was clearly in view, the Western scholars had a strong hesitation to accept it. Soon after, India was dropped and the original home was searched in Pamir, Caspian Sea etc., inspite of the fact that the most original and orthodox Indo-European speech, Sanskrit was spoken in India. No strong ground has ever been shown for dropping India.

The following ground may be assumed for dropping India. This was a nice place to live. People would not like to go to places like Europe which was half-civilized in such early days. But I have shown above that we have evidence of movement of Aryans from India to the outside world on several occasions, in NIA, MIA and OIA stages and perhaps also in the Indo Iranian stage. Therefore, migration of the people in still earlier stages is quite likely. Besides there is no evidence of Aryans coming to India from an outside world. Thus, there is no evidence from Indo-Aryan sources that the Aryans came to India from outside. There is also no evidence of their spreading from north-western part of India to other parts of India. Many modern books describe that the Aryans came from outside through the north-west and from that area they gradually spread to other parts of India. I have searched thoroughly and found no archaeological evidence for this type of hypothesis. There is no literary evidence for the same in *Vedic* and classical. *Manusamhita* which is a *Smriti* and therefore belongs to a considerably late date gives us the description of Brahmavarta, Brahmarsidesa and Aryavarta, but never speaks of the spread of Aryans from one to the other. The description of the three areas has an altogether different basis. Therefore, we have no evidence for even spread of Aryans from one to another area in India.

On the other hand, there is definite evidence of spread of Aryans (or Indo-Europeans) in different parts of Europe. There is also evidence that an area was peopled by other tribes and was subsequently occupied by the Indo-European speaking tribes (such as Greeks). There is no evidence that one Indo-European speaking tribe (such as Celtic), was wide spread in an area which was driven away by another Indo. European speaking tribe (such as Italic and Germanic).

A brief sketch may be presented here without going into greater details. As far as the Hellenic branch of Indo-European is concerned, it is said that they destroyed the Minoan civilization and that they were rude barbarians. But after they settled in Greece they mastered the arts of the people they had subjugated.[5] Thus, the Greeks were invaders and came to Greece from outside. Besides "Numerious inscriptions in non-Greek languages prove beyond every doubt the existence of an older civilization in the Aegean world. Some of them are written in alphabets which are yet unknown and therefore, cannot even be read. Such non-Greek inscriptions in Crete prove that the Eteocretans, mentioned in the Odysseus, were still living there in the 4th century BC. The inscriptions definitely prove that the Eteorcretans, (i.e., Original Cretans) were a pre-Indo-European race inhabiting not only Crete and the Aegean islands, but also the mainland of Greece but the Eteocretans were not the only the pre-Greek inhabitants of Greece. An inscription of the 6th century BC discovered in Lemons shows remarkable similarities with Etruscan. All these definitely prove that there was a vast substratum of pre-Greek languages and culture on which was foisted at a later date the ruder civilization of the early Greek. The range of this pre-Greek culture extended from Asia Minor to Italy, including all the Aegean islands."[6] Thus, there is sufficient evidence that the Indo-European speaking Greek people were invaders into Greece from outside.

The Celtic branch of Indo-European was fortunate enough to spread over a large part of the Europe in the beginning. "At a time when Latin was no more than a local dialect, Celtic language was used over a vast area from Britian to Spain and from Spain to Danubian plain and beyond. But their was an unlucky star. And it was Latin which was destined to strike the mass telling blows against Celtic to storm its main strongholds on the continent and finally to isolate it in the less accessible parts of the British Isles".[7] "Judging by references in Greek writings and by archaeological evidence, Celtic tribes-man began to move into the Balkan area and settled among Illyrians and Thracians during the course of the 4th century BC...".[8] Thus, the Celtic people came from outside to Europe and were later driven away by Italic speaking people.

That the Italic people were invaders is well-known. As shown above they have driven away the Celtic speakers from a large part of Europe.

The Hittites present archaeological evidence which shows that before the Hittite invasion to the area it was peopled by another tribe called Hattic. The Indo-Aryan local words in Hittite documents have been discussed above which prove that Indo-Aryans were going to that area even after the Hittites were settled there. It is therefore, likely that the Hittite speakers might have gone there in very early days from an original home (which was perhaps India) and before these Hittite people, the Hattic people were residing there and finally the conqueror and conquered had been amalgamated.[9]

The Slavonic people also present enough evidence that they were invaders. 'The Slavs have expanded enormously at the expense of the speakers of Finno-Ugrian and Baltic languages. The Volga was Finnish and so also the Don area and Moscow. In the north the Baltic Lithunians held the basins of the Neimen and the Dvino. It is significant that Novgorod situated in this region means 'new town'. None of these wild tracts could, therefore, have been included in the original hibitant of the Slavs, which according to Niederle's widely accepted theory, should have originally comprised eastern Poland, the south of white Russia and the north of Ukraine. In modern Russian the word 'Ukarine' means 'beyond the frontier'. This shows that due to later political changes, a part of which was probably the original homeland of the Slavs came to be regarded as a foreign country by the Russians. Radiating from this comparatively narrow homeland, the Slavs have gradually expanded to the heart of Europe in the west and upto Vladivostok in the east despite the fact that the Slav territories were repeatedly ravaged by Mongolian hordes.[10] Thus, the Slavonic people also spread this way they present some evidence of their movement from an outside world to the Slavonic areas.

The Germanic speaking Indo-Europeans present evidence for spreading to different parts of Europe much later. "At the time when Celtic dominated in Western and Central Europe and was making its impact on Mediterranean countries, Germany was still effectively isolated in its northern home and scarcely noticed by the classical world until the closing years of the 2nd century BC. It was then that the migrating Cimbri and Teutones made their war-like appearances in Cisalpine Gaul. All the same, Germanic tribesmen had been in touch with Mediterranean civilization before this".[11]

The spreading of Germanic people also speaks of their possibility of coming from an outside world.

Much has been said about the movement of Iranians from India to Iran. Some material is presented above about several Indo-European branches which speaks of the possibility of their spreading from another area to their present area. The Indo-Aryans present no such evidence. On the otherhand Iranians present evidence that the Indo-Aryans were going to that area from India. the Finno-Ugrian contact with Indo-Aryans speak of the movement of Vedic Aryans from India to that area.

Therefore, it is likely that the Pre-*Vedic* Aryans also might have gone out from India in several waves.

The migrations from India to the outside world might have taken the following order. The Centum speakers might have left India first of all, of course gradually in several waves. Out of the Satem speakers Armenian left first, then Albanian, next Baltic followed by Slavonic. The Iranian people were the last to leave India. This order is based on the linguistic analysis of relative affinity with Sanskrit. Similarly out of the Centum groups Greek might have left India last of all.

Notes and References

1. Ralph L. Turner, "The Position of Romani in Indo-Aryan", *Collected papers,* pp. 269.
2. L. Bloomfield's review article in *Language,* vol. V, 1929, pp. 270.
3. S.S.Misra, *NLIECG,* pp. 37.
4. Louis H. Gray, *op. cit.*, pp. 304-5.
5. B.K. Ghosh, *A Survey of Indo-European Languages,* pp. 33.
6. *Ibid.*, pp. 35.
7. W.B. Lockwood, *A Panorama of Indo-European Languages,* pp. 62.
8. *Ibid.*, pp. 62
9. Sturtevant, *Comparative Grammar of the Hittite Language,* rev. edn., pp. 4.
10. B.K. Ghosh, *op. cit.*, pp. 148.
11. W.B. Lockwood, *op. cit.*, pp. 95.

Abbreviations

Alb	Albanian,
Arm	Armenian,
Av	Avestan
Cer	Ceremis,
Finn	Finnish,
Gk	Greek,
IE	Indo-European,,
IIr	Indo-Iranian,
Lat	Latin,
Lith	Lithuanian,
MIA	Middle Indo-Aryan,
NE	New English,
NHG	New High German,
NIA	New Indo-Aryan,
NLIECG	*New Lights on Indo-European Comparative Grammar*;
OCS	Old Church Slavic,
OE	Old English,
OHG	Old High German,
OIA	Old Indo-Aryan,
O Irish	OldIrish,
Russ	Russian,
Skt	Sanskrit,
Tokh	Tokhavian.

17

On Colours and Classes: The Invasion Myth*

Nisha Rathore**

The writings on caste and class have recently sprung into existence like mushrooms. The Western anthropologists, sociologists and historians have recently written more on caste than even the philosophers. A contemporary Western scholar finds the Indian caste system as an archaic phenomenon. And he is attracted towards this curious Indian phenomenon, and wishes to record it before it disappears from history. The attitude of the contemporary Western Scholars is only slightly different from the attitude of the British officials of India who acted as the anthropologists, sociologists and historians at the close of the 19th century. The revolt of 1857 led the British officials to "learn something of the life of the uncivilized races", the races which were at "the lower stages of culture".[1] These official academicians discovered that the Indian people "were a living memorial of the past", and hence worked with a view that "the past, once lost, can never be recovered".[2] In their writings the contemporary Western scholars continue to have this attitude.

The myth which is most popular for analyzing the caste-system among the contemporary Western scholars is the myth of the 'conquerors and the conquered'. This myth was used by the British officials sometimes after the revolt of 1857. Of course these officials had the blessings of so

---

* The Possibility of Sanskritization, or the upward mobility of a caste, presupposes the rejection of the definition of "varna" in terms of "colour". So the present paper is in support of my earlier paper on "Hinduization, Sanskrtization, De-*Brahmanization* and the Oudh peasant Revolt of 1921", *New Quest*, No. 83, September-October 1990. I thank Professor K.N. Chitnis, Head of the History Department, University of Poona, for his encouraging remarks on this paper.

** Young researcher in History at Hyderabad University. The article was first published in th bimonthly "*New Quest*" May-June 1991.

many European scholars, including the great indologist, Max Muller. The British wished to show that their invasion of India was only the second great event, the first great event being its invasion by the Indo-Aryans or Indo-Iranians. The educated elite of India continues to accept this myth in spite of all the odds against it, such odds as the discovery of Harappan people and the exposure of the motive of the British to distort the history of the Indian people. In order to obtain currency the official Myth tries to justify itself through *Purusasukta* which is accepted by the Hindus for the origin of four varnas.

The official myth considers 'caste' as an English synonym of '*Jati*', it only tries to define and interpret the concept of '*Varna*'. The propounders of this myth define '*Varna*' in terms of 'colour'. *The Census Report of India,* 1911, mentions Manu's 'four *varnas*' as "four colours".[3] And the report further adds concerning these colours that "they are classes, not castes in any sense of the term".[4] According to this view the emergence of castes exhibits the degradation of Hindu society which was originally a society with the class distinctions (colour distinctions?)

Before we proceed further it may be interesting to point out that even Risley, one of the most reputed British officials, considers Aryan invasion of India as a myth. As he says:[5]

> The 'Aryan brother' is indeed a much more mythical being than Rama or Krishna, or any other of the popular heroes of Hindu tradition whom writers of the Aryan school have vainly striven to attenuate into solar myths.

Yet Risley has treated the white Aryan brother as a historical figure and Rama and Krishna as mythical figures. This is an exhibition of contradiction in the colonial thinking. One can have glimpses of truth in the system of lies propounded by the colonial thinkers.

In order to study the official myth we will discuss the views of Max Weber. Though Weber is not the propounder of this myth he has accepted this myth without questioning it. Weber has been chosen for discussion simply because he continues to have impact on the Indian academic world. Weber considers the development of caste-system in India in terms of the invasion of India by the Aryan hordes. The Aryans conquered the original inhabitants of India and converted them into their *dasas*. As Weber writes:[6]

> Only the antagonism of the *Arya* and the *Dasyu* appears in the ancient *Vedic* period. The name *Arya* remains as a term for the distinguished, the 'gentleman'. The *Dasyu* was the dark coloured enemy of the invading conqueror.

This kind of analysis has been accepted by most of the great historians who have written on India recently. As the late Professor A.L. Basham writes that the Aryans had:[7]

> a sense of solidarity against the *Dasas* or *Dasyus*, who evidently represent the survivors of the Harappa culture, and kindred people of the Punjab and the North-West.

Similar views have been expressed by Professor Romila Thapar who says, referring to the age of invasion by the Aryans, that "society was divided into two main groups, the *Arya-varna* and *Dasa-varna*".[8]

First, Weber, Basham and Romila Thapar have not used the word '*Asura*' which is a synonym or near-synonym of the word '*Dasyu*'. There is an easy transition from *Dasyu* to *Dasa,* but no such transition from *Asura* to *Dasa*. Secondly, Weber does not refer to the conquered people as the *survivors* of 'Harappan culture' and 'kindred people of Punjab' as does Basham. The Harappan culture has come to light in the twentieth century. When the European scholars were preparing the story of Indo-Iranian invasion of India, they were ignorant of the dead Harappans. Max Muller is no exception. He too was ignorant of Harappa. In their ignorance of the past of India the British officials baptized the Indian races into the Aryan type, the Australoid type and the Mongoloid type. As their baptism of races suggests, these races originally belonged to the foreign lands, and they invaded India at different points of time. The history of India was made to look as if it is a land of invasions; it is an invader's paradise, the British were the last to enter not this paradise. The British biographers of the Indian races never thought that beneath the Indian soil are buried the civilized people. They thought that the buried people did not make any advancement over their stone implements, and hence posed no challenge to the invading forces, for the invading forces had iron weapons with them. But the buried Indians posed a real challenge to the invading forces, for the buried could not be enslaved, either physically or mentally.

Crooke's knowledge of Max Muller and Risley coupled with his own study of the *Vedic* hymns made him accept that "from the earliest times the vallet of the Five Rivers must have been the land of the white man. Here the Aryans did not intermarry with the dark daughters of Heth".[9] How very distanced is the view of Crooke from the view of Basham! For Crooke not only North-West but even Punjab was free from the clash of white with black races. In Punjab the Aryans had their white wives, and did not come in contact with the natives. It is only when the Aryans moved towards the east and the south of the valley of the Five Rivers that they came in contact with the natives. As Crooke further writes, "If caste, as many authorities believe, was the result of the clash of a white with a black race, it could not have originated in this region."[10] Thus the region of Punjab was purely an Aryan region, for the Aryans had no war with the natives in this region.

What about the Harappans? Who fought and defeated the Harappans? If the foreign invaders, then they must have come from outside Harappa. If these foreign invaders were the same as the Indo-Iranians then they could not have reached Punjab without losing their purity of blood. In such a situation Punjab could not have remained 'the land of the white man'. For prior to their reaching Punjab the foreign Aryans had already clashed with the Harappans. It is certainly not the Iranian-Aryans but the Indian-Aryans from Punjab who had clash with the Harappans.

The Jigsaw puzzle of Aryan invasion is solved. Punjab must be accepted as the original homeland of the Aryans, call them Indo-Aryans if you like. They remained pure in Punjab because Punjab was the cradle of their culture, the *Rigvedic* culture. Because of the excessive population a time came when the Aryans of Punjab branched off into two directions, one going towards the south-east and the other moving towards the north-west of Punjab. Those Aryans who moved towards the north-west of Punjab clashed with the Harappans, and those Aryans who were moving towards the south-east of Punjab clashed with the other Indian races and tribes. It is only in this way that Punjab could retain its white colour. The Aryans remained white in Punjab because of its cold climate; its climate produces a whiter complexion. The war between Aryans and non-Aryans (*Asuras*, *Dasyus*, etc.) is a *national* issue rather than an *international* event. The Aryans were Indians and so were coming from different climatic conditions. India is a vast country where geographical conditions differ. According to *Rigvedic* tradition "the *Devas* (gods) and Asuras both of them sprang from the creator Prajapati."[11] It is no surprise that the Aryans have described the non-Aryans as snubnosed and bull-lipped, etc., described them in all kinds of derogatory ways. But we should not be surprised about it. An enemy is described as a demon. But once he is defeated, and the war is over, he does not remain a demon. The victors establish matrimonial relationship with the defeated enemies.

The move of the Official Historians to change the venue of the first war between Aryans and *Dasyus* will not do. According to the revised version of the Official view it is not the Indo-Gangetic plain or the Central India where the clash between the Aryans and the *Dasyus* occurred first time. The venue of the first clash was Harappa. Basham considers

Harappa as the place where the Indo-Iranians clashed with the *Dasyus*, by equating *Dasyus* with the Dravidians. But the excavations of Harappa acquired a multi-racial character. After the discovery of 57 graves by Sir Martimer Wheeler in 1945, it is now maintained that the Harappans were of several racial type, some of them were Dravidians (Australoid type). But the Dravidians alone did not dominate the scene, for there were also the races of the Mediterranean type, Mongoloid type and the Alpine type. This shows that the term '*Dasyus*', like the term '*Asura*', is only a synonym of the term 'enemy', and the descriptions of the *Dasyus* in derogatory terms are only a part of the propaganda machinery.

The multi-racial people of Harappa were certainly not demons. Basham himself accepts that "Harappa was the meeting place of many races".[12] But this implies that the situation of Harappa was not at all different from the situation of India in the 20th century. Since the days of Harappa India has remained a multi-racial country. There is no doubt that the races of India had their points of concentration. The Aryans concentrated in Punjab, Dravidians in the south and the Mongoloids in the Himalayas. But there is no reason to think that these races were not moving around and forming multi-racial and multi-lingual groups and cultures. The different races of India had their points of contact. The Indus civilization is the best example of the achievement of multi-racial groups and cultures. The different races of India brought their own experiences and succeeded in doing what they could not have done singly. Neither the Aryans alone, nor the Dravidians alone nor the Mongoloids alone could have achieved what they achieved when they came in contact with one another on the places where the Harappan culture is spread out. When the people belonging to different races came together some of them certainly became multi-lingual. According to Kosambi Brahui language is undoubtedly of the Dravidian origin, but the "Brahuis are not of the Dravidian race".[13] He further points out that "The Brahui language in the North-West is a solitary Dravidian 'island' among speakers of Aryan languages".[14] Though it is an island, it is a very significant island. For, it shows the mobility of the races of India, and also the possibility of one race adopting the language of the other race. From the ancient times Indians had a secular outlook.

It seems that after defeating the Indus people the Aryans from Punjab moved further to the North-West of Indus. As Basham accepts that "some of the inhabitants of the Indus cities were of a type widely found further to the west".[15] This shows that the Indian Aryans moved towards Iran, and after running over Iran they reached the mountains north of the Mesopotamian Plain. While running over Iran the Aryans carried with them their early *Rigvedic* thought which includes the distinction between *daevas* and *Asuras*. The Aryan-Iranian hostility is well known. Since the Aryans worshiped *daevas* the Iranians (Zoroastrians) started considering them as demons. And the demons of the Aryans, i.e., *Asuras,* became the objects of worship for the Zoroastrians. The Zoroastrian term '*Ahura*' is derived from '*Asura*'. Referring to the distinction between *Daevas* and *Asuras* developed in India and Iran, Zaehner point out:[16]

> The two different classes of deity met with a very different fate in the sister civilizations: for whereas, in India, the *asuras* were gradually reduced to the status of demons and the *daevas* alone retained their divinity, in Iran it was the *Ahuras* who retained their divine character and the *daevas* who were reduced to demonhood.

In changing the Aryan gods into demons, and the Aryan demons into gods, the Iranians were showing anger against the invading Aryans. The enemy of one's enemy is one's friend, and the friend of one's enemy is one's enemy. The Indian Aryans also invaded Mesopotamia is proved by the fact that the Mittani tribe settled there worshiped *Varuna.* This tribe, according to Ninian Smart, "inhabited mountains north of the Mesopotamian plain."[17] Varuna, according to an Aryan tradition, is an *Asura*. Thus, Asuras were given the highest regard outside India because they stood as symbols of hostility against the invading Aryans. But there is no doubt that in spite of the negative reactions the invading Aryans left their marks on the tribes and races of the Western countries.

Instead of seeing the movement of the Indian Aryans towards Iran and the West, the British biographers of the Indian races have been propagating the invasion of India by the West. Crooke's worry is the retention of the Aryan purity in Punjab. How could Punjab retain its white colour? There is no worry, no problem to be solved, if it is accepted that Punjab was the cradle of Indian-Aryan culture; it was the original home of the Aryans. In order to bring the foreign Aryans, the Indo Iranians, to Punjab Crooke remarks, "If the race remained pure in Punjab, in seems obvious that they must have been accompanied by their wives".[18] Crooke is clear about the fact that there was no clash between Aryans and non-Aryans till they reached Punjab. The safe route to Punjab is discovered via Baluchistan. As he says:[19]

> It is assumed that a migration of this kind could not have been accomplished through the north-western passes, like the Khyber, which offers a difficult route for the heavily laden caravans. It has, therefore, been suggested that they used the southern route through Baluchistan.

But this kind of solution and wild guess makes sense only when one is ignorant of the Indus people. Indo-Aryans or Iranians could have avoided the Indus people only in one way. The way is air-lift from the Tehran airport to the Chandigarh airport. If the Indo-Iranians had come with their families by air, then, they would have certainly avoided the surface-based Indus people. But not only their wives and white children, even their horses are required to be air-lifted. The horses too are supposed to have come from outside India. The Aryans, their iron weapons, their *Rigvedic* thoughts, and all the items of a superior culture and civilization were brought to India from outside. At the time of the Aryan invasion India had nothing but the demons inhabiting the thick forests. Then what attracted the Aryans to come here? They should have gone to some better place.

Suppose it is accepted that the original Aryans were foreigners, and not the indigenous people of Punjab, the question arises why were they not diffused with the natives, and remained white till they reached central India and other parts of the country? What led to the introduction of the caste-system in India, when the Aryans invaded other parts of the world without introducing any such system? In order to answer these questions Weber compares the Aryan invasion of India with the invasion of Anglo-Saxons by the Normans. As he points out:[20]

> The most striking contrast in external appearance happens to be different skin colour. Although the conquerors replenished their insufficient supply of women from among the conquered, colour differences still prevented a fusion in the manner of the Normans and Anglo-Saxons.

Normans had the same colour as the Anglo-Saxons. Therefore, fusion occurred. But the Aryans had a different colour altogether from the non-Aryans, and therefore, fusion did not occur. But fusion did occur at a later stage. The later development of four *varnas* goes back to the ultimate fusion of white with black colour. Weber accepts the usual distinction "by typical skin colour: *Brahmans*, white; *Kshatriyas*, red; *Vaishyas*, yellow; *Shudras*, black".[21] The evolution of four different skin colours is the result of interbreeding. As the Indian historian Nirpendra Kumar Dutt writes with approval:[22]

> The *Brahmanas* were white, the *Kshatriyas* red, and the *Vaishyas* because the large absorption of black blood were yellowish like the Mulatto's of America, and the *Shudras* black, as is described in *Mahabharata*.

Fortunately or unfortunately the conqueror-conquered myth can be obtained even if the Aryans were originally from Punjab rather than from Iran or any part of Europe. The climatic conditions of Punjab produce a whiter complexion. In order to contain white complexion it is not required for a race to travel from Europe to India. And then the

British officials themselves accept that interbreeding occurred outside Punjab where people had darker complexion.

To translate *varna* in terms of 'colour' is completely absurd. For 'colour' here refers to the skin-colour. We have to consider only the fusion of white skin with black skin, for the skin of Aryans was white and that of the non-Aryans black. But the fusion of white with black can produce only one new colour, in Dutt's example, the colour of American Mulattos. From where will come the colour called 'red', the skin-colour of *Kshatriyas*? Colour theory requires four colours, not three. The best example of the *varna* system is not the ancient India at the time of Aryan invasion but the present U.S.A. where people having all the four skin-colours are found, the European settlers, migrants from the countries of the far-east, the Red Indians who are the original inhabitants of America and the Negroes who were originally brought as slaves. The difficulty is not only about the genesis of the yellow colour which has been produced by combining white with black colour, but the most difficult situation is the genesis of the red-skinned *Kshatriyas*. What kind of interbreeding would lead to the production of *Kshatriyas*? And could they be considered as the result of interbreeding? For it is the *Kshatriyas* who fought and defeated the non-Aryans. Referring to the colour of the *Kshatriyas* and the *Vaishyas*, Morton Klass writes that the colour of the *Kshatriyas*:[23]

> was red, a colour many people identify with blood and therefore with violence. The *Vaisyas*, according to Manu, were concerned, among other things, with "trade and commerce, usury" and so it is not unreasonable that yellow, the colour of gold, is associated with them. And if not gold since *Vaisyas* also perform agriculture—the colour yellow might reflect ripening wheat.

These remarks clearly exhibit that the colour chart is applied not only to the human skins, rather it is applied to all kinds of material objects. If Klass is right then the *Kshatriyas* could very well be black, the only requirement is that they should be violent. So also the *Vaishays* are not required to have the colour of the American Mulattos, what is required is that they should be concerned with the business of wheat and gold. This is to give up the skin-colour theory. The views of Klass do not support the racial theory propounded by the official ethnologists.

While referring to the skin-colour of the races and tribes of North India, Crooke remarks, "The Northern India was peopled by three distinct strains—the white, the yellow, the black".[24] What happened to the red strain? Where has it disappeared? If the Northern Indians do not have red strain why describe the skin of *Kshatriyas* as red? If red is not considered as the skin-colour of *Kshatriyas* then why should white, yellow and black be considered as the skin-colours of *Brahmanas*, *Vaishyas* and *Shudras*?

So many historians have written and emphasized the point that the early Aryans stratified their society in terms of classes. It is only at a later stage that the stratification of society in terms of caste was accepted. In what way have the early Aryans stratified their society in terms of classes? The definition of 'class' has been reduced to its definition in terms of 'colour'. Consider the view of Basham again:[25]

> In India class stratification grew more rigid when, in *Vedic* period, a situation arose rather that prevailing in South Africa today, with a dominant fair minority striving to maintain its purity and supremacy over a darker majority.

To know the class-character of the *Vedic* Aryans Basham draws our attention to the present situation of South Africa.

If 'class' means 'colour of the skin of a person', as Basham clearly means to say, then the development of Hindu society in terms of *caste* is really its progressive step. In the case of *caste*, according to the Official doctrine, irrevocable occupation, endogamy, etc. are supposed to work rather than the colour of one's skin. This step gives up the colour prejudices, for 'colours' are restricted to 'classes'; they are not extended to castes. Then how can these historians also maintain that the evolution of castes is a backward step of the Hindu society?

Since ages Hindus have been talking about *varna*, not in terms of colour but in terms of *janma* (birth) and *karma* (action). Someone may be *Brahmana* by birth but *Kshatriya* by action, or a *Kshatriya* by birth but *Brahmana* by action. Similarly, Visvamitra is not cited as a *Kshatriya* by birth but *Brahmana* by action. When these descriptions are given the skin-colour of Parsuram or Visvamitra is not taken into consideration. The *Purusasukta,* which tells about the genesis of *varnas*, does not mean that *Purusa* is multicoloured, his head being white, arms red, thighs yellow and legs black, so that it gives birth to white *Brahmanas*, red *Kshatriyas*, yellow *Vaishyas* and black *Shudras*. The concept of *Purusa* is free from the colour descriptions. It is quite possible that in the beginning the decision about one's *varna* depended purely on action. At this stage there was no question about irrevocable occupation or endogamy. However, the Hindu society degenerated, and the *varna* came to be decided by birth. Once birth considerations became a rule rather than an exception, varna gave birth to caste or *jati*. Thus Manu describes the way in which different castes were produced from the original four *varnas*.

The *Purusasukta* model has been used by the historians according to their convenience. The British biographers of Indian races have interpreted it in such a way that it justifies their Aryan invasion theory.

The inconsistencies in the interpretation are over-looked. The translation of *varna*–hierarchy into colour-hierarchy can be accepted if it is further accepted that the Indo-Aryan armies which were advancing towards Harappa from some site in Iran had a number of Red Indian soldiers with them. So when the conquering armies "were compelled to take wives from the dark-skinned conquered races",[26] they produced the new skin-colours. When the invaders settled down in India, the Indo-Aryans became *Brahmanas*, Red Indian *Kshatriyas*, and the conquered black races were converted into the *Shudras*. The *Vaishyas* were produced as a result of interbreeding between the white Aryans and the black *Dasyus*. If we are faithful to the colour theory we can also successfully talk about the fifth *varna* which, according to the indologist, was later added to the four *varnas*. The fifth *varna* can be considered as the result of the inter-breeding between the Red Indians and the black Indians. The Red Indians too were part of the conquering forces and, therefore, they too should be provided with the native wives. Since '*varna*' means colour, fifth *varna* too must be considered as a colour, independent of all the other four colours. I do not know whether any historian is so revolutionary as to accept the colour theory on such terms. But this is the simplest way in which classes can be introduced in terms of colours.

People who migrate from one place to the other continue to remember their original homeland. The *Vedic* hymns clearly show that the original homeland of the Aryans was Punjab. One can identify the geographical features of Punjab in the *Vedic* literature. This literature does not exhibit at all that Germany or Yugoslavia was the homeland of the Aryans. Referring to the literary evidence of the Aryans even Crooke accepts, "When literary evidence—that of the *Vedic* hymns—begins, we find them settled in the Holy land of the Hindus in the South-Western Punjab".[27] Why settled? This evidence does not at all show that the Arynas came from outside Punjab. Rather the evidence shows that they moved from Punjab to other places. There is no doubt that the Aryans invaded Iran. From which direction did the invaders come is a matter to be decided. Either they came from the north-west of Iran, from some European country, or from the north-east of Iran, i.e. from the direction of India. For the Aryans who invaded Iran had the equipment of early *Rigvedic* thought, particularly the distinction between the *daevas* and the *Asuras*. Since those Aryans from India who invaded Iran were warriors other than philosophers, no further development of the *Vedic* thought occurred outside India. The *Vedic* thought developed fully only in India which was the cradle of their culture and civilization. The hierarchy of four *varnas*, the distinction between *varna* and *jati*, etc. were the product of those Indian-Aryans who continued staying in India, and moved only to other parts of India.

As happens with the invading forces, the Indian-Aryans who invaded Iran and later Mesopotamia and other parts of Europe were ultimately absorbed by the local races and tribes.

The Arya-*Dasyu* conflicts which occurred in India were more of an ideological kind. There is no doubt that the Aryans were in constant conflict with the *Dasyus*. This is for the reason that the ideology of *Dasyus* was very different from the ideology of the Aryans. *Dasyus* were pure consumerists. But the Aryans were not in a position to afford pure consumerism. They thought that consumerism without production would annihilate society. And production is possible only when there is land. The fact that the *Dasyus* accepted pure consumerism shows that they had considerable amount of land, and they were well established people. They already reached a stage of development where they could afford consumerism. Concerning the life of the *Dasyus*, Basham accepts that they lived in "fortified palaces called *pur*, of which the Aryan war-god Indra has destroyed hundreds".[28] Since the Aryans were not in a position to afford consumerism, they thought that the *Dasyu* way of life would lead to the annihilation of society. No society can survive without land, because land is the basis for production. Hence for the sake of preserving society, i.e. the Aryan society, *Dasyus* must be annihilated. Thus, the Aryan-*Dasyu* conflicts were not very different from the conflicts of ideologies going on today. It is quite misleading to consider them simply as racial conflicts. Not colours but food and land were responsible for these conflicts. The spiritual food is good, the Aryans had lot of it, but it does not fill stomachs. The search for food led the Aryans to invade *Dasyu* lands.

Notes and References

1. W. Crooke, *Landmarks in Indian Anthropology: Races of Northern India,* Vol.2, first published 1896, Cosmo publication, New Delhi, 1987, pp. v.
2. *Ibid.*, pp. vi.
3. *Census Report of India,* 1911, pp. 324.
4. *Ibid.*
5. Risley, *Tribes and Castes of Bengal,* vol. 1, pp. xxi-xxii.
6. Max Weber, *The Religion of India,* New York, 1958, pp. 124.
7. A.L. Basham, *The Wonder that was India,* London, revised edition, 1967, pp. 32.
8. Romila Thapar, *Ancient Indian Social History,* Hyderabad, 1984, pp. 154.
9. Crooke, pp. 34.
10. *Ibid.*

11. Margaret and James stutley, *Harper 'sDictionary of Hinduism— Its Mythology, Folklore, Philosophy, Literature and History,* New York, 1817, edition of 1977, p.28. If *Devas* had the same ancestors as Asuras then it would be difficult to accept the location of *Devas* in the Arctic region or even in Europe, particularly when the *Asuras* are located in the Indian sub-continent. It is more rational that both *Devas* and *Asuras* are located in the Indian sub-continent. Because of the diversity of its climatic conditions this sub-continent can accommodate both, the white skinned Aryans and the black skinned *Asuras*.
12. Basham, pp. 24.
13. D.D. Kosambi, *The Culture and Civilization of Ancient India in Historical Outline,* New Delhi, first published in 1970, impression of 1977, pp. 41.
14. *Ibid.*
15. Basham, pp. 24.
16. R.C. Zaehner, 'Zoroastraianism',, pp. 200-14 in *The Concise Encyclopedia of Living Faiths,* ed. R.C. Zachner, London, edition of 1977, pp. 202.
17. Ninian Smart, *The Religious Experience of Mankind,* Glasgow, impression of 1976, pp. 305.
18. Crooke, pp. 34.
19. *Ibid.*
20. Weber, pp. 125.
21. *Ibid.*, pp. 123-4.
22. Nirpendra Kumar Dutt, *Origin and Growth of Caste in India,* Vol. 1, London, 1931, pp. 22.
23. Morton Klass, *Caste*, Philadelphia, 1980, pp. 40-1.
24. Crooke, pp. 35.
25. Basham, pp. 137.
26. *Census Report of India*, 1911, pp. 324.
27. Crooke, pp. 35.
28. Basham, pp. 32.

18

Ambedkar Rejects Aryan Race Theory

Koenraad Elst*

Dr. Ambedkar has, naturally, written a lot about the genesis and history of the caste system. First of all, Dr. Ambedkar rejected what we could call the conspiracy theory of caste, esp. the belief that caste was cunningly and maliciously imposed on Indian society by the mechinations of the sly Brahmins. This was the view fed to Jotirao Phule by the missionaries, and is nowadays the most popular and politically exploited belief about caste.

The conspiracy theory of caste is a variation on the pop-Marxist view of religion as "opium for the people". Marx saw religion as a genuine reflection (though a mistaken belief) of people's actual condition: without needing outside inspiration, the common people themselves would create religion as a source of consolation for their misery. But his followers saw it as "opium for the people", a false belief system concocted by exploiters who sat down one day, thought of a way to fool the people into submissiveness, and then improvised the Bible, or the *Veda* etc., which they fed to these unbelievably gullible masses. In this view, sly exploiters could make the millions accept a religion which they had hitherto not known nor needed, and similarly, the sly *Brahmins* (esp. the law-giver Manu) could make the millions adopt a rigorous and all-encompassing system of practices which they had not known nor needed and which moreover went against their own interests.

In his paper *Caste in India*, Ambedkar wrote:

> One thing I want to impress upon you is that Manu did not *give the law* of caste and that he could not do so. Caste existed long before Manu. He was an unholder of it and therefore philosophized about it, but certainly he did not and could not ordain the present order of Hindu Society...The spread and growth of the Caste system is too gigantic a task to be

---

* A young Belgian scholar, took courses in Indian Philosphy at B.H.U. Varanasi, author of many books on Indian history and politics. Here we reproduce some portion from his "*Indigenous Indians: Agastya to Ambedkar*" (Voice of India, N. Delhi, 1993).

achieved by the power or cunning of an individual or of a class..... Similar in argument is the theory that the Brahmins created the Caste. After what I said regarding Manu, I need hardly say anything more, except to point out that it is incorrect in thought and malicious in intent. The *Brahmins* may have been guilty of many things, and I dare say they were, but the imposing of the caste system of the non-*Brahmin* population was beyond their mettle.[1]

Dr. Ambedkar goes on to describe how *Vedic* society knew a class system, just like other societies, with as classes for four *varnas*: "1. *Brahmins* or the priestly class; 2. the *Kshatriya*, or the military class; 3. the *Vaishya*, or the merchant class; and 4. the *Shudra*, or the artisan and menial class. Particular attention has to be paid to the fact that this was essentially a class system, in which individuals, when qualified, could change their class, and therefore classes did change their personnel."[2]

Secondly, Dr. Ambedkar also rejected the racist theory of caste:

'European students of caste have unduly emphasized the role of colour in the caste system. Themselves impregnated by colour prejudices, they very readily imagined it to be the chief factor in the Caste problem. But nothing can be farther from the truth, and Dr. Ketkar is right when he insists that all the princes whether they belonged to the so-called Aryan race or the so-called Dravidian race, were Aryas. Whether a tribe or a family was racially Aryan or Dravidian was a question which never troubled the people of India, until foreign scholars came in and began to draw the line.'[3]

Dr. Ketkar and Dr. Ambedkar uphold the traditional Hindu view that the word "Arya" has a social and not an ethnic meaning, precisely like the related word "aristocracy" has had in European history.

Dr. Ambedkar concludes:

My study of the Caste problem involves four points: (1) that in spite of the composite make-up of the Hindu population, there is a deep cultural unity; (2) that caste is a parcelling into bits of a larger cultural unit; (3) that there was one caste to start with; and (4) that classes have become castes through imitation and excommunication.[4]

Again, in his famous address *Annihilation of Caste,* Dr. Ambedkar has specifically rejected the racial theory of caste:

The *Brahmin* of Punjab is racially of the same stock as the *Chamar* of Panjab...Caste system does not demarcate racial division. Caste system is a social division of people of the same race.[5]

In his detailed study *Who were the Shudras*? Dr. Ambedkar has exhaustively refuted the Aryan Invasion theory and its pretence at explaining the institution of caste. He starts by noticing what no propounder of this theory has so far been able to put in doubt:

> So far as the *Rig Veda* is concerned, there is not a particle of evidence suggesting the invasion of India by the Aryans from outside India...So far as the testimony of the *Vedic* literature is concerned, it is against the theory that the original home of the Aryas was outside India.[6]

The famous theory of a racial conflict between *Dasas*/*Dasyus* and Aryas is also refuted. Dr. Ambedkar points out:

> "the paucity of references in the *Rig Veda* of wars between the Aryans on the one hand and the *Dasas* and *Dasyus* on the other". The *Rig Veda* is a bulky literature by itself, and yet the term Arya occurs only 33 times in it. Moreover, only in 8 places is it used in opposition to *Dasas* and in 7 places is it used in opposition to the word *Dasyus*. This may show the occurrence of sporadic riots between the two. It is certainly not evidence of a conquest or subjugation.[7]

The *Dasas* were not entirely alien to the Aryas, for:

> whatever conflict there was between them and the Aryans, the two seem to have arrived at a mutual settlement, based on peace with honour. This is borne out in the *Rig Veda* showing how the *Dasas* and Aryans have stood as one united people against a common enemy.[8]

In fact, it is pretty well established that the *Dasas* were one of the Iranian tribes, generally close to the *Vedic* people in language, customs and religion, but in a position of rivalry and therefore, frequently scolded in the *Vedic* texts.

Finally, Dr. Ambedkar points out how the opposition between Aryas and *Dasas*/*Dasyus* is described as a cultural and religious difference (*Dasas* are "without rites", without sacrifices", without prayers" etc.), but never as an ethnic and racial difference. He deals exhaustively with the few words in the *Rig Veda* that have been invoked as a support for the racial theory. These are the terms *Mrdhravak, Anasa* and *Krshnayoni*, which are used in describing the *Dasas* or the *Dasyus*.

The term *Mrdhravak* occurs four times (RV 1:174.2; 5:32.8; 7:6.3; 7 :18.3), and Dr. Ambedkar affirms that it means "one who speaks crude, unpolished language". And he comments: "It would be childish to rely upon this as a basis of consciousness of race difference."[9] Let alone difference in race, even difference in language is not implied in this expression.

The word *Anasa,* upon which so much racial theory has been built, occurs exactly once (RV 5:29.10). Max Muller analyzed it as *a-nasa,* meaning "noseless", to be understood as "snub-nosed". There are few people in India to whom this discription applies, and even then "noseless" would be an inaccurate way of saying "snub-nosed". There is nothing else in the *Rig Veda* that would confirm this interpretation. Dr.

Ambedkar therefore supports Sayanacharya's classical analysis of the word as *an-asa,* meaning "speechless" (related to Latin *os*, mouth).

The word *Krshnayoni,* often translated as "black-skinned" or indeed "of black race", is applied to the *Dasas* exactly once (RV 6:47:21), and no synonymous terms are applied to them. That in itself, Dr. Ambedkar argues, makes the reading "black-skinned" improbable. Indeed, a difference in skin colour would be an ideally simple way of identifying friend and enemy, and in a real report of the epic Aryan Invasion, it would have been used all the time. It is quite certain that a collection of speeches by Ku Klux Klan leaders or by South African racists, of equal size as the *Rig Veda*, would contain the words *kaffer* or *nigger* many more times than just once. Dr. Ambedkar opines that the term may be used in a figurative sense, or be used as a term of abuse rather than as a description of fact.

Others have said that *Krshnayoni* also has the meaning of "black-covered", i.e. "operating under the cover of darkness", indicating activities incompatible with the light of day. The simplest explanation is that in the *Rig Veda*, the word "black" generally refers to the night, the darkness as the opponent of the light, as when the dawn-goddess Usha "puts the black monster in hiding" (4:51:9) and "drives away the black monster" (1:92:5). The word *krshnayoni* would then mean "breed of the darkness". Another reason why "black" can hardly refer to skin colour, is that in the most probable hypothesis the *Dasas* were Iranians, and these were obviously not blacker than the Indo-Aryans.

Then, he quotes some *Vedic* verses which are explicitly incompatible with the race theory: "Oh Vajri, thou hast made Aryas of *Dasas*, good men out of bad by your power." (RV 6:22.10) *Dasas* could become Aryas, but even Vajri's (=Indra's) power has not made a black man white or vice-versa. Indra himself is made to say: "I have deprived the *Dasyus* of the title of Aryas." (RV 10:49.3) So, "conversion" in the opposite direction also occurred. A third verse reads: "Oh Indra, find out who is an Arya and who is a *Dasyu* and separate them." (RV 1:151.8) Dr. Ambedkar comments:

> These verses...indicate that the distinction between the Aryans on the one hand and the *Dasas* and *Dasyus* on the other was not a racial distinction of colour or physiognomy.[10] We may surmise that Arya was an honorific term, and that both contending parties claimed it for themselves and denied it to the opponent as a matter of combative rhetoric.

Dr. Ambedkar also refutes the common belief that *varna* means "skin colour". On the basis of the use of the related terms in the Avestan tradition, he concludes that its effective sociological meaning was "religious adherence", "(belonging to a) sect or tradition", derived from a root-meaning "choice" (*var*, from the root *vrt*, as in *swayam-vara,* "a girl's free choice of a bridegroom"). Many modern Hindus claim that this was indeed the original meaning, suggesting that one's *varna* was originally conceived as a matter of personal choice or inclination (*varana*) towards a profession. The proper translation of *varna* in the Indian context would then be: "chosen membership of a professional guild or social class".

In the *Vedas* (which represent an earlier stage of the Aryan tradition than the Avesta), the term is mostly applied to the gods. According to Dr. Ambedkar:

The word *varna* is used in the *Rig Veda* in 22 places. Of these, in about 17 places the word is used in reference to deities such as "Ushas, Agni, Soma, etc. and means lustre, features or colour."[11] It is not impossible that *varna* in the sense of "colour, lustre", attested in the *Veda*, and *varna* in the sense of "choice, conviction, chosen community", attested in the Avesta, are two different though homonymous words, with a different etymology.

The five remaining *Rig Vedic* occurrences of the word *varna* do not indicate the sense of "skin-colour" either. In 3:34:5 and 9:71:2 it indicates the lustrous colour that appears with the receding of darkness, as at dawn. Unlike the sky, human beings do not usually change skin colour. In 1:179:6 it is said that the two *varnas* prospered as a result of *Rishi* Agastya's sexual intercourse with Lopamudra; it is hard to interpret this as 'the two races'. In 1:104:2 and 2:12:4, the term is applied to the *Dasas*, and seems to have the same meaning as in the Avesta: a religious tradition, a sect. This would eminently fit Srikant Talageri's theory (see ch 2.11) that the *Dasas* are the early Iranians whose conflict with the *Vedic* people is given a religious colour by emphasizing the differences regarding rituals and the worship of *Asuras*. At any rate, Dr. Ambedkar correctly concludes that the term *varna* "had nothing to do with colour and complexion."

To be sure, Dr. Ambedkar was not a *Vedic* scholar, and his opinion should not be used as an argument of authority. But he had common sense and a healthy skepticism regarding the biased Western interpretation of the puzzling *Vedic* literature. He did not read his preconceived notions into the text. Applying his intellect to the historical sources available, he has shown reasonable grounds to reject the racist theory of caste. He explicitates his conclusions as follows:

My conclusions are:

1. The *Vedas* do not know any such race as the Aryan race.

2. There is no evidence in the *Vedas* of any invasion of India by the Aryan race and its having conquered the *Dasas* and *Dasyus* supposed to be the natives of India.

3. There is no evidence to show that the distinction between Aryans, *Dasas* and *Dasyus* was a racial distinction.

4. The *Vedas* do not support the contention that the Aryas were different in colour from the *Dasas* and *Dasyus*.

Dr. Ambedkar also uses the evidence of physical anthropology. In his book *Who Were the Shudras*?, he quotes with approval the pioneer of the physical-anthropological mapping of India's population past and present, Dr. Guha:

> From the beginning of the 4th millennium BC (i.e. since the oldest dated finds), north-western India seems to have been in the occupation of a long-headed race with a narrow prominent nose. Side by side with them, we find the existence of another very powerfully built race also long-headed but with lower cranial vault, and equally long-faced and narrow nose, though the latter was not so high-pitched as that of the former. A third type with broader head and apparently Armenoid affinities also existed, but its advent occurred probably somewhat later judged by the age of the site at Harappa from which most of these type of skulls came.

The two long-headed varieties are elsewhere referred to as Nordic and Mediterranean, while the broad-headed one is the Alpine type. If these were the Aryans, they were not the destroyers of the Harappan civilization, nor were they invaders any time after 4000 BC.

In his book *The Untouchables,* he brings in the research findings of Prof. G.S. Ghurye. The latter has found a few cases where skull and nose measurements show a marked differences between castes of the same region, esp. in U.P., where the *Brahmin* is markedly different from the untouchable *Chamar* (but surprisingly) close to the untouchable *Chuhra* of Panjab, which fits the hypothesis that the *Vedic* tradition was brought from Saptasindhu eastward along with a part of the population, presumably after the decline of the Saraswati basin. However, in general the situation is the opposite: high and low castes from one area are closer to each other than to their respective caste fellows from another area:

> The table for Bengal shows that the *Chandal* who stands sixth in the scheme of social precedence and whose touch pollutes, is not much differentiated from the *Brahmin*...In Bombay the *Deshastha Brahmin* bears a closer affinity to the Son-Koli, a fisherman caste, than to his

> own compeer, the *Chitpavan Brahmin*. The Mahar, the Untouchable of the Maratha region, comes next together with the Kunbi, the peasant. They follow in order the *Shenvi Brahmin*, the *Nagar Brahmin* and the high-caste Maratha. These results...mean that there is no correspondence between social gradation and physical differentiation in Bombay.[13]

Next he quotes Prof. Ghurye's comparative lists of social precedence and nasal index in the Kannada-Telugu and Tamil speaking regions of Madras presidency. In all three cases, there is by far no one-to-one correspondence between the two lists. Thus, in the Kannada region, the Holaya and the Deshastha *Brahmin* castes, who are at the opposite ends of the caste hierarchy, have a similar nasal index. with their extreme nasal index, the broad-nosed tribal communities like the Krumba and Solaga are low but not the lowest in the caste hierarchy. Dr. Ambedkar observes that while the picture is not altogether uniform, one can broadly say that, for instance, the nasal indexes of the *Chamar* and the *Brahmin* of Bihar are nearly the same, as are the nasal indexes of the Cheruman ("an Unapproachable lower than the Pariah") and the *Brahmin* of Tamil Nadu.

Therefore he concludes: "If anthropometry is a science which can be depended upon to determine the race of a people, then the results obtained by the application of anthropometry to the various strata of Hindu society disprove that the Untouchables belong to a race different form the Aryans and the Dravidians. The measurements establish that the *Brahmins* and the Untouchables belong to the same race. From this it follows that if the *Brahmins* are Aryans the Untouchables are also Aryans. If the *Brahmins* are Dravadians the Untouchables are also Dravidians. If the *Brahmins* are Nagas, the Untouchables are also Nagas.[14]

In the course of his refutation of the racial explanation of caste, Dr. Ambedkar makes an observation which, if he had developed it further, would have made redundant much of his more speculative work on the origin of certain features of the caste system (see ch. 5.4 and 5.5). He shows that the families (*kula*) and exogamous clans (*gotra*), on the evidence of their names, cut across different castes, e.g. in Panjab the Jats and the (untouchable) Mazhabis have some *Gotra* names in common. Whether this really proves a kinship between homonymous clans of different castes, as Dr. Ambedkar claims, is a matter for debate. More important is the point he makes off-hand, concerning the structural continuity between caste and tribes:

> The racial theory of Untouchability not only runs counter to the results of anthropometry, but it also finds very little support from such facts as we know about the ethnology of India. That the people of India

were once organized on tribal basis is well-known, and although *the tribes have become castes,* the tribal organization still remains intact. Each tribe was divided into clans and the clans were composed of groups of families.[15]

And this tribal structure continues in the system of endogamous clan or sub-castes, indicating that caste is in fact a continuation of tribal organization in a supra-tribal or post-tribal society.

At any rate, Dr. Ambedkar was very clear about the one belief which is now crucial to many self-styled champions of the Dalit cause: he rejected the explanation of caste from the Aryan invasion theory. In his view, the caste system does not have a racial basis, and does not perpetuate an Apartheid system imposed by invaders on natives.

Who were the Shudras?

Dr. Ambedkar has launched remarkable theories concerning the genesis of the *Shudra varna* and of untouchability. About the *Shudras*, Dr. Ambedkar summarizes his thesis as follows:

1. The *Shudras* were one of the Aryan communities of the Solar Race.
2. There was a time when the Aryan society recognized only three *varnas*, namely *Brahmins*, *Kshatriyas* and *Vaishyas*.
3. The *Shudras* did not form a separate *varna*. They ranked as part of the *Kshatriya varna* in the Indo-Aryan society.
4. There was a continuous feud between the *Shudra* kings and the *Brahmins* in which the *Brahmins* were subjected to many tyrannies and indignities.
5. As a result of the hatred towards the Shudras generated by their tyrannies and oppressions, the *Brahmins* refused to perform the *Upanayana* of the *Shudras*.
6. Owing to the denial of *Upanayana*, the *Shudras* who were *Kshatriyas* became socially degraded, fell below the rank of the *Vaishyas* and thus came to form the fouth *varna*.[16]

Notes and References

1. Dr. Ambedkar: *Writings and Speeches,* vol. 1, pp. 16. Emphasis in the original.
2. *Ibid*, pp. 21, with reference to Ketkar: *History of Caste,* pp. 82.
3. *Ibid*, pp. 22.
4. *Ibid*, pp. 49.
5. Dr. Ambedkar: *Writings and Speeches*, vol. 7, pp. 74.
6. *Ibid*, pp. 75.
7. *Ibid*, with explicit reference to Rig Veda 6:33.3; 7:83.1; 8:51.9; 10:102.3.
9. *Ibid*, pp. 76.
10. *Ibid*, pp. 77.
11. *Ibid*, pp. 82.
12. *Ibid*, pp. 85.
13. *Ibid*, pp. 301.
14. *Ibid*, pp. 302-303.
15. *Ibid*, pp. 303, Emphasis added.
16. Dr. Ambedkar: *Writings and Speeches,* vol. 7, pp. 11-12.

19

Vedic Studies Provide Valuable Clues

Subhash C. Kak*

The controversies of the past century about India's earliest chronology offer a rich case study of the sociology of rise and fall of paradigms. Max Muller is credited with the popularization of the theory that nomadic hordes of horse-riding. Aryans invaded India in mid-second millennium BC, subjugated the original inhabitants and imposed their culture and language on them. This theory explained the fact that the languages of North India and Europe belonged to the same family and that the myths of the Indian and the European worlds had some commonality. This theory also assumed an expansion of the Indo-European into Europe at about the same time as the supposed invasions into India. The epoch of mid-second millennium BC was based on the evidence that references of *Vedic* gods dating back to this period had been found in Mesopotamia and Turkey. It was assumed that these were records of the Aryans on their way to India from their original homeland.

While this theory provided an explanation within the framework of the then emerging field of archaeology, it suffered from serious flaws. Also the context in which the word Aryan was used was wrong as this word in the earliest Indian literature refers to culture and not any specific race or linguistic background. A major flaw of the invasion theory was that it had no explanation for why the *Vedic* literature that was assumed to go back into the second millennium had no references to any region outside of northwest India. Furthermore, the astronomical references in the *Vedic* literature allude to events in the third millennium BC and earlier. Then there was the fact that the earliest Indian sciences and literature and philosophy were very advanced indicating a very long tradition of scholarship which the invasion model did not posit. Most importantly, the discovery of the archaeological sites of the Indus-Saraswati tradition, which go back to at least 6500 B.C. and which show cultural continuity

* Professor, Electrical and Computer Engineering, Louisiana State University, U.S.A. Discovered astronomical code in *Rigveda*.

with the later Indian civilization, created a fundamental contradiction for the model. If one could explain the cultural continuity by arguing that the invading Aryans eventually adopted the culture of the original inhabitants, then how was one to explain the fact that they were able to impose their language also on the same people.

Theories of Horse-riding

More recently it has been found that the date for horseback riding should be pushed back to earlier than 4000 B.C. (Anthony, Telegin, and Brown 1991) so that even if the questionable assumption of the horse providing the impetus for the expansion of the Indo-Europeans is accepted, it invalidates many of the crucial details of the invasion model.

Once the theory of horse riding invaders took root, any evidence that went against this view was ignored or simply brushed aside as being ambiguous.

It has been argued by many scholars that a peculiar complex of intellectual and political attitudes current in Europe in the nineteenth century were responsible for the ascendancy of the invasion theory. Although the discovery of the ancient Sanskrit literature by the Western scholars first led them to assume that the regions of the Himalayan ranges might have been the original homeland of the Indo-Europeans, this was based primarily on the priority of the Indian literature. In the 1860's, physical anthropology was pressed into service by a new generation of scholars to argue that the original homeland must have been Europe since their readings of the literature implied that the Indo-Europeans were light-skinned blondes. That such an inference rested on flawed readings and a variety of unproven assumptions was ignored. A considerable part of the literature of this period is purely polemical, inspired by the conviction that no region outside the European part of the Indo-European world could have created a great civilization centuries before Europe. There also was the attempt to compress the chronologies of the ancient world within the framework of biblical chronology. The significance of this theory will be apparent when it is recalled that many of the prominent Indologists of the nineteenth century were missionaries, not wholly versed in the scientific temper. There was linguistic abuse in giving a racial connotation to the word Aryan although it had no such implications in Sanskrit.

European Conquest of Americas

Another reason for the popularity of the invasion theory was that parallels were seen with the conquest of the Americas by the Europeans.

It is only in the past couple of decades that the preponderant evidence from archaeology and literary sources has caused the proponents of the invasion model to modify many of their assumptions. The continuity in the Harappan and the later art and religion is now being explained as a wholesale adoption of the entire civilization, to the minutest detail with regard to adoption of symbols and words suitably transliterated, by the Aryans. This position is similar to that of the believer in creation science who claims that God placed on earth at the same time not only man but also the fossil evidence.

Invasion Theory Knocked Down

In the absence of any archaeological evidence to support it, the theory of invasion of the Aryans has been, more generally, characterized as a myth (Shaffer 1984, Shaffer 1992). The Brahmi script has been shown to be derived from the Indus (Saraswati) script in the third millennium BC (Kak 1987). Research on earliest Indian geometry has shown that there exist reasons to reopen the question of the dating of the *sutra* literature. Seidenberg has argued (Seidenberg 1978) that the late dating of *sulbhasutras* was partly prompted by the attempt to see Indian geometry as following the rise of Greek geometry. His demonstration that *Shatapath Brahmana*, which is conservatively dated centuries before earliest Greek geometry, itself contains geometry that compels a new look at the entire question.

Furthermore, geological studies indicate that the Saraswati river dried up early in the second millennium B.C. This requires a revision in the chronology of the *Rigvedic* era, since the Indo-Aryan people were settled mainly in the valleys of that river in that age.

Meanwhile, the epoch for the influx of the Indo-Europeans into Europe is also being pushed back to the sixth millennium B.C. According to one model their expansion into Europe was a result of their introduction of farming which permitted families to be larger, resulting in new settlements and intermarriage with the native inhabitants. There are other models that speak of expansion of a different type (e.g. Mallory 1989) where the proto-Indo-European era is dated to 4500-2500 BC But this model conflicts with the astronomical evidence from the Indian texts.

Astronomical Code in the *Rigveda*

Recently, I discovered an astronomical code in the structure of the *Rigveda* (Kak 1992b Kak 1993a-e, Kak and Frawley 1992), which pushes back the dates for the rise of measurement astronomy by at least a millennium and credits the *Rigvedic* Indian with the knowledge of the data about the planet periods as well as the motions of the moon and the sun. Knowledge of fairly advanced astronomy by the *Rigvedic* Indians flies in the face of all invasion theories by barbarians. Judicious use of the astronomical and literary evidence suggests antiquity for the earliest Indian literature not at much variance from the traditional view.

History of science and civilizations shows that scientists and scholars often do not abandon paradigms even when new evidence compels such a revision. Once scientists and scholars invest parts of their career in support of a paradigm, it becomes a sort of a self betrayal to abandon it. This explains why many authorities of the day rejected Champollion's decipherment of Egyptian hieroglyphs, or in recent times the decipherment of Mayan writing being rejected by many scholars. Even in scientific theories where one has the advantage of predictive power, believers in old theories have resisted the new. This is why Planck claimed that often only death can separate scientists from their pet theories (Planck 1950). This is the only explanation one can provide for the reiteration in new texts of the invasion model that has no archaeological or textual evidence.

This essay considers several issues related to the earliest Indian chronology and the Aryan question by a juxtaposition of the literary and the archaeological evidence. After an account of the larger Indo-European context of these issues, it considers the system of *Vedic* science and knowledge to establish that it must have had a very long pre-history in India. The Greek notices about India's calendar are analyzed. It is shown that the above arguments as well as the recent discoveries in *Vedic* astronomy compel a view that the Indo-Aryans have been present in India for the entire duration of the Indus-Saraswati tradition that goes back to at least 6500 BC.

Some Influential Views

Consider first a summary of some of the influential views on the Indo-European problem. The last ice age in Europe ended around 8000 BC when glaciers started retreating northwards. The earliest farming communities in Europe are to be found in Greece around 6500 BC and by 3000 BC most of Europe excepting the extreme north was occupied by a variety of farming communities who must have represented different ethnic and linguistic groups. It has been argued that copper and bronze metallurgy was established around 4000 BC and 3000 BC respectively. These technological advancements have led to increased trade and surplus leading certain communities becoming stronger than others. Around 2000 BC a kingdom with a literate bureaucracy emerged in Crete. In another five hundred years we see the rise of the Mycenaean civilization of Greece. Iron-working on a significant scale is seen in Greece and southeast Europe around 1000 BC.

With the development of archaeology, pottery types and other cultural complexes were studied as evidence of the expansion of the Indo-Europeans. Gordon Childe in 1926 suggested that proto-Indo-European culture was characterized by graves covered with red ochre and surmounted by a mound or *kurgan.* This theory was expanded into Europe in the late bronze age aided by the horse-drawn chariot and the war horse. More recently Marija Gimbutas has suggested in her *Kurgan* theory that the homogeneous Kurgan culture of the Pontic and Volga steppes characterizes the proto-Indo-European culture and that it was widespread in east Europe at the end of the copper age (Gimbutas 1973), Gimbutas 1985). In this view proto-Indo-Europeans is generally assigned the period 4500-2500 BC.

Diffusionists *vs* Migrationists

There are two extreme views regarding the spread of culture: the diffusionists maintain that learning leads to the adoption of new ways, whereas migrationists see the movement of people as the key to ancient economic and social changes. The third view sees culture as expanding by forces that include learning as well as migration. Ammerman and Cavalli-Sforza (1984) proposed that the spread of farming increased population densities so that the offsprings set up new farms, intermarrying with the native population, absorbing native genes but imposing their language and culture. They argued that such an expansion would have occurred at the rate of about one kilometer a year.

Colin Renfrew suggested (Renfrew 1987) that the spread of farming in Europe around 6500 BC. was the vehicle that led to the expansion of the Indo-Europeans there. Of the specific technological or social changes outlined above, it is hard to pick any particular one as having greater intrinsic worth unless such a choice is corroborated by other independent evidence. Analysis of the genetic evidence from the European population shows some correlation of the genes with the spread of farming in a southeast to northeast direction.

Vedic Models of Knowledge

The situation of the Indo-Europeans in the east has not been as thoroughly debated as the one in the west. Often the scholars who have generalized from the European evidence to the Indo-European model have had a flawed understanding of the Indo-Iranian evidence. Most of the linguistic evidence marshalled by these scholars has been based on Sanskrit and the wealth of independent linguistic evidence from the Prakrit languages has been unavailable to them. The use of the Sanskritic evidence has in itself been hampered by the assumption that the analysis of this evidence should not be based on *Vedic* models of knowledge. A reasoned analysis of the Indian evidence allows us to find other independent arguments that have a bearing on understanding the general Indo-European question.

Physical anthropology has been at the basis of many popular theories regarding the origins of the Indo-Europeans. In a recent review, J.P. Mallory concludes that "[it] has failed, at least so far, to produce substantial support for any particular theory of Indo-European origins" (Mallory 1992). Although Mallory only considers origins in Europe, Near East, and Central Asia in his analysis one can add Northwest India to this list and his conclusion still holds. For a review of the theories that claim that the Indo-Europeans originated in Northwest India, see Majumdar (1951).

Earliest Indian Chronology and the *Vedic* Sciences

The present author's study of the question of Indian Chronology stemmed from the puzzle that *Vedic* conception of science is astonishingly modern and its achievements are very advanced. The contributions of the *Vedic* world to philosophy, mathematics, logic, astronomy, medicine and other sciences provide one of the foundations on which rests the common heritage of man. What is amazing is that new applications of ancient Indian sciences are still being found. As an example consider artificial intelligence, the science of designing computers to mimic human reasoning, which has been one of the most intense areas of research in the past three decades. It is now being realized that the contributions of ancient Indian linguists, logicians and psychologists can have applications in the developments of powerful computers. The distinguished linguist Frits Staal writes:

> We can now assert, with the power of hindsight, that Indian linguists in the fifth century BC knew and understood more than Western linguists in the nineteenth century AD. Can one not extend this conclusion and claim that it is probable that Indian linguists are still ahead of their Western colleagues and may continue to be so in the next century? (Staal 1988)

The tradition of scholarship and inquiry must have had a long history in India during the Vedic era. The theory that such a development took place just in a span of a few centuries in rural setting does not appear convincing.

True Nature of *Vedic* Literature

To understand the *Vedic* tradition it is essential to examine the process by which *Vedic* knowledge was accumulated. This can not be done by considering the main *Vedas* as literary documents without using the six supplementary *Vedangas* that consist of: *kalpa,* the performance of sacrifice; *shiksha,* correct pronunciation; *chhandas,* meter and prosody;

nirukta, etymology; *vyakarana,* grammar; and *jyotisha,* astronomy and calendrical science. Notice should also be made of the four supplementary fields of knowledge or *Upavedas; arthaveda,* economics and politics: *gandharvaveda,* music and the fine arts; *dhanurveda,* warfare; and *ayurveda,* medicine and biology. These in turn were classified into the thirty-two sciences and the sixty-four arts.

What is the method of science? One isolates a phenomenon, observes cause-effect relationships, and then describes the phenomenon, in terms of its components. But before observation can begin it is essential to believe that the world is knowable and that it follows natural law. The *Vedas* make precisely this declaration.

The theory of knowledge in the *Vedic* world was based on a belief in the interconnectedness and unity in the whole universe. According to *Vedic* knowledge, the macrocosm (*adhidaiva*), the living beings (*adhibhuta*), and the human spirit (*adhyatma*) are intimately connected. It was for this reason that the *Vedas*, that were the compendium of knowledge of its times, were to be interpreted in three ways. So the *Vedas* speak of the *rishis* in the sky as stars, on the earth as sages, and in the head as cognitive centres. Paralleling the Ganga of the sky (the Milky Way) is the Ganga river of our planet, and the Ganga of neural pathways inside the brain. Ayurveda speaks of the parallel between 360 days to the year and the 360 bones (308 bones of the child plus 32 teeth, and 20 nails) of the human.

Thc knowledge about the universe as well as the theory behind this knowledge were communicated through the theatre of the ritual. Astronomical knowledge was represented in the design of the altars and in the *Vedic* ritual (*adhiyajna*).

Cosmic Science in the *Vedas*

The *Vedic rishis* apparently thought very deeply about the limits of logic and science and they were the first to recognize that straight logic could not answer all questions. They recognized that each scientific metaphor will have its own paradoxes. It was perhaps because of this that they enjoin the use of logic and questioning without fail so that the person would discover these paradoxes for himself. Many paradoxes of the *Vedas* are about time and consciousness; but there are others as well.

The scientific structure of the *Vedas* may be viewed at three different levels. First is the level of logic and philosophy where it is asserted that explanations lead to paradox which is why the understanding of the nature of consciousness is of fundamental importance. This is the reason why the hymns are full of paradoxes and riddles. At another level the *Vedas* deal with the representation of the mystery of reality in the framework of the theatre of ritual. This leads to the realm of sacrifice. The third level deals with astronomical phenomena which are often described in the grab of myths. The potentiality that underlies nature is seen to emerge through the paradoxical process of sacrifice. The word sacrifice (Skt. *yajna*) has several connotations including creation through transcendence. The whole universe is the altar of sacrifice out of which its potentialities emerge.

The background of this science provides us with various clues that have a bearing on the chronology of that period. In particular we argue that astronomy was central to the *Vedic* people and that the astronomical markers in literature were based on actual observations and should not be considered as later interpolations.

Geometry and Mathematics

A few years ago Seidenberg analyzed the geometry and mathematics of the *Shatapatha Brahmana* and the *Shulbasutras* (Seidenberg 1962, 1978). He argued that the earliest geometry and mathematics arose in relation to problems of altar design. In his view the philosophy that equivalent altars were to have equal areas led to the posing of basic problems of geometry leading to results such as the theorem of the diagonal. Textbooks of the history of mathematics have begun to weave Seidenberg's arguments in their accounts of the rise of early geometry and mathematics. But Seidenberg's analysis was very limited as far as the ancient *Vedic* texts were concerned, although his conclusions were quite significant for a history of mathematics. Seidenberg dated the rise of the earliest mathematics in the Indo-European ritual dating back to about 1700 BC but new results push this epoch back further as we shall see.

The earliest mathematics may be seen as a tool of the earliest astronomy in all civilizations. Mathematical knowledge should therefore be analyzed within the context of contemporary astronomy. *Shatapatha Brahmana* provides us an overview of certain aspects of *Vedic* astronomy that are generally misunderstood. The sixth chapter of the book provides significant clues. Speaking of creation mention is made of the mergence of *Ashva, Rishbha, Aja* and *Kurma* before the emergence of the earth. Clearly these refer to stars or constellations. It appears that these be identified as the Sun (*Ashva*), *Rishbha* (*Gemini*), *Aja* (Capricorn) and *Kurma* (Cassiopeia). Other constellations mentioned in the *Vedic* books include the *Rikshas* (the Great Bear and the Little Bear), the two divine Dogs (Canis Major and Canis Minor), the heavenly Boat (Agro Navis), the constellation of *Mriga* or Deer (Orion) and the star *Nrigvyadha* (Sirius). What is most fascinating about the creation process is that the earth is supposed to emerge after the emergence of several constellations.

The Calendrical Evidence

Consider now the question of calendrical tradition in India. What were the earliest eras and how back do the genealogies take us? The earliest era used by Indian astronomers from the time of Aryabhatta (500 AD) onwards is the *Kaliyuga* era that is taken to have begun in 3102 BC, 35 years after the conclusion of the *Mahabharata* war. However, there is no reference to this era in earlier texts and so it has been claimed that the *Kaliyuga* era was devised by Aryabhatta or his contemporaries.

Now consider that the tradition of the seven *Rishis*, the stars of the Ursa Major, in India is an ancient one and it goes back to the *Rigveda*. *Shatapatha Brahmana* speaks of a marriage between the *Rishis* and the *Nakshtras*; specifically it is mentioned that the *Rishis* were married to the *Krittikas*. In the *Puranas* this notion of marriage is elaborated when it is clearly stated that the *Rishis* remain for a hundred years in each *Nakshatra.* The *Puranic* elaboration implies a centennial reckoning system with a cycle of 2700 years. Such a system has been in use in parts of India for a long time that goes back centuries before Christian Era and it is called the *Saptarshi* era. Each cycle of 2700 years was called a *chakra*, or cycle. By current reckoning in Kashmir, that goes back at least to Kalhana, *Saptarshi* era began in 3076 BC Cunningham (1883) provided a careful analysis of the traditions related to this era.

Saptarshi era of 6676 BC

Mitchiner (1982) has suggested that the *Saptarshi* era goes back to 6676 BC. He argues that it is the beginning of this era that is quoted by the Greek historians Pliny and Arrian.

Apart from the reference to *Mahabharata* related to the *Kaliyuga* era, there are two other important traditions that address it. Varahamihira reports that Yudhishthira became king 2526 years before the Shaka era (2249 BC); on the other hand, the *Puranas* say that 1050 years elapsed between the birth of Parikshit and the coronation of Mahapadma Nanda (e.g. Roy 1983, Kak 1987).

Cunningham (1883) argued that the *Kaliyuga* and the Varahmihira traditions about the *Mahabharata* war can be reconciled if it is assumed that a change in reckoning from a system of 28 *Nakshatras* to that of 27 *Nakshatras* took place sometime after the time of Chandragupta. He and Mitchiner suggest that the original list of 28 *Nakshatras* which is given in the *Atharva Veda* was amended in the medieval times to 27. Since the notion of 27 *Nakshatras* also goes back very far as in *Taittriya Samhitā*, it appears that the two traditions on the *Mahabharata* war go back much further than suggested by Cunningham and Mitchiner. It has also been suggested that the *Kaliyuga* tradition might be authentic and the Varahamihira one was derived from it.

But the evidence from the *Rigveda* supports the notion that the original system of *Nakshatras* was 27 and that it was modified to 28 later. For example, the sum of the hymns of the middle four books is 324, which equals the *Nakshatra* year of 27 *Nakshatras*. If it is assumed that the reckoning had been by the *Nakshatra* centennials then the increase in the *Nakshatra* count by one required the change of the beginning of the *Kali Yuga* from 2414 BC to 3102 BC to ensure that the events remembered about the war would square with the reckoning scheme. Further support for such an idea comes from the internal astronomical evidence of the *Mahabharata* as analyzed by Sengupta (1983a). It is also more plausible to see the flowering of the *Vedic* age to have occurred during the Harappan phase.

It is conceivable that the original text of *Mahabharata* was remembered from the third millennium B.C. and expanded much later in the first millennium B.C. when the events and the geography got a contemporaneous colouring, but the main astronomical associations remain altered.

It is likely that the *Saptarshi* era was known during the *Shatapatha Brahmana* times. Notice that the altar is made in an area 7½ times that of one *Purusha*. With 360 years considered one divine year, 2700 years equal 7½ divine years. It may be that such a theory led to the popularity of the system of 27 *nakshatras*. It is also significant that the epoch of 6676 BC is exactly 3600 years earlier than the starting point of 3076 BC for the *Saptarshi* era as accepted now. Since it is clear that at the time of the Maurya, the cycles of the *Saptarshi* era were counted back to 6676 BC, it appears that the new count that goes back to 3076 BC was started later to make it as close to the start of the *Kali* era as possible.

There is no reason to assume that the centennial system of reckoning was not used in the second millennium BC and earlier.

The Astronomical Frame of the Myths

Myths of different cultures have an astronomical basis (Brecher and Feirtag 1979, Deppert 1983). Varuna, Ouranos (Greece), Tammuz (Sumer-Babylon), Adon (Canaan, Cyprus), Osiris (Egypt), Telipinus-Sharruma (Hittie) can be viewed as being fundamentally the same. These gods were born to the great mother goddesses of their cultural fields: Aditi, Ishtar, Astarte, Isis, the Sun goddess of Arinna Kybele (Attis). These gods were often represented by the night sky. From another point of view they encode the constellation of Orion and their myths refer to the vernal equinox in it (7th-5th millennium BC). The precession of the vernal equinox was noted by transferring Orion's mythology to Taurus and Aries. Thus Tammuz was killed by his hostile brother Sirius, Osiris by his hostile brother Seth (Ursa Major), Tvashta, Dyauspita, Prajapati were killed by their youngest son Indra or Rudra (Sirius). Terrible events in ancient myths usually refer to dramatic celestial phenomena. Therefore, many myths provide chronological markers. But to use them as such, without other supporting evidence, is fraught with danger since these myths could have been adopted at a late stage from another culture. But the parallels in the symbols that cut across different cultures also suggest that interaction between these civilizations goes back very far.

That many myths represent astronomical knowledge was known to the ancients and many gods symbolized stars or planets. The dramatic incidents of the myths referred to departure from an expected clockwork of the stars. This departure was a result of the precession of the earth that changed the orientation of the earth's poles slowly. Other layers of stories added to myths over time may have had nothing to do with astronomical phenomena but rather provided a framework to understand the vicissitudes over time experienced by the culture.

The earth's axis of rotation is tipped at an angle of 23½ degrees with respect to the direction of its orbital motion around the sun. This is what causes the changing seasons because the length of the day keeps on varying. The longest and the shortest days, also called summer and winter solstices, occur roughly near the 21st of June and December, respectively. The date of a solstice can be marked by noting that around this date the sun appears to linger at the same extreme at dawn.

The two Equinoxes

The days when the days and nights are equal are called equinoxes. The two equinoxes, vernal in spring and autumnal in fall, mark the halfway points between summer and autumn. The equinoxes occur at the two intersections of the celestial equator and the ecliptic. The motion of the moon is more complex since its orbit is inclined approximately 5 degrees to the earth's orbit around the sun, and the earth's gravitation perturbs the moon in its orbit. The resultant precession completes a cycle in 18.61 years.

The stars present a way to calibrate calendar. Thus some groups of stars dominate the winter nights and others the summer nights. One would look for the first or last appearance of a group like the Pleiades. Another calibration could be done with respect to a star's heliacal (pre-sunrise dawn) rising. Thus the heliacal rising of Sirius was extremely important to the Egyptians. During one period of their history, the heliacal rising of Sirius occurred at the same time as the summer solstice and, by coincidence, at the same time as the annual Nile flood. The calendar was calibrated, and the year began, with the heliacal rising of Sirius.

Due to the precession of the earth's polar axis, the direction of the north pole with respect to the fixed background stars keeps on changing. The period of the precession is roughly 26,000 years. Polaris (*alpha Ursae Minoris*) is the Pole star now but around 3000 BC it was *alpha Draconis* which was followed later by *beta Ursae Minoris*; in 14000 AD it will be *Vega*. The equinoxes and the solstices shift with respect to the background stars. Tilak in his Orion (1893) and Georgio de Santillana and Hertha von Dechend in their Hamlet's Mill (1969) argue that much of mythological narrative is a symbolic description of the changing orientation of the earth against the background of the stars.

The precession of the polar axis leads to a precession of the equinoxes and solstices. The equinoxes move along the ecliptic in a direction opposite to the yearly course of the sun (Taurus to Aries to Pisces rather than Pisces to Aries to Taurus and so on).

The vernal equinox was usually taken to be the first day of the year. The sun's position among the constellations at the vernal equinox was an indication of the state of the precessional cycle. This constellation was noted by its heliacal rising. The equinoctial sun occupies each zodiacal constellation for about 2200 years. Around 5000 BC it was in Gemini; it has moved since into Taurus, Aries, and is now in Pisces. In India the ancient mapping of the stars constellations was in 27 or 28 *Nakshatras* or lunar mansion; the moon spending about a day in each. The sun spends about 13-1/3 days in each *Nakshatra*, and the precession of the equinoxes takes them across each *Nakshatra* in about a thousand years.

The moon returns to a starting position in the zodiac in about 27 days. Each day was marked by the asterism (*Nakshatra*) near which the moon was seen resulting in the use of 27 *Nakshatras*. The *Atharva Veda* lists these together with their presiding deities. The list begins with *Krittika* (Pleiades) where the spring equinox was situated at that time. Thirteen and a half *Nakshatras* ending with *Vishakha* were situated in the northern hemisperes; these were called *Devanak-shatras*. The remaining *Nakshatras* ending with *Bharani* that were in the southern hemisphere were called *yamanakshạtras* (yama: twin, dual). This classification in *Taittiriya Brahmana* (1.5.2.7) corresponds to 2300 BC.

The *Shatapatha Brahmana* (2.1.2.3) has a statement that points to an earlier epoch where it is stated that *Krittika* never swerve from the each. This corresponds to 2950 BC.

Maitrayaniya Brahmana Upanishad (6.14) refers to the winter solstice being at the mid-point of the *Shravishtha* segment and the summer solstice at the beginning of *Māgha.* This indicates 1660 BC.

Vedanga Jyotisha (Yajur 6-8) mentions that winter solstices was at the beginning of *Shravishtha* and the summer solstice at the mid-point of *Ashlesha*. This corresponds to about 1370 BC.

Sumerian, Babylonian, Egyptian and Greek mythology likewise point to very early epochs. This can be guessed also from the design of early observations, as well as the origin of a great number of ancient rituals. An example of this is the *upanayana* ritual that dates back to the *Vedic* times.

Now consider Shiva. Many of the stories about him are meant to highlight paradoxical aspects of reality. But there are other stories which are clearly astronomical. There is the well-known story about Agni fathering Skanda on the *Krittikas* (Pleiades). In later mythology Agni is replaced by Shiva and he is identified with the star Sirius. Now the famous story about Shiva cutting off the head of Daksha Prajāpati (Orion) or God of Time is nothing but a retelling of when the vernal equinox moved away from *Mrigashiras* (Orion's head) toward *Rohini*. This analysis is brilliantly presented by Tilak in his *The Orion*.

The Greek notices indicate that *Puranic* king lists were in existence in the fourth century BC. From the *Puranic* genealogies we have the testimony that the first compilation of the *Puranas* took place at the end of the *Mahabharata* war. Many of the *Puranic* myths have an astronomical basis, therefore it appears probable that the original myths were themselves thus inspired, and the grammar passed on the later redactors of the Gupta age and onwards. Astronomical references and allusions in the *Vedas* confirm this view. The *Vedic* hymns were supposed to have been composed by the seven *rishis* (*Saptarshi*). The solstitial colure, called the "Line of the Seven *Rishis*" ran through these stars starting about 4000 BC.

The Archaeological Evidence

The setting for the hymns of the *Rigveda* is the area of *Sapta Saindhava,* the region of Punjab bounded by the Indus and the Ganga rivers. There are also geographical references in the *Rigveda* that are of chronological value. In the past ten millennia, north India has undergone major tectonic and hydrological upheavels, and so it becomes impossible to correlate certain geographical references to different time epochs. Other significant references are to seagoing vessels and to settlements on the Saraswati. The archaeological record suggests that this river turned dry around 1900 BC.

The genealogies of the *Puranas* and the later *Vedic* literature also reach back at least into the third millennium BC (Pargiter 1922, Roy 1983). Using synchronisms in the various *Vedic* texts, one estimate lists 94 generations before the *Mahabharata* War. Furthermore, the later *Vedic* literature, starting with the *Shatapatha Brahmana,* describes an expansion of the civilization outside of the original area of the Indus and the Saraswati valleys.

Archaeological investigations have shown that the Indus-Saraswati cultural tradition represents the beginnings of the Indian civilization. This tradition has been traced back to about 6500 BC in remains that have been uncovered in Mehrgarh and other sites (Jarrige and Meadow 1980, Possehl 1982, Kenoyer 1989, Shaffer 1992). It reached its flowering during the period 2600-1900 BC, called the Harappan age, when several cities and towns were established and writing, based on the so-called Indus script, was used. In the 1970's it was found that most of these towns and settlements were on the banks of the Saraswati river. Hydrological changes and the socio-economic evolution of the groups led to an abandonment of large areas of the Indus valley. A second urbanization began in the Ganga-Yamuna valley around 900 BC. The earliest surviving records of this culture are in Brahmi script. This second urbanization is generally seen at the end of the Painted Gray Ware (PGW) phase (1200-800 BC) and with the use of the Northern Black Polished Ware (NBP) pottery. Late Harappan was partially contemporary with the PGW phase. In other words, a continuous series of cultural developments link the two early urbanizations of India.

Indus-Saraswati Script

The restructuring of society that occurred between the two urbanizations is partially mirrored in the restructuring of the Indus-Saraswati script. The Brahmi script, which was in use throughout India during the Mauryas was highly systematic, reflecting clearly the theories of Indian grammarians. Literary evidence as well as signs on early punch-marked coins suggest that writing in India during the second urbanization goes back much before the middle of the first millennium BC. The punch-marked coins that go far back to at least the seventh century BC (Mitchiner 1973) use a Harappan weight standard. It appears that the coins were originally issued as silver blanks by traders and the weights checked by traders. The checking was represented by marks that are strikingly similar to the Harappan signs. By the sixth century BC the kings began putting their own issuing marks on the coins. These pictorial marks were generally representative of the meaning of the king's name. The Saraswati script uses many more signs than Brahmi and it is generally written from right to left, in a direction opposite to that of Brahmi. On the other hand, there are instances of both the scripts being written in the *boustrophedon* style, that is, written in opposite directions in alternate lines. But the change in the normal direction of writing does indicate a fundamental shift. Whether this shift took place between the two urbanizations or just prior to the Mauryan empire is not clear.

The spread of the Indian civilization, as indicated by the literary and archaeological records, can further be checked by an analysis of the processes that might have supported this spread. Ammerman and Cavalli-Sforza (1984) argue for the parallel situation in Europe that the spread there of farming after 7000 BC could be seen as a diffusionary process brought about by a combination of cultural diffusion, and population growth and displacement, which they call *demic* diffusion. Sokal, Oden, and Wilson (1991) have published genetic evidence supporting this model. Genetic variation across the Indian sub-continent suggests that a diffusion model might be at the basis of the spread of the Indian people as well.

The evolution and restructuring of the ethnic groups (Shaffer 1992) can be seen in the archaeological record. No evidence for any break in the Indian tradition due to any invasions has been found. Since the Indo-Aryans were the dominant group in northern India by the late second millennium BC, one is compelled to conclude that they must have been one of the ethnic groups in the Indus and the Saraswati valley areas as early as 6500 BC.

There is enough convergence in the Archaeological evidence about the Indus-Saraswati tradition and the literary and the geographical evidence of the *Vedic* literature to infer that this tradition was essentially Indo-Aryan (Kak 1992a). Nevertheless, since the Indus tradition appears to have been characterized by several ethnic groups (Shaffer 1992, Kenoyer 1991), it is very likely that several languages, some of them non-Indo-Aryan, were also present in the area. Our conclusion that the Indo-Aryans represented the Harappan ethnic group is based on our analysis of the Indus script which seems to have been used for an Indo-Aryan language (Kak 1998, 1989, 1990) and on the geographical evidence from the *Vedic* literature.

Phases of the Indus-Saraswati Tradition

In its earliest phase the Indus-Saraswati tradition was characterized by cultivation and animal husbandry. Cattle pastoralism was an extremely important component of the economy. It is estimated that as early as 5500 BC, domesticated cattle were already central to food production. In this respect the Indus-Saraswati tradition is different from the tradition of Mesopotamia which emphasized domesticated sheep and goats. Jim Shaffer (Shaffer and Lichtenstein 1989, Shaffer 1992) views the evolution of the culture in the Indus region in four broad eras. The first is the early food producing era (*c.* 6500-5000 BC) that is characterized by an absence of ceramics. The next is the regionalization era (5000-2600 BC) where distinct artifact styles (including ceramics) develop regionally. The third is the integration era (2600-1900 BC) where we see pronounced cultural homogeneity and the development of urban centres. The fourth era is that of localization (1900-1300 BC) where characteristic patterns from the integration era are seen to blend with regional ceramic styles. This era indicates decentralisation and restructuring of the interaction networks.

Amongst the many factors at the basis of the evolution of this tradition, changes in farming are considered to be quite important. According to Richard Meadow (1989:61):

> Two distinct agricultural revolutions can be identified for the northwestern region of the South Asia during the pre and protohistoric period. The first involved the establishment by the sixth millennium B.C. of a farming complex based principally on the rabi (winter sown, spring harvested) crops of wheat and barley...The second saw the addition by the early second millennium B.C. of kharif (summer sown, fall harvested) cereals including sorghum, various millets, and rice.

In the arid and semi-arid areas, buildings were made out of mud bricks and fired bricks and stone but it is likely that wood structures were used in regions where wood was easily available. There was public architecture as in plazas, streets, public buildings, wells, drains, and tanks. Pottery was mass produced by using wheels and sometimes by moulds. Painted decorations used a variety of geometric, animal, and floral motifs which are still popular in India. A network of long distance trade existed. Turquoise from central Asia, lapis lazuli from northern Afghanistan, and shells from the coast of the Arabian sea have been found at Mehrgarh.

Cultural and Ethnic Diversity

The Indus-Saraswati tradition consists of several styles, that probably represent different ethnic groups. The richest period of this tradition is named Harappan after the site of Mohenjo-Daro was discovered. Since then other major sites of Dholarvira, Ganweriwala, Kalibangal, Lothal and Rakhigarhi as well close to 2500 smaller settlements have been discovered. The Harappan world covered an area of 650,000 to 800,000 square kilometers that stretch from the Himalayas in the north to the Tapti river in the south, and from the Indus river valleys in the west to the plains of the Ganga and Yamuna rivers in the east. According to a recent estimate (Misra 1992), nearly two-thirds of the sites have been found along the Saraswati river, a majority of the remaining one-third of the sites are located in Gujarat and Uttar Pradesh; the Indus valley proper has less than 100 sites (Fig.1).

A temporal pattern underlying the settlements is also clear. Indus and Saraswati valleys, Kutch, and parts of Saurashtra were the focus of the early and mature Harappan settlements, whereas the upper course of Satluj, trans-Yamuna region of Uttar Pradesh, and Saurashtra were the focus of the post-Harappan settlements.

While the Harappan city seemed to evolve out of an irregular net plan, it had two distinctive elements. In many cases to the west lay a 'citadel' on a high platform that based the public and ceremonial buildings. To the east was the lower city with straight, wide main streets that divided the city into large blocks. The blocks in turn were served by narrow curving lanes. The houses were built of generally standardized burnt bricks. They were planned as several rooms around a square courtyard, and were often of two or more stories. Some houses had bathrooms which were connected by bricklined drains to sewers under the main streets. Many windows were screened with grilles of terracotta or alabaster. Houses presented blank walls to the streets and, in many cases, the doors opened on the side lanes in a manner that would not be out of place in a traditional city in contemporary Punjab.

Monument at Mohenjo-Daro

On of the striking buildings in the citadel at Mohenjo-Daro is the great bath. The oblong bath is 39 feet long, 23 feet wide, and 8 feet deep. It was sunk into the paving of a courtyard and it was approached from the north and south by brick steps with possible wooden stair-treads. The floor of the bath sloped to an outlet that led in turn to an arched drain deep enough for a man to stand upright. Just north of the pool were eight small bathrooms drained by little tunnels in the floor. Each bathroom had its own staircase leading to the second storey which may have housed cells for the priests, if the whole complex was like a tank of a Hindu temple.

The largest building uncovered at Mohenjo-Daro was probably a palace of size 230 feet long and 78 feet wide. At Harappa a building twice this size, that may have served as a granary, has been discovered. It is significant that the dimensions of these monuments are in units that are related to each other. If the dimensions of the bath are in the proportion 1:1.7, that of the palace are 10:3.4. The relationship between the sides suggests a normative approach to architecture reminiscent of *Vedic* architecture. This conclusion is reinforced by the directional symmetries in the buildings.

There are distinct differences in the brickmaking of the two urbanizations. The Harappans used several brick sizes of which the most common had length, breadth, thickness ratios of about 4:2:1. The bricks used during the second urbanization of the Ganga valley are not as per this ratio, one type encountered there has the ratio 7:4:1. But this departure may merely be a result of the popularization of one of the existing styles in a multi-ethnic and multi-cultural society. We do not observe a complete break with the earlier tradition, but only reorganization and re-adjustment. Thus corbelled drains, characteristic of the Harappans, persist in Ganga valley.

The Harappan settlements along the Saraswati were located on the desert scarp above the entrenched river. On the other hand, the settlements during the age of Painted Grey Ware (1200-800 BC) are found within the entrenchment on the bed of the river (Possehl and Raval 1989). This establishes two important chronological markers. First, the river had dried up before the PGW era. Second, the *Rigvedic* age which describes the Saraswati river as one of the largest of its times lies prior to the drying up of Saraswati. Recent satellite remote sensing has shown that the river was as wide as 8 kilometers at places (Francfort 1992). There are reasons to assume that the abandonment of the Harappan sites in the Saraswati valley region was caused by this drying up. This suggests the epoch of 1900 BC for this change.

Fire Altars and Script

Ceremonial structures that appear to be fire altars have been found in Lothal and Kalibangan (Rao 1979, Lal 1984, Thapar 1985). A brick-lined fire pit at Kalibangan has five layers of bricks just as a *Vedic* altar would. A platform in the 'citadel' at Kalibangan has seven fire altars in a north-south row, which parallels the six *Vedic dhishnya* hearths that are also placed in the same directional orientation. Another significant building at Mohenjo-Daro has been identified by Dhavalikar and Atre (1989) as a fire temple (Fig. 2). The building is 62 feet long and 50 feet wide; it has a central courtyard and a symmetric arrangement of rooms. Every alternate room has a low brick platform and one of the rooms has a staircase leading to an upper floor. It appears that a fire altar was placed in the central courtyard. This fire temple has symmetric features that have much commonality with the architectural *mandalas* discovered in North Afghanistan that have been dated to 2000 BC (Sarianidi 1977).

I have recently proposed that the writing of the Harappan era, which has hitherto been called Indus writing, be properly called the Saraswati writing (Kak 1993 d), Saraswati is connected in the Indian tradition with writing and learning; on the other hand the Harappan settlements where

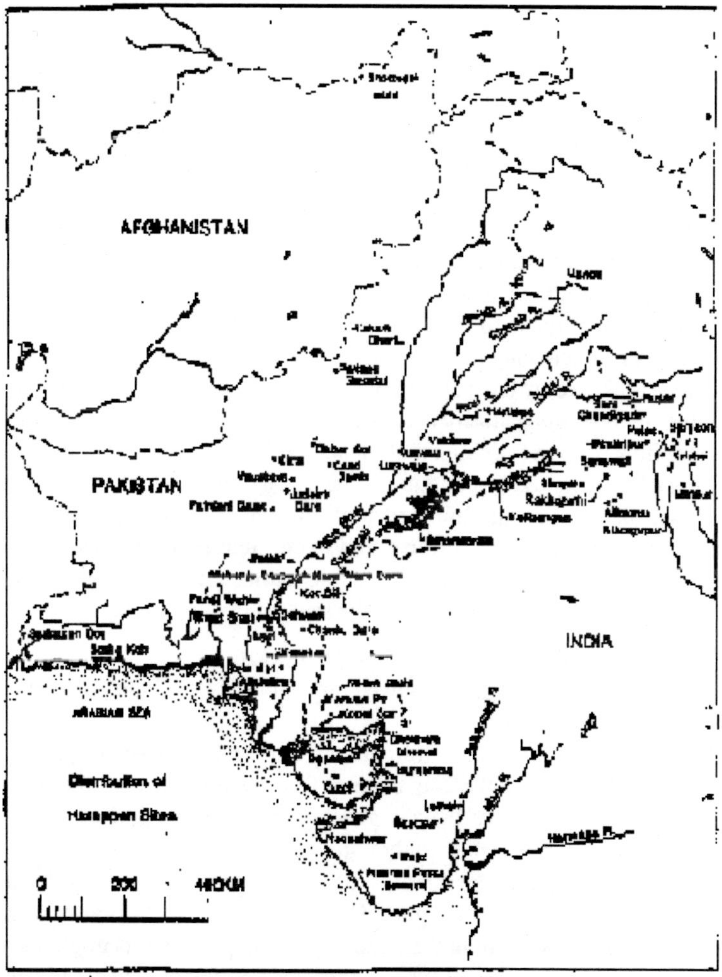

Figure 1. **Harrapan sites of the 3rd millennium B.C.E.**

the earliest writing was used were based primarily along the Saraswati river. In later mythology Saraswati is remembered as the wife of Brahma, or as Brahmi, representing thereby the transformation in the script.

The writing of the Harappans has survived in carvings on seals, small pieces of soft stone, and copper tablets. The total number of inscribed objects is around 4200, but many of these are duplicates (Mahadevan 1977, Joshi and Parpola 1987). But it should be remembered that many of the large Harappan towns have not yet been excavated and therefore it is likely that our written records in the Saraswati writing will go up. The number of different signs used is close to 400, but these include the various numeral signs as well as the conjuncts of the more basic signs. Most texts are very brief, the average length being 5 signs, and the longest text, on a three-sided 'amulet', is 26 signs long. The longest inscription on a single side is 17 sings, in three lines, on a seal. The primary purpose of the seals was perhaps to mark ownership and the copper tablets may have served as amulets. A large number of seal impressions on clay have also survived. These are likely to have served as tags which were attached to bales of goods, for the reverse sides often show traces of packing materials. The impressions of the seals are likely to have served as signatures. The pictorial motifs that accompany the writing include the humped bull, buffalo, elephant, tiger, rhino, crocodile, antelope, fish, tortoise, and so on. Geometric designs include the swastika, spoked wheel, and a circle with a dot. These pictures are similar to the ones that show up in the seals of two thousand years later.

Extensive Foreign Trade

Signs of extensive trade between the world of the Indus-Saraswati tradition and central and west Asian regions have been found. The Harappans also did maritime trading, and their seals have been recovered in Mesopotamia from the 24th century BC onwards. On the other hand Persian Gulf seals have been found in the Harappan port of Lothal. Inlands the Harappans moved their goods using wheeled carts, camels, and boats. They used strikingly accurate weights in a series that is preserved in later Indian weights. The same unique series is also found on the island of Bahrein in the Persian Gulf suggesting this might have been their colony. Some of the weights are so tiny that they could have been used by jewellers to measure gold, others are so big that they must have been hoisted by ropes. Their products would have included fine pottery wares, jewellery, copper and bronze vessels, and woven cotton goods. The variety and extent of this trade indicates that credit-keeping and calculations were very important to the Harappans. The length measurements also appear to have been preserved in the later Indian length measures.

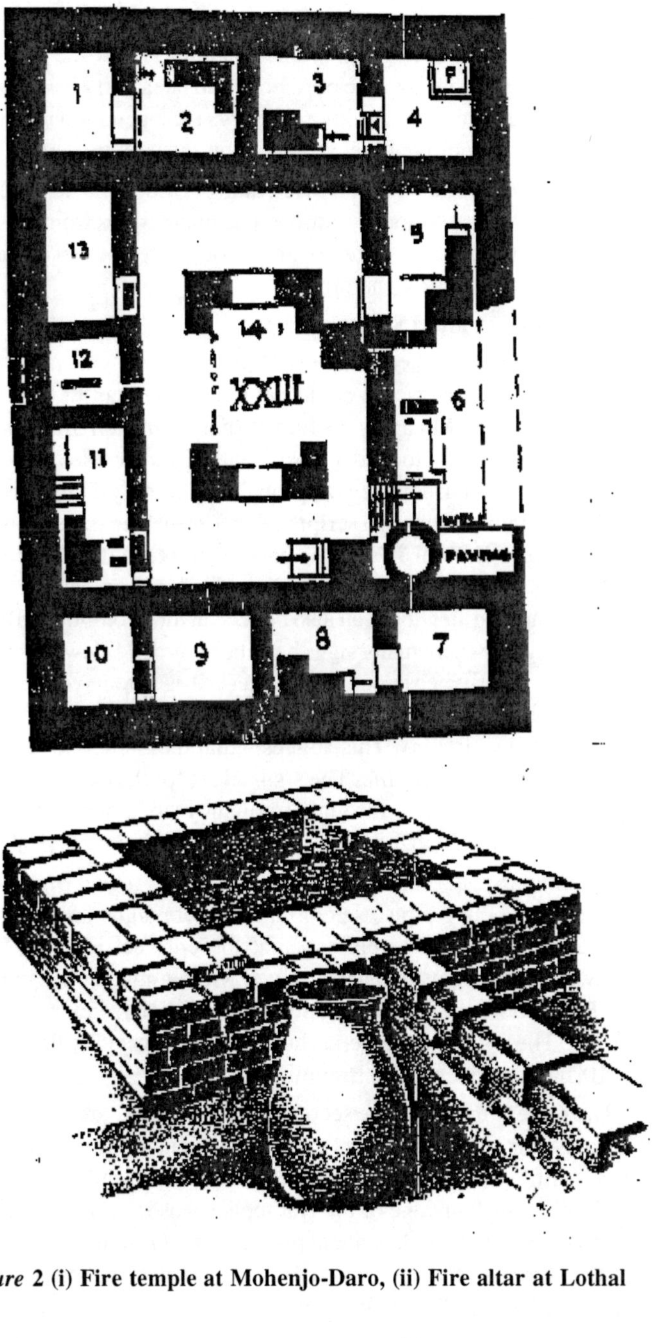

(i)

(ii)

Figure **2 (i) Fire temple at Mohenjo-Daro, (ii) Fire altar at Lothal**

Pran Nath noted the striking similarities in the iconography of the Harappan seals and the punch-marked coins of the first millennium BC (Fabri 1935, Mainkar 1984). Another parallel is that the seals of the historical period, from the time of Ashoka and later, carry brief texts like-the Indus-Saraswati seals. In almost all cases the legends on the historical seals end in the genitive case, representing ownership.

The exceptions are where no case-ending is used, or where the ending is nominative as in religious formulae. The impressions from these seals, like the earlier seals of the Harappan period, were used to authenticate records, or to serve as signatures.

Saraswati and Brāhmi Scripts

An analysis of Saraswati and Brāhmi reveals obvious connections between the two scripts that could not have arisen out of chance (Kak 1988, 1989, 1990). My analysis showed that the most frequent letters of Saraswati and Brahmi looked almost identical and besides, they were in the same order of frequency. A probabilistic analysis confirmed the connection between the two scripts (Kak 1988). The transformation of Saraswati into Brāhmi is seen to have occurred with changes in the orientations of some signs. For example the fish sign has been flipped over. Similar modifications can also be seen in the evolution of Brāhmi to the later Nāgari, where many signs have been turned sideways or upside-down. The genitive case-ending in Sanskrit is often *sya* or *sa* and in Prakrit the ending is generally *sa* or *ssa* and this is what we frequently see in these inscriptions. This suggests that the Saraswati language is likely to have been *Prākritic.* The sign values for the case-endings were obtained independently through frequency considerations. Further checks were obtained in the readings of some specific signs (Kak 1992a).

To summarize the connections between Saraswati and Brahmi, it may be noted that both scripts use conjuncts where signs are combined to represent compound vowels and that the core set of most frequent Saraswati signs seems to have survived without much change in shape into *Brāhmi* where it corresponds to the most frequent sounds of Sanskrit. The writing of numerals in Saraswati, especially the signs for 5 and 10, have carried over to Brāhmi.

The pottery marks in late second millennium BC are reminiscent of the Saraswati signs (Rao 1982) as are the signs on the punch-marked coins a millennium later. The other evidence on cultural continuity suggest that the language of the Harappans was Indo-Aryan. This is in consonance with the independent proposals by Gimbutas (1973, 1985), T.V. Gamkrelidze and V.V. Ivanov (1985), [see also Diakonov 1985] and Colin Renfrew (1987) that posit a dispersal of the Indo-European languages much earlier than previously thought. The relationship between Saraswati and Brāhmi is one more piece of evidence that interlocks with other similar evidence from archaeology and literature linking the Harappan and Ganga civilizations.

Geographical Evidence from the *Vedic* Books

The main home of the *Vedic* Indians was the region between the Saraswati and the Drishadvati rivers. There is reference in the *Rigveda* to the performance of the fire ritual on the banks of these rivers. The various references to the rivers suggest that the *Vedic* world extended from central India to Afghanistan. The heartland is described as a region that is bounded by four seas (lakes). Bhargava (1964) theorizes that these lakes were in the courses of Indus, Ganga, Saraswati to the three sides of Punjab and the lake in the valley of Kashmir. There is also several descriptions of the rivers of this region draining into a sea and of ships, some of which were equipped with sails. In the *Vājasaneyi Samhita* it is mentioned that five rivers feed into the Saraswati. This suggests that trade via rivers and the sea must have been important then. Saraswati is praised the most out of all the rivers which indicates that many of the *Rigvedic* hymns must have been composed at its banks.

In *Rigveda* 6.61 there is reference to the Saraswati occupying three abodes; in *Rigveda* 5.43 it is explained that one of these abodes is the sky. This suggests a celestial origin as was attributed later to Gangā. When in the *Brāhmana* period Saraswati dried up its mythology was transferred to Ganga. The name Yamunā is likely to have represented its being the twin to Saraswati; later this appelation became correct for Ganga.

Also after the period of the *Samhitas,* the river Indus is rarely mentioned, suggesting that the focus of the civilization had shifted. In the *Rigveda* itself Gangā is mentioned only once (10.75.5) in contrast to the frequent references to Saraswati.

There are references to major tectonic changes in the literature that follows *Rigveda*. For example, the Jain book *Kahakosu* (35.1-3) speaks of how the Yamuna river changed its course to flow north of Mathura. Such changes led to extensive flooding and draining of many lakes as well as desiccation of rivers. The decline of Mohenjo-Daro is likely to have been the economic collapse of the heartland owing to the drying up of Saraswati around 1900 BC. This then represents a terminus and quem for the *Rigvedic* age.

There are references to Saraswati reaching the sea in Gujarat in the *Mahabharata* (see Bhargava 1964) and the *Puranas* (for example *Brahmapurana* 77.2). This suggests that the original core of the epic and the *Purana* must also date back into the *Rigvedic* era.

It is believed that sedimentation and tectonic movement led to the capture of the Saraswati system by the Satluj (Shatadru) river of the Indus system and the Yamuna river of the Ganga system (Francfort 1992. Gentelle 1986, Kenoyer 1991). This led to the drying up of the Saraswati and the Drishadvati rivers, in whose valleys most of the Harappan settlements were situated. Francfort (1992) claims that a network of canals was used by the Harappans for irrigation. He further suggests that Drishadvati (modern Chautang) might have been dry before the Harappan phase.

The corroboration for the conclusion that Saraswati became dry at the end of the Harappan phase comes from the fact that there are no Harappan sites on the Yamuna although they are present on its easterly seasonal tributaries. At the same time we do find Harappan sites along a westerly earlier course of Yamuna that connects to the Saraswati river.

The disruption in the economy of the heartland caused cities like Harappa to decline. A fundamental shift took place in the economic life of the Harappans. Theirs had been a dual economy based on agriculture and pastoralism. The emerging society was more intensively focused on agriculture. There was therefore an emigration away from the earlier towns to new communities in less arid regions. The farming practices changed. The new economy did not at first generate surplus wealth to lead to urban centres of the same size as in the earlier age. Eventually new powerful cities were established due east at Kaushambi, Atranjikhera, and Mathura. The *Vedic* literature also speaks of a gradual relocation from the area of Sapta Saindhava which is practically identical to the Harappan domain.

Saraswati–the mighty river

During the *Rigvedic* period Saraswati was the most important river. Sindhu (Indus), Saraswati, and Sarayu are called great streams in *RV* 10.64 and in *RV* 7.95 Saraswati is declared to be the mightiest of all rivers. *RV* 10.75 speaks of three groups of seven rivers that reflects the tripartite system of classification, characteristic of *Vedic* knowledge.

The earliest *Vedas* describe a society that is partly urban and partly agricultural and pastoral like the Harappan society. This may be seen most easily from the many occupations listed in *Yajurveda*. The *Rigveda* describes fortified towns. *Rigvedic* ritual requires construction at altars out of bricks. On the other hand, certain structures in the lowest layers of the Harappan sites are clearly fire altars. The *Brahmanas,* which are appendices to the *Vedas*, describe the phase of slow expansion to the east, a region that was originally densely forested. They, in turn, are followed by *Āranyakas* and *Upanishads* that capture the cultural transformation, also paralleled in the Harappa evidence, that values living in forests and small farming communities. The farming described in the *Vedic* books parallels that of the Harappans. Copper is the metal used in the *Vedic* ritual.

That writing was used by the *Vedic* people is indicated partially by a reference to the mark of eight that occurs in the *Rigveda* itself. *Atharva Veda* 19.72 speaks of the book being taken out and placed back in a chest although this might have been meant in a metaphorical sense. *Chhāndogya Upanishad* has several references to syllable counts and to analysis of words in terms of vowels and consonants. *Aitareya Āranyaka*, of the period of forest dwelling, also describes the distinction between vowels and consonants and has reference to writing (*Aitareya Āranyaka* 5.3.3). Several *Upanishads* describe different aspects of the alphabet.

The Expansion of the *Vedic* Culture

The parallels with the work of Ammerman and Cavalli-Sforza (1984) on the spread of farming in Europe are of relevance here. According to this model, which bridges archaeology and population genetics, introduction of farming led to increase in fertility rates and in population density. Their study indicates that the rate of this diffusion was about one kilometer a year. Renfrew has postulated that these early farmers were Indo-Europeans who started out from Near East around 7000 BC.

One may hypothesize a similar process of diffusion at work in the Indo-Aryan expansion across the Yamuna-Ganga plains and beyond. Considering the same rate of expansion of one kilometer/year as in Europe, one would expect the Indo-Aryans to reach the Bay of Bengal from the Punjab region in about 2500 years. If we accept the traditional date of *c*. 3000 BC for the composition of the later parts of *Rigveda,* this agrees with the rise of the Indo-Aryan city states in eastern India in the first millennium BC.

As regards the appearance of *Vedic* gods in the Hittite-Mitanni treaty, it is generally accepted that this proves of an intrusion by the Indo-Aryans (e.g. Burrow 1973, Sethna 1980). The hypothesis that such an intrusion represented one branch of migrating Aryans when another branch moved on to India at about the same time has been invalidated by the accumulated evidence presented in this paper. We propose that after the collapse of the Harappan economic system upon the desiccation of Saraswati, one branch of the *Vedic* Indians migrated west. Such a tradition is in fact remembered by the *Puranas*. But it is also likely that Aryans might have already been present in Iran and further west. The Zoroastrians remember having spent time in Sapta Saindhava before

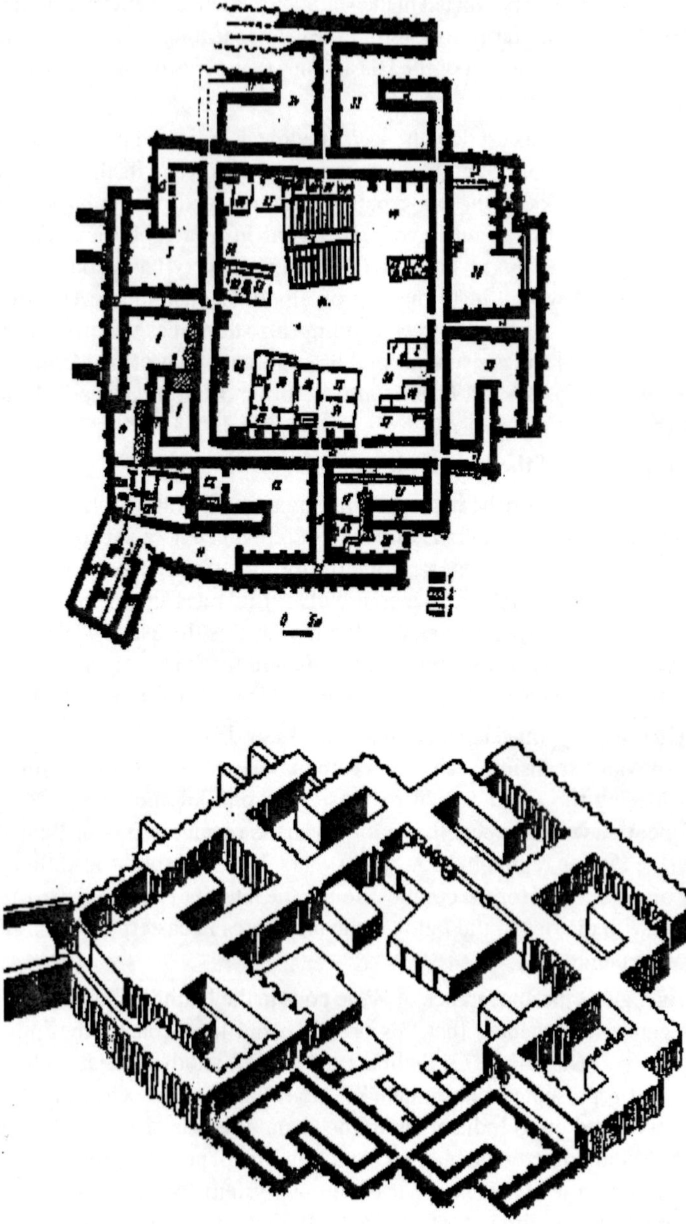

***Figure* 3. The Tantric palace at Dashli-3 in North Afghanistan *c* 2000 BC**

entering Iran. This suggests that such a time might have been spent before the epoch of 1900 BC And as Benvesnsite (1973) argues the struggle between the Aryans and the *Dasyu* represented the struggle between the Indo-Aryans and the Iranians. The Iranians moved into Iran in stages and they struggled to suppress worship of *Vedic* gods in their western regions for a long time. Nevertheless, their religion continued to have close parallels with the *Vedic* religion.

Evidence for the present of the Indo-Aryan theories in the periphery of their world is to be found in the palaces and forts found in North Afghanistan which have been dated to 2000 BC that are according to *tāntric* designs (Sarianidi 1977). Fig. 3 shows a palace from Dashli-3 that is clearly a *mandala*. Note also the building of Fig. 4 from the same region that is dated to the first millennium BC. Architecturally this building is related both to the fire temple of Fig. 2 from Mohenjo-Daro as well as the mandala of Fig. 3.

Conclusions

The astronomical, geographical and other literary references in the *Vedic* literature make sense only if this tradition remembers events in India that go back to the third millennium BC and earlier. The heartland of the *Vedic* people was the region around the Saraswati river. Settlements along this river were abandoned by 1900 BC. The Saraswati valley area was the breadbasket of the Harappans and the large urban centres of Harappa and Mohenjo-Daro appear to have served as gateway cities at the borders (Ratnagar 1982). These parallels imply the identity of the Harappans and the *Vedic* Indians. The memory of the literate phase of the *Vedic* history was mythologised in naming Saraswati as the goddess of learning and wisdom. Since the Harappan phase is merely one manifestation of the Indus-Saraswati tradition that shows great continuity and goes back to at least 6500 BC, we conclude that this tradition was principally *Vedic*. These conclusions agree broadly with the traditional chronology of India.

Notes & References

Ammerman, A.J. and Cavalli-Sforza, L.L. 1984. *The Neolithic Transitions and the Genetics of Populations in Europe,* (Princeton University Press).

Anthony, D., Telegin, D.Y., Brown, D, 1991. "The origin of horseback riding", Princeton. *Scientific American,* December, 94-100.

Beveniste, E. 1973. *Indo-European Language and Society*. Coral Gables: University of Miami Press.

Bhargava, P.L. 1964. *The Geography of Rigvedic India*. Lucknow: Upper India Publishing.

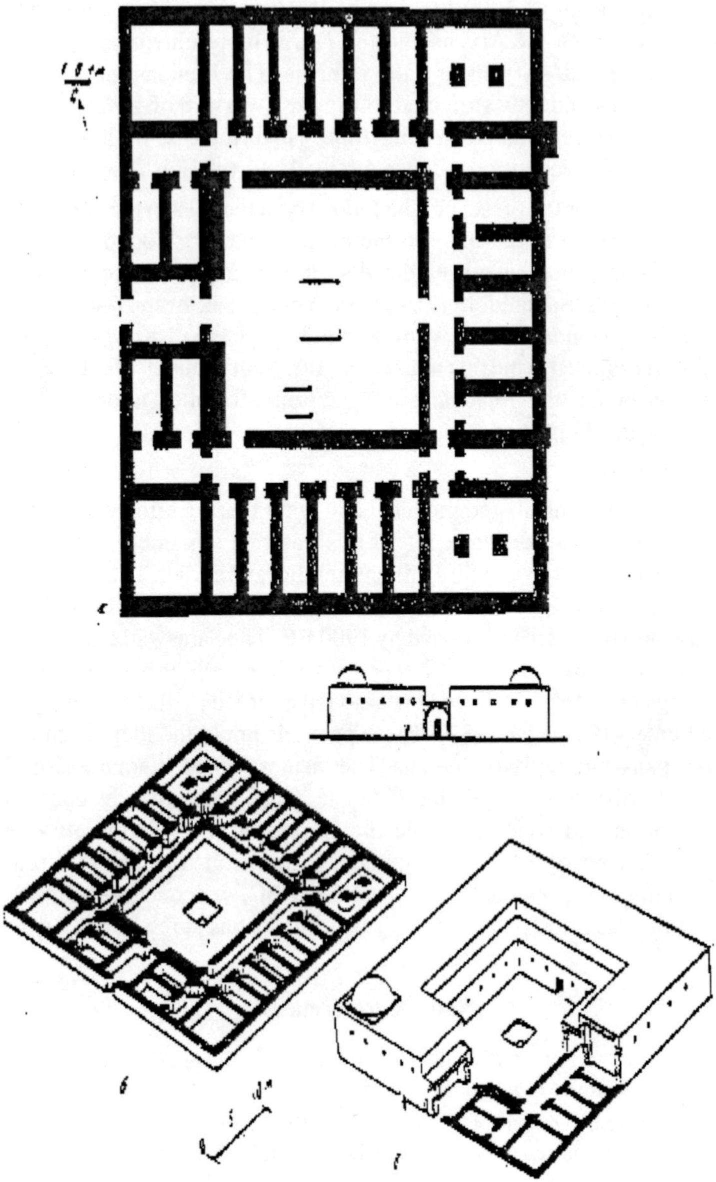

***Figure* 4. Building plan at Kutlug Tepe in Bactria *c* 1st millennium B.C.E.**

Brecher, K. and Feirtag, M. 1979. *Astronomy of the Ancients.* Cambridge: The M.I.T. Press.

Burrow, T. 1973. "The proto-Indo aryans". *Journal of the Royal Asiatic Society,* 1973, 123-140.

Cavalli-Sforza, L.L. 1991. "Genes, peoples and languages", *Scientific American*, November, 104-110.

Cunningham, A. 1883. *A Book of Indian Eras.* Calcutta; reprint Benares, 1970.

Deppert, Joachim, 1983. *India and the West,* Delhi.

D'iakonov, I.M. 1985. "On the original home of the speakers of Indo-European", *Journal of Indo-European Studies,* 13, 92-174.

Dhavalikar, M.K. and Atre, S. 1989. "The fire cult and virgin sacrifice: some Harappan rituals". In J.M. Kenoyer (ed.), *Old Problems and New Perspectives in the Archaeology of South Asia,* Wisconsin Archaeological Reports, Vol. 2. University of Wisconsin, Madison.

Fabri, C.L. 1935. "The punch-marked coins: a survival of the Indus civilization". *Journal of the Royal Asiatic Society*, 307-318.

Francfort, H-P, 1992. "Evidence for Harappan irrigation system in Haryana and Rajasthan", *Eastern Anthropologist,* 45, 87-103.

Frawley, D. 1991. *Gods, Sages, and Kings,* Salt Lake City: Passage Press.

Gamkrelidze, T.V. and Ivanov, V.V. 1985. The ancient Near East and the Indo European question: Temporal and territorial characteristics of proto-Indo-European based on linguistic and historico-cultural data. *Journal of Indo-European Studies,* 13. 3-91.

Gentelle, P. 1986. "Landscapes, environment and irrigation: hypotheses for the study of the 3rd and 2nd millenniums", *Man and Environment,* 10, 101-110.

Gimbutas, M. 1973. "The beginning of the bronze age in Europe and the Indo-Europeans 3500-2500 BC". *Journal of Indo-European Studies,* I, 163-214.

Gimbutas, M. 1985. "Primary and secondary homeland of the Indo-Europeans". *Journal of Indo-European Studies*, 13, 185-202.

Gonda, Jan 1075, *Vedic Literature,* Wiesbadan: Otto Harrassowitz.

Jarrige, J.-F. and Meadow, R.M. 1980. "The antecedents of the civilization in the Indus valley", *Scientific American*, 243, 2, 122-133.

Joshi, J.P. and Parpola, A. 1987. *Corpus of Indus Inscriptions.* Memoirs of the Archaeological Survey of India, Delhi.

Kak, Subhash C. 1987. "On the chronology of ancient India". *Indian Journal of History of Science,* 22, 222-234.

Kak, Subhash C. 1987. "A frequency analysis of the Indus script". *Cryptologia,* 12, 129-143.

Kak, Subhash C. 1989. "Indus writing", *Mankind Quarterly* 30, 113-118.

Kak, Subhash C. 1990. "Indus and Brahmi: further connections". *Cryptologia* 14 169-183.

Kak Subhash C. 1992a. "The Indus tradition and the Indo-Aryans". *Mankind Quarterly,* 32, 195-213.

Kak, Subhash C. 1992b. "The Astronomy of the Vedic Altars and the Rgveda", *Mankind Quarterly,* 33, 43-55.

Kak, Subhash C. 1993a. "Astronomy in the Shatapatha Brahmana", *Indian Journal of History of Science,* 28, 15-34.

Kak, Subhash C. 1993b. "Planetary periods from the Rigvedic code". *Mankind Quarterly,* 33 (in press).

Kak, Subhash C. 1993c. "Astronomy of the Vedic Altars". *Vistas in Astronomy,* 36, 117-140.

Kak, Subhash C. 1993d. "The structure of the Rigveda", *Indian Journal of History of Science,* 28, 71-79.

Kak, Subhash C. 1993e. "The Verse Structure of the Vedas". *LSU Report,* June 1993.

Kak, Subhash C. and Frawley, David 1992. "Further Observations on the Rigvedic Code", *Mankind Quarterly,* 33, 163-170.

Kenoyer, J.M. 1991. "The Indus valley tradition of Pakistan and Western India". *Journal of World Prehistory,* 5, 331-385.

Lal, B.B. 1984. "Some reflections on the structural remains at Kalibangan". In B.B.Lal and S.P. Gupta (ed.), *Frontiers of the Indus Civilization.* New Delhi: Books and Books.

Macdonell, A.A. 1886 *Katyayana's Sarvanukramant of the Rigveda,* Oxford: The Clarendon Press.

Mahadevan, I, 1977. *The Indus Script.* Memoirs of the Archaeological Survey of India, Delhi.

Mainkar, V.B. 1984. "Metrology in the Indus civilization". In B.B. Lal and S.P. Gupta (ed.), *Frontiers of the Indus Civilization.* New Delhi: Books and Books.

Majumdar, R.C.(ed.) 1951. *The Vedic Age,* London: George Alien and Unwin.

Mallory, J.P. 1989. *In Search of the Indo-Europeans.* New York: Thames and Hudson.

Mallory, J.P. 1992. "Human populations and the Indo-European problem". *Mankind Quarterly,* 33, 131-154.

Meadow, R.H. 1989. "Continuity and change in the agriculture of the greater Indus valley". In J.M. Kenoyer (ed.), *Old Problems and New Perspectives in the Archaeology of South Asia,* Wisconsin Archaeological Reports, vol. 2, University of Wisconsin, Madison.

Misra, V.N. 1992. Research on the Indus civilization: a brief review, *Eastern Anthropologist,* 45, 1-19.

Mitchiner, J.E. 1978, *Studies in the Indus Valley Inscriptions*: New Delhi: Oxford & IBH.

Mitchiner, M. 1973. *The Origins of Indian Coinage,* London: Hawkins Publications.

Moore, W. 1989, Schrodinger: *Life and Thought,* Cambridge: Cambridge University Press.

Pargiter, F.E. 1922, *Ancient Indian Historical Tradition,* London: Oxford University Press.

Parpola, A. 1985. *The Sky-Garment. Helsinki: Studia Orientalia.*

Planck, M. 1959, *Scientific Autobiography,* Williams and Norgate, London.

Possehl, G., (editor) 1982. *Harappan Civilization, A Contemporary Perspective,* Aris & Phillips, Warminster.

Possehl, G. and Raval, M.H. 1989, *Harappan Civilization and Rojdi,* E.J. Brill, Leiden.

Rao, S.R. 1979, *Lothal: A Harappan port town,* New Delhi: Memoirs of the ASI, 78.

Rao, S.R. 1982, *Decipherment of the Indus Script,* Asia, Bombay.

Raster, P. 1992. *Phonetic Symmetries in the First Hymn of the Rigveda.* Innsbruck.

Ratnagar, S. 1982. "The Location of Harappa". In Possehl, G.L. (ed.), *Harappan Civilization,* Aris & Phillips, Warminster.

Renfrew, C. 1987. *Archaeology and Language:* The Puzzle of the Indo-European Origins. Jonathan Cape, London.

Roy, S.B. 1983. "Chronological framework of Indian protohistory-the lower limit". *Journal of the Baroda Oriental Institute,* 32, 254-274.

Santillana, Giorgio de and Dechend, Hertha von 1969. Hamlet's Mill, *An essay on myth and the frame of time.* Boston: Gambit.

Sarianidi, V.I. 1977. *Drevnie zemeldel'tsy Afganistana.* Moskva.

Seidenberg, A. 1962. "The ritual origin of geometry", *Archive for History of Exact Sciences,* 1, 488-527.

Seidenberg, A. 1978. "The origin of mathematics". *Archive for History of Exact Sciences,* 18, 301-342.

Sengupta, P.C. 1947. *Ancient Indian Chronology.* University of Calcutta Press, Calcutta.

Sethna, K.D. 1980. *The Problem of Aryan Origins.* Calcutta: S&S Publishers.

Shaffer, J.G. 1984. "The Indo-Aryan invasions: cultural myth and archaeological reality". In J.R. Lukacs (ed.), *The People of South Asia.* Plenum Press, New York.

Shaffer, J.G. 1992. "The Indus valley, Baluchistan, and Helmand traditions: neolithic through bronze age". In R. Ehrich (ed.), *Chronologies in Old World Archaeology* (3rd Edition), University of Chicago Press, Chicago.

Shaffer, J.G. and Lichtenstein, D.A. 1989. "Ethnicity and change in the Indus valley cultural tradition". In J.M. Kenoyer (ed.), *Old Problems and New*

Perspectives in the Archaeology of South Asia, Wisconsin Archaeological Reports, vol. 2, University of Wisconsin, Madison.

Sokal, R.R., Oden, N.L., and Wilson, C. 1991. "Genetic evidence for the spread of agriculture in Europe by demic diffusion". *Nature,* 351, 143-145.

Staal, F. 1988, *Universals,* Chicago: Chicago University Press.

Thapar, B.K. 1985, *Recent Archaeological Discoveries in India,* Paris: UNESCO.

Tilak, B.G. 1893. *The Orion.* Poona (Reprinted 1989).

20

The Aryans : A Reappraisal of the Problem

B.K. Thapar*

During the present century, perhaps very few subjects have been so absorbing as those relating to the problems of the Aryans. Despite the restraining pleas of some distinguished scholars to give Aryans a holiday, the subject continues to attract the attention of the archaeologists, anthropologists and philologists all over the world. The stage of flogging the dead horse has not, therefore, been reached in this subject which still remains purposeful.

Philologists are not unanimous over the terms Aryans and Indo-Europeans. While the former is used variously in the context of language, race, nobility and even citizenship, the latter is considered clumsy and inappropriate. Gordon Childe who made an analytical study of the Aryans[1] felt that the literary evidence was inconclusive and that it must be supplemented by archaeological and anthropological data. Since then, various scholars have investigated the fascinating problem of (a) the origin and diffusion of the Indo-European languages and (b) the homeland of the Aryans. While the study of the former problems, bearing on the distribution of *Satem* and *Centum* groups of languages and their phonetic peculiarities being essentially an objective one, has yielded some tangible results, the homeland of the Aryans still remains elusive, the study being based on comparison and abstraction, and thus beset with pitfalls.

There is a wide divergence of views among scholars[2] regarding the homeland of the Aryans, the suggested regions being as disparate as Scandinavia on the one hand and Tibet on the other—Arctic region, Baltic region, Danube basin, central European steppes, including the Carpathian plains, Siberia, Ukranian steppes, lower Volga area (between the Altai and Kazakistan), southern Russia (between Caucasus and eastern Europe), Turkmenia, north-western Kirghiz steppes, Pamirs, Asia

---

* Former Director-General, Archaeological Survey of India, Excavated more than a dozen sites in India including the famous Indus-Saraswati site of Kalibangan.

Minor, Bacteria or Sogdiana, great plateau of Central Asia and the land of the Sapta Sindhu. The last named region is taken by some scholars to include eastern India as well.[3] It will be seen that all potentially habitable regions lying roughly between 30° and 70° north parallels and 5° and 95° east meridians, some of them almost cheerless and marked by sterility, have variously been enumerated as the possible primitive habitat of the Aryans. Equally divergent are the theories regarding the date of their first appearance, ranging as they do between 8000 BC and the middle of the second millennium BC. Which of these theories, relating both to the cradle-land and the date of the first appearance of the Aryans, is correct, cannot, at the present stage of our research, be established with any certitude. Some of these conclusions have been received with scepticism and the solution of the problem does not appear to be as simple as generally believed. The present paper attempts to review the evidence from the Indian standpoint.

Philological Background

The first appearance of the Aryan people is reported from the northern borders of Iraq. That they were intruders is clear from archaeological records. It is surmised that the leaders of the Kassites (*circa* eighteenth century BC), who introduced the horse for drawing chariots in Ancient East, were actually Aryan princes. In the names of the Kassite rulers of Babylonia, names of Indian deities are found to form a significant element, though in other respects, the Kassite language is of a different kind. It has also been demonstrated by the Czech scholar Hrozny that the Hittie language had affinities with that of the Indo-European group, representing perhaps a distinct branch other than that of *Satem* and *Centum*. The presence of Indo-European element in Cappadocia is attested as early as the beginning of the second millennium BC as evidenced by some recognizable names in the Kultepe tablets.[4] The exact position of the Hittite within the Indo-European family, being highly controversial, does not concern us here. A more convincing evidence about the existence of the Aryan dynasty in upper Euphrates and Asia Minor around 1400 BC was obtained from the Mittanian and Hittite archives, found at Tell-el-Amarna and Boghaz-Koy, which mention divine[5] and personal names and numerals, usually believed to be the oldest actual specimens of any Aryan speech, very nearly pure Indic. Jacobi[6] had felt that the names of these Mittanian divinities were Indian and were introduced into Mesopotamia by a body of Sanskrit-speaking people from Punjab. This theory, though endorsed by Pargiter[7] was not accepted by other philologists particularly Eduard Meyer[8] and Husing[9] who felt that these dynasts were Indian, but 'Indian on their way to

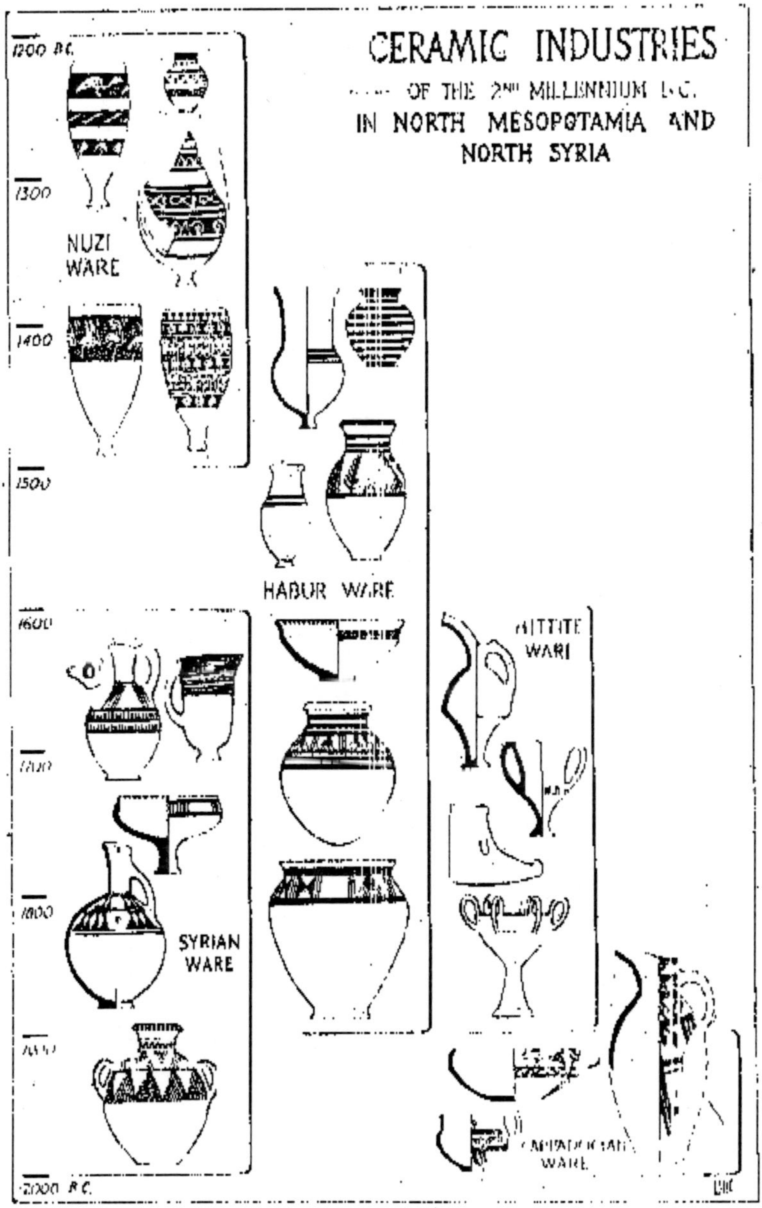
CERAMIC INDUSTRIES
IN NORTH MESOPOTAMIA AND
NORTH SYRIA
1200 B.C.
1300
1400
1500
1600
1800
2000 B.C.
NUZI
WARE
HABUR WARE
SYRIAN
WARE

Fig. **1**

India' and that they had lived with Iranians as one body somewhere north of Caucasus.

It is widely known that on the tablelands of Iran and the north-western part of ancient India, Aryan languages continued, while in the Mittani region these had succumbed to local dialects. Unfortunately, however, in the former region, no written records of these languages are available till about the sixth century BC. For any investigation of the problem connected with the Aryans, therefore, we have to depend upon the material remains of that period (fourteenth-sixth century BC) in these areas. In view of the fresh archaeological discoveries made in India and Pakistan during the last two decades or so, and the considerable advance in the analytical process, it is worthwhile examining the available archaeological evidence bearing on this issue.

Archaeological Evidence: India and Her Neighbours

We may now pass on to the domain of culture-groups, defined by pottery, tools, weapons, etc., belonging to the second millennium BC which is the normally accepted period of movement of the Aryan people from their primitive habitat. In India and Pakistan, claims for the identification of the Aryans have been put forward in respect of the following groups:[10] (i) the Gandhara Grave Clause, (ii) Cemetery 'H' culture, (iii) the Banas culture (iv) the post Harappan Chalcolithic Cultures of Central India and Northern Deccan (v) the Copper Hoard Culture; and (vi) the Painted Grey Ware Culture. In the present scope of this paper it seems proper to pass over in silence theories about the identification of the Indus Civilization with the *Rigvedic* Aryans, for the evidence is of an involved kind based either on the claimed decipherment of the script on the seals[11] or on the professed chronology of the *Rigveda* (*circa* fifth millennium BC), or on the reported occurrence of husk and rice at Lothal or on the promiscuous anthropological evidence obtained from the two cemeteries at Harappa—R 37 and 'H'. Of these culture-groups, only the Painted Grey Ware Culture and Period III of the Gandhara Grave Culture attest the use of iron, the remaining cultures representing the copper/bronze using economy. We may now review each of the above postulates, all of which, it may be stated at the outset, point to an extra-Indian homeland of the Aryans.

The Gandhara Grave Culture and Aryans

The Gandhara Grave Culture is characterized by: (a) three distinct types of burial practices (inflexed articulated, cremation in urns, and fractional or partial); (b) two classes of pottery (red ware and grey ware); (c) use of copper during Periods I and II, and of iron and copper during Period III; and (d) the knowledge of horse-breeding (definitely attested in Period III). On the basis of the C-14 determinations, Period II is dated to the ninth century BC. Dr. Bernhard,[13] on the basis of the detailed study of the skeletal material obtained from the various graves, has recognised two predominant groups of foreign people in the graves: *Eurydolichomorph* or *Proto-Europoid* in Period I and *Leptodolichomorph* or *Mediterranean* in Period III, and maintains that they are 'closely connected with the southern migration of the foreign people into India, which began in the second millennium BC and continued in the first'. On the basis of this evidence the excavator felt that these migrations represented two waves of invasions of the plain grey ware culture, the first association with copper or bronze in about the middle of the second millennium BC and the second with iron towards the beginning of the first millennium BC.

On circumstantial evidence (for no written records are available), the people associated with these migrations are identified with Aryans, the two waves being further explained by the use of the words *ayas*, (generally taken to be copper) in *Rigvedic* literature and *tamra-ayas* (copper) and *krsna-ayas* (iron) in the later *Vedic*. Furthermore, it is seen that Period III marks a new tradition not only in the ritual of the disposal of the dead but also in the use of iron. The evidence suggests that these people were invaders who quickly spread out in the area. Both archaeological and ethnological parallels of the Gandhara Grave Culture have been cited in the cultures of the comparable period in the Central Asian steppes (Sakae tribes and Andronovo Culture). In case we assume that the occupation of this culture, covering Periods I to III, represent the settlement of the Aryan people, may be of two waves, the anthropological differences between Period I and III 'destroyed the earlier populace' for whom they had no regard and whose graves they disturbed, as though sacrilegiously, by robbing stones and building their own houses atop.[14] We have yet to be convinced if a second wave of the people of the same stock would behave in the aforesaid manner. The identification of both the groups, the Proto-Europoid with the massive and bugged bony skull of Periods I and II, and the Mediterranean, with the gracile skull of Period III with the Aryans, therefore, seems to be presumptuous. Or, on the analogy of Scythian Sarmatian series, we have to conceive of a nomadizing Indo-Aryan people penetrating the region and destroying the settlement of their kinsfolk who had arrived earlier.

The possibility of Cemetery 'H' Culture people being Aryans was first suggested by Gordon Childe in 1934[15] and was made out into a plausible hypothesis in 1947[16] by Mortimer Wheeler who averred that cemetery 'H' people were responsible for the distraction of the strongholds of the Indus Civilization, and sought to explain the occurrence of skeletons of men and women in the upper levels of Mohenjodaro, which he thought implied a massacre to the hostile attack of the Aryans. This theory did not carry much,[17] for it was observed that a Harappa cemetery 'H' occupation did not immediately follow the collapse of the Indus settlement but appeared after a lapse of some time, as indicated by an intervening deposit of debris, both in the cemetery and in the habitation area. One could argue that the conquerors having destroyed the strongholds had to level it for making it suitable for habitation and thus explain the intervening deposit which may not represent a hiatus in the cultural sense. But at the same time it must be conceded that the cultural remains of the conquerors, if they are identified with the Aryans, should be found widespread in the area, which is not the case with the Cemetery 'H' Culture. The limited distribution of the Cemetery 'H' Ware (two sites in Bahawalpur, West Pakistan) precludes its association with the Aryans who, according to the literary sources, initially settled in the Ghaggar (Saraswati), Sutlej and upper Ganga valleys. Equally debatable is the postulate regarding evidence of the 'massacre' in the upper levels of Mohenjodaro. It has been demonstrated that not all skeletons belonged to the uppermost levels of the site.[18] The causes of the collapse of Indus Civilization do not concern us here. All that emerges out of the present investigation is that the Cemetery 'H' people were not Aryans.

The Banas Culture and the Aryans

Another evidence of a postulated contact of the Harappan with the Aryan is claimed to be provided by the Banas Culture[19] which in time range extends from *circa* 2000 to 1200 BC[20] and is characterized principally by the use of copper and the White-painted Black-and-red Ware. In the material equipment of this culture, as revealed from the excavations at Ahar and Gilund, Agrawal recognizes two strains: western Asiatic and Harappan. An antecedent stage of this development is sought to be provided by the evidence at Desalpur in Kutch, where in a continuously evolving sequence, the appearance of the new pottery tradition,[21] particularly the cream-slipped bichrome Ware and the White-painted Black-and-red Ware, etc. in Period I B is shown to mark the arrival of new people. The latter, on circumstantial evidence, have been identified with the Aryans. It has been postulated that these very people were also responsible for the collapse of the Indus Civilization in the Kutch region, the Banas Culture being the first attempt at settlement in India by the Aryans. The spread of the Black-and-red ware in the Ganga-Yamuna, *doab*, the lower Ganga basin and central and western India is

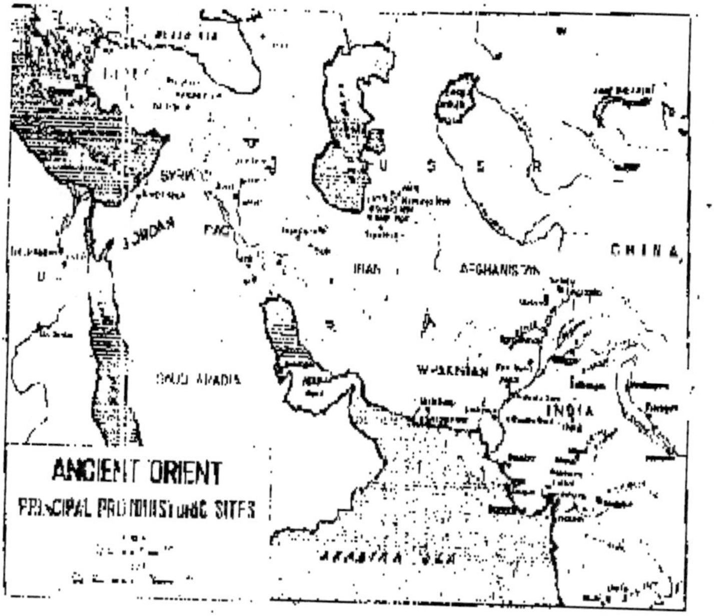

Fig. 2

also attributed to the early colonization by the Aryans. This hypothesis has not been found to be tenable.[22] First, the western Asiatic strain or the Banas Culture (incised decorated spindle whorls, animal-headed handles and a few other pot forms, particularly, the Chandelier type dish-cum-bowl stand) is based on tenuous links of superficial similarities of certain objects found at Ahar and at Tepe Hissar, Shah Tepe, Troy, Geo Tepe and Anau,[23] sometime in disparate chronological horizon. Second, the White-painted Black-and-red Ware does not present any comparable ceramic tradition in western Asia, particularly at the sites where the aforesaid similarities have been noticed. Third, the evidence for the contact of these nomadic Aryans (authors of the Banas Culture) with the Harappans, resulting in heavy borrowing from the latter, and also leading to the final collapse of the latter's culture, seems to be more apparent than real, unless the reported identification of some skeletal remains at Lothal[24] with the Aryans is mentioned as a significant supporting evidence. Fourth, the cream slipped bichrome ware of Period I B at Desalpur does not seem to be a characteristic component element of the Banas Culture. Fifth, it is inconsistent with the views of the philologists,[25] according to whom Rajasthan area was not settled by the first wave of Aryans but by a later wave associated with the Sauraseni

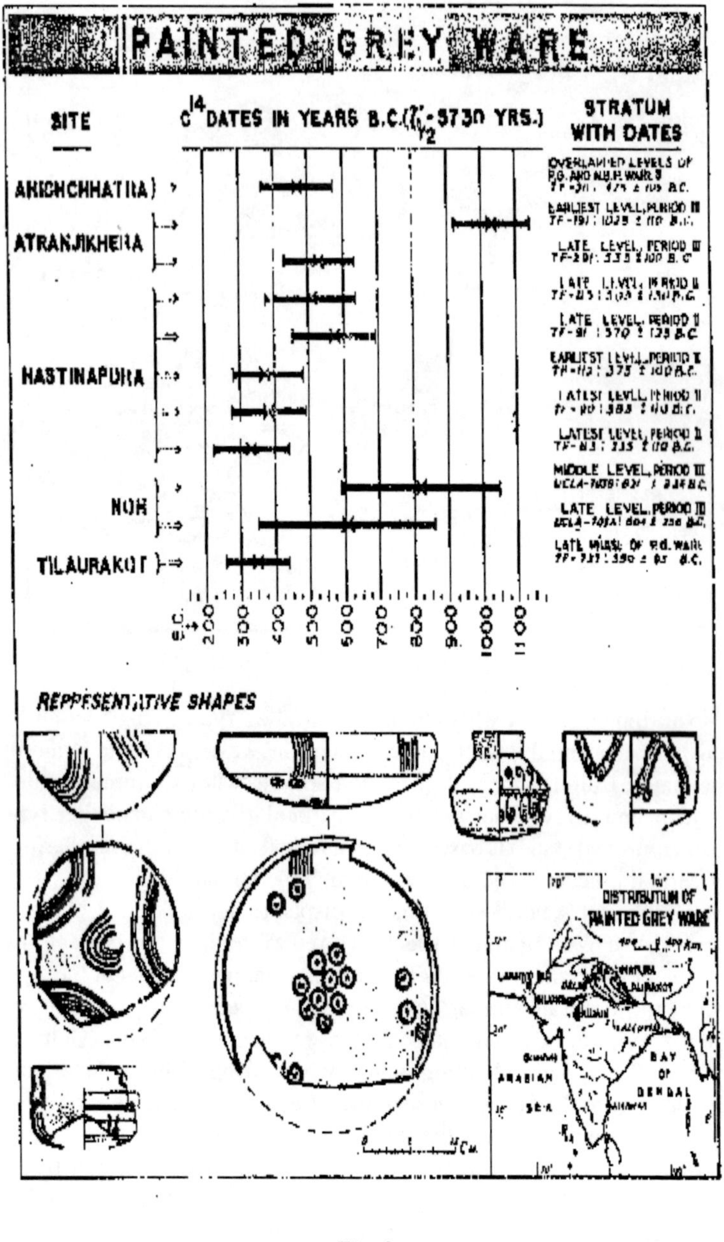
PAINTED GREY WARE
SITE
DATES IN YEARS B.C.
STRATUM WITH DATES
AHICHCHHATRA
ATRANJIKHERA
HASTINAPURA
NOH
TILAURAKOT
200
300
400
500
600
700
800
900
1000
1100
REPRESENTATIVE SHAPES
DISTRIBUTION OF PAINTED GREY WARE
ARABIAN SEA
BAY OF BENGAL

Fig. 3

language. Sixth, it seems to raise new problems regarding the route which the Aryans took on their way to India, the usually accepted view being that they migrated into northern India through the passes in the Hindu Kush mountains located on the north-western frontiers of the present day West Pakistan.

The Chalcolithic Cultures and the Aryans

An equally problematic identification of the Aryans has been suggested by Sankalia with the authors of the post-Harappan Chalcolithic Cultures of Central India and Northern Deccan.[26] On the basis of the *Puranic* evidence, the colonization of the Narbada valley had commenced much earlier than the *Mahabharata* war which was dated by Pargiter[27] to about 950 BC. The only remains of settlement prior to 1000 BC in this area relate to the chalcolithic cultures of Central India and Northern Deccan, dated to *circa* 1700-1000 BC and characterized by (a) distinctive black-painted red wares, (b) microliths and blades, (c) restricted use of copper and (d) distinctive modes of burials. Their level of economy was essentially agrarian and pre-urban. A few pottery types, including certain decorative themes, belonging to these cultures have analogues on some sites in Iran and Iraq.[28] Do these similarities indicate a migration of Aryan tribes from West Asia and their subsequent settlement in central India, etc. around 1700 BC? If so, do these latter settlements represent colonization by Askakas or Assokas[29] or by the Yadavas and Haihayas of *Puranic* tradition? In the latter case, their relative position in a time-sequence of Aryan colonization in India would be later than the settlements in the Ganga-Yamuna *doab* which, on the basis of the *Puranic* history, were colonized by the forebears of the Hailhayas-the Iksvakus-some generation earlier.

The Claim of Kausambi

This brings us to the evidence brought forth by the excavations at Kausambi.[30] Here, out of a total of twenty-five structural phases, the first four are reported to have yielded certain pottery forms which resemble those obtained from Navdatoli, Rangpur, Somnath, Mehgam, Motamachiala, etc., in post-Harappan and late Harappan contexts. On the basis of the close affinity in pottery types, Sharma claims that the earliest settlers of Kausambi and those of Navdatoli belong to the same culture community, representing perhaps the first Aryan immigrants. As an additional support to this hypothesis, the theory of Hoernle, relating to the two waves of Aryan immigrants into India, has been cited. It is also surmised, though not without subjecting reasoning, that this group 'sacked the Harappan cities and conquered them'. Elaborating this postulate, it has been professed that 'urban revolution in the Ganga valley was achieved by a people who lived in close proximity of the Harappans from whom they borrowed not only the conception of a town and a citadel but also the various elements of architecture'. Except for the superficial similarities of pottery types mentioned above, these extrapolations are not warranted by archaeological evidence. In which area of the Harappan empire—Sind, Punjab, Rajasthan or Gujarat—was this contact or conquest made has nowhere of the Harappan cities (Rangpur, Somnath, Mehgam, Motamachiala) and the early phase of the Central Indian Chalcolithic Culture (Navdatoli) could be conceived, there is no evidence of any borrowing of the element of urban architecture from or conquest of the former by the latter. From the fairly intensive evidence of excavation at more than half-a-dozen sites in central and western India, it is clear that the chalcolithic cultures of the region had predominantly a rural economy. Furthermore, as a composite assemblage, the Central Indian Chalcolithic Culture (typified here by Navdatoli) does not compare with the culture represented by Period I at Kausambi. One of the principal component elements of the former culture, viz. microliths and blades, is conspicuously absent at Kausambi. Conversely, the use of iron and the building of massive fortifications (battered clay rampart, revetted externally with baked bricks laid in english boding) in the upper half of Period I at Kausambi does not find any parallel development in the chalcolithic cultures of Central India and Northern Deccan. Besides, according to the known time-brackets of these cultures, the earliest settlement at Kausambi began sometime around 1100 BC, by which time the Chalcolithic Cultures of Central India and Northern Deccan were already drawing to a close. In case the similarities of pottery types have still to be given any weight for the argument of Aryan settlement of Madhyadesa, we have to think in terms of a movement of Aryans from Central India towards Ganga-Yamuna *doab* with a chain of sites showing comparable elements of the cultural millieu along the line of transmission. The available evidence does not permit any such conclusion.

The Copper Hoards and Aryans

The next hypothesis, put forward in 1936 by R. Heine Geldern,[31] and initially supported by Stuart Piggott[32] relates to the identification of the *Vedic* Aryans with the authors of the Copper Hoards. The conclusions were based on the typological study of the tools, particularly on the analogies of (i) the trunnion celt from Shalozan, (ii) the fan-hilted sword from Fort Munro, (iii) the shaft-hole axe from Shahi Tump and Chanhudaro, (iv) the tubular shaft hole axe-adze from Mohenjodaro, (v) harpoon-heads from the sites in the Ganga Valley and (vi) the antennae swords from Fatehgarh and Kallur with those from sites in west Asia, including northern Caucasus, Afghanistan and southern Russia, dated to circa 1200-1000 BC.

It was asserted that these tools represent archaeological traces of the Aryan invaders on their way from western Asia. By a careful analysis of the material, the above hypothesis was found to be unworkable.[33] In fact, the very basis of the whole argument was undermined by showing that the first four tool-types listed above did not form a part and parcel of the 'Copper Hoards' as presumed by Heine-Geldern. In fact, on typological grounds, two zones of the area of distribution of these Hoards were distinguished:[34] the eastern zone characterized by simpler types (flat axes, bar celts and shouldered axes) and the central *doab* by advanced types ('barbed harpoons, anthropomorphic figures, double-edged antennae swords, etc.). The discovery, during the last decade, of three more 'Copper Hoards' [from (i) Khurdi[35] in District Nagaur of Rajasthan, (ii) Mehsana,[36] (iii) Karakoram],[37] has not substantially altered the position. Daggers of Fort Munro type, trunnion celts and axe-adzes were never found in the Ganga plains. The distinctive typology of the 'Copper Hoards', therefore, indicates a separate cultural pattern. Technological studies[38] revealed that in the technique of both alloying and forging, the Copper Hoards were unrelated to the Harappans or other chalcolithic traditions of western and central India. Furthermore, it has also been demonstrated that the 'Copper Hoards' of the central *doab* (notably upper Ganga basin) were associated, on circumstantial evidence, with a ceramic, labelled the 'Ochre Colour Ware',[39] which has recently been also dated[40] by thermoluminescence methods to circa first half of the second millennium BC.

In 1956, Heine-Geldern again reviewed[41] the available archaeological evidences, and citing further parallels of bronze and copper objects (particularly those pointed out earlier by Piggott,[42] viz. animal-headed pin from Mohenjodaro, rod from Harappa and macehead from Chanhudaro besides the seals from Chanhudaro), re-affirmed his earlier conclusions (though in a modified form) that the authors of these objects were Aryans who invaded India between 1200 and 1000 BC. He held the view that these types belonged to a single cultural complex in western Asia and inferred that the same was the case in India. The hypothesis too remains untenable, for the evidence relating to the objects from Mohenjodaro, Harappa and Chanhudaro seems to have been examined in isolation. While our present knowledge, there is nothing to suggest that the occupation at these sites continued till about 1200 BC to witness the invasion,[43] the presence of these findings, essentially stray and without any diagnostic associated material equipment, precludes their identification with the movement of the Aryans. It is difficult to subscribe to the view that a dynamic equestrian people like the Aryans, should have left only these traces which again are not available in the area of their further expansion in the Ganga-Yamuna *doab*. If Jhukar levels at Chandudaro represent the Aryan occupation, as believed by Hiene-Geldern, the material equipment of the Jhukar Culture, including the distinctive pottery, is not consistently represented even at Mohenjodaro and Harappa, not to speak of sites further east of the Indus plains. Besides, apart from the metal objects referred to above, at Harappa the only non-Harappan tradition met with is represented by the occupation of the Cemetery 'H' Culture. At Mohenjodaro, direct evidence for a non-Harappan occupation of a comparable affiliation is wanting. Are we to agree to the explanation given by Stuart Piggott that the new arrivals were predominantly conquerors who travelled light bringing with them only the portable property of seals, spears and battle axes, and adapting the pottery traditions of the regions in which they established themselves.[44]

The Quetta Valley Ghul Ware and the Aryans

Related to this hypothesis is the suggestion of Fairservis[45] to associate two distinctive Wares in the Quetta valley with the period of the Aryan occupation. One of these, labelled the Ghul Ware, is reportedly 'a heavy handmade ware decorated rather coarsely with simple designs', sometimes in polychrome, while the other, with a distribution in northern Baluchistan, is a wheel made ware decorated with geometric and curvilinear motifs, suggesting Jhukar style. Although the stratigraphic relationship of this ware with the Ghul Ware is not sufficiently established, there is some indication to infer that the former is somewhat earlier. Both of these, however, fall within the time-span of Rana Ghundai IV. It is claimed that these ceramic traditions entered Sind via Derajat or the Zhon valley along with the Aryan invaders through Gomel Pass. This postulate suffers from the lack of internal consistency. Do these two ceramic traditions represent two different waves of Aryan immigrants? If so, how do we explain the absence of the potter's wheel and sophisticated pottery in the latter group (viz. represented by Ghul Ware), unless we assume that the users of the Ghul Ware came from an area of isolation. The claims of the Jhukar Culture have already been commented upon above and need not be repeated.

The Painted Grey Ware and the Aryans

The hypothesis put forward by Lal[46] relates to the identification of the authors of the Painted Grey Ware with an early wave of the Aryans in India. The relevant evidence, though entirely circumstantial, rests on four incontrovertible facts: (i) the Painted Grey Ware has been found to occur in the lower levels of a large number of sites associated with the *Mahabharata* story: (ii) the distribution of this distinctive ceramic fits with the geographical foci of *Vedic* literature, being virtually co-terminous with the land *Brahmavarta* and *Brahmarsi desa*, held holy in the Aryan literature; (iii) the people who occupied the Ghaggar (the ancient Saraswati Valley)—traditionally an early home of the Aryans in India—in the wake of the Harappans used the Painted Grey Ware; and (iv) a considerable part of the Painted Grey Ware settlement at Hastinapura was washed away by a heavy flood resulting in the desertion of the township for the time being. The occurrence of the skeletal remains of the horse (*Equus caballus*), though in the late levels of the Painted Grey Ware strata, has also been emphasized as a significant evidence. (Fig. 1).

The Painted Grey Ware might not have come from Outside

This hypothesis has been disputed on two principle issues: first, the antecedent stages of the Painted Grey Ware along the route which the Painted Grey Ware flourished. Regarding the former, Lal had cited some similarities between the Painted Grey Ware obtained from Indian sites and the Minyan Ware found on sites in Thessaly, 47 ascribable to the Bronze Age. Here it was found to be an intrusive element in a local culture continuum. Apart from sites excavated by Wace and Thompson (Tsani, Tsangli and Zerila) and referred to by Lal. Painted Grey Ware has also been found from Otzaki (also in Thessaly),[48] a site excavated by Vladimir Milojic, the industry being represented by only a few sherds. Besides, the straight-sided bowls, no other form, much less the distinctive Indian dish with incurved sides, was available. One of the bowls had in addition, at mid-height, a sloping lug handle, painted on the upper surface, a feature altogether absent in the Indian examples. The painted patterns consisted of thick rim band with regularly spaced verticals, horizontal bands, rim-band joined by oblique lines with dots, etc. The designs in each case showed a disciplined style with no blurrings. This evidence, though alluring, failed to carry conviction largely because no chain of transmission of the pottery tradition could be built between the two regions, viz. Thessaly and India. Likewise, the suggested similarity in fabric of the fine grey ware from south of Lack Urmia with the Painted Grey Ware from the Ganga-Yamuna *doab* and the Saraswati valley seems to be more apparent than real, for its is not supported by any close correspondence in characteristic pot-forms excepting the corrugated stem, of which the complete shape in the Indian assemblage remains unknown. The occurrence of a few Painted Grey Ware sherds of the patent Ganga-Yamuna *doab* fabric in sieslaw, including

Lakhyopir in Said, however, provides some weight to the hypothesis, but has sencauied geographically separated from the known area of distribution of the war in India. Similarly the approach sesenable between the painted grey ware of the *doab* and that of Shahi Tump does not seem to be fully consistent in forms, decoration, etc.[48a]

While conceding that the available evidence was essentially a *disjecta membra,* Lal felt that, for working out the movement of the Aryans in western Asia and southern Europe, it was desirable that the distribution of the painted and plain grey wares should be studied. Painted Grey Ware in India seems to indicate a tradition long established and fully developed outside India. Although Baluchistan, Indus valley, and Pakistan part of the Punjab still remain largely unexplored from this angle, it would be worthwhile to review the evidence brought forth by the excavations in the Swat valley, including the Gandhara region (Gandhara Grave Culture) which has some bearing on the subject[49] especially on the attributed source of inspiration of the Painted Grey Ware.

It has already been stated above that the middle of the second millennium BC, grey ware, marking the introduction of a completely new ceramic tradition in Pakistan, was the harbinger of the Gandhara Grave Culture and that of the two waves of invasion of the grey ware culture, the first was associated with bronze and the second with iron. The Painted Grey Ware of the Ganga-Yamuna *doab* was also associated with iron. Comparing the two assemblages, Dani holds the view[50] that it may not be improper to seek the origin of the latter to the development of the grey ware of the Gandhara Grave Culture in the as yet unexplored intervening plains between the Indus and the Beas. While future investigations would no doubt extend the areas of distribution of the respective wares in this region, what is needed is a site where a stratigraphic correlation of the ware could be established. At the present stage, the evidence seems to be only indicative and not proved. Further, no specific resemblance has been noticed in the shapes represented in the two respective ware; the distinctive type of Gandhara Grave Culture is the tall drinking vase while that of the Painted Grey Ware the flat dish or thali. Does it not imply differing food habits with reflections on the social economy of the corresponding culture-group?

Coming to the date of the Painted Grey Ware, excepting a single date, 1025 BC, most of the C-14 dates for this Ware are concentrated between 800 and 500 BC.[51] This incidentally falls within the same time-bracket as proposed by Dani for Period III of the Gandhara Grave Culture (*circa* ninth to the middle of the sixth century BC) There is thus no possibility of the Painted Grey Ware being inspired by the pottery traditions of Period III of the Gandhara Grave Culture. In fact, the frequency graph of the Grey Ware shows a descending trend in the latter assemblage.

Archaeological Evidence : West Asia

It is widely known that in the first quarter of the second millennium BC there was a general break-up of Western Asiatic Civilizations, following migration of peoples. This period saw the rise of the Hittite Empire in Asia Minor. In Mesopotamia, the Guti tribes rudely, if not ruthlessly, shook the kingdom of Akkad. In the Iranian tableland, the arrival of the newcomers, who were mostly barbarian potentates, is attested at Hissar II-III, Giyan III, Anau-III, Shah Tepe II and Turang Tepe. In Soviet Central Asia, the period is marked by the appearance of nomadic tribes. These movements reflect insecurity, raids, etc., as attested by the promiscuous traits in the associated assemblages.[52] (Fig.2).

For an archaeological phenomenon of the above evidence, we may examine the ceramic industries of the comparable period in Anatolia, north Mesopotamia, including Syria, northern Iran and Soviet Central Asia (notably Tajikistan).[53] (Fig. 3)

The exotic hand-made polychrome Cappadocian Ware along with the wheelmade monochrome red or black burnished ware formed the ceramic industries of the Hittites, covering also the period of the Assyrian colonists in Anatolia. The designs in grey, black or red on a light background is the caphagouian ware included, occasionally, stigliged representations of birds, tigzag bards, bogeges, double axes, etc. The Anatolian character of spouts and handles is amply clear in the forms (fondness for cutway lip, rhytons in the form of animals and model-shoes). An eastern derivation for this Ware is indicated by its connections of Anau and the occurrence of some cognate forms of Geo Tepe in Azerbaijan.[54] The monochrome ware was unrelivedly black or red with a tendency to burnishing polish and showing individualistic shapes, more characteristic of local taste. This ware gradually became predominant as the Cappadocian Ware went out of use. Another ceramic which is associated with the movement of peoples in Anatolia and Palestine is the Khirbet Kerak Ware (circa second half of third millennium BC) which is associated by some archaeologists with Hittites or proto Hitites. The original home of this ware is hand made and heavy furnished occassionally red all-over, more often black, but quite often black-and-red with the inside showing red and outside black or red below and black above is believed to be in the Araxes valley. In the Jordan valley (Amuq plains), it was an indicator of a foreign ethnic, element.[55] In northern Mesopotamia, the ceramic industries of the period, meriting our attention comprised the Habur and the Nubi wares. The form (Core Ir or+200 BC) which both preceded and one lapped the latter in chronological sequence, is painted in black over light-red background and shows in its design repertoire notably the double axe motif, horizontal triangles in bands, zigzag metops, etc.—influences from north Iran (Tepe Giyan II-III) and Armenia, both nuclear regions of potential cultures in the beginning of the second millennium BC. The Nuzi Ware (alternatively termed as the Hurrian, Subartu or the Atchana Ware) which is widely known as a Mittani ceramic dates from the sixteenth to the twelfth century BC and is considered as a fashion adaptation from Crete with an impulse from mural paintings. It is painted in white over dark surface. The patterns, showing zonal form of decoration, have an ornamental character and consist of tendrils and creepers, geometric elements and sometimes even birds.

All these ceramic traditions are sudden intrusions in their respective areas, and as such could have resulted only from the admixture of a new element in the population.

In northern Iran, towards the middle of the third millennium BC, the existing pottery traditions at Tepe Hissar,[56] Tepe Giyan,[57] and Shah Tepe,[58] are found to be interrupted by the appearance of plain, burnished grey or black ware. At Turang Tepe,[59] where no earlier occupation of painted pottery was reached, the habitation started with the grey ware occupation. At Sialk[60] similar ware has been attested in Cemeteries A and B (respectively Periods V and VI), assignable evidence of grey ware intruding upon and finally supplanting the painted pottery tradition is available at Anau. The unpainted grey ware, marked by different traditions of kiln and firing, seemed to be more than a change in ceramic fashion and could only mean the arrival of new comers in this region with decisive outer influences. As regards the associated objects of this striking ceramic, attention may be drawn notably to the occurrence of a new type of tools and weapons of copper or bronze; (i) gypsum seal with the omnipresent filled cross; (ii) double spiralheaded pin; (iii) pins with animal or mace heads; (iv) copper stamp seals with terraced square design; (v) axe-adze with tubular shaft-hole; and (vi) a distinctive type triple jar with tubular connections joining all the three. The use of iron was not attested in this assemblage. Some of these types would permit an excursion from Iron through Baluchistan to Mohenjodaro (above). This widespread distribution is not without significance. Equally noteworthy, however, is the evidence regarding the existence of the domesticated horse (*Equus caballus*) at Shah Tepe, both of Periods II and III.[62]

The problem concerning the origin of the grey ware is much too complex. It is not sure whether this ware is representative of an originally homogenous culture. Some analogues are known from Anatolian sites including Alishar and from the Uruk Ware in Mesopotamia,[63] but cannot offer a reasonable explanation.

In south Russia, the basic culture towards the end of the third millennium BC and early part of the second was that of agriculturists, partly nomadic, but sufficiently sedentary, as evidenced by the existence of cemeteries,[64] including the great tombs such as that of Maikop which contained metalwork types similar to those obtained from Tepe Hissar and Turang Tepe.

Anthropological Evidence

Let it be stated at the outset that owing to the lack of a sufficient series of skeletons of the respective periods in the areas under study, the anthropological evidence on the subject is sadly deficient. Besides, most of the anthropological studies in these regions have been based on outmoded concepts of race without the application of scientific concept of population-genetics.[65] It is, therefore, difficult to formulate any definite theory on the subject. As such our inferences on the affinities of people, represented by the skeletal remains, will be tentative.

The carniological evidence from the excavated skeletons from the Anatolian sites, including Kultepe, indicates that an extensive invasion of brachycephals occurred roughly at about 2000 BC. The archaeological and philological evidence points to the Hittites (predominantly Alpine) as the invaders.[66]

As regards the Iranian sites under study, the position is as follows: among the crania available at Shah Tepe[67] no brachycephals were recorded in any of the Periods (I-III), the skulls being either dolichocephalic or mesocephalic; at Tepe Hissar,[68] in periods I and II, among the twenty crania (respectively 4 and 16) no brachycephals were recorded and in Period III, out of the one hundred and thirtyseven crania, only one was brachcephalic (Alpine), the majority (eighty-five) of the remaining being dolichocephalic (Mediterranean); at Sialk,[69] brachycephals were found to be present in Cemeteries A and B (periods V and VI).

Turning to the evidence obtained from the graves of the Gandhara Grave Culture, excavated in the Swat valley of Pakistan, we find that five different morphological types were represented: rugged bony proto-Europoid (Eurydolichomorph); both robust and gracile Mediterranean (Leptodolichomorph)! Mongoloid; and Veddiform (Paedoeury dolichomorph). Of these commonest type was the gracile. Mediterranean (Leptodolichomorph) met with in the graves of Period III, followed by the robust Eurydolichomorph and the robust Leptodolichomorph of Period I. According to Bernhard,[70] this evidence would suggest an immigration of new people or at least a biological contact with a foreign population group during Period III. The gracile Mediterranean Leptodolichomorph of Period III was a widespread type in Central Asia during the Neolithic and the Bronze Ages, and was represented in Bronze Age skull series from sites in Tajikistan, South Turkmenia, Aral sea region, west Kazakistan as also from Shah Tepe and Tepe Hissar III. Statistical comparison, based on multivariate statistical method, also yielded significant similarities with the series from Tepe Hissar III, middle and east Europe and Central Asia. Identifying the- gracil Mediterranean of Period III as the Aryan and the robust Leptodolichomorphs of Period I as the non-Aryan does not have any convincing anthropological or physical basis. Racially, Aryan did not comprise a single physical type but included such races as Nordic, Alpine, Armenoids, etc.[71]

In India, the anthropological evidence for the comparable period is sadly lacking. No burials have so far been recorded, belonging either to the Banas Culture or to the Copper Hoard Culture, or to the Painted Grey Ware Culture, and those found associated with the post-Harappan Chalcolithic Culture of Central India and Northern Deccan are small in number to permit any generalization.

Conclusions

From the foregoing it would be clear that the archaeological and the anthropological evidences, represented by the various culture-groups of the second millennium BC, are inconsistent with the philological evidence. Even the archaeological and anthropological evidence have been found to vary from region to region—Anatolia, northern Iraq, northern Iran, Soviet Central Russia, Swat valley and Gandhara region of Pakistan and Ganga-yamuna *doab*, southern Rajasthan, and Malwa plateau and northern Deccan of India. It is obvious, therefore, that there was no single culture associated with the Aryans in all these regions. At the same time, an interrelationship between the cultures of each region is fully attested by the occurrence of some common objects, including potter forms. Are we to assume that the Aryans were migrants with no defined culture but an adherence to a linguistic equipment? Two things, however, emerge out of this discussion: First, between the close of the third millennium BC and the middle of the second, there have been movements of land hungry people, marked by armed invaders in various regions of Western Asia, notably Anatolia. Among plains, northern

Mesopotamia, northern Iran and north-western parts of Pakistan. These conquerors mingled with the survivors of the old stock in each region and with a sudden intrusion introduced their characteristic handicrafts. Secondly, the period was marked by the sudden appearance of a burnished grey ware. A tangible connection between these two phenomena and some major historical event, such as the movement of the Indo-Europeans, must be found.

In India, among the various culture groups for which identifications with the Aryans has been claimed, the Painted Grey ware alone seems to fit into the sequence. The evidence admitedly is not definitive, primarily because of disputed chronology and lack of specific resemblance of the ware in areas further west of Punjab, but it has the merit of providing a workable hypothesis. The Painted Grey Ware of the Ganga-Yamuna *doab* seems to belong to the grey ware complex which had suddenly intruded upon the ceramic traditions of northern Iran towards the end of the third millennium BC. At the same time it may be admitted that besides similarity in the tradition of firing and kiln there is little to compare the forms, fabric and the decoration of the Painted Grey Ware with those of the Iranian Ware. The latter complex probably sent out feelers far to the east, by a route that is as yet imperfectly understood. Perhaps this may explain (a) the reported likeness between certain pottery forms of grey ware found in the Gandharva grave Culture of the swat valley and Periods II and III at Hissar in northern Iran, and (b) the absence of such corresponding resemblance between the Painted Grey Ware and the Swat Iranian Ware. The link of grey ware complex, howsoever tenuous, is reinforced *a fortiori* by (a) the evidence about the use of the horse (*Equus caballus*) in association with the grey ware in northern Iran (Shah Tepe II and III). Swat valley and the Gandhara region of Pakistan (Gandhara Grave Culture) and upper India (Painted Grey Ware Culture late levels) and (b) the association of the predominantly Mediterranean type of people with this grey-ware at least in northern Iran and in the Swat valley. With this generalization a loop is left open at this stage for other intermediate developments which future investigators may uncover. We must also keep in mind the inherent capacity of a culture to expand or to develop in response to local environments, which would mean that while formulating theories, due allowance for the process of Indianization should also be given.

To which wave of the movement of Indo-Aryans does the Painted Grey ware belong, if at all it belongs to one, still remains to be established. Although its sophistication, as evidenced both by form and decoration, the date of its association with the use of iron seems to be a few cogent points for ascribing the Ware to a later wave, the archaeological remains of the earlier wave[72] of Indo-Aryans in India still eludes us.[73] At the same time, it be reiterated that during the interregnum following the collapse of the Indus Civilization, Painted Grey Ware Culture constituted the earliest representation of an organized society in the Sutlej and the Ghaggar valley. In the Ganga-Yamuna *doab*, being the major part of the remaining area of its distribution, this culture followed either that represented by the Ochre Colour Ware (as at Hastinapura, Ahichchatra and Jhinjhana) or that attested by the black-and-red ware (at Atranjikhera and Noh), neither of which, as already demonstrated above, could be identified with the material remains of the Indo-Aryans. In the present impasse, can surmise be hazarded, without however any claim for a definitive assertion, that the Painted Grey Ware belongs to the early wave of Indo-Aryan immigrants in India, and that the earlier of the two floods mentioned in the *Puranas*[74] which might conceivably have submerged the Ochre Colour Ware sites,[75] occurred before the arrival of the Aryans in India with whom it was perhaps a living memory for rendering the story of the great deluge from which only Manu the great progenitor, as mentioned in the Aryan lore, was reported to have survived.

Lest the conclusions be bedevilled by extrapolations and surmises, it must be re-affirmed that the available objective evidence of the movement of Aryans into India is still inconclusive. In the present state of our knowledge or, for that matter of our ignorance, which is not as despairing as it was two decades ago, calls for a sustained work on the problem including the ancestry of the Painted Grey Ware if it was at all there outside India.

Notes & References

1. V. Gardon Childe, *The Aryans, a study of the Indo-European Origins* (London, 1926); also cf. Isaac Taylor, *The Origin of the Aryans* (London, 1889).
2. Buddha Prakash, *Rgveda and the Indus Valley Civilization* (Hoshiarpur, 1966), pp. 121-46; also Gregary Bongard Levin, 'Is Arctic the Original Home of Indians', *Soviet Land*, no. 12, June 1968 and no. 13, July 1968.
3. H.C. Chakladar, Aryan Occupation of Eastern India', *Indian Studies, Past and Present,* Vol.III, no.1 (Calcutta, October-December, 1961), pp.
4. Seton Lloyd, *Early Anatolia* (Harmondsworth, 1956), p. 119; also Bedrich Hrozny, *Ancient History of Western Asia Indian and Crete* (Prague), p. 106.
5. Hugo Winckler, *Mitteilungen der deutscher Orient-Gesellschaft,* vol. XXXV (Berlin, 1907), p.51; also cf. *Zeit-schrift der deutschen Morgenl and gesell schaft*, vol. LXXVI (Berlin), pp. 250 ff; Paul Thleme, "The Aryan Gods of the Mittani treaties', *Journal of the American Oriental Society*, vol. 80, no. 4 Oct.-Dec. 1960; and O.R. Gurney, The Hittites (Harmondsworth, 1961).

6. H. Jacobi in *Journal of the Royal Asiatic Society,* (London, 1909), pp. 721 ff.
7. F.E. Pargiter, *Ancient Indian Historical Tradition* (Oxford, 1922).
8. Eduard Meyer, *Reich und Kultur der Chetiter* (Berlin, 1914).
9. Husing, 'Volker-schichtern in altem Iran,' *Mittelungen der anthropologishcen Gesellschaft in Wien,* vol. XLVI, p. 210.
10. For a previous discussion of the evidence Cf. Dilip K. Chakrabarti, 'The Aryan hypothesis in Indian Archaeology', *Indian Studies, Past and present* vol IX, no. 4 (Calcutta, July-September, 1968), pp. 343-58; Shivaji Singh; Archaeological evidence on the pluralistic make-up of the Aryan Culture' paper read at the All Indian Oriental Conference October, 1968 and N.R. Banerjee, *The Iron Age* (Delhi, 1965).
11. Swami Sankaranad : *Rigvedic Culture of the Prehistoric Indus,* Vol I-II (Calcutta, 1943-44) Buddha Prakash, *op. cit.*; L. Sarup, 'The Rigveda and Mohenjodaro, *Proceedings of Oriental Congress* Vol. VIII, pp. 122; K.N. Sastri, *New Light on the Indus Civilization* (Delhi, 1965) A.D. Pusalkar, Pre-Harappan and Post-Harappan Cultures and the Aryan Problem', *The Quarterly Review of Historical Studies,* Vol. VII, no. 4 1967-68, pp. 233-44.
12. Ahmad Hasan Dani, 'Timargarh and Gandhara Grave Culture, *Ancient Pakistan*, vol. III (Peshwar, 1967).
13. W. Berhard, 'Human skeletal remains from the Cemetery of Timargarh', *Ancient Pakistan*, Vol III (Peshawar, 1967), pp. 289 ff.
14. Dani, *op.cit.*, p. 48.
15. V. Gorden Childe, *New Light on the Most Ancient East* (London, 1934), p. 223.
16. R.E.M. Wheeler, 'Harappa 1946: The defences and cemetery R-37' *Ancient India* no. 3 (New Delhi 1947), pp 58-130. Also see D.H. Gordon, 'The early use of metals in India and Pakistan,' Jour *Roy. Anthrop.* vol. LXXX (1950), pp. 56 ff. and 'The pottery industries of the Indo-Iranian border: a re-statement and tentative chronology', *Ancient India,* nos. 10 and 11 (1954 and 1955), pp. 157 ff.
17. B.B. Lal, 'Protohistoric Investigation', *Ancient India,* no. 9 (New Delhi, 1953), pp. 88, also 'Excavation at Hastinapura and other explorations in the Upper Ganga and Sutlej basins 1950-52', *Ancient India,* no. 10 and 11 (New Delhi, 1954-1955), p. 151.
18. G.F. Dales, 'The Mythical Massacre at Mohenjodaro', *Expedition,* vol. 6, no. 3 (Philadelphia, 1964) pp. 36-43; for subsequent discussion, cf. Mortimer Wheeler in *Antiquity,* no. 152 (December, 1964) pp. 307-309 and *Civilization of the Indus Valley and beyond* (London, 1966), pp. 79-83.
19. D.P. Agarwal, 'C-14 dates, Banas Culture and the Aryans', *Current Science,* 35, no. 5 (March 5, 1968), pp. 114-17.
20. H.D. Sankalia, S.B. Deo and Z.D. Ansari, *Excavations at Ahar* (Tamabavati, Poona, 1969), pp. 5 and 6.

21. *Indian Archaeology 1963-64—A Review,* (New Delhi, 1967) pp. 11-12. It is however, not very clear whether white-painted or plain black-and-red ware was only accidently absent in the lowest levels. It may by recalled in this connection that both at Lothal and Rangpur, white-painted black-and-red ware occurs along with the Harappan pottery from the earliest levels.
22. Cf. D.K. Chakrabarti, 'Origin of Ahar Culture', *Man in India,* vol. 48, no. (April-June 1968), pp. 5 and 6.
23. H.D. Sankalia et al, *op. cit.* (1969); also 'New links between Western Asia and the India of 4,000 years ago; excavations in the huge dust heap of Ahad near Udaipur, *Illustrated London News,* September 1, 1962; 'New light on the Indo-Iranian or western Asiatic relations between 1700 BC-1200 BC', *Artibus Asiae,* vol. XXVI (1963) pp. 312-32; and 'Iranian influence on early Indo-Pakistani Cultures, *Indica,* vol. 6, no. 2 (Bombay, September 1969), pp. 59-80.
24. D.K. Sen, 'Ancient traces of India and Pakistan–A Study of methods', *Ancient India,* nos. 20-21 (New Delhi, 1964 and 65), p. 186. According to Chatterjee one of the three morphological types identified at Lothal in is large and rugged long-headed Proto-Nordic or Caucasoid type also identified at Harappa Cemetery R.37 and Tepe Hissar III, cf. B.K. Chatterji and G.D. Kumar, "Racial elements in Post Harappan skeletal remains at Lothal," in Anthropology on March Ed. Bal Ratnam (Madras, 1963) pp. 104 ff.
25. A.F.R. Hoernle, *A Grammar of the Eastern Hindi Compared with the other Gaudian Languages* (London, 1880).
26. H.D. Sankalia, 'Excavations at Maheswar and Nevasa and their possible bearing on the Puranic History', *The Sardhasatabdi Commemoration Volume,* 1804-1954 (Asiatic Society of Bom. Bombay), pp. 229-39.
27. Pargiter, *op. cit.*
28. H.D. Sankalia, (1963), *op. cit.*
29. Bimla Charan Law, *Tribes in Ancient India* (Poona, 1943), pp. 130-83.
30. G.R. Sharma, *The Excavation at Kosambi* 1957-59 (Allahabad, 1960), pp. 7-16.
31. R. Heine, Geldren, 'Archaeological traces of the Vedic Aryans', *Journal of the Indian Society of Oriental Art,* IV (1936), pp. 87-115; 'New light on the Aryan migration to India' *Bulletin of the American Institute for Iranian Art and Archaeology,* v (1937), pp. 7-16.
32. Staurt Piggott, 'Prehistoric Copper Hoards in the Gangese basin', *Antiquity,* XVIII (1944), pp. 173-82.
33. B.B. Lal, 'Further Copper Hoards from the Gangetic basin and a review of the problem', *Ancient India,* no. 7 (1951), pp. 20-39.
34. S.P.Gupta, 'Indian Copper Hoards' *Journal of the Bihar Research Society,* Vol.XLIX pts I and or to IV (Patna, 1963), pp. 147-66; also, 'Further Copper Hoards' a re-assessment in the light of new evidence; *Journal of the Bihar Research Society,* Vol. LI, Pt. I-IV (Patna 1969) pp.1-7. Also see

Bridget and Raymond Allchin. *The Birth of Indian Civilization* (Harmondsworth, 1968), pp. 204-206.

35. *Indian Archaeology 1960-61—A Review* (New Delhi, 1961), p. 66, p;. LXXVIIB, also cf. *Handbook to the Centenary Exhibition,* (New Delhi, 1961), pl.3 and Bridget and Raymond Allchin, *op.cit.*,pp. 152-53, pl. 21A.

36. Unpublished, recently acquired by the National Museum. Information supplied by Sri S.P. Gupta.

37. K. Jettmar, 'Bronze axes from the Karakoram', *Proceedings of the American Philosophical Society,* vol. 105, (1961).

38. D.P. Agarwal, 'The Copper Hoards problem : a technological angle', unpublished paper.

39. B.B. Lal, 'A deluge? Which deluge? Yet another facet, of the problem of the Copper Hoards Culture', *American Anthropologist,* vol. 70, nos. 5, (October, 1968), pp. 857-63.

40. Information from Prof. S. Nurul Hasan who got a few sherds of the Ochre Colour Ware from four sites, viz., Atranjikherea, Jhin-Jhana, Lal Qila and Nasirpur dated by the Research Laboratory for Archaeology and the History of Art. Oxford.

41. Robert Heine-Geldern, 'The Coming of the Aryans and the end of the Harappa Civilization, *Man*. vol. LVI, (October, 1956), p. 135-40.

42. S. Piggott, 'Notes on certain metal pins and a macchead in the Harappa Culture', *Ancient India,* no. 4 (New Delhi, 1947-48), pp. 33-38.

43. Walter A. Fairservis, Jr's estimation of 1200 BC or later for the end of the Harappan Civilization in 'The chronology of the Harappan Civilization and the Aryan invasion', *Man*, LVI (London, 1956), pp. 153-56, does not stand the test of the numerous C-14 dates and the general chronological setting of the area.

44. Stuart Piggot, *Prehistoric India* (Harmondsworth, 1950), pp. 220 and 239.

45. Fairservis, *op. cit.*, 155-56.

46. B.B. Lal, *op.cit.*, (1955) and Presidential Address at the Seminar on Painted Grey Ware (Aligarh, 18-19th August 1968); also A. Ghosh, editorial notes, *Ancient India,* nos. 10 and 11 (1954 and 1955) pp. 1-3.

47. A.J.B. Wace and M.S. Thompson, *Prehistoric Thessaly* (Cambridge, 1912).

48. Author's personal examination of the material at the Institute of Pre-and Proto-History, University of Heidelberg.

48a. H.D. Sankalia, 'The Painted Grey Ware of the Genetic Valley and Shahi Tump-Baluchistan', paper read at the Seminar on Painted Grey Ware (Aligarh, 18-19th, August, 1968).

49. S.P. Gupta, 'Gandhara Grave Culture : Its bearing on the problems of the Painted Grey Ware and Aryan migration', paper read at the Seminar on painted Grey Ware (Aligarh, 18-19th August, 1968).

50. Dani, *op. cit.*, p. 25.

51. D.P. Agarwal, An integrated study of the Copper bronze technology in the light of chronological and ecological factors, Ph.D. Thesis presented at the Banaras Hindu University pp. 107-12; fig. 8. Also see Lal *op. cit.*, (1968).

52. B.K. Thapar, 'The West Asian background to the protohistoric pottery of India in the second and first millennium a.c.; paper read at the First International Conference on Asian Archaeology, held at New Delhi in December 1961; also 'Relationship of the Indian Chalcolithic cultures with West Asia: *Indian Prehistory.* Ed. V.N. Misra and M.S. Mate (Poona, 1965), pp. 157-76.

53. Marian Welkar, 'The painted pottery of the Near East in the 2nd millennium a.c. and its chronological background', *Transactions of the American Philosophical Society,* New Series, vol. 38, 2 (Philadelphia, Septr. 18\948); Bethel Hrouds, '*Dei bemalte Keramik des Zivelten Jahrtausends in Nordmesopotamien and Nordsvrien, Istambular Forschungen,* Band 19 (Berlin, 1947).

54. M.V. Seton William, 'A painted pottery of the second millennium from southern Turkey and northern Syria', *Iraq*, vol. XV, pp. 57 ff; also cf. H.H. Von der Osten, 'Buntkeramilk in Anatolien', *Orientalla Secana,* col. I (Uppsala, 1952), pp. 15 ff.

55. Leonard Wooley, *A Fargotteu Kingdom* (Harmondsworth, 1953) pp. 31-6.

56. Erich F. Schmidt, *Excavations at Tepe Hissar Damgham* (Philadelphia, 1937).

57. G. Contenau et R. Ghirshman, *Fouilles du Tepe Giyan pres de Nehavend* 1931 et 1932 (Paris, 1935).

58. T.J. Arne, *Excavations at Shah Tepe,* Iran (Stockholm, 1945).

59. F.R. Wulsin, 'Excavations at Turang Tepe near Asterabad', *Supplement to Bulletin of the American Institute for Persian Studies,* Vol. II (1932).

60. R. Ghirshman, *Fouilles de Sialk,* vols. I and II (Paris, 1938-39).

61. R. Pumpelly, '*Explorations in Turkestan-prehistoric Civilizations of Anau I and II,* Carnegie Institute Publication XII (1934).

62. Arne, *op. cit.*, p. 325.

63. Donald E. McCown, *The Comparative Stratigraphy of Early Iran.* Studies in Ancient Oriental Civilization, no. 23 (Chicago, 1941).

64. B.A Litvinsky, "Recent Archaeological discoveries in south Tajikistan and problems of cultural contacts between the peoples of Central Asia and Hindustan" in *Antiquity* (Moscow, 1967).

65. About methodology of the anthropological evidence cf. Sen. *op. cit.* pp. 178-205.

66. Seton Lloyd, *op. cit.* pp. 326-30.

67. Arne, *op. cit.* pp. 326-30.

68. Henery Field, *Ancient and Modern Man in South-western Asia* (University of Miami Press Coral Galiles, Florida, 1956), pp. 127-28.

69. H.V. Vallois 'Les Ossements humains de Sialk' in *Fouilles de Sialk,* vol III (Paris, 1939), pp. 113ff.

70. Bernhard, *op. cit.*, pp. 375 ff.

71. A.K. Mitra, "The Aryan Problem in Indian Anthropology", *Anthropology on the March* (Madras, 1963), pp. 116 ff.

72. D.P. Agarwal, 'The P.G. Ware: a revaluation' paper read at the Seminar on Painted Grey Ware (Aligarh, 18-19th August, 1968).

73. Shivaji Singh, 'The theory of the Aryan association of the Painted Grey Ware: an analysis' paper read at the Seminar on Painted Grey Ware (Aligarh, 18-19th August, 1968).

74. Lal. *op. cit.*

75. At the present stage of our knowledge, the theory regarding the flood is largely a tentative one. Dr. B.B. Lal, Chief Archaeological Chemist of the Archaeological Survey, does not subscribe to the view of water-logging of the deposits containing the Orchre Colour Ware. According to him, 'when the Ochre Colour Pottery people were living, there was a gradual deposition of wind-blown material on the site under arid conditions and the pottery became weathered. Of B.B. Lal, 'The Ochrecoloured pottery', *Potteries in Ancient India,* Ed. B.P. Sinha (Patna, 1969), pp. 92-93.

21

On the Mythical Massacre at Mohenjo-Daro

Prof. George F. Dales*

Nothing delights the archaeologist more than excavating the ruins from some ancient disaster—be it a flood, earthquake, invasion, or massacre. This does not reflect any inordinately ghoulish tendency in the character of archaeologists. It is simply that a much more complete picture of the lift and times of an ancient site is preserved if it was the victim of some quick, devastating disaster than if it had just died a slow natural death or had been abandoned or remodeled.

The classic example of the rewards that we can reap as the result of an ancient natural disaster is Pompeii where the eruption of Vesuvius preserved for posterity a full-scale authentic model of daily life in an ancient Roman town. But more popular with historians are disasters that can be blamed on mankind itself. Scholars and laymen alike have always delighted in being able to boo and hiss the evil villain, the murderous invader, the barbarian hordes. Only the approach is different—the one flicks on the "Late Show", the other writes learned footnotes.

One of the most enigmatic whodunits of antiquity concerns the decline and fall of the Indus Valley (Harappan) civilization. Remains of this vast civilization of South Asia are scattered over an area considerably larger than those covered by either ancient Egypt or Mesopotamia. The life cycle of this third major experiment in the origin and development of the world's earliest civilization is at present highly speculative and is the subject of increasingly intensive investigation by archaeologists, historians, linguists, and natural scientists alike.

It is now apparent that a re-evaluation is necessary of some of the earlier theories that have come to form, over the past thirty years, the

---

* Late Prof. Dales was the head of the Deptt. of South Asian Archaeology and Anthropology in the Berkeley University, U.S.A. He directed archaeological field work in West Pakistan since 1960; excavated important Indus-Saraswati sites including reexcavation of Mohenjodaro and Harappa.

basic structural members in the framework of early South Asian history. It is especially necessary to call for a retrial concerning the placing of guilt for demise of the Indus civilization. Evidence was published some 30 years ago suggesting that Mohenjo-Daro, the southernmost of the two major cities of the Harappans, was destroyed by armed invaders and that the hapless victims—including a large percentage of women and children—were massacred on the spot. The excavators of Mohenjo-Daro were content—at least at first—to put the blame for the "massacres" on several dissociated causes and incidents. The "massacre" idea immediately ignited and has been used as a torch up to the present day by some historians, linguists, and archaeologists as visible, awful proof of the invasion of the subcontinent by the Aryans. It provided a seemingly pat answer to one of the most vexing questions in South Asian history. The arrival into northern India of the Aryans—the eastern branch of the vast Indo-European language family—heralded the beginning of the historical era in South Asia. The social and religious life of the times is described in detail in the hymns of the Sanskrit *Rig-Veda,* the earliest book known in India. The *Vedic* hymns describe the principal god, Indra, as the "fort destroyer" who "rends forts as age consumes a garment." In attacking the fortresses of the *dasyus* (the name applied to the non-Aryan enemies, be they mortal or supernatural), Indra is specifically described as setting fire to the buildings—

...in the kindled fire he burnt up all their weapons, and made him rich with kine and carts and horses. See Fig. 1.

The texts describe how the Aryan warriors were protected by armor and shields. In addition to the bow and arrow—the chief weapon—they used the javelin, axe, and sword. Horses were common but were probably used to pull the chariots rather than for riding.

It seems logical to assume that, as Sir Mortimer Wheeler puts it, "India stands accused" of destroying the cities of the Harappan civilization and of the responsibility for the "massacre" at Mohenjo-daro. Apart from a few dissenting comments in rather obscure publications, the general literature on the subject current today still repeats vivid, dramatic descriptions of the barbarian hordes descending upon the once great and proud cities of the Indus civilization. For example:

> The Indus cities fell to barbarians who triumphed not only through greater military prowess, but also because they were equipped with better weapons, and had learnt to make full use of the swift and terror-striking beast of the steppes (i.e. the horse). (Basham, 27)

(Above): ***Mohenjodaro: Wheeler called it "the last massacre" but Dales has proved that these are the skeletal remains of the people caught in a sudden, and surprise flood because none of them shows any cut-mark.*** **(Below):** ***Dales found these skeletal remains in his excavations conducted in 1964. One can see how men were caught in a flood within their.***

It is still premature to talk in terms of absolute dates—the entire chronology of South Asia down to the 6th century BC is a web of pluses and minuses of hundreds of years—so, on purely chronological grounds, we cannot even establish a definite correlation between the end of the Indus civilization and the Aryan invasion. But even if we could, what is the material evidence to substantiate the supposed invasion and massacre? Where are the burned fortresses, the arrowheads, weapons, pieces of armor, the smashed chariots and bodies of the invaders and defenders? Despite the extensive excavations at the largest Harappan sites, there is not a single bit of evidence that can be brought forth as unconditional proof of an armed conquest and destruction on the supposed scale of the Aryan invasion. It is interesting that Sir John Marshall himself, the Director of the Mohenjo-daro excavations that first revealed the "massacre" remains, separated the end of the Indus civilization from the time of the Aryan invasion by two centuries. He attributed the slayings to bandits from the hills west of the Indus, who carried out sporadic raids on an already tired, decaying and defenseless civilization.

What of these skeletal remains that have taken on such undeserved importance? Nine years of extensive excavations at Mohenjo-daro (1922-31)—a city about three miles in circuit—yielded the total of some 37 skeletons, or parts thereof, that can be attributed with some certainty to the period of the Indus civilization. Some of these were found in contorted positions and groupings that suggest anything but orderly burials. Many are either disarticulated or incomplete. They were all found in the area of the Lower Town—probably the residential district. Not a single body was found within the area of the fortified citadel where one could reasonably expect the final defence of this thriving capital city to have been made.

It would be foolish to assert that the scattered skeletal remains represent an orderly state of affairs. But since there is no conclusive proof that they all even belong to the same period of time, they can not justifiably be used as proof of a single tragedy. Part of this uncertainty results from the unsatisfactory methods used by the excavators to record and publish their finds. But even allowing for this serious methodological shortcoming, it is possible to reevaluate the published evidence and to come to some definite conclusions concerning the massacre myth.

The most celebrated group of skeletons, the photograph of which is usually published to provide visible proof of the "massacre", was found in the area of Room 74, House V (HR area). The interpretation of this grisly discovery was not even agreed upon by the excavators themselves.

Mr. Hargreaves, who did the actual excavating, states that because four of the fourteen skeletons were found above the ruins of the southern wall of the room, the entire group belongs to a date subsequent to the decay of the building and thus to a period posterior to the abandonment of the latest stage of the city.

Marshall, the over-all director of the excavations, says on the other hand "this does not seems to be proven." He points out that the building belongs to the Intermediate period of the city and that this entire area was covered over and rebuilt in the Late period (the assumed Late period remains were not preserved at this part of the city; it is probable they had eroded away.) Marshall suggests that the skeletons could belong to the interval between the Intermediate and Late periods, "though the possibility of their being posterior to the Late period may be admitted." He also disagrees with Hargreaves over the circumstances that produced this gruesome"...in the agony of death that those of a number of corpses thrown into a room." Marshall reads the evidence differently. He believed that the bodies were intentionally interred "within a few hours of death" or else they would have been prey for animals and birds. "There is no reason whatever for doubting that these burials date from the declining years of Mohenjo-daro's prosperity," stated Marshall, but he didn't suggest they represent any final massacre of the population.

During the removal of the thick accumulation of debris covering a courtyard of the Intermediate period (House III, HR area), incomplete remains of three skeletons were found. Their location in the debris shows, however, that they did not belong to the time of the courtyard but to sometime after it had fallen into disuse and had been filled in, possibly in preparation for the buildings of the Late period. The excavator suggests that it represents a late funerary deposit and doesn't intimate any connection with a final "massacre" of the city's population. Those who have so stated have misread the archaeological evidence.

One reads about "the slaughtered Harappans" who "lay unburied amid their streets." This melodramatic description was prompted, in part, by the reported find of six skeletons in a lane between two houses in the VS area of Mohenjo-daro. And yet, the excavator stated in his report that "from their position they appear to be posterior to the adjacent remains". They were covered with loose earth, free from bricks and other debris that would indicate any violent destruction. There is no suggestion in the report that they were lying on the actual street surface. Marshall suggests again that they were probably burials of the Late period that just accidentally penetrated down between the building walls bordering the lane—the lane itself having been long before covered over. Had the skeletons really been found directly on the street surface, there would still be no case for a final "massacre" because the lane belongs to the Intermediate period of the city.

Deadman's Lane in the HR area of the city was the scene of another well publicized but mythical street slaughter. One fragmentary skeleton (part of a skull, the bones of the thorax, and the upper arm of an adult) was found lying on its back diagonally across the narrow lane. But this incomplete skeleton was not resting directly on the walking surface of the lane. It appears to have been in the debris that accumulated between the walls of the building facing the lane some time after the lane had fallen into disuse. The lane itself belongs to the Intermediate period of the city. This area was rebuilt during the Late period and houses covered the location of the earlier lane. The excavator suggests that this partial skeleton was interred under the floor of a house of the Late period. Thus, it was just accidentally located in the proximity of the lane and was not associated with it at all.

Another celebrated group of "victims" consists of the nine skeletons that "lay in strangely contorted attitudes and crowded together" (Block 10A, DK area). Ernest Mackay, the excavator, expressed considerable doubt about the date of these remains. They were reportedly found at a level corresponding to the early part of the Intermediate period. For "convenience sake," Mackay termed the find-spot a burial pit although he admitted that he noticed no definite walls for the "pit" nor any traces showing that the area had been dug. Only two objects were found with the skeletons—an ivory comb that is not like the known Harappan period combs, and a copper bracelet. On the evidence of the bracelet, Mackay dates the remains to "the period of the occupation of the city." The technical report on the skeletal remains states that they probably do not represent a massacre *per se* because many of the skeletons were incomplete, represented by only a few fragments of cranium and odd bits of bone.

Mackay suggests that these were the remains of a family who tried to escape from the city with their belongings at the time of a raid but were stopped and slaughtered by the raiders. Their bodies were then "thrown pell-mell into a hurriedly made pit." He says it is "quite possible" that the tragedy took place in the final period of the city but can offer no supporting evidence. That at least five of the nine skeletons were of children prompted the anthropologist who studied the remains to conclude that "the riders nursed a consistent hatred of the people of Mohenjo-daro as a whole, and total extermination appears to have been their endeavour."

Finally, in bringing this rather macabre account to an end, mention must be made of the lone bit of evidence from Mohenjo-daro that could conceivably be used as positive evidence of some murderous tragedy during the Late period of the city. In what we might call the "Well Room Tragedy" (DK area, G section), two skeletons were found on a flight of stairs "evidently lying where they died in a vain endeavour with their last remaining strength to climb the stairs to the street." But the circumstances surrounding this tragedy are unknown and it would be presumptuous to cry "massacre" on this bit of evidence alone.

Thus stands the evidence in the case against Indra and the Aryans, or to be less specific, against the idea of a "final massacre" by whomever your refer. The contemporancity of the skeletal remains is anything but certain. Whereas a couple of them definitely seem to represent a slaughter, in situ, the bulk of the bones were found in contexts suggesting burials of the sloppiest and most irreverent nature. There is no destruction level covering the latest period of the city, no sign of extensive burning, no bodies of warriors clad in armor and surrounded by the weapons of war. The citadel, the only fortified part of the city, yielded no evidence of a final defence.

The evidence that is being gathered by present investigators from various branches of the natural and physical sciences is tending to support—in part—the theory expressed years ago by Mackay. Regarding the decay of Mohenjo-daro and the Harappan civilization, he suspected the cause to be "the vagaries of the Indus rather than pressure by invader, of whose existence we have, in fact, little positive evidence."

The details of the story of the decline and fall of the Indus civilization are, as yet, far from clear, but a pattern of contributing factors is taking shape. This pattern does not include invasion and massacre as basic factors. On the contrary, it appears that a series of natural disasters occurred—possibly as swiftly, certainly more devastating than any hypothetical invasion. A sudden rise in the Arabian Sea coastline of Pakistan apparently took place sometime around the middle of the second millennium BC. This resulted in a disastrous increase in the already serious floods in the major river valleys with the subsequent rise of the underground water table, contributing to an increase in the soil salinity to the point where it was impossible to sustain the population of the vast urban settlements. The economy must have decayed rapidly; the Harappans were forced to migrate gradually to more fertile territory. There is now incontrovertible archaeological evidence that the major population shift was to the southeast into the area of the Kathiawar peninsula, north of Bombay. Here the Harappans mingled with other

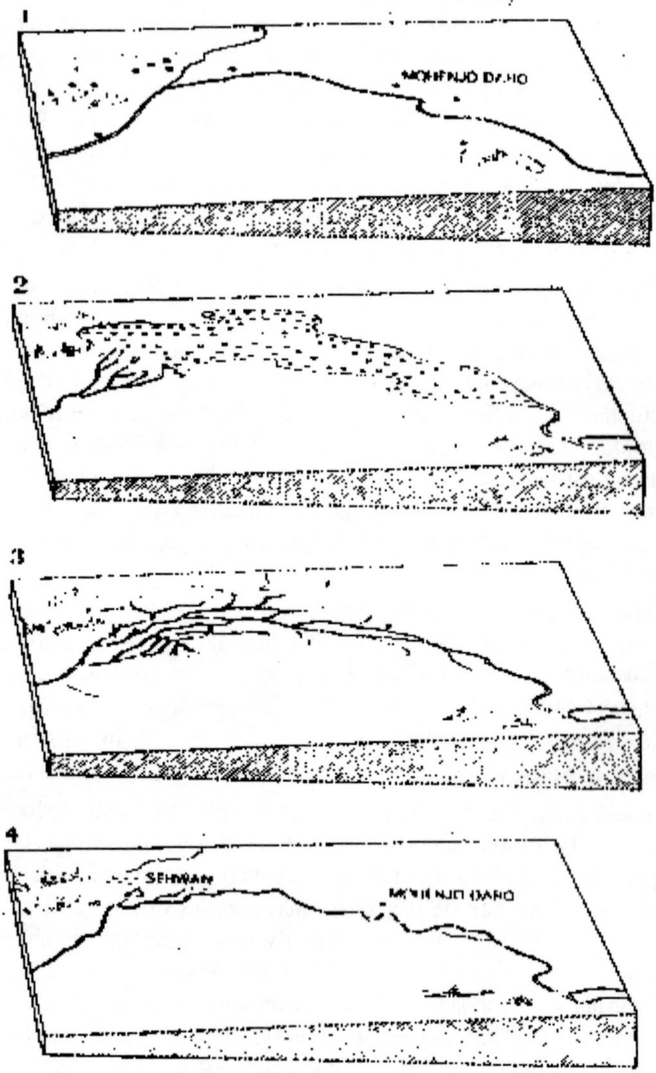

Periodic flooding of Mohenjo-daro and other Harappan settlements in the Indus River valley was apparently caused by geologic disturbances in the vicinity of modern Sehwan in 1 the Indus follows an unhindered course to the sea (south is at left, north at right). In 2 a massive mud extrusion or a rock fault dams the river and produces a shallow, marshly lake upstream, flooding Mohenjo-daro; In 3 the lake waters have topped the barrier; as it erodes the lake empties. In 4 the cycle is complete and the valley is habitable again.

Illustration by Bunji Tagawa

indigenous populations and gradually there was a complete absorption and transformation of the remnants of the formerly great Harappan culture into what we are coming to recognize as a distinctive chalcolithic culture of Central India. The former capitals of Mohenjo-daro and Harappa were virtually abandoned and became easy prey for bandits from the Baluchistan hills.

The enemy of the Harappans was Nature aided and abetted by the Harappans themselves, who accelerated the spoilation of the landscape through improper irrigation practices, and by denuding the watersheds through overgrazing and deforestation. They would have eventually put themselves out of business through such malpractices—just as the Sumerians did in southern Mesopotamia—but the process was speeded up by a sardonic twist of the earth's surface. Thus ended one of the three earliest civilizations of antiquity—Indra and the barbarian hordes are exonerated.

Notes & References

Sir R.E.M. Wheeler, *The Indus Civilization* (Supplement to the *Cambridge History of India*). Cambridge, England (2nd Revised Edition), 1960.

George F. Dales, "Harappan Outposts on the Makran Coast," *Antiquity*, Vol. XXVI, 1962.

R.L. Raikes and R.H. Dyson, JR., "The Prehistoric Climate of Baluchistan and the Indus Valley." *American Anthropologist*, Vol. 63, 1961.

22

Anthropological Data Re-examined

Kenneth A.R. Kennedy*

The cultural achievements of the people of the Indus Valley Civilization extended in time from 2400 to 1750 BC and in space across a thousand mile east-west tract from the present Iran-Pakistan border to Delhi and from the banks of the Sutlej to the Narmada, even as far south as Maharashtra. Were these a people of unique origin who founded the cities of Mohenjo-daro, Harappa, Kalibangan and hundreds of towns and hamlets? Were they the Aryans of *Vedic* tradition? Do their descendants survive today?

These questions about the racial identity of the Indus Valley, or Harappan people were raised coincidentally with the recognition of their archaeological remains by Sir John Marshall in 1924, although the mounds of Harappa had been visited by Charles Masson in 1826, and by Alexander Cunningham in 1853 and 1873. Excavations at this site and at Mohenjo-daro began in the early 1920s, and were coordinated by Marshall in these early years. Since that period, other archaeologists from South Asia and foreign countries have continued work at these ancient cities as well as discovered new sites, of which Kalibangan in northwestern Rajasthan is as impressive an urban center as the earlier known cities of the Indus Valley. At the localities of Mohenjodaro, Harappa and Chanhudaro in the Indus Valley and at Lothal in Gujarat archaeologists have encountered human skeletal remains. These have been examined by native and foreign physical anthropologists interested in establishing the racial identity and biological affinities of these ancient urban folk.

The mortuary sample which was collected is a heterogeneous one, including skeletal specimens from both urban and rural sites and these are broadly distributed in space and time. The sample is extended further

---

* Distinguished biological anthropolist in the Biological Sciences Division of the Cornell University, Ithaca, U.S.A.; has published many papers based on his field work in India.

if we include, as some physical anthropologists have done, human remains from certain pre and post-Harappan sites in Afghanistan and Baluchistan (Nal, Shahitump) or from post-Harappan sites in Maharashtra (Nevasa, Chandoli, Inamgaon) and Gujarat (Langhnaj). A single skull found many years ago at Sialkot in West Punjab has been included within this sample by some investigators. Mortuary data from the Harappa deposits of Cemetery H.Strata I and II, are dated as Post-Harappan, but the skeletons from Cemetery R37 and Area G of the same site are datable to the Mature Harappan period, as are most of the human remains from Mohenjo-daro. However, no cemetery has been found at Mohenjo-daro thus far. Skeletons removed from this site were encountered under circumstances indicative of hasty interment in different sectors of the city. At its fullest, the mortuary sample associated with these Indus Valley Civilization sites includes about three hundred individuals, some represented by very fragmentary remains. This figure becomes reduced by two-thirds when the sample size is restricted to well-preserved skeletons from archaeological contexts dated to the periods of the Mature Harappan Culture.

Historiography of Skeletal Studies

The first scientific study of these mortuary data appeared in 1931 with the anthropometric description of the Mohenjo-daro specimens by R.B.S. Sewell and B.S. Guha (1931). Their work was succeeded by Guha in collaboration with P.C. Basu (Guha and Basu 1938). The small skeletal collection from Chanhudaro was described by W.M. Krogmman and W.H. Sassman (1943). It was not until 1962 that a study of the Harappa specimens was published, and then by two teams of investigators: P. Gupta, P.C. Dutta and A. Basu, (1962) and by B.K. Chatterjee and G.D. Kumar, (1963). The latter two investigators published their study of the small skeletal series from Lothal in the following year. It has been my privilege to examine all of these specimens as well as those found at Harappa and Mohenjo-daro by Pakistani and foreign archaeologists since 1947. During partition, the bulk of the skeletal and cultural collections from the Indus Valley cities went to Calcutta where they are preserved today in the Indian Museum under the aegis of the Anthropological Survey of India. The skeletons from the cemetery at Kalibangan are also in Calcutta and these specimens are in the process of being described by Indian physical anthropologists.

Theories concerning the racial origins and biological affinities of the ancient Harappans are legion but may be separated into: (1) those studies which are typological and inspired by Guha's work, and (2) those which are based upon the data of demography, systematics, ecology and population genetics. Physical anthropologists inclining towards the latter strategy, among whom I count myself as one, do not approach skeletal biology with the assumption that mankind is naturally divisible into a number of subspecific categories called 'races' and that what we need to do is measure skulls and fit our metrical and morphological data into already existing or conveniently invented typological classifications. But such was Guha's philosophy of human diversity and it is not surprising that his colleagues followed a traditional racial approach to the biological study of their materials. This was a common practice in the thirties.

Racial typologies were based originally upon linguistic classifications. It was assumed that living speakers of Munda, Dravidian and Indo-European languages must have distinctive physical characteristics and, consequently, different biological histories. But the developing science of craniology had its part to play too, and terms such as "Australoid" "Veddoid" "Pre-Dravidian" and "Negritorid" found their way into the earlier anthropological literature concerning tribal peoples, outcaste groups, and the occasional lucky find of a prehistoric skull. Finally, there is the racial classification intrinsic to the *Vedic* literature itself where in a dichotomy of pure Aryan and impure *Dasas* is based as much upon differences of cultural and linguistic purity as it is upon stature, body form, skin colour, nasal form and head size. Mass migrations and invasions were the explanation for phenotypic diversity in the paradigm of racial typology which persisted for some two centuries of anthropological speculation.

In supervising the anthropological survey for the Census of India of 1901, Sir Herbert Risley (1915) defined seven physical types in the subcontinent which he identified by linguistic terms. His work has significance as the first scientific survey of biological diversity of living human populations throughout South Asia. Furthermore, Risely's racial classification served as a model to later anthropologists who proposed their own interpretations as to the numbers and kinds of races in India. Among the best known racial typologists apart from Guha were Egon von Eikstedt (1939), and D.N. Majumdar (1961). It was Guha's (1935) anthropological survey for the 1930 Census of India which has endured in South Asia, being represented even today as a massive illustrated diagram on a wall of the Indian National Museum in New Delhi. It is reproduced frequently in textbooks published by South Asian countries. Guha was influenced by Risley's classification, but he included in his census report many elements of the racial taxonomy of his professor at Harvard, Roland Burrage Dixon (1923). Guha gave attention to prehistoric skeletal remains in his discussion of the races of India and he found a place for them all within his racial categories with their subdivisions, a scheme based upon the examination of some 2500 living individuals from various parts of the subcontinent.

The Discarded Racial Theory

Guha's racial scheme is reflected in his 1931 and 1938 studies of the Mohenjo-daro skeletons as well as in the works of those whom he influenced who went on to describe the mortuary data from Harappa. Chanhudaro and Lothal. However, these later authors tended to alter in name, if not in meaning, Guha's racial labels: the names were changed but the typology remained the same! Guha's identification of four racial elements at Mohenjo-daro, which he called "Mediterranean," "Proto-Australoid," "Alpine" and "Mongoloid," was based upon a relatively small number of physical criteria of which the most common variables were indices of cranial height, length and breadth, facial and nasal indices, degrees of robusticity of the frontal bone and conformation of the occiput. Many more anthropometric observations have been recorded for skulls and post-cranial bones, but traditional racial typologies are based upon a finite number of traits. Cranial specimens which depart in their anthropometric values from what was considered "typical" were ascribed to "foreign" invading elements absorbed within the population. Thus the one or two broad-headed (brachycranic) skulls from Mohenjo-daro and Harappa were held to belong to foreign residents from lands to the east; those with rugged facial features were low caste people of peasant or barbarian stock who lurked on the fringes of Harappan cities. Since the dates of the mature Harappan culture are earlier than the period of the reputed Aryan invasion in the fourteenth century BC, Guha and his followers did not ascribe the Indus Valley people to this category, although some writers (Wheeler 1952) attributed the decline and fall of the Indus Valley cities to the Aryans.

Modified Approach

Although we may not be attracted today to racial classification, we are not dismissing the enduring questions of the origins and biological affinities of the ancient Harappans. Rather, in freeing ourselves from a taxonomic approach we may find better answers in the data of multivariate statistical studies of skeletal variability, such as has been undertaken by Mario Cappieri (1959). In a comparative analysis of Harappan skeletal data with those from archaeological sites outside of South Asia but of comparable antiquity, Cappieri has produced convincing evidence that the closest biological ties of the people of the Harappan Civilization are with the ancient populations of the Mediterranean basin and Near East rather than with the peoples of peninsular India and lands lying to the east of the Brahmaputra. Our own study of this problem confirms Cappieri's conclusions. It suggests, too, that when multivariate studies are made using data from populations of the Mediterranean, western Asia and the area influenced by the ancient Harappans in South Asia, a biological continuum extending over some five millennia is demonstrable. In short, the ancient Harappans are not markedly different in their skeletal biology from the present-day inhabitants of north-western India and Pakistan which do, in turn, share a high frequency of phenotypic characters with both ancient and living peoples of Afghanistan, Iran and the lands bordering the Aegean and Mediterranean. This existence of ancient and widely distributed phenotypic pattern is neither explained nor is its significance enhanced by recourse to typological classification. The physical traits considered in these multivariate studies assume independent gradational, or clinal, distributions over the geographical areas considered. Some reflect adaptive responses to specific ecological settings and are of evolutionary significance. The search for "Urrassen": among ancient cemeteries or between the pages of *Vedic* literary accounts seems purposeless within this evolutionary paradigm.

Collapse of Old Racial Theory

If it is true that the ancient Harappans represent an eastern sector of a Mediterranean-western Asiatic phenotypic pattern, how can we account for those particular specimens of the Harappan skeletal series which are described earlier by Guha and others as representatives of foreign peoples? In answering this we first observe that the so-called "Proto-Australoid", "Alpine" and "Mongoloid" specimens have been designated as such on the basis of a limited number of physical features of cranial architecture. Other anatomical characters, which are potentially sound indicators of biological diversity and affinity, have been neglected. In short, criteria used for racial classification are arbitrary. If we look at other phenotypic features than those traditionally selected by anthropometrists, we find that most of them fall within the normal range of variation for the Indus Valley population as a whole. This circumstance is paralleled by the study of the living populations of north-western India and Pakistan. Here we have the advantage of supplementing the data of skeletal biology with a number of biochemical, growth and development and pathological markers of which some are under known genetic control. When more and different sorting criteria are used than were included in most typological studies, the so-called foreign elements in the Harappan population are not separable. Instead we recognize an urban-type population with a normal range of physical variations such as we should expect to encounter in any metropolitan setting today or in the past.

Furthermore, we know that the broad-headed feature of the so-called Alpine or Mongoloid racial elements is better understood as a general evolutionary trend towards bracycephalization which has taken place in *Homo sapiens* since the close of the Pleistocene some 10,000 years ago. Broad heads appears in varying frequencies in populations inhabiting all of the world's continents. It is an inadequate indicator by itself of specifically non-Indian biological affinities. Broad skulls occur in the modern population of South Asia and, as at the Harappan cities, have frequencies which fall within the normal range of variation for many local groups elsewhere on the continent or in Europe.

A New Approach

We must conclude at this point that the existence of phenotypic diversity of some cranial features is not a spectacular element of the ancient Indus Valley people. However, where differences of cranial form and muscular robusticity do appear we are perceiving the same degree of diversity that we anticipate finding in any urban population. Such a population is never static, an evolutionary fact commonly overlooked by racial taxonomists who treat the Harappan series as though all specimens were contemporary in time. Nor is due regard given to geographical and regional differences. Since the populations of Mohenjo-daro, Harappa, Chandudaro and Lothal and those from other centers of the second and third millennia BC were never rigidly stable, it seems reasonable to conclude that whatever trends towards biological homogeneity that they may have been drifting towards were continuously being effected by the immigration of rural peoples coming from the outlying Harappan townships and hamlets. Then, as in South Asia today, peasant agriculturalists constitute low or outcaste groups which are made up in large part of acculturated tribal populations. This part of the world has been experiencing an evolutionary dynamic whereby already biologically heterogeneous urban populations regularly receive relatively homogeneous tribal populations. The latter have become partially acculturated in village settings. Once defined into the social category as low caste people, many individuals and families leave as migrant enclaves for the urban centers. Tribal populations have been relatively isolated, despite long standing symbiotic relationships with settled agriculturalists in their territories. It is not surprising that multivariate studies of a wide range of physical features of lower caste peoples in villages and cities indicate their ultimate derivation from tribal populations, many of which have undergone acculturation quite recently. From a position of being small and isolated breeding populations, they tend to find themselves moving into the socially segmented configuration of urban life and mixing with the longer settled inhabitants.

The high degree of polytypism in South Asia today is due to this overlap of relatively homogeneous tribal and outcaste groups and their penetration into villages, then into urban environments of more heterogeneous people. Indeed, urban diversity is increased by this ancient and continuous process. This dynamic rather than mass migration and invasions of nomadic and warlike peoples better accounts for the biological constitutions of those earlier urban populations in the Indus Valley. Gregory Possehl (1976) has recently suggested the close symbiotic ties of the hunting-gathering peoples of Gujarat with Indus valley leaders or their intermediaries who used Lothal as a trade station. This is the beginning of the kind of acculturation we see represented in the form of Harappan urban life and eventual phenotypic diversity.

Anthropology of the Aryans: No Evidence

Of the Aryans, we must defer to literary and linguistic scholars in whose province lies the determination of the arrival and nature of the linguistic phenomenon we call the Aryans. Surely, as a linguistic and traditional element its influence is profound and real. But archaeological evidence of Aryan-speaking people is questionable and the skeletal evidence is nil. Even if we were presented with an Aryan skeleton, how should we be able to identify it? We know nothing about the skeletal biology of the bringers of Indo-European languages to South Asia, least of all the early composers of the *Vedic* accounts. Nor is there any sound evidence to indicate that the so-called Aryan invasion was coincident with and contributory to the decline of the Harappan Civilization. The massacre at Mohenjo-daro is questionable, and to ascribe the fate of its victims to the Aryans would be unfounded indeed. S.R. Rao (1973) would have us believe that the ancient Harappans were racially and linguistically pre-Aryans who preceded the *Vedic* Aryans and were demolished by them. But he brings forth no biological evidence to convince us and such questions of biological origin and affinity are never settled outside the data of biology itself, namely the results of skeletal analysis by trained professionals. We are happy to note that of late he has discarded his own theory made under the influence of Wheeler.

Physical Anthropology Today

But what the physical anthropologist has to say today which is new and, I believe, more exciting, concerning the ancient Harappans, has to do with their demographic characteristics rather than with their racial classifications. Today the issues have shifted from settling the question of who were the Harappans? To what were they? This is asked with the purpose of measuring not their skulls but their biological adaptability to the settled agricultural lifeway. What has been the biological cost of shifting from a hunting-gathering lifeway with its relatively isolated sphere of activity and gene flow to the complexities of urban life maintained by food production, animal domestication, foreign trade, artisan crafts and experimental technologies? This change is reflected in characteristic modifications of dental attrition which tell us about food preparation and the quality of the environment, in the markers of arrested growth on bones and dental enamel, in the general health profile which is related to nutritional as well as pathological variables including markers of such chronic diseases as malaria, certain cancers, arthritic disease and many hereditary diseases. The vital statistics of extinct populations are defined by measures used by the physical anthropologist to determine rates of fecundity, fertility, mortality and morbidity. These adaptive mechanisms are critical to understanding the biological nature and affinities of the ancient Harappans for they are interpreted today not within the framework of racial typology but in the light of seeing the Indian subcontinent as an ever-changing evolutionary field within the greater landmass of Asia.

Our own work of the past few years has focused upon these questions of measuring the degree of biological costs in man's adjustment to the lifeway demanded by food production, herding, mass production of goods, and trade with the larger world outside the walls of the city. Some of my colleagues have investigated these questions in various parts of the world: J. Lawrence Angel in the Aegean region, Jane Buikstra in the pre-Columbian American midwest, and Philip Rightmire in Africa. Palaeodemography is a well-established field of anthropological inquiry. But we are just beginning to learn about these kinds of problems on the Indian subcontinent.

Notes & References

Cappieri, M. 1959 "La popolazoine priestorica della civilta dell' Indo." *Rivista di Scienze Preistoriche* 14: 123-174.

Chatterjee, B.K. and G.D. Kumar 1862 "Etude comparee et analyse raciale des restes humains de Harappa, Pakistan Occidental." *L'Anthropologie* 66: 335-337.

1963 *Comparative Study and Racial Analysis of the Human Remains of Indus Valley Civilization with Particular Reference to Harappa.* Calcutta: W. Newman and Company.

1963 Racial Elements in Post-Harappan Skeletal Remains at Lothal. In *Anthropology on the March: Recent Studies of Indian Beliefs, Attitudes and Social Institutions.* Bala Ratnam (ed) Madras: Social Sciences Association.

Dixon, R.B. 1923, *The Racial History of Man* (London: Charles Scribner's Sons).

Guha, B.S. 1935 The Racial Affinities of the Peoples of India. In *Census of India,* 1931. 1: (3A), i-lxxi+1-116. (Simla: Government of India).

Guha, B.S. and P.C. Basu 1938 Report on the Human Remains Excavated at Mohejo-daro, in 1920-29. In Further Excavations at Mohenjo-daro, Being an Official Account of Archaeological Excavations Carried out by the Government of India Between the Years 1927 and 1931. (With chapters by A.S. Hemmy, B.S. Guha and P.C. Basu), E.J.H. Mackay, (ed.) 1:613-638 (New Delhi: Government Press).

Gupta, P., P.C. Dutta and A. Basu 1962 *Human Skeletal Remains from Harappa,* 9: 13-188+i-lxl, Pls. 2-711. (Calcutta: Anthropological survey of India.)

Krogman, W.M. and W.H. Sassman 1943 "Skull Found at Chanhu-daro." In *Chanhu-daro Excavations1935-36*. E.J.H. Mackey (ed.) New Haven, (Connecticut: American Oriental Society). pp. 252-263.

Majumdar, D.N. 1961 Races and Cultures of India, 4th ed., rev. (Bombay: Asia Publishing House).

Possehl, G.L. 1976 "Lothal: a Gateway Settlement of the Harappan Civilization." In *Ecological Backgrounds of South Asian Prehistory.* K.A.R. Kennedy and G.L. Possehl, (eds.) South Asia Occasional Papers and Theses, (Cornell University, Ithaca, New York), pp. 118-131.

Rao, S.R. 1973 *Lothal and the Indus Civilization.* (New York: Asia Publishing House).

Risley, H. 1915 *The People of India,* 2nd ed. (Calcutta and Simla: Thacker, Spink and Company.).

Sewell, R.B.S. and B.S. Guha 1931 Human Remains. In *Mohenjodaro and the Indus Civilization,* Being an Official Account of Archaeological Excavators Carried out by the Government of India Between the Years 1922 to 1927. J. Marshall, (ed.) 2: 599-648. (London: Arthur Probsthain).

von Eickstedt, E. 1939 The History of Anthropological Research in India. In *The Travancore Tribes and Castes* 2.

Wheeler, R.E.M. 1952 Archaeology and the Transmission of Ideas. *Antiquity* 26: 180-192.

Related Sources

Dutta, P.C. 1972 "The Bronze-Age Harappans: a Re-examination of the skulls in the context of the Population Concept." *American Journal of Physical Anthropology* 36: (3) 391;396.

Kennedy, K.A.R. 1969 "Palaeodemography of India and Ceylon Since 3000 BC" *American Journal of Physical Anthropology* 31: 315-320.

„ 1972 "The Paleontology of Human Populations." *The Biologist* 54: 97-114.

,, 1973 Biological Anthropology of Prehistoric South Asians. *The Anthropologist* 17: 1-13.

„ 1980 Prehistoric Skeletal Record of Man in South Asia. *Annual Review of Anthropology* 9: 391-432.

23

Studies in the Indus-Saraswati Civilization: Some New Developments

S.P. Gupta*

The common man's knowledge of the third millennium BC civilization of India is generally based upon the views of Sir Mortimer Wheeler contained in two of his major publications—*The Indus Civilization* (1953) and the *Early India and Pakistan* (1960). However, some of his major postulates put forward therein have now been found extremely questionable by many leading field-archaeologists working for the last 25 years both in India and Pakistan. These are anthropologists who have re-examined the skeletal remains of the people who once lived in the cities of the Indus Civilization. These are scholars of palaeo-religious, who have interpreted a whole class of new structures unearthed at some Indus sites. And these are palaeo-zoologists, who have re-studied the animal bones from these sites. An attempt will be made here to bring at one place the results of some new excavations, new explorations and new works done in the laboratories of these anthropologists, archaeologists, and palaeontologists which throw new light not only on the problems of origin and decline of the Indus Civilization but also on a few problems related to the phenomenon of the first urbanisation of India, called variously as the Indus Civilization or Harappan Civilization.

First, some of Wheeler's postulates. To begin with, Wheeler used all his talents and literary skill to prove that the Indus Valley Civilization was the outcome of the Mesopotamian experiment in city-life; at one place he even goes to the extent of suggesting that the master-craftmen came from a foreign country to Mohenjodaro to build the first houses! In other words, he looked at this civilization not as a 'primary' civilization, like the ancient Egyptian and Mesopotamian, developing on its own soil and produced by its own genius, but a 'secondary' civilization built by

* Chairman, Archaeological Society of India; former Director, Allahabad Museum; teaches Art and Archaeology at National Museum Institute of History and Art, New Delhi; published and edited many research publications on Archaeology and history of Art.

foreigners. Though the theory is dead since long in some quarters it is still persisting, either in its original form or some modified version.

Wheeler's second major postulate was regarding the end of this civilization. He squarely blamed the *Vedic* war-lord Indra for it. He repeatedly wrote that the Aryans came from beyond the north-western frontiers of India, attacked the fortified townships of the Indus people, like Harappa and Mohenjodaro, and destroyed them once for all by massacring people; and that this was, for all practical purposes, the end of the Indus Valley Civilization in Sind and Punjab at least; in Gujarat it lived a little longer, he conceded in a later publication.

Some of his other conclusions were related to nomenclature, chronology, presence or absence of horse, fire worship, etc. These will also be dealt with at the appropriate places.

The Nomenclature: A Plea for the 'Indus-Saraswati' Civilization

The two archaeological sites which for the first time, in the year 1921-22, revealed the existence of a city-oriented culture in India, belonging to the third millennium BC, were Mohenjodaro and Harappa, the former located on the Indus in Sind, and the latter on the Ravi, a tributary of the Indus, in Punjab. In the subsequent years, a few more sites of the same culture-complex were found in the Indus basin, such as

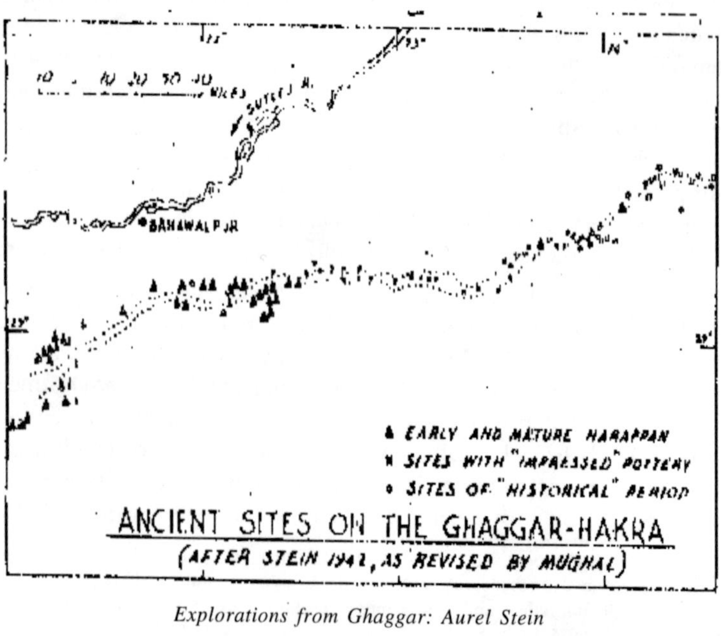

Explorations from Ghaggar: Aurel Stein

Chanhudaro, Mohenjodaro and Dabar Kot. It was, therefore, thought fit at that point of time to name it as the 'Indus Valley Civilization', although then, and even now, in many quarters it is called the 'Harappan Civilization', after the name of the site where the remains of this civilization were discovered first, in the mid-19th century itself by Charles Masson, Alexander Cunningham and others, although none of them could understand its real significance even in terms of chronology; for all of them it remained just an enigma.

When India was partitioned in 1947 both Harappa and Mohenjodaro remained in Pakistan due to which Wheeler wrote a book in 1950, entitled *Five thousand Years of Pakistan*. Suddenly, an absolutely new nation claimed to be the ancient-most. Very few people know that this was deliberately done by Wheeler, in retaliation to a rebuff that Sardar Vallabh Bhai Patel, the then Deputy Prime Minister of India, had given to him. It was 1948. Wheeler was under the impression that after the partition also India would retain his services because he had done so much of field-work here and trained so many young men in the new methodology of excavations he introduced not only in India but in the whole world. Thus, when asked to give his choice, he arrogantly wrote on the file 'whosoever would like to have my services'. To his greatest surprise, he found the note of Sardar Patel on his file 'we do not need your services'. Crest-fallen and bitter to the core, Wheeler went to Pakistan and joined them as the Advisor for Archaeology.

This incident, though an unhappy one, and of no other value except for historiography, impressed upon the Indian archaeologists to put their heart and soul in the search of Indus Valley or Harappan sites in the new boundaries of India, if these were there; afterall, an ancient country was divided in 1947 and not its culture and cultural heritage which is still and shall always remain one and the same. Some hint was already available to them. Sir Aurel Stein[1] had already explored in 1940-41 a part of the dried up course of the river Saraswati in the Old Bahawalpur State as well as in Distt. Ganganagar, Rajasthan, bordering Pakistan; at that time the country was not divided. Here he had identified some 90 sites as 'Harappan' and 'later'. (Fig. 1) In Gujarat, as far back as 1935, the site of Rangpur was explored and also excavated, though only partially, but extensive enough to prove that it was also 'Harappan'; at that time it was called 'late Harappan' since it was believed that only the Indus Valley could produce the evidence of the early phase of this civilization; archaeologists believed that this alone was the epicentre of the culture. Thus, for the Indian archaeologists, specializing in the Indus Valley Civilization, the partition of the country and the departure of Wheeler did not, at all prove any deterrent; if anything, the unhappy incident became a blessing in disguise.

Explorations in the Saraswati Basin

A. Ghosh,[2] in the year 1951, picked up the thread left by Aurel Stein in the Bikaner deserts, and undertook intensive explorations along the old channel of the Saraswati inside the new boundaries of India, from Hanumangarh to Anupgarh, through Suratgarh. His work was thus only an extension of the work done a decade earlier by Stein. Here he found as many as 25 sites of the Indus Civilization. It included the now famous site of Kalibangan which was a decade later excavated by B.B. Lal and B.K. Thapar,[3] from 1961 through 1968. In recent years, starting from 1974 through 1980, M.R. Mughal[4] undertook a similar exercise, of intensive explorations in the old basin of the Saraswati, locally called 'Hakra', in the Bhawalpur region of Pakistan; the region is sometimes called 'Cholistan' also. He covered 480 kms in length and 16 to 20 kms in breadth the basin of the lost Saraswati, starting from the Indian border. He found around 264 sites, large and small, which belonged to this civilization: 40 Early Harappan, 174 Mature Harappan and 50 Late Harappan; 99 were the 'pre-Early Harappan' sites of the "Hakra Culture", which in fact belonged to the Formative Period of the Indus Valley Civilization. The efforts of these and many other Indian and Pakistani scholars, like Henery Field, K. Dalal, K.N. Dikshit brought more fruits. It was further augmented by similar projects undertaken in areas further eastward, in Haryana, by R.S. Bisht, U.V. Singh, Suraj Bhan, J.P. Joshi[5] and others, both in the basin of the Saraswati and the basins of its tributaries like Drishadvati, locally called 'Chitang' or 'Chautang'. Now even the region of mega Delhi is within the Harappan or the Indus cultural zone; the site of Alamgirpur, excavated by Y.D. Sharma, lies only 28 kms from the city of Delhi, on the river Hindon, in Distt. Meerut. Thus, we have now more than 500 known large and small sites of the Indus Civilization on the river Saraswati and its tributaries in the Indus-Yamuna Divide (Fig.2).

Explorations in the Indus Basin

Equally serious efforts were made by scholars to explore the basin of the Indus and its tributaries in Sind and Punjab on both sides of the international boundary between India and Pakistan. Several foreign scholars joined the Pakistani colleagues to do the job, for almost three decades now, like J.F. Jarrige from France who excavated Mehrgarh, Raymond Allchin and Bridget Allchin from U.K., who excavated Lewan, and G.F. Dales from U.S.A. who excavated Harappa, Mohenjodaro, Balakot and Sutkgendor. There are many others from Italy, France and

USA who have worked on this problem in Pakistan. They have, however, not been able to find even 100 sites; the known number in fact does not exceed 90 to 96, which includes both Harappa and Mohenjodaro. We have, therefore, a clear case of 700 versus 100; 700 and odd sites on the Saraswati and its tributaries and around 100 sites on the Indus and its tributaries. Many archaeologists, therefore, thought it proper and logical to coin a new term, the 'Indus-Saraswati Civilization', to name the same Civilization which was so far known by terms like 'Indus Valley' and 'Harappan' civilization. It has now been fully realised that this civilization was the gift of both the rivers, the Indus as well as the Saraswati, perhaps more of the latter, hence only the new nomenclature will reflect the archaeological ground-realities.

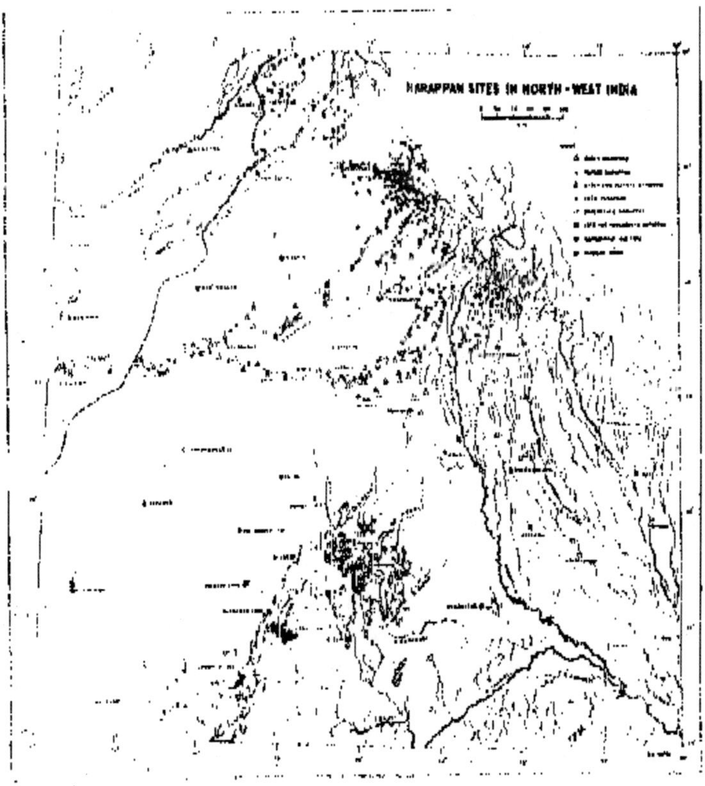

The Beginning : What was Below the Cities?

When Marshall and his colleagues excavated Mohenjodaro and Harappa, for almost a decade, from 1921, and they published the excavations report in 1931, entitled *Mohenjo-daro and the Indus Civilization*, the sub-soil water was so very high around Mohenjodaro that they could not reach the earliest level of human occupation at this site. Hence, whatever they found, belonged to the city or highly developed urban phase of the Indus-Saraswati Civilization. When Wheeler also tried to reach the lowest depth of Mohenjodaro in 1950 he too failed, since his trenches were soon filled with the gushing sub-soil water, hampering all efforts to reach the bottom. Dales, therefore, used in 1965 the geological method of boring the ground with a pipe to know at least the total depth of the deposit at the site. The results were revealing: the earliest level appeared to have been reached at the depth of 68 ft. below the ground level. It also indicated that the lowest level people used pottery which was not cent-per-cent 'mature Harappan'; in all probability it was Kot Dijian or Early Indus-Saraswati. This fact has been reconfirmed by several boring which the UNESCO conservators of Mohenjodaro have laid round the site to pump out the subsoil water.

In 1946 Wheeler had re-excavated the site of Harappa and he took had encountered a group of pottery below the fortification wall, in layers '26' and '26a', which was non-Harappan in character; at that point of time he thought that it belonged to one of the Baluchistan chalcolithic cultures, such as Periano Ghundai.[6] Since, the deposit of this 'non-Harappan' pottery was very thin, found only in two layers, he failed to appreciate its implications which were in fact far-reaching as it is now fully proved, after the excavations conducted at Kot Diji by F.A. Khan[7] and re-excavation of Harappa by G.F. Dales.[8]

Excavations at Kot Diji : Turning Point

From the year 11955 to 1957, the site of Kot Diji on the Indus exactly opposite Mohenjodaro, some 25 kms away, on the east bank, was excavated on a large scale till the bedrock was reached. It revealed to the world for the first time that much before the birth of the highly developed city of the 'Harappans', at this very the birth of the highly developed city of the 'Harappans', at this very site, people had been living for at least 500 to 600 years in a fortified settlement, with public and domestic structures of stones and mud-bricks. It was a township with houses built along roads and lanes. At one stage the town got burnt. The new township built on the ashes of the old township was, however, much mor elaborate. It was a city with a citadel. It started using a script, seals and sealings as well as weights which were found by Marshall and others at Harappa and Mohenjodaro. It was, however, also established that all the cultural elements of the previous people, called by the excavator 'Kot Dijian', continued to be used by the 'Harappan' people. In other words, there was no cultural break as such between the 'Kot Dijian' and the 'Harappan' culture-complexes, even though there did occur a burnt layer between the two levels which may at best mean temporary abandonment of the site which was necessary to re-plan and re-build the township; this time on a larger scale, and with better drainage system.

The 'overlap' between the so-called 'Kot Diji' and the 'Harappan', or respectively the Early Harappan and Mature Harappan, cultures was soon re-verified and fully established and B.B. Lal and B.K. Thapar at Kalibangan: most of the cultural items of the Kalibangan-I or lower level settlement, characterised by pottery used at Kot Diji and Sothi, were found in use during the period called 'Kalibangan-II' or upper level settlement characterised by pottery used at Mohenjodaro. Like Kot Diji, Kalibangan had also to pass through a severe catastrophe, an earthquake which had destroyed the township of the Kalibangan-I period. When it came to re-building the city after the earthquake, here also the people re-planned the settlement on a massive scale—enlarging the fortification wall and adding huge religious and secular structures; of course, over a long period of time and one by one.

Now arose the problem of interpreting this archaeological record: how exactly to do it?

'Pre-Harappan' or 'Early Harappan'?

In the beginning, the thinking of scholars both in India and Pakistan was of great caution. They did concede the point that the 'Kot Diji' culture (A. Ghosh had called it 'Sothi culture', after the name of a site on the Saraswati which he had explored in 1950s and where he had got a largely similar pottery) was the *immediate precursor* of the 'Harappan' culture since they overlapped stratigraphically in a big way, through several layers, still both did not appear to belong to one and the same culture-complex because of some marked differences in the cultural items of the two complexes. They, therefore, used the term 'Pre-Harappan' for the Kot Diji-Sothi culture-complex. Shashi Asthana took this line of argument in the very title of her book *The Pre-Harappan Cultures of India, and the Borderlands* (1985), and D.P. Agrawal also used the same terminology in his book *The Archaeology of India* (1982).

However, in 1970s itself the usage of the term 'Pre-Harappan' for the Kot Diji culture-complex was challenged by M.R. Mughal. The title that he gave to his Ph.D. thesis, submitted to the Pennsylvania University, was "*The Early Harappan Period in the Greater Indus Valley and Northern Baluchistan (c. 3000-2400 B.C.)*".

The Battle of Approaches

This led to a serious debate amongst all the archaeologists of the world who were dealing with the Indus-Saraswati Civilization, directly or indirectly. What one group called 'Pre-Harappan', the other group called 'Early Harappan'. Why this controversy cropped up?...It is all a question of 'approaches' in archaeological studies which are primarily two—the 'culture historical' and 'culture processual'.

The 'culture-historical' approach to the Indus-Saraswati Civilization, in which the 'Kot Diji' and 'Harappan' culture-complexes are considered two entirely different entities, puts emphasis on the differences which exist in archaeological cultural-items of the two complexes, overlooking the phenomenon of overlap between the two cultures and the continuity of all the items of the 'Kot Diji complex' into the 'Harappan complex'; these two features this approach tries to explain away on factors other than cultural continuity. Thus, the practitioners of this approach, mostly in India, say that since writing cubical chart weights and steatite square seals, with perforated and grooved knobs at the back are found only in the 'Harappan' levels and not in 'Kot Dijian' levels, the two cultures cannot be considered as part and parcel of one and the same culture-complex. For them the phenomenon of overlap can hardly be over-emphasised since to the separate cultures exemplified in two different potteries, come close to each other and thus lived together without losing the material items of their individual cultures.

The 'culture-processual' approach to the Indus-Saraswati Civilization, on the other hand, argues that a dynamic culture like the one the Indus and the Saraswati produced, kept on evolving and changing slowly and gradually, over a vast area of its settlements. The change is, however, neither uniform nor identical everywhere because it can never be fully controlled and directed by the authorities whatever their form may have been. Changes occur because of two reasons—local fusion of people and ideas. The two together produce automatically similarities in certain respects and dissimilarities in other respects of culture. Both are, in fact, seen in the Indus-Saraswati context.

The practitioners of this approach, mostly those who are working in Pakistan, including foreigners, therefore, do not go by the culture-items of single periods of single sites; they try to locate first the common cultural elements existing at different contemporary sites, and then the elements which are uncommon. This exercise gives them an insight into the *process* which brought about cultural commonness and cultural distinctiveness in a large culture-complex spread over a vast area. In the Indus-Saraswati context, they emphasis, there is no case for two separate cultures, one 'Kot Diji' and the other 'Harappan'; the two complexes formed part of a single developing process of culture-change. They, therefore, decided to follow Mughal and called the Kot-Diji complex as 'Early Harappan' and the Harappan complex as 'Mature Harappan,' or else 'Urban Harappan'. On the commonness of certain pottery types and decorative designs on them, Mughal plotted the 'Kot Dijian' sites as well as 'Harappan' sites on one and the same map. The discovery was startling: more than 3/4th of the area covered by the two culture-complexes has been one and the same.

Moreover, none of the two cultures is found located in too distant geographical areas with large spatial gap between them to allow enough scope of migration in the Indus-Saraswati country from regions outside India.

The Victory of Processual Archaeological Approach

The logical conclusion, according to these scholars, is that the birth of the urban phase of the Indus-Saraswati Civilization, called 'Harappan', lies in the proto-urban phase of the Indus-Saraswati Civilization, called 'Kot Diji'—both the terms are used for convenience sake, denoting only the economic status of the two stages of one and the same culture-complex.

Thus, in the model of the processual archaeologists not individual cultural items but their cumulative effect on culture as a whole matters most. The Kot Diji culture-complex is called 'Early Indus-Saraswati' because when spread on a table cultural items from the pre-burnt levels of Kot Diji; Sothi; Balakot; Kalibangan I; Lower levels of Harappa; upper levels of Jalilpur (Jalilpur II); Sarai Khola II; Rehman Dheri; Gumla II; Amri lower levels or Period I; Chanhudaro, lower levels; Mohenjodaro lowest level in D.K. area, section 6; Nausharo, lower levels; Sothi, Banawali I, Dholavira, Stage III, etc. *We find that practically every important item of the Harappan, or the Mature phase of the Indus-Saraswati Civilization, is present there*—pottery, ornaments, seals, weights and even writing. We may now consider two sites which bring to our notice some new features.

Excavations at Balakot

At Balakot, on the dried up course of the Windar on the Arabian coast, Dales[9] excavated in 1973 the 4m thick deposit of which phases I to XI are Early Indus-Saraswati, phases XII to XIII represent Transition, and phases XIV to XVII Mature Indus-Saraswati. The Early Period (Pd.I) has yielded the evidence of houses built with mud-bricks of the standard size in the ratio of 1:2:4, the Mature Period standard. The pottery is wheel-thrown with forms and polychrome paintings resembling Nal cemetery ware. On one of the pots a motif is identified by Dales as 'proto-Siva'. Chert blades, grinding stones and pounders, tumblers, paste beads, humped bull terracotta figurines and lumps of copper along with Amri, Anjira pottery etc. make it an extremely crucial site for the Early Harappan phase.

These include more than a dozen types of pottery shapes, including deep and shallow bowls, wide shouldered globular vessels with very short neck decorated with painting using a broad band on the neck and a large horned bull-head decorated with six petalled flowers (also found at Gumla III, Sarai Khola near Taxila, and Burzahom in Kashmir Valley), cylindrical vases, dishes-on-stand, ring stands, etc. The pottery is generally dull red on the surface with paintings done in sepia, black and white.

Excavations at Kunal

In recent years, from 1990, a site Kunal, located in Distt. Hissar of Haryana, has been put to excavations by the Haryana State Department of Archaeology. It is near the famous Harappan site of Banawali where Kot Diji-Sothi material was found in a 3m thick deposit in the lower levels (Ph. I). Kunal has also yielded a large number of painted pottery types identical with those from Banawali (Pd.I) in an equally thick deposit indicating long life.

The excavators have divided this Kot Diji-Sothi or 'Early Harappan' deposit into overlapping cultural levels. The former, or the lower level, yield evidence of 'pit-dwellings' of the Kashmir Neolithic type microliths, copper arrow-heads and fish-hooks, and remains of post-holes indicating that people were at the Neolithic-Chalcolithic stage which may be dated to 3500-300 BC period and may belong culturally to the Hakra or Jalilpur 'neolithic' phase since the character of the dwellings and the presence of microliths would clearly indicate that. The second or upper phase is characterised by typical Banawali I and Kalibandgan-I Kot Diji-Sothi culture-complex of the Early Harappan type. The houses were built of standardized 1:2:3 size moulded mud-bricks; such bricks were also used for lining the 'pit-dwellings', the largest measuring 2.75m in diameter; some of these were found containing hearths at the bottom. The settlement was planned and the houses discharged their waste water through the soakage jars and pits. In order to store grains, they made silos in the from of pits of different sizes with sides plastered with clay and lime to save the material from insects. Copper artifacts, like arrow-heads and blades, bone points, beads of terracotta, steatite, faience, lapis lazuli, several kinds of which were found even in Phase I levels, are some of the other materials. The paintings on earthen pots—vases, jars, globular vessels, basins, troughs, dishes, etc.—generally using geometric patterns, were done in black and white colours. All the so-called pre-Harappan pottery fabrics, A to F, have been found here also which clearly shows that here we are dealing with just another site of one and the same culture, although like all other sites, Kunal also had its own individual elements of culture, such as the pit-dwellings. It had also a black-and-red ware, not found at Kalibangan but reported from Lothal. A medium-sized pottery kiln was also found. It is reported that square and rectangular, houses came up in Phase III although, to our mind, these must have been there from the early times. In addition, it has yielded half a dozen uninscribed square steatite seals with a variety of geometric motifs engraved on them; some of them appear in the Mature Indus-Saraswati deposits. But, undoubtedly, the most startling discovery is the presence of two silver tiaras, one large and the other small, decorated with designs in gold. These were found kept in an earthern pot buried in the habitational areas.[10]

But items like typical Indus-Saraswati seals, writing and weights and measures were not found so far either at Kot Diji or Kalibangan. Recently, some of these items have also been found at a site where it was hardly expected, for example at Dholavira in Kutch.

New Discoveries at Dholavira

Uninscribed but typical Harappan square steatite seals, at least three of them, have been found at Dholavira; cubical weights of agate, at least one example was also found at Dholavira; writing (a couple of signs written in black on a red pot-sherd) too was found at Dholavira. A large number of graffiti marks, some resembling Indus-Saraswati script-signs, are, however, found at Rehman Dheri as well as several Quetta Ware sites in Baluchsistan and beyond, belonging definitely to an still earlier period. Painted designs and motifs, including pipal leaf, intersecting circles, fish-scale pattern; shell bangles; terracotta objects, including pots like 'perforated jars', bull figurines, and the so-called 'cakes' etc. anticipate in clear terms all such items which are found in larger numbers in the mature or urban phase of the Indus-Saraswati Civilization.

It may be noted in this context that Mughal has separated Sothi sites in India, now around 150, spread over Haryana, Punjab and Rajasthan, where Kalibangan I type potteries, divided into six fabrics, called A B C D E F, are found; but to our mind, Sothi pottery forms part of the Kot Diji pottery complex, a fact which emerges out of half-a-dozen excavated sites of this culture-complex in India alone. The Kot Diji sites in Pakistan number 63 of which as many as 40 are located in the Saraswati basin, in

Cholistan, which it may be noted, is only an extension of the Suratgarh deserts in which Kalibangan is located.

The Collapse of Mesopotamian theory of Indus-Saraswati Origin

The earliest Calibrated radiocarbon date for the Kot Diji culture comes from lower levels at the citadel of Kot Diji, two layers above the lowest; it is 3370 BC, and it tallies well with the date obtained from the contemporary levels at Harappa where it is 3300 BC. In fact, the lowest level of Kot Diji may easily go back to 3500 BC since the two lowest most layers still remain to be dated.

The Kot Diji contemporary site of Rehman Dheri, Level I, is also dated to 3380 BC Kalibangan I, however, begins in 2980 BC Sarai Khola II near Taxila is dated to 2905 BC, i.e., around 3000 BC.[11]

It would, therefore, indicate quite clearly that there were at least two phases in the Kot Diji or the Early Indus-Saraswati culture: Old (3500-3000 BC) and New (3000-2700 BC). The period between 3500 BC and 3000 BC was very crucial—the Early Indus-Saraswati Civilization was spreading far and wide, informing us that it was the proto-urban phase in which new townships were getting established in and also beyond the Indus and Saraswati basins; the large cities of Harappa, Mohenjodaro, etc. were the culmination of the long process of urbanisation and not its beginning.

Wheeler's hypothesis of West Asian or Sumerian origin of the Indus-Saraswati Civilization has, therefore, completely collapsed; it has now been replaced by the indigenous origin theory as it has been fully realised that the Mature or Developed Urban phase of the Indus-Saraswati Civilization, called 'Harappan', had all its roots deeply buried in the proto-urban phase of the Indus-Saraswati Civilization, called the 'Kot Diji'. The Indus-Saraswati Civilization had no moorings in the civilizations existing outside India, even though it had contacts over a very large area beyond its boundaries, from the 4th millennium BC itself, such as Afghanistan and Turan because such contacts were limited to trade. Therefore, why 'thank' Mesopotmia for the *idea* of civilization, that is 'city', coming to India at the end of the 4th millennium on its *wings* and giving her the impetus and model for the 'production of a mature and literate civilization', afterall fortified townships were already there at Harappa, Kot Diji, Dholavira etc. by the middle of the fourth millennium. Mesopotamia had also nothing to contribute to the origin of the Indus-Saraswati writing, the two scripts were poles apart. The same was true of weights and measures, seals and sealings, town-planning, etc. Mesopotamia had no priority over India in most of these respects.

The Chronology

Wheeler's third postulate was in the field of chronology. In 1953, in the first edition of *The Indus Civilization,* Wheeler had dated the Indus-Saraswati Civilization to the maximum time-bracket of 2500 BC and 1500 BC; the lower limit he, however, later on, in the third edition, brought down to 1700 BC, apparently under the impact of the Radiocarbon dates which were then taken by many scholars in absolute terms. In fashion was 'shorter chronology' as proposed by D.P. Agarwal; he had proposed 2300 BC-1700 BC as the 'comprehensive' time-bracket for the urban phase of the civilization.[12] However, 1980s dealt a cruel blow to the so-called absoluteness of the radiocarbon dates; Agrawal knew about it. It was by then fully realised by scientists in cognate disciplines, such as dendrochronology, that the absoluteness of the radiocarbon dates was a myth, these dates were much younger than the real ones; as we go back in time we have to add hundreds of more years in order to arrive at the absolute or near absolute dates. After a lot of trials and errors, it has now been generally agreed to follow a conversion table, called 'CALIB program' as worked out by Stuiver and Reimer.

According to this system a radiocarbon date of 2500 BC is calibrated to 3180 BC, i.e., an addition of 580 years, to arrive at the correct dates. And so on and so forth. The 'shorter chronology' has now been finally replaced by the 'longer chronology'. The Urban or Mature phase of the Indus-Saraswati Civilization is now fixed between 2700 BC and 1900 BC.

Since the proto-urban or Early period of the Indus-Saraswati Civilization is now also considered as part and parcel of the Indus-Saraswati Civilization, we have to add at least 300 years more to it. The time-bracket for the Early Period is fixed between 3500 BC and 2700 BC, divided into two phases, as noted earlier—Old phase (3500 BC-3000 BC) and New phase (3000 BC-2700 BC).

The things have, however, not stopped here. Extensive field-work conducted during the last more than one decade has further sharpened our understanding of the beginning of the Indus-Saraswati Civilization. It has added some 500 years more, pushing back the beginning to about 3800 BC or even to 4000 BC. This is called the Formative Period of the Indus-Saraswati Civilization. The glimpses of this are available at Jalilpur, at Harappa, at Mehrgarh, at Amri, at Balakot and at about 90 sites in the Saraswati basin.

Excavations at Mehrgarh in Bolan Basin: Another Turning Point

On the present showing it appears that these people originally belonged to the piedmont region of the Baluchi hills. The site of

Mehrgarh[13] is very crucial in this respect because it is here that we get the evidence of Neolithic settlement which goes back to the 8th millennium, like a number of Neolithic sites in Iran, Mesopotamia, Syria and Asia Minor. What is, however, much more significant to note is that here we have the longest sequence of cultures, without any break whatsoever, upto the Early Indus-Saraswati. In other words, this sequence does not allow any outside agency to come and effect changes in the step-by-step growth of culture. If this is realised clearly, it will not leave any scope for doubt in the indigenous theory of origin and growth of the Indus-Saraswati Civilization; at Mehrgarh from around 4000 BC we start getting all those characteristic features which went directly into the make-up of the Early Indus-Saraswati Civilization, D.P. Agrawal once observed (he uses the term 'Pre-Harappan' for Kot Diji or Early Harappan):

> The Pre-Harappan and the Harappa cultures are not two disparate entities but urban and rural aspects of the same cultural phenomenon. The Harappan phases at Kot Diji, Amri and Kalbangan, should not be understood as one culture supplanting another, but like a city corporation taking over a sub-urban village to urbanise.[14]

The Absence of Horse: Yet Another myth About the Indus-Saraswati Civilization

Marshall, and following him Piggott in his *Prehistoric India,* categorically stated that the Indus-Saraswati people did not domesticate the horse and use it because the bones of the domesticated horse, *Equus cabalus* Linn., was not found at any of the Indus-Saraswati sites. They relied on the report of Sewell and Guha published by Marshall in Volume II of his *Mohenjodaro and the Indian Civilization* (1931) even though they did mention the presence of fragments of mandible of *Equus cabalus* Linn, at Mohenjodaro. In 1936 B. Prasad[15] maintained the same in the context of Harappa. Unfortunately, this *negative evidence* was subsequently used by at least three generations of historians, including the present one, of R.S. Sharma and Romila Thapar, of ancient India as the *positive proof* that the Indus-Saraswati Civilization was non-Aryan because the horse was extensively used by the *Vedic* Aryans right from the *Rigvedic* times; the horse has been mentioned at least 250 times in the *Vedic* literature. What is the archaeology of domesticated horse vis-a-vis the Indus-Saraswati Civilization?

Domesticated Horse: Its Presence at Indus-Saraswati Sites

Bhola Nath, the most leading archaeo-zoologist of India of the sixties, identified some of the bons from Lothal as definitely of the horse of the domesticated variety—*Equus cabalus* Linn.[16] S.R. Rao, the excavator of

Lothal, informs us that such bones were found both from the 'Mature Harappan' and 'Late Harappan' levels.[17] As far back as 1963, Bhola Nath had already examined the then unexamined lot of animal bones from Area G of Harappa and declared that there were bones of the true domesticated horse mixed with the bones of elephants.[18]

Bhola Nath also identified identical bones from Ropar, an Indus-Saraswati site in Punjab, excavated by Y.D. Sharma.[19]

V.V. Rao had reported the bones of true horse from Kalibangan, another very important Indus-Saraswati site, in Rajasthan, excavated by B.B. Lal and B.K. Thapar. Recently, A.K. Sharma has reported on 30th Nov. 1992 he was supplied a report on the bones of true or domesticated horse from Kalibangan by the Zoological Survey of India whose archaeo-zoologists have examined the bones. In 1964-65 he too had collected identical bones from Kalibangan.[20]

In 1974 A.K. Sharma had published in *Puratattava* No. 7, pp. 75-76, photographs of the bones of *Equus cabalus* Linn. which J.P. Joshi had collected from his digs at Surkotada, another very important Indus-Saraswati site, in Kutch. The bones came from all the levels of the site—from the earliest to the latest.

In 1972-73 the site of Malvan in Gujarat was excavated by J.P. Joshi and F.R. Allchin. Here also A.K. Sharma had identified the bones of the true horse.[21]

In 1991 Prof. Sandor Bokonyi,[22] an acknowledged authority on the horse in the world of archaeology, came from Budapest and re-examined the animal bones from Surkotada which A.K. Sharma had already identified as the bones of *Equus cabalus* Linn, as mentioned earlier. On 13th Dec. 1991 he delivered a personal note to M.C. Joshi, the then Director General, Archaeological Survey of India, wherein he categorically stated that the identification of Dr. A.K. Sharma was absolutely correct.

That Col. Ross had identified the bones of horse at Rana Ghundai, decades back need repetition here because F.E. Zeuner once opined that the bones could have been of onager, i.e. half ass. Mackay had found a terracotta figurine of a domesticated horse from the upper levels of Mohenjodaro is well known. S.R.Rao had also found a similar figurine from Lothal.

Once Sethana[23] had very pertinently remarked, in 1980, when he found scholars like Asko Parpola repeatedly using the negative evidence, the absence of horse on seals, sealings and terracottas, to prove that the Indus-Saraswati people were Dravidians and not *Vedic* Aryans, "As there are no depictions of cow in contrast to the pictures of the bull, which are abundant, should we conclude that Harappa and Mohenjodaro had only bulls? What about that mythical animal, the unicorn, which is the most common pictorial motif on the seals? Was the unicorn a common animal of the protohistoric Indus Valley? Surely, the presence or absence of depictions cannot point unequivocally to the animals known... "The depicted male animals do not cover all the fauna known to the Harappan Culture." It is true of camel also—not depicted for too many times in art but found in bones. It is also true of the onager—not depicted in art but found in bones. Wolf, cat, deer, nilgai, fowl, pigeon are rarely or never found in art but their presence has been attested by bones found at Kalibangan and several other sites.

One thing more. Habitational areas yield bones mostly of those animals which were killed and eaten—the horse, the camel, the elephant are only rarely represented in actual bones, very few indeed at every site, simply because these animals are not likely to have been as regularly eaten as sheep and goats as well as fish whose bones are abundantly found at all Indus-Saraswati settlements. Wheeler seems to accept this position and never uses the absence of horse in Indus-Saraswati art to prove that the civilization was non-Aryan or Dravidian.

It will indeed be surprising if the horse is not there—long-distance trade usually requires speed animals. It is common knowledge that bulls are no match to horse—while the former may cover at best twenty to twenty five miles of distance a day, the horse may cover thrice that distance in the same span of time—ten hours of maximum running. In fact, the bull becomes tired very soon and, therefore, eventually he may prove to be only slightly better than the human being but certainly not the horse, which is several times faster than man. In the deserts, camel is the quickest—neither bull nor horse, because of the morphology of their hoofs.

If, therefore, horse's absence was interpreted in the past as a very important evidence to prove that the Indus-Saraswati Civilization was non-Aryan, then now its presence at Mohenjodaro, Harappa, Kalibangan, Ropar, Lothal, Malvan, Rana Ghundi, etc. may also be produced as one sure ground to accept that the Indus-Saraswati Civilization was the Aryan. But, in our view, the initial argument itself was methodologically faulty hence the historians need not rush to contradict the archaeologists in order to prove their theory in this regard.

Evidence of Fire Worship and Animal Sacrifice at Indus-Saraswati Sites

Archaeology is a very poor guide to reconstruct the religion or religions of the Indus-Saraswati people. Excavators of Harappa, Mohenjodaro and Chanhudaro, like Vats, Marshall and Mackay respectively, have emphasised, on the basis of terracotta female figurines that they were the worshippers of 'mother-goddess', but most of the other sites have only rarely yielded this imagery; possibly there were regional differences in religions. On the basis of some seal-representations from Mohenjodaro these scholars said that the Indus-Saraswati people were the worshippers of 'Siva in his Pasupati form, in the form of *Yogi*, in the form of phallus, etc., but then there again such representations are very few, the so-called 'lingas', as Dales[24] has questioned, may not at all have been the phallus symbol. On the basis of the Great Bath at Mohenjodaro they felt that the people were the water-worshippers. On the basis of some terracotta figurines and seal representations they observed that the Indus-Saraswati people were bull worshippers, tree worshippers, snake worshippers, etc. Marshall felt that the present-day Hindu beliefs and rituals have direct connection with the Indus-Saraswati religious practices. It is quite possible that through the Oral Traditions, these beliefs continued in the post-Urban phase of the Indus-Saraswati Civilization till they re-emerged in the early historical period.

M.S. Vats, the excavator of Harappa, on the other hand, interpreted many seal imageries and imageries on pottery in terms of *Vedic* beliefs, such as the one (seal) with seven human beings in one line; narrative pictures on a few of the Cemetery 'H' burial-pots; and pots with post-cremation ashes. Be that as they may, in recent years at Kalibagan and Banawalli series of fire-altars have been found, which the excavators associate with the public rituals; that in the individual household at Lothal, Mohenjodaro and Harappa also fire-worship was practised is, of course, another mater and may only strengthen the belief of B.B. Lal and R.S. Bisht, the former excavated Kalibagan in Rajasthan and the latter Banawali in Haryana. At Kalibangan there is the evidence of animal sacrifice also. The evidence is as follows.

> The fortified citadel of Kalibanga had two parts, divided by a wall--the southern part had five mud-brick platforms, existing side by side; three to four more are suspected. One could reach their tops by staircases or ramps, there is the evidence of both the kinds. On tip of one of these platforms a series of seven 'fire-altars' were found. "The 'altars' were in fact clay-lined pits, each measuring 75 x 55 cm. Within each pit were noted ash, charcoal and the remains of a clay stele as well as of what are known as 'terracotta cakes'. Of the last named item, complete examples were found in some of the 'fire-altars' in the residential houses of the Lower Town. The clay-stele, as seen from relatively more intact examples in the Lower Town, stood vertically up, was either cylindrical or slightly faceted, and measured about 30-40 cm. in height and 10-15 cm. in diameter.

> The row of these altars ran north-south and immediately behind it was a burnt-brick wall. To the west of the row, but within easy reach of the worshipper was the lower half of a jar partly embedded in the ground and full of ash and charcoal. Perhaps in it was kept some ready fire to be used for the ritual. A short distance away were a well and the remains of a few bath pavements with attached drains. This kind of layout clearly suggests that ceremonial bathing constituted a part of the ritual...

There are many other details of these 'fire-altars' but here this should suffice to note that one of the dominant modes of worship, in which the Indus-Saraswati people engaged themselves at Kalibangan, was fire-worship. The *Vedic* people were primarily the fire-worshippers.

At Kalibangan, there is also the evidence of 'animal sacrifice'. Prof. Lal informs us this.[25]

> To take up the nature of the remains on the top of another such platform within the southern rhomb where the platform with fire-altars is located. On it were noted not only a well and a 'fire-altar' but something more; it was a rectangular pit, measuring 1.2x1 m and lined with kiln-burnt bricks. Within it lay bovine bones and antlers, evidently representing some kind of a sacrifice. That the offering of animals was a Harappan practice is also suggested by certain seals, for example one from Mohenjo-daro. It depicts a deity in front of whom kneels a devotee. Behind the latter is an animal, in all likelihood brought as an offering. Indeed at Kalibangan itself may have some thing more to convey with regard to animal sacrifice. On a terracotta cake are depicted a deity on one side and, on the other, a person drawing an animal with the help of a rope(?) tied round its neck...the deity is clearly suggested by the headgear, comprising two horns and a central feathered crest which is on the lines of what one sees on the head of the 'Siva-pasupati' figure on the well-known Mohenjo-daro seal." Animal sacrifice also figures in the Vedic literature.

At Banawali, on the other hand, there is a double apsidal or oval shaped mud-brick platform surrounded by a row of small rooms—at least one row was clearly made out. In the centre, along a low wall, a series of Kalibangan type fire-altars with ash and terracotta cakes have been found. The details have not been published but personal observation, the available photographs and a film made during the excavations, clearly establish the fact that Fire Worship was prevalent here also on a high mud-brick platform of the citadel.

Whether this evidence will further support the hypothesis that the Indus-Saraswati Civilization represents one very important aspect of the developed *Vedic* Civilization or not is, of course, anyone to guess.

Notes & References

1. Stein, Aurel, *An Archaeological Tour Along the Ghaggar-Hakra* (Ed. S.P. Gupta) (Kusumanjali Prakashan, Jodhpur, 1989).
2. Ghosh, A. "The Rajaputana Desert—Its Archaeological Aspect", *Bulletin of the National Institute of Sciences of India,* No.1, pp. 37-42.
3. Lal, B.B. "Kalibangan and the Indus Civilization", in *Essays in Indian Protohistory* (Eds.) D.P. Agrawal and Dilip K. Chakrabarti: (D.K. Publishers, New Delhi, 1980) pp. 65-67.
4. Mughal, M.R. "Recent Archaeological Research in the Cholistan Desert", in *Harappan Civilization,* (2nd Edition, 1982, Oxford & IBH Publishers, New Delhi) pp. 97-106.
5. Joshi, J.P. *et al,* "The Indus Civilization, A Reconsideration on the Basis of Distribution Maps", in *Frontiers of the Indus Civilization* (Eds. B.B. Lal and S.P. Gupta) (Books & Books, New Delhi, 1984) pp. 511-530.
6. Wheeler, R.E.M. "Harappa, 1946: The Defence and the Cemetery R-37", *Ancient India,* No.3 (1947), pp. 59-130.
7. Khan, F.A. "Excavations at Kot Diji", *Pakistan Archaeology* No.5 (1995) pp. 11-85.
8. Dales, G.F. and Kenoyer, J.M. "The Harappan Project, New Investigation at an Ancient Indus city", in *Harappan Civilization,* pp. 469-520.
9. Dales, G.F. "Excavations at Balakot", *Jr. of Field Archaeology* Vol.I, Nos. 1-2, (1974) pp.3 22.
10. Only Newspaper reports have appeared in early 1994, for example in *Times of India,* dt. 14th Feb. (1994).
11. Gupta, S.P. "Longer Chronology of the Indus-Saraswati Civilization", *Puratattva,* No. 23(1992-93) pp. 21-29.
12. Agrawal, D.P. *The Archaeology of India,* (Curzon Press, Scandinavian Institute of Asian Studies, Copenhagen, 1982) p.188.
13. Jarrige, J-F. "Excavations at Mehrgarh: Their Significance for understanding the Background of the Harappan Civilization" in *Harappan Civilization* (Ed. G.L. Possehl) pp. 79-84.
14. Agrawal, D.P. *op. cit.*, p.141.
15. Prasad, B. *"Animal Remains From Harappa",* Memoir, Archaeological Survey of India, No. 51 (New Delhi, 1936).
16. Bhola Nath, "Advances in the Study of Prehistoric and Ancient Animal Remains in India, A Review" *in Rec. Zoological Survey of India,* Vol. 61, (Calcutta, 1968), pp. 1-13.
17. Rao, S.R. *Lothal and the Indus Civilization,* (Asia Publishing House, Delhi, 1973).
18. Bhola Nath, "Animals of Prehistoric India and their Affinities with those of the Western Asiatic countries", in *Rec. of the Zoological Survey of India,* Vol. 59, pp. 335-367.

19. *Ibid.*
20. Sharma, A.K. "The Harappan Horse was Buried under the Dunes of...." *Puratattva,* No.23 (1992-93) pp. 30-34.
21. *Ibid.*
22. *Ibid.*
23. Sethna, K.D. "*Karpas' in India* (Impex India, New delhi, 1981).
24. Dales, G.F. "Sex and Stone at Mohenjodaro", in *Frontiers of the Indus Civilization,* pp. 109-116.
25. Lal, B.B. "Some Reflections on the Structural Remains at Kalibangan" *in Frontier of the Indus Civilization,* pp. 55-62.

24

Lost Saraswati : The Cradle of Harappan Civilization

V.N. Misra*

The largest concentration of Harappan sites of the three earlier phases is on the Hakra-Ghaggar river in the Cholistan desert (Pakistan) and on its tributaries in north Rajasthan, Haryana and Punjab (India). In comparison, the Indus valley, especially its upper course is very poor in Harappan sites[1] (Fentress 1979). Today, the Hakra is a totally dead river. Its bed has been much encroached upon by sands, showing that the river has been extinct for a very long time. However, the bed of the river has been traced from its source in the Siwaliks through Punjab, Haryana, Rajasthan, Bahawalpur and Sind to its mouth in the Rann of Kutch with the help of surviving geomorphic traces and the presence of numerous archaeological sites along its course. Sir Aurel Stein (1942)[2] discovered many archaeological sites along its course in the former Bikaner and Bahawalpur states. A Ghosh (1952)[3] traced a branch (Drishadvati) of this river in north Rajasthan and located many Harappan, Painted Grey Ware (P.G.W.) and Rang Mahal culture sites along its course. Later, Henry Field (1959)[4] continued the work of Stein in Bahawalpur and located more sites further east. More recently, Mughal (1981)[5] has discovered nearly 400 sites of Pre-Harappan Hakra Ware, Early Harappan, Mature Harappan, Late Harappan (Cemetery 'H' Related). Painted Grey Ware and Medieval period cultures on this river between the Indian border and south of Rahimyar Khan. On the lower course of the river, Louis Flam (1981)[6] has located several Harappan sites. In the Indian part of this river in recent years a large number of Harappan and P.G.W. sites have been discovered on its various tributaries by Suraj Bhan (1971-72a, 1972, 1973, 1975)[7], U.V. Singh (1977),[8] Katy F. Dalal (*nee* Frenchman) (1972, 1981),[9] and several officers of the Archaeological Survey of India (Bisht 1976, 1977; Dikshit 1979b, 1981; Joshi 1978a, 1978b; Joshi and Madhu Bala 1979; Lal 1977; Madhu Bala 1981; Thapar 1973a).[10]

* Emiment Archaeologist, Director, Deccan College, Pune; specialises in Prehistoric archaeology and Palaeo-Environement.

In its upper course, the bed of this river runs in a more or less east-west direction, up to the Indo-Pakistan border and is known variously as the Ghaggar (Ghosh 1952).[11] Hakra and Sotra (Oldham 1893).[12] From

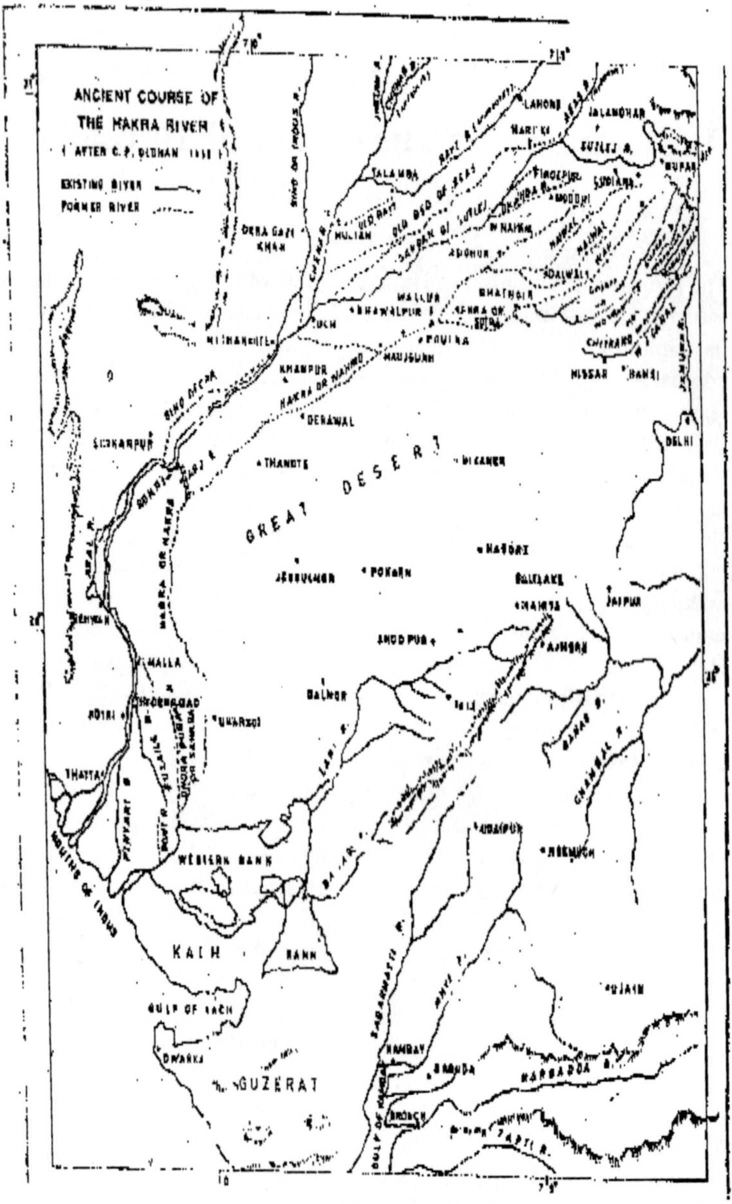

this point onward, it takes a south-westerly course into Bhawalpur and is known as the Hakra or Wahind. After entering Sind, it turns southward and flows in that direction right down to its mouth in the Rann of Kutch, and is known variously as the Narra (Nara), Hakra or Sagara, Wahind, and Dahan. For the greater part of its course, the bed of the Hakra runs parallel to, and east of, that of the Indus.

The width of the Hakra bed varies from 3 to 10 km in different parts of its course. It was obviously, therefore, a very large river during its lifetime. The large number of settlements found along its course dating broadly to the period 4000-6000 BC, also shows that it must have been a perennially flowing mighty river. Today no permanent settlement along its course is possible except where artificial irrigation has been provided. It is also significant that, except in the uppermost part, the river receives no feeders, and, therefore, the only source of its waters must have been the rainfall and snowmelt in the Himalayas. No amount of increased rainfall (as compared to today's) could have, however, filled such a wide and enormously long bed. Indeed, as Oldham (1893:52) pointed out nearly a century ago:

> It would have involved the existence, previously, of such meteorological conditions as must have rendered the holy land of the *Brahmanas* as uninhabitable swamp. The neighbouring large rivers, too, must in such case have been vast in proportion. This, as their channels show, they were not. Some of them, in fact, which are mentioned in the *Vedas* as being fordable, are so with difficulty at the present day.[13]

It is, therefore, clear that the Ghaggar-Hakra could have flowed as a mighty perennial river from its mouth to the sea only if some other equally large river was flowing in its channel in the past.

Hydrological Fluctuations: Yamuna and Sutlej

What was this river? And where did it go leaving the Hakra as a dry channel?

The question has attracted the attention of geographers, historians and archaeologists now for more than a century (Oldham 1874, 1893, R.D. Oldham 1886; Stein 1942; Ghosh 1952; Erikson 1959).[14] The ancient river has been identified by most scholars with the Saraswati of Hindu tradition. Saraswati is one of the holiest rivers of the Hindus. According to living Hindu tradition, the river flows through a subterranean channel and joins the Yamuna at Prayag (Allahabad) to form, together with the Ganga, the Triveni Sangam (confluence of three holy rivers). The myth or legend would appear to enshrine the folk memory of a period when the Saraswati and the Yamuna did actually converge above ground. Subsequently, the Yamuna probably shifted its course leaving the

Saraswati in possession of a dry channel, and helped create the myth of the river having gone underground. In the *Rig Veda*, the Saraswati is described as a large and rapid river flowing from the mountains to the sea. It is called "the mother of rivers" and a river that "surpasses in greatness all other waters" (Oldham 1893: 49).[15] But in the *Mahabharata*, the river is described as having lost itself in the sands. Although it is not possible to assign precise dates to these events, most scholars put the beginning of the *Vedic* period around the middle of the second millennium BC. The *Mahabharata* period has, on archaeological grounds, been shown to coincide with the P.G.W., culture (Lal 1954-55, 1981)[16] which can be dated broadly to c. 1000-600 BC. It can, therefore, be said that the Saraswati was a fully flowing river in the second millennium BC (and by implication earlier) but had dried up by c. 1000 BC.

At present, the Saraswati is a small stream which originates in the Siwaliks a little to the west of the point where the Yamuna enters the plains. After flowing for nearly 150 kms it joins the Ghaggar. Although below the confluence, the combined stream is shown on the maps as the Ghaggar,

> 'It was formerly the Saraswati, that name is still known amongst the people, and the famous fortress of sarasuti or Saraswati was built upon its banks, nearly 100 miles below the present junction with the Ghaggar'
>
> (Oldham 1893: 51-52)[17]

This small Saraswati which carries water for only a short distance, still possesses the sacred character assigned to the river of that name since *Rig Vedic* times. There can, therefore, be little doubt that the existing Saraswati is the Saraswati of the *Vedic* and Epic periods. The names Ghaggar, Sotra, Hakra, Nara, etc. which the river carries in different parts of its course do no occur in ancient literature. They all seem to have been acquired in later historical or recent times.

What river did then flow into the Saraswati (or present day Hakra) channel to make it a functioning river, and when and how did it leave the Saraswati bed?

The Other Rivers

There are only two large rivers—the Sutlej and the Yamuna—which are close enough to the Saraswati to have performed this role. Between these two Himalayan rivers there is no other gap in the Siwaliks through which a third large river could have entered the plains and flowed into the Saraswati bed. It is also significant that there are no Harappan sites on the Sutlej except in its upper course near the Siwaliks. Nor are there any Harappan sites on the present Yamuna channel. It, therefore, seems certain that neither the Sutlej nor the Yamuna flowed in their present respective channels during Harappan times (3rd-2nd millennia BC). Both of them could, therefore, have flowed in the Saraswati channel. (C.f. Oldham 1874, 1893),[18] considered both these alternatives and came to the conclusion that the Sutlej rather than the Yamuna was flowing in the Saraswati channel. However, we have to remember that when Oldham wrote, he did not have, at his disposal, the enormous volume of archaeological evidence pertaining to Harappan and other cultures that has become available in the last sixty yeas. His historical reasoning depended mainly upon the information available in *Vedic* and Epic literature and from the ruins of the antiquity of which he had no clear idea. The new archaeological evidence has made it possible to consider the question in a new perspective. Besides recent research, especially by Raikes (1968)[19] and Suraj Bhan (1972, 1973, 1975,1977)[20] has produced archaeological geomorphic and sedimentological evidence to show that the Yamuna did flow into the Saraswati in the past. It has, therefore, become necessary to examine the alternatives in the light of this new cumulative evidence.

For such a re-examination, it is necessary to have a clear picture of the living and defunct river courses of the area in which the postulated vital changes in the course of the Sutlej and the Yamuna must have taken place.

There are a number of, mostly dry, river-beds between the Yamuna and the Sutlej in Haryana, Punjab and Rajasthan. They all rise within a very limited area on the western slopes of the Siwalik Range, bounded on the south by the drainage area of the Yamuna, and on the north by that of the Sutlej. None of them ever had any connection with the glaciers of the higher levels nor with other, larger, catchment areas. The upper courses of these rivers run through steep narrow gorges in the mountains, but below the 500 m level they broaden considerably and gradually peter out further westward where the head of water diminishes rapidly as the landscape levels out. Below the 250 m contour, the country is almost horizontal with only a slight westward cant. Here the width of these rivers varies from 2 to 10 kms. They carry water, however, seasonally or throughout the year only in a narrow channel of the bed and only for short distances. Over most of their courses, the rivers meander through a flat topography, the vast area covered by these rivers is, and has always been, susceptible to flooding by the waters of the Sutlej. This leads to the formation of vast lakes and their filling up by abundant silt and clay sediments brought in by the rivers. This process sometimes necessitated the scouring out of new courses by spring floods. This is the only way one can explain the presence of so many river courses in a very limited area with a limited supply of water. The lower courses of these rivers, already silted up, have been, and are being encroached upon by sands (Oldham 1893 and Erikson 1959).[21]

Because of the excessive silting and encroachment by sand of these river-beds, they are only discontinuously visible on the ground. For this reason, there are some discrepancies in the courses as traced by different scholars. All the courses may probably be visible on 1:50,000 sheets, but this author has not had access to them. The map (Fig. 1) showing the river courses of the area has been drawn from 1:1,000,000 National Atlas sheets. It shows only some of the river-beds, C.F. Oldham (1893),[22] however, has shown many more beds, specially between the Ghaggar and the Sutlej (Fig.2). His map is probably based on the work of R.D. Oldham (1886).[23] B.M. Pande (1977: Fig...)[24] has also shown the same rivers, though his alignments differ slightly from those given by C.F. Oldham. The picture that emerges from a study of these maps as also from the accounts of Ghosh (1952), Erikson (1959) and Suraj Bhan (1972, 1973) can be summarized as follows:[25]

The Ghaggar or Hakra is formed by a combination of two rivers which meet near Wallur or to the west of Anupgarh on the Indo-Pakistan border. These are named the eastern and western Hakra by Oldham, while Ghosh who explored the 'eastern Hakra' uses the name Ghaggar for it. The eastern arms of the Hakra is formed by a combination of four rivers which are named, from east to west: (1) Chautang (Chitrung of Oldham) or Drishadvati: (2) Saraswati; (3) Ghaggar; and (4) Wah or Sonamwal or Sirhind Nadi, the Chautang flows almost parallel and close to the Yamuna from the hills down to a little north of Karnal where the two rivers diverge, the Chautang taking a south-westerly course and the Yamuna turning south. At present, the Chautang dries up near the village of Safidon, but Ghosh (1952)[26] was able to trace its course for a considerable distance further to the south-west, past the towns of Bhadra and Nohar to near Suratgarh where it must have joined the Ghaggar. The Hansi branch of the Western Yamuna Canal runs through this dry bed. Another river running west of, and parallel to it, is also known as Chautang[27] (Erikson 1959: 22, Ref. 21) and joins the Saraswati at the town of Pehowa. The Harappan site of Banawali is probably located on its dry bed. To its west is the Saraswati (also known as the Markanda in its upper course) which joins the Ghaggar near the village of Rasula, a few kilometers south-east of the small town of Shatrana. Although the Ghaggar is the smaller of the two rivers, from the confluence it takes the name of the combined river. Wah, the westernmost branch of the eastern

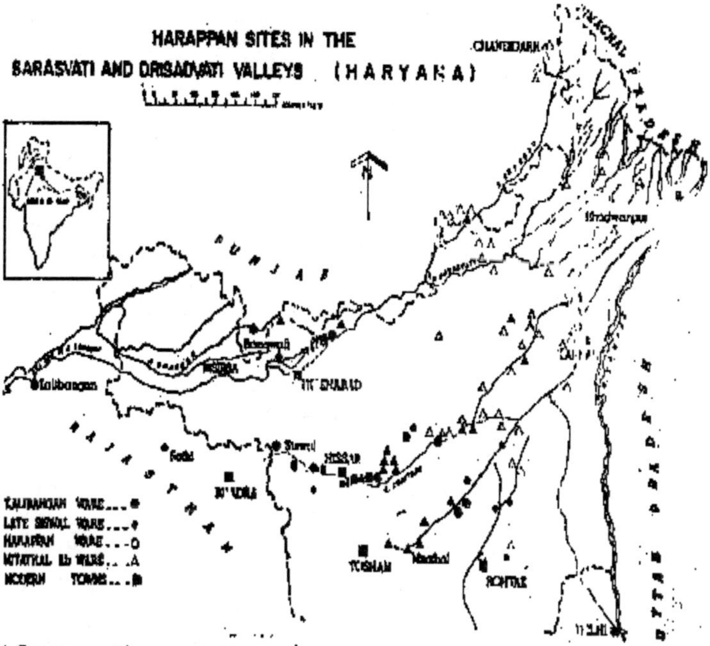
HARAPPAN SITES IN THE
SARASVATI AND DRISADVATI VALLEYS (HARYANA)
PUNJAB
RAJASTHAN
Kalibangan
HISSAR
TOSHAM
ROHTAK

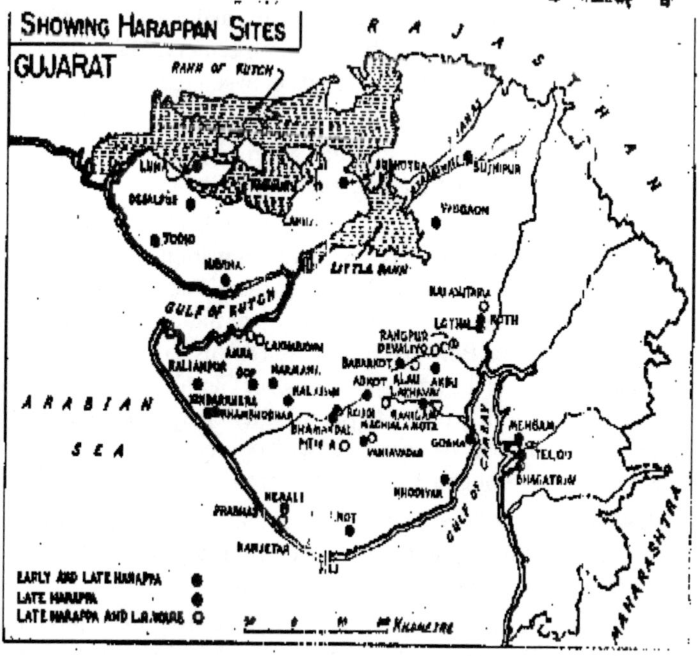
SHOWING HARAPPAN SITES
GUJARAT
RANN OF KUTCH
RAJASTHAN
LITTLE RANN
GULF OF KUTCH
ARABIAN SEA
GULF OF CAMBAY
MAHARASHTRA
LOTHAL
RANGPUR
MEHGAM
EARLY AND LATE HARAPPA
LATE HARAPPA

arm of the Hakra, at one time joined the latter east of Sirsa, but today it dries up nearly 100 kms north-east of this town.

The western arm of the Hakra is formed by a combination of three rivers, each of which is known as Naiwal. They are designated eastern middle and western Naiwal. According to Oldham (1893:58)[28] these streams meet near Kurrulwala (29 33'N: 73 52'E) south of the town of Abohar in Punjab. In the map published by Pande (1977[29]: Fig.2) the eastern and middle Naiwals are shown joining the Ghaggar south of Hanumangarh, as well as the western Naiwal a little further west. Between the western Naiwal and the Sutlej, Oldham has shown two more dry beds both of which join the Sutlej. The eastern of these beds is known as the Dhunda.

Oldham was of the opinion that the Sutlej flowed into the Hakra or Saraswati through each of these dry beds, gradually shifting its course from east to west. When the Sutlej shifted its course westward

> 'and abandoned the eastern arm of the Hakra, the Saraswati, which had been a tributary, was left in possession of the deserted channel, in the sands of which its waters were swallowed up' (Oldham 1893: 59).[30a]

This event took place between the period of the *Rig Veda* and that of the *Mahabharata*. After this, the Sutlej flowed into the western arm of the Hakra through each of the three Naiwals, and finally changed its course more or less due west in the thirteenth century AD to flow into the Beas valley through the two dry beds between the western Naiwal and the present Sutlej.

Oldham's arguments in support of his hypothesis are quite convincing, and can be summarised as follows.

1. The application of the name Sutlej to the combined Beas-Sutlej stream, below the confluence, is a modern innovation, and is not to be found in old writings, Hindu or Mohammedan. The united stream of Beas and Sutlej was never known as Satadru or Satludra. Instead it has been known as Vipasa, Beas and Beah. Even to this day, the river below Ferozepur is known to the boatmen as Beah or Garrah. All this seems to show pretty clearly that the Sutlej is an interloper, and the Beas the original stream. Had it been otherwise, the greater river must have retained its name throughout its course.

2. Several of the old river beds which combine to form the Hakra have been traced to within so short a distance of the Sutlej that they could not possibly have belonged to any other stream.

3. All the old channels of the Hakra diverge from the direction of Roper where the Sutlej enters the plains and each is said to have been in

turn the bed of that river. On the banks of each of them are towns which, though now more or less decayed, were once places of importance.

4. The local traditions of the land between the Sutlej and the Saraswati all agree that until Muslim times, the Sutlej flowed into the Hakra channel and that till then the country along its banks was fertile and prosperous.

5. There is a tradition that the Wah was once the old bed of the Sutlej.

Oldham's another inference that the Yamuna could not have flowed into the Saraswati bed is, however, not based on convincing arguments. In fact, he does admit that:

> It is not beyond the bounds of possibility that the Jumna may at some very remote period have taken a westerly instead of an easterly course and joined the Hakra; for, as observed by R.D. Oldham of the Indian Geological Survey, this old riverbed lies between the fan or talus of the Jumna, and that of the Sutlej (Oldham 1893:55).[30b]

Elsewhere he says:

> Near Bhatnair the eastern arm of the Hakra is joined by a dry river bed, marked in our maps as Chitrung. If the Jumna ever joined the Hakra it must have been by this channel, which however is only traceable for a short distance. It is supposed to have once been continuous with the Chitrung stream, which has been identified with the Drishadvati.[31] (*Ibid*:58)

Yet, he is disinclined to accept this alternative because

"Tradition, however, is silent on the subject, and so are the *Vedas*".[32] (*Ibid*: 55)

What Oldham means by tradition in this context is not very clear, for as has been mentioned earlier and is indeed too well known, Hindu tradition strongly associates the Saraswati with the Yamuna but never with the Sutlej. How a percipient scholar like Oldham could be unaware of this is difficult to comprehend.

The Yamuna River

Oldham's view in this matter is mainly influenced by the references to Yamuna in the *Vedic* and Epic literature, namely:

(i) In the only place in which the river Ganga is mentioned in the *Rig Veda* (X. 75.5) the Yamuna is coupled with it; and

(ii) There is ample evidence from the *Mahabharata* and the *Ramayana* to show that the Yamuna was flowing in its present channel during the period of these epics.

In other words, since literary tradition says that the Yamuna was flowing in its present course, it could not have flowed elsewhere.

Here it is important to remember that Oldham was writing at a time when the history of India was not known to extend beyond the period of the Epics and the *Vedas*. With our present archaeological knowledge, however, we know that there is no contradiction in the Yamuna having flowed during the Epic and probably even during the Early *Vedic* time in its present course, and during pre-*Vedic* or Harappan times in a different course.

The available archaeological evidence suggests that this indeed was the case:

1. The total absence of Harappan sites along the present course of the Yamuna shows that the river was not flowing in its present course during the Harappan period.

2. The presence of many P.G.W. sites on the Yamuna shows that the river had shifted to its present channel by P.G.W. time. The association of the P.G.W. culture with the *Mahabharata* epic has been fairly convincingly demonstrated (Lal 1954-55, 1981).[33]

3. Raikes (1968)[34] has shown, on geomorphic and sedimentological evidence that the Yamuna was actually flowing in the Ghaggar channel during Harappan times. The geomorphic evidence consists of the migration of the meandering channel of the Yamuna across of 10-15 km width of the plain. To the west, the plain slopes gently towards the Indus. The present Western Yamuna Canal evidently incorporates considerable parts of a former channel that followed the extreme western boundary of the plain. The sedimentological evidence consists of the discovery of

> 'a coarse, greyish sand very similar in mineral content to that found in the bed of the present-day Yamuna'.

in bore holes in the Ghaggar bed at Kalibangan 11 m below the present flood plain level (Raikes 1968: 287).[35] Above the 11m depth, Raikes found mainly clays and silts typical of present-day flood-plain deposits. Basing his arguments on calculations for the rates of sedimentation, location of archaeological sites of early cultures (Harappan, P.G. Ware and Rang Mahal or Kushan) in the Ghaggar valley, and the thickness of the deposits at these sites, Raikes has postulated alternate captures of the Ghaggar channel by the Indus and the Ganga systems. In effect, these episodes imply simply the capture or abandonment of the Ghaggar channel by the Yamuna. Raikes has correlated these episodes with archaeological cultures in the following manner.

1.	Westward diversion to Indus (coinciding with Harappan occupation)	2500-1750 BC (750 years)

2.	Eastward diversion to Ganga (coinciding with abandonment)	1750-1100 BC (650 years)
3.	Westward diversion to Indus (coinciding with Painted Grey Ware)	1100-500 BC (600 years)
4.	Eastward diversion to Ganga (coinciding with abandonment)	500-100 BC (400 years)
5.	Westward diversion to Indus (coinciding with Early History)	100 BC-AD 500 (600 years)
6.	Eastward diversion to Ganga in about AD 500 (coinciding with abandonment)	

Raikes' second and third westward diversions take into consideration only the archaeology of the Ghaggar valley and totally ignore the archaeological and historical evidence of the Yamuna valley. They appear to be forced upon to explain the presence of Painted Grey ware and Rang Mahal cultures on the Ghaggar. However, basing on the total archaeological evidence both on the Ghaggar and the Yamuna, there seems little doubt that, during Harappan times, the Yamuna was flowing in the Ghaggar channels, and subsequently, it has always flowed in its present channel.

The question then arises as to through which of the many existing and obsolete channels of the Ghaggar did the Yamuna flow into the Ghaggar (or Saraswati). From the archaeological point of view, the most important of these channels appears to be the Chautang or the Drishadvati since a large number of Early and Mature Harappan sites have been located on it. Though today the Chautang dries up east of Safidon,.Ghosh (1952) was able to trace its course right up to the Ghaggar near Suratgarh.[36] As suggested by Oldham also, Yamuna is most likely to have flowed through this channel during its westward course in prehistoric times.

Eastward Diversion of Yamuna

The eastward shift of the Yamuna must have taken place through the channels which have recently been traced by Suraj Bhan (1972).[37] One of these starts from near Indri, 20 km north of Karnal and is traceable for a distance of 180 kms up to Tigrana near Tosam in the south-west. This channel runs along the course of the West Yamuna Canal up to Mundak and then along the Jind branch of the same canal up to Safidon. The channel is marked by sand dunes along its banks, a regular band of fresh water vegetation in its course and thick deposits of the grey sands so typical of the Yamuna, in the well dug along the channel. Local tradition also associates this channel with the old course of the Yamuna. East of

Tigrana, the channel is lost in the sands. Suraj Bhan has located 18 Harappan and 2 P.G.W. sites on this channel. The scarcity of P.G.W. sites here suggests that the Yamuna had already shifted eastward during the late Harappan period. Suraj Bhan has located two more channels further east with late Harappan and P.G.W. sites on them, thus providing further evidence for the eastward shift of the Yamuna. This eastward diversion of the Yamuna to its present channel and the westward diversion of the Sutlej into the western arm of the Hakra, sometime in the Late Harappan times, must have left the channel of the Ghaggar (Saraswati) dry over a long distance (up to Wallur where the western arm of the Hakra joined it). This must have created the myth that Saraswati went underground to join the Yamuna.

Decline of Indus Civilization–A Fresh Look

The third hypothesis of Singh's, namely, that a decrease in rainfall around 1800 BC led to a decline of the Indus Civilization can now be examined.

Here it may incidentally be mentioned that the date of the decline in rainfall is not certain. While at Lunkaransar in the arid belt, the lake had started drying up around 2000 BC, the same event at Sambhar, in the semi-arid belt, took place a thousand years later. It is difficult to explain such a long time difference between two points only 200 kms apart. Singh's dating of this event therefore seems to be influenced by the need of reconciling the climatic evidence with archaeological data.

But first let us examine the evidence for the decline of the Indus Civilization.

It is undeniable that in the 18th-19th centuries BC, Harappan cities declined, and some of them were even abandoned. In the lower Indus valley many causes for this event have been suggested: reduction in rainfall (Marshall 1931),[38] exhaustion of the economic resources (Wheeler 1968; Fairserivs 1961, 1967),[39] excessive flooding (Raikes 1964, Dales 1966);[40] and Aryan invasion (Wheeler 1953).[41] Though some of these explanations have been questioned (Dales 1964, 1966; Possehl 1967; Lambrick 1967),[42] the fact of decline and abandonment of the cities is accepted by all critics. There is also an undeniable decline in material prosperity and in civic standards. But this decline did not lead to a decrease in population. It only forced the population to migrate from the lower Indus Valley into Saurashtra and from the Hakra Ghaggar valley into north Punjab, Haryana and the upper Yamuna-Ganga Doab. The sudden proliferation of Late Harappan sites in Saurashtra, north-east Punjab and Haryana and the upper Yamuna-Ganga doab attests to this migration.

At least in the case of north Punjab and the upper Yamuna-Ganga doab, rainfall is not significantly higher than in the adjoining parts of Punjab and Haryana which had witnessed dense human settlements during the Early and mature Harappan times. Therefore, these new regions of colonization could not have conferred any significant advantages to the immigrants. On the other hand, the shift of the courses of the Yamuna and Sutlej to the east and west, respectively, would have considerably reduced the availability of both surface and sub-surface water in the Ghaggar valley. This would, in due course, have adversely affected both natural vegetation and agriculture, and forced the population to shift to areas like north Punjab (Sutlej channel) and the upper Yamuna-Ganga doab where the rivers provided the ecological conditions the Harappan had long been accustomed to exploit. It is, therefore, quite unnecessary to invoke the deterioration of climate to explain this migratory phenomenon.

In the case of the lower Indus valley, some or all of the various explanations suggested, could have accounted for the shift of the Harappan population into Gujarat.

The phenomenon of Degenerate Harappan (same as OCP or OCW) culture represents a continuation of the eastward migration of the Late Harappans. This would appear to be due to excessive population pressure in the limited land available in the upper doab. The density of Late Harappan sites in the districts of Ludhiana and Saharanpur is eloquent proof of this demographic pressure.

Aridity : Second Millennium–Fresh Look

The fourth and final hypothesis of Singh is that aridity between 2000 and 1000 BC is responsible for the 'hiatus' between the Harappan and P.G.W. cultures. This too does not stand the scrutiny of new archaeological evidence. Recent excavations by the Archaeological Survey at Bhagwanpura, in the district of Kurukshetra (Haryana); Dadheri in the district of Ludhiana, Nagar and Katpalon, both in the district of Jullandur (Punjab), and Manda on the Chenab in Jammu have shown that the P.G.W. culture coexisted with the Late Harappan at these sites (Joshi 1977, 1978; Lal 1979).[43] Gupta (Gupta and Ramachandran 1977)[44] suggests, 1300 BC for this overlap phase. This new evidence eliminates the 'hiatus' between the Harappan and P.G.W. cultures and effectively knocks the bottom out of the desiccation hypothesis of Singh. Even in the north Rajasthan part of the Ghaggar valley, the new evidence available suggests that there was no 'hiatus' between the Harappan and the P.G.W. cultures. Black-and-red Ware has been found in profuse quantities in association with Painted Grey Ware both in surface explorations and in the excavation at Sardargarh in this region (Pande 1977:56).[45] Archaeological research during last two decades has amply demonstrated that in north-east Rajasthan (Jodhpura and Noh) and in the central Yamuna-Ganga doab (Atranjikhera), Painted Grey Ware was preceded by an independent phase of Black-and-red Ware culture which, in turn at many sites, was preceded by OCP or Degenerate Harappan. Fresh field research in Ghaggar valley in Rajasthan and a re-evaluation of the older evidence is most likely to show a continuity of occupation in this area from Harappan to Painted Grey Ware.

However, there is evidence to show that population during the Painted Grey Ware period was much sparser in the Ghaggar valley. In the Pakistan part of the this valley, only 14 sites of this culture have been found and all these occur in the eastern part (south-east of Bahawalpur) near the Indian border. This is in sharp contrast to the dense concentration of Mature Harappan sites further down in the same valley (south-west of Bahawalpur) (Mughal 1981: map).[46] Further, Ghosh (1952)[47] has shown that the Painted Grey Ware sites are often located on the Ghaggar bed. These two factors show that during the P.G.W. period: (1) the Ghaggar (or Saraswati) no longer flowed all the way to the sea, but only in the upper part of its course; and (ii) that its original bed had considerably shrunk. This must naturally have been the consequence of the diversion of the Yamuna from the Ghaggar channel to its own present channel.

Summing up

We can now summarize the conclusions of this lengthy review of archaeological and palaeoenvironmental evidence as follows:

(1) The Ghaggar river originates in the Himalayas and its channel passes through Punjab, Haryana, Rajasthan, Bahawalpur and Sind to its mouth in the Rann of Kutch. It should therefore be possible to explain the presence of Harappan sites on this river in the north-east corner of Rajasthan by factors which are also applicable to other sites on the rest of the course of this river.

(2) The geographical distribution of the Harappan sites reveals the following pattern: most of the Early Harappan sites are located in the middle Ghaggar-Hakra valley and a few in the lower and upper Indus valley. The Mature Harappan sites occur on the Indus, in Kutch-Saurashtra, and on the Ghaggar, but the greatest concentration is again in the middle Ghaggar-Hakra valley. In Late Harappan times, there is a decline in the number of sites in the middle Hakra valley (Cemetery 'H'-related) and in the Indus valley (Jhukar culture), but there is a remarkable expansion of settlements in Saurashtra and in the upper Ghaggar-Sutlej valleys. The Harappans also cross the Indus system to colonize the

upper Yamuna-Ganga doab during this period. The Degenerate Harappan (OCP) sites are mainly located in the upper Yamuna-Ganga doab but there is also a sporadic expansion in the central doab and even further east.

(3) This pattern of settlements shows that, except in Saurashtra, Harappa culture was essentially a riverine culture, flourishing in the valleys of the Himalayan rivers whose flood plains are annually inundated by monsoon floods which spread fresh fertile silt and provide adequate subsoil moisture for agricultural crops.

(4) The Harappan agricultural economy was mainly based on the cultivation of wheat, barley, gram and peas which are winter crops and can be grown in the flood plains of large, annually inundated rivers without artificial irrigation. This pattern of agriculture could have been practised in the river valleys existing in the Harappan zone in the present climatic conditions. Higher rainfall during Harappan times was not necessary for the flourishing of this economic pattern in these river valleys.

(5) The Ghaggar-Hakra today is a dead river, except near its source in the Siwaliks. But during the time of the *Rig Veda* (middle of second millennium BC) it was a mighty river and was flowing from the mountains to the sea. Its very wide bed (up to 10 kms) also shows it to have been a mighty river like the Indus. This bed can be traced right from its source in the Siwaliks through Punjab, Haryana, north-east Rajasthan, Bahawalpur and Sind to its mouth in the Rann of Kutch. The river could have supported the large populations represented by the dense concentration of Hakra Ware, Early Harappan, Mature Harappan and Late Harappan and (Cemetery 'H' related) sites only if it was perennially flowing with the volume of water commensurate with the width of its bed.

(6) No amount of reasonably possible higher rainfall in the Himalayas could have filled this bed, unless one or more of the large Himalayan rivers flowed through its channel. For geomorphic considerations, this function could have been performed only by the Sutlej and the Yamuna.

(7) The absence of Harappan sites on the Sutlej (except in its uppermost course along the Siwaliks) and on the Yamuna shows that these rivers were not flowing in their present channels during Harappan times. Indeed, the Sutlej was not flowing in its present course until the late medieval period. There is geomorphic, archaeological and folkloristic evidence to show that both the Sutlej and the Yamuna were flowing into the Ghaggar channel in the past, and that they shifted to their present channels during early medieaval times and Late Harappan times, respectively.

(8) The shifting of the Yamuna from its ancient course must have considerably reduced the volume of water in the Ghaggar bed. This would have reduced the extent of annual flooding and consequently the potential for agriculture along the Ghaggar course. The Harappan population must, therefore, have been forced to moved eastwards along the course of the perennial rivers and into areas with more assured rainfall. The sudden proliferation of Late Harappan settlements in the upper reaches of the Sutlej and of the Ghaggar tributaries, and in the upper Yamuna-Ganga doab is symptomatic of this hydrological change.

(9) There is definite evidence for the decline of the Mature Harappan culture and the abandonment of the cities in the Indus valley. These phenomena have been explained as due to the depletion of ecological resources caused by over-exploitation, sapping of the population morale due to recurrent and disastrous flooding (caused perhaps by the damming of the Indus by tectonic uplift), and tribal movements. The population from this region spilled over into Kutch and Saurashtra as is seen by the dramatic increase in Late Harappan settlements in these areas. The Harappans here adapted their agricultural strategy by taking recourse to the cultivation of rice (in the Hakra delta and along river valleys) and the dry farming of millet crops.

(10) The 'hiatus' between the Harappan and P.G.W. cultures has been bridged by recent researches in Haryana, Punjab and Jammu. The postulated decline in rainfall between the Harappan and P.G.W. periods can, therefore, no longer be sustained by archaeological evidence. The smaller number of P.G.W. sites (as compared to Harappan) in the Hakra valley is easily explained due to the reduced volume of water in its bed caused by the shifting of the Yamuna from the Ghaggar to its present channel.

In sum, the enormous volume of archaeological evidence now available from north-west India completely fails to sustain the overall hypothesis proposed by Gurdip Singh that fluctuations in rainfall played a decisive role in the emergence, diffusion, prosperity and decline in farming-based cultures in the region. The only role the increased rainfall played was to arrest the hyperaridity of the Upper Pleistocene, stabilize the sand dunes, accelerate the growth of vegetation and help in the emergence and spread of a nomadic hunting-gathering-pastoral economy. This pattern of life has persisted in the semi-arid and arid environments to this day. Agriculture based on dry farming of millet and related crops appeared in these regions only during the past 2000 years and was probably a consequence of the increasing population pressure in neighbouring areas. With the appearance of agriculture and permanent habitation, overall vegetation density and cover as also wild fauna was reduced, leading to a decline in the role of hunting in the economy. Pastoralism, however, proved to be the best adaptive strategy and has persisted to this day.

Notes & References

1. Fentress, Marcia A. 1979. From Jhelum to Yamuna—City and Settlement in the 2nd-3rd Millennium B.C. In the Conference on *The Harappan Civilization: A Contemporary Perspective*, Srinagar: AIIS.
2. Stein, Sir Aurel, 1942. A Survey of Ancient Sites along the 'Lost' Saraswati River. *The Geographical Journal*, 99 (4); 173-182.
3. Ghosh, A. 1952. The Rajputana Desert--Its Archaeological Aspect. *Bulletin of the National Institute of Sciences of India*, 1; 37-42.
4. Field, Henry, 1959. An Anthropological Reconnaissance in West Pakistan. *Papers of the Peabody Museum of Archaeology and Ethnology.* Harvard University. Vol. 3 Cambridge (Mass): Peabody Museum.
5. Mughal M.R. 1981. New Archaeological Evidence from Bahawalpur. In *Indus Civilization: New Perspectives.* A.H. Dani ed. 33-42, Islamabad: Quaid-Azam University.
6. Flam Louis, 1981. Towards an Ecological Analysis of Prehistoric Settlement Pattern in Sind, Pakistan, *Man and Environment*, 5; 52-58.

7a. Suraj Bhan, 1971-72a, Siswal: A Pre-Harappan Site on the Drishadvati Valley *Puratattva*, 5; 44-46. See also

7b. 1971-72b OCP and NBP: 1971, *Puratattva,* 5; 16-21.

7c. 1972, Changes in the Course of Yamuna and their Bearing on the Protohistoric Cultures of Haryana. In *Archaeological Congress and Seminar papers.* S.B. Deo ed. 125-128. Nagpur: Nagpur University.

7d. 1973, The Sequence and Spread of Prehistory Cultures in the Upper Saraswati Basin. In *Radiocarbon and Indian Archaeology.* D.P. Agarwal and A. Ghosh eds. 252-263. Bombay: TIFR.

7e. 1975, *Excavations at Mitathal (1968) and other Explorations in the Sutlej-Yamuna Divide.* Kurukshetra: Kurukshetra University Press.

7f. 1977, The Protohistoric settlement pattern in Haryana. In the Seminar on *Indus Civilization Problems and Issues.* Simla: IIAS.

8. Singh, U.V. 1977. Late Harappan Culture as revealed by the Excavations at Mirzapur and Daulatpur District Kurukshetra (Haryana). In the Seminar on *Indus Civilization Problems and Issues,* Simla: IIAS.
9. Dalal, Katy F. 1980. A Short History of Archaeological Explorations in Bikaner and Bahawalpur along the 'lost' Saraswati River, *Indica,* 17(1); 1-40.

   1981, RD-89. A New Hakra Ware Site. *Man and Environment* 5; 77-86.

9a. Frenchman, Katy F. 1972. Prehistoric Pottery Industries along the 'Lost' Saraswati River of the Great Indian Desert. Unpublished Ph.D. Thesis, Pune: Poona University.

10. Bisht, R.S. 1976. Transformation of the Harappan Culture in Punjab with special reference to the excavations at Sanghol and Chandigarh. In *Archaeological Congress and Seminar,* U.V. Singh ed. 16-22. Kurukshetra; Kurukshetra University.

10a. 1977, *Banawali: A Look Back into the Pre-Indus and Indus Civilization,* 1-14. Chandigarh: Government of Haryana.

10b. Dikshit, K.N., 1979b. The Late Harappan Culture in India. In *Essays in Indian Protohistory.* D.P. Agrawal and D.K. Chakrabarti ed. 123-133. Delhi: B.R. Pub. Corp.

10c. Dikshit, K.N., 1981. The Excavations at Hulas and Further Exploration of the Upper Ganga-Yamuna Doab, *Man and Environment,* 5; 70-76.

10d. Joshi, J.P. 1978a. Overlap of the Late Harappan Culture and Painted Grey Ware Culture in the Light of Recent Excavations in Haryana, Punjab and Jammu. In the Seminar on *Indus Civilizations: Problems and Issues.* Simla: IIAS. Also:

1978b. Interlocking of Late Harappa Culture and Painted Grey Ware Culture in the Light of Recent Excavations. *Man and Environment,* 2; 98-101.

11. Ghosh, A, 1952. The Rajputana Desert–its Archaeological Aspect. *Bulletin of the National Institute of Sciences of India,* 1; 37-42.

12. Oldham, C.F., 1893. The Saraswati and the Lost River of the Indian Desert. *Journal of the Royal Asiatic Society* 1893, 49-76.

13. *Ibid,* p. 52.

14a. Oldham, C.F. 1874. Notes on the Lost River of the Indian Desert. *Calcutta Review,* 59; 1-27.

14b. Oldham, R.D. 1886. On Probable Changes in the Geography of the Punjab and its Rivers; an Historico-Geographical Study. *Journal of the Asiatic Society of Bengal,* 55; 322-343.

14c. Ghosh, A 1965. The Indus Civilization: Its Origins, Author, Extent and Chronology. In *Indian Prehistory* 1964. V.N. Misra and M.S. Mate eds. 112-156. Poona Deccan College.

15. See 12.

16. Lal, B.B., 1981. The two Indian Epics vis-a-vis Archaeology. *Antiquity,* 55; 27-34.

17. Same as 12.

18. *Ibid* and 14.

19. Raikes, R.L. 1968. Kalibangan: Death from Natural Causes. *Antiquity.* 42 (168); 286-291.

20. Same as 7.

21. Erikson, K. Gosta, 1959. The Dry Bed of the River Ghaggar. In *Rang Mahal,* Hanna Rydh. 22-40. Lund (Sweden): C.W.K. Gleerup.

22. See 12.

23. See 14.

24. Pande, B.M. 1977. Archaeological Remains on the Ancient Saraswati. In *Ecology and Archaeology of Western India,* D.P. Agrawal and B.M. Pande ed. 55-59. Delhi, Concept.

25. See 21.

26. See 25.

27. See 12.

28. See 24.

29. See 12.

30a. *Ibid.*

30b. *Ibid.*

31. *Ibid.*

32. *Ibid.*

33. Lal, B.B. 1954-55. Excavations at Hastinapura and other Explorations in the upper Ganga and Sutlej Basins. *Ancient India,* 10-11:5-151 & See 16.

34. See 19.

35. *Ibid.*

36. See 3.

37. See 7.

38. Marshall, Sir John, 1931. *Mohenjo-daro and the Indus Civilization* (3 Volumes), London: A Probsthain.

39. Fairservis, Jr. W.A. 1961. The Harappan Civilization: New Evidence and More Theory *Novitates,* 2055; 1-35. New York: American Museum of Natural History.

1967, The Origin, Character and Decline of an Early Civilization. *Novitates,* 2302; 1-48, New York; American Museum of Natural History.

40a. Raikes, R.L. 1964. The End of the Ancient Cities of the Indus. *American Anthropologists,* 66 (2); 284-299.

40b. Dales G.F. 1966. The Decline of the Harappans. *Scientific American.* 241 (5); 92-100. Also Raikes 40.

41. Wheeler, Sir Mortimer, 1953. The Indus Civilization. Cambridge: Press.

42a. Possehl, G.L. 1967, The Mohenjo-daro Floods: A Reply, *American Anthropologist*, 69(1); 32-40.

42b. Lambrick, H.T. 1967, The Indus Flood Plain and the 'Indus' Civilization, *The Geographical Journal*, 133 (4); 483-495.

42c. Dales, G.F. 1964. The Mythical Massacre at Mohenjo-daro. *Expedition.* 6(3); 36-43.

43. See 10.

44. Gupta, S.P. and Ramachandran, K.s. 1977 *Mahabharat: Myth and Reality,* Agam Prakashan, New Delhi. Introduction, pt. II, by Gupta.

45. See 24.

46. Mughal, M.R. 1970. The Early Harappan Period in the Greater Indus Valley and Northern Baluchistan. Unpublished Ph.D. Dissertation; Department of Anthropology, Philadelphia: University of Pennsylvania.

47. See 3.

25

Harappan Vedic Civilization—A Continuum

Robert H. Dyson, Jr.*

The abandonment of the catastrophe paradigm for the demise of Harappan Civilization has led to the realization that we are dealing with a complex process of cultural change which took place over a prolonged period of time, and which manifested itself in different ways in different areas. Thus, the invasion thesis also becomes a paradigm for limited usefulness. By freeing themselves from this hypothesis drawn from earlier linguistic studies, archaeologists may now focus their attention on the archaeological evidence in its own terms. There is a continuing lack of agreement over the criteria by which the presence of the Indo-Aryans can be demonstrated and, even more surprisingly evidence against the cultural content of traditional *Vedic* literature. Thus, there must be a change of concern from trying to identify the date and direction of movement of an "event' like an invasion to the complexities of the processes of cultural change and adaptation.

Even, the subject of the history of the Indo-Aryans cannot help but continue to haunt the study of this period of subcontinent archaeology and sooner or later it must be better understood. It is interesting in this regard to note the tendency among Iranian and Central Asian scholars to accept the growing evidence for the continuity of population in the Turanian area from Neolithic times onward—from the painted pottery through the grey pottery of the Bronze Age (e.g. Deshayes 1969) and probably onward through the Iron Age and Parthian Periods (Hlopina 1972 : 213-14). The suggestion of an indigenous Indo-Aryan population going far back into pre-history in North-eastern Iran and nearby Turkmenia is now taken quite seriously. With this trend in mind it is interesting that the discussion between present scholars indicated a parallel trend. Both scholars B.B. Lal and B.P. Sinha feel the need to trace the continuity of elements back through the Harappan into the Pre-

* Former Director, University Museum of the of Pennsylvania, Philadelphia, U.S.A., Distinguished archaeologist excavated several sites in Asia.

Harappan and to relate these elements to the *Vedic* literature. Carl Lamberg-Karlovsky also suggests that Indo-Aryan elements were already present in the Harappan Culture. I. Mahadevan suggests that Indo-Aryan priests married into the local population and that a long period of bilingualism and racial fusion ensued. The hearths at Kalibangan identified as fire-altars was suggested by B. Allchin as indicating the presence of the Indo-Aryans. Thapar (1973:101) describes this as a ritual hearth with a clay or brick pillar at the center. This feature immediately brings to mind a hearth of this type in room seven of the Burned building at Tepe Hissar (not indicated in the plan in the site report) and a group of three other such hearths on the Main Mound dated by radiocarbon to the mid-third millennium B.C. (Schmidt 1937; Fig. 162, Fig. 84 square DG 20l; Dyson and Remsen, in Press). If these were ritual hearths then B.B. Lal's point that Aryans were present at the very beginning of the site is a good one. This is so because there is a close association between such features and Indo-Aryans in India. F.R. Allchin agrees with this correlation.

In relation to the so-called "massacre" at Mohenjodaro, traditionally cited to demonstrate the invasion thesis, Kennedy points out that there is no evidence of injury to the bones of the so-called victims at the time of death. In some cases, however, there are partially healed cranial lesions which indicate wounds several months old. He argues on the basis of the available skeletal evidence that a biological continuum exists with many of the Harappan morphometric variables continuing in the modern population of the Sind and Punjab, thus supporting a concept of population continuity rather than displacement.

The disagreements as to the attributes suitable to the identification of Indo-Aryans spills over to a discussion of Cemetery H at Harappa. Allchin felt that the birds on the jars represented the sun and fire combined, but Gupta objected that the manner of disposing of the dead in Cemetery H was wrong for the *Vedic* literature. Deo agreed that basic concepts drawn from the Indo-Aryans were already present in the Indus Civilization. Fairservis expressed his opinion that Indo-Aryans could have been in the Indus Valley a thousand years before we traditionally think so. Jarrige's discoveries at Mehrgarh of direct linkages between the site and Namazga III and IV in Turkmenia in Pre-Harappan times provides an important piece of new evidence for culture contact between these regions which will have to be taken into consideration in any further speculation on this subject.

26

The Quest for Krishna's Dwarka

S.R. Rao*

Every year thousands of pilgrims visit the holy town of Dwarka to pay homage to Lord Krishna, at the temple of Dwarkadhish. According to the *Sabha Parva* of the *Mahabharata,* Krishna accompanied by his Yadava followers migrated to Dvaraka** to escape Jarasandha's attacks on Mathura.

The Yadavas led by Sri Krishna sought shelter on the west coast where the town of Kusasthali built by Kakudmin Riavata, a Yadava, once stood. The *Rigveda* refers to the Yadus in Anarta country, that is Gujarat, which was named after Anarta, the son of Manu, Kakudmin Raivata was one of the descendants of Anarta. From the statements made in the *Sabha Parva,* impregnable forts were built to make the town habitable.

The *Vishnu Parva* of the *Harivamsa,* an appendix to the *Mahabharata,* throws light on the initial steps of reclamation taken by Krishna. The sea is said to have yielded twelve yojans of land at his behest.

Addressing the sea Krishna says, 'If you respect me, withdraw yourself.' The *Harivamsa Vishnu Parva* significantly describes Dvaraka as a fortress in water, *varidurga,* 'being made impregnable on account of the sea all round.'

All texts unanimously agree on the catastrophe that befell Dvarka. The *Mausala Parva* of the *Mahabharata* says, 'This city is going to be swallowed by sea.' The residents of Dvaraka forewarned by Krishna, vacated the city before the sea submerged it.

---

* Renowned archaeologist, who excavated the Indus-Saraswati port city of Lothal and Rangpuri; deciphered the Harappan Script; pioneer of marine archaeology in India; discovered the lost city of Dwarka under sea water.
Presently Emeritus Scientist and Advisor, National Institute of Oceanography and Marine Archaeology, Goa.

** The author distinguishes Krishna's Dvaraka from modern Dwarka.

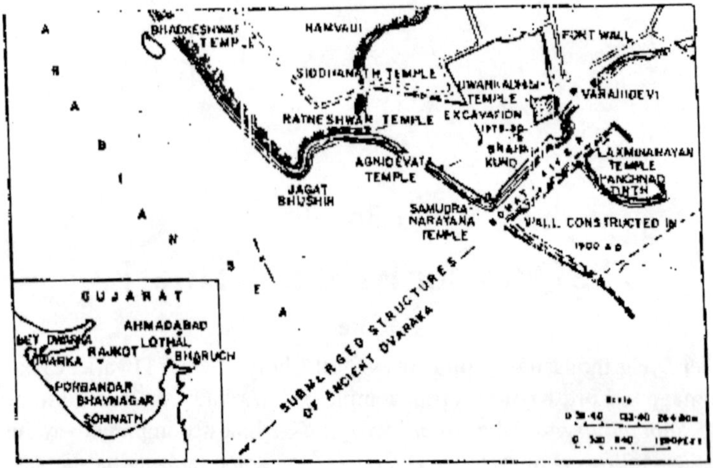

It is important to ascertain the truth of the statements about Dvaraka in the epics and *Puranas* for, if the city was built three or four thousand years ago it would convincingly prove a second urbanization long before 500 BC when Pataliputra and Takshasila were built. It would also narrow the gap in Indian history between the end of the Indus (Harappan) civilization in 1900 BC and the beginning of the Buddhist period in 500 BC. The submergence of Dvaraka is also of oceanographic interest because the undersea structures, if discovered, would provide reliable data for calculating the rate of rise in sea level, a matter of great concern for planners of coastal towns. Finally, the oft-repeated theory that a dark age descended on the Indian sub-continent after the decline of the Harappan civilization can be effectively refuted if there is concrete archaeological evidence for the advanced technology which produced iron weapons, built piers and anti-erosion walls in the sea.

Before undertaking onshore and offshore excavations at Dwaraka, it was necessary to first explore Mul Dwarka in the Una taluk of the Junagadh district, Madhavpur Ghed fifty-six kilometers southeast of Porbandar and Visavada, forty kilometres south of Dwarka, all of which claim, in varying degrees, to be Krishna's Dvaraka. Mul Dwarka excavated by Hirananda Sastry in the thirties yielded no evidence of any human settlement before the first century AD. His findings were confirmed when I explored Mul Dwarka in 1979. The Madhavpur Ghed and Visavada sites show no trace of any settlement before the present era. Junagadh is another site suggested by some scholars as Dvaraka because of the presence of a hill called Raivataka, but this is a later appellation. Its original name was Urjayanta. The hillock Raivata near Dvaraka mentioned in the *Mahabharata* seems to have been submerged.

Having disposed of the claims on other sites, Dwarka in Okhamandal was the only one which remained to be thoroughly explored. The earliest reference to Dvaraka appears in a 574 AD copperplate grant issued by Garulaka Simhaditya, who says his father, a brave warrior, cast in the mould of Sri Krishna, conquered the land of Dvaraka. By the sixth century AD, according to tradition, Krishna founded Dvaraka at the site where modern Dwaraka stands. By the third century BC Krishna was deified and Bhagavatta-Krishna-Vishnu cult became popular.

An inscription by Heliodorus, the Greek ambassador, refers to Vasudeva as *devadeva,* god of gods. Earlier in the fifth century BC the grammarian, Panini mentions an aphorism which suggests the divinity, *devatavisesha,* of Vasudeva. The still earlier *Chandogya Upanishad* refers to Krishna-Devakiputra. A careful examination of the earlier part of the *Mahabharata*, namely Jaya, suggests that Krishna was a historical person and it was only later that he was deified. The very fact that he had to leave Mathura on account of Jarasandha's threat indicates that he behaved like a human strategist. He tried a bring about a reconciliation between the Kaurava and Pandava princes, but when he found war was inevitable, he spared no means to win with the sole purpose of establishing *dharma*. Even his end was human and unlike that of a god. It is rightly said that Krishna was intensely practical and intensely spiritual. If he was a historical person, as is evident from his

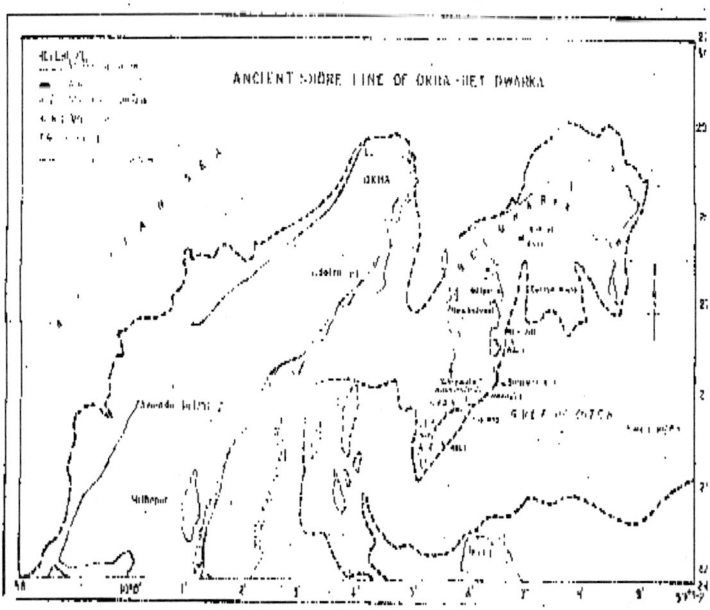

actions, the founding of Dvaraka must be a reality and it is possible to trace the submerged remains of the city.

Below Harrapan Bronze Chariot

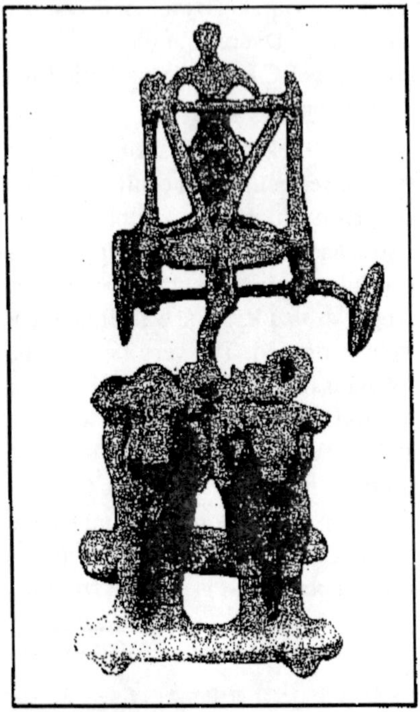

In 1963, excavations carried out by the Deccan College, Pune, a few hundred metres away from the Dwarkadhish temple complex, revealed evidence of a settlement dating to the first century AD which the excavators concluded was the Dvaraka mentioned in the *Mahabharata, Ghata Jataka, Dwarkamahatmya* of the *Skanda Purana.* But the date assigned to it was apparently wrong because it takes the *Mahabharata* was and building of Dvaraka city to the first century AD whereas by the fourth century BC Krishna was already deified. A fresh excavation at Dwaraka was therefore an urgent necessity.

During clearance operations at Dwarka in 1979, a two storeyed modern building which concealed a view of the Dwarkadhish temple was demolished. Systematic excavations revealed a temple of Vishnu with its beautifully carved plinth and walls intact, though the roof was missing, perhaps blown away by a storm wave. The sand deposited by the receding sea had preserved the rest of the temple. Further excavations revealed the plinth and foundation of two earlier temples. According to ceramic and numismatic evidence the earliest temple dates to the first century BC/AD. Below this temple we encountered the habitation deposit of a human settlement destroyed by the sea. A distinct pottery known as the Lustrous Red Ware, identical with the fourteenth-fifteenth century BC pottery found at Prabhasa (Somnath), was recovered from the lowest layers. It was thus obvious that a township of the *Mahabharata* age existed here. The generally accepted data of the *Mahabharata* war is 1424 BC. But conclusive evidence that a fortified town or city was

Late Harappan script on the shoulder of an eathern vessel.

submerged was necessary to corroborate the *Mahabharata* tradition. Such evidence could be possible if expert marine archaeologists were to excavate the sea-bed off Dwarka. Not a single marine archaeologist existed in India in 1980, nor had any offshore survey of shipwrecks and submerged cities been made along the Indian coast, even though Indian ships had visited Sumerian ports as early as 2400 BC, and the earliest dockyard in the world was built at Lothal in 2300 BC.

A Marine Archaeology Unit was established at the National Institute of Oceanography (NIO), Goa, in 1981 to explore submerged Dwarka as well as shipwrecks along the Indian coast. Before venturing an offshore survey, the submarine topographical features of the Gulf of Kutch and the ancient shore line and landmarks in and around Dwarka, were studied. From their study of the calcareous sandstone of intertidal origin, NIO scientists concluded that ten thousand years ago the sea level in the Gulf of Kutch was sixty metres lower than at present. They also observed that six to thirty metre high pinnacles separated by flat terraces lie submerged in the Gulf. The sea level, three thousand years ago, must have been ten to fifteen metres below the present level exposing some of these hillocks and connecting the island of Bet Dwarka (thirty kilometres from Dwarka) with the mainland near Okha by a landstrip. The maximum water depth along the Bet Dwarka coast is only three to six metres and the tidal range is four metres. It became necessary to explore Bet Dwarka before undertaking an offshore survey of Dwarka because the *Harivamsa* describes Dwaraka as a 'fortress in water' which may refer to an island. Bet Dwarka, also called Shankhodhara because of a rich harvest of conch shells, or sankha, is considered as Krishna's pleasure resort.

Hirananda Sastry's onshore excavation in the thirties pushed the antiquity of Bet Dwarka to the third century BC. In 1981 the Marine Archaeology Unit (MAU) discovered a massive stone wall in the cliff section at the site designated BDK-I-BDK II near the southern end of the east coast, and recovered pottery of the protohistoric period from the intertidal zone. The damaged section of the wall suggested that it was a landward gravity wall of a protohistoric town and further seaward, submerged structures may lie. This assumption was proved correct when underwater surveys, from 1982 to 1984, revealed another wall made of large stone blocks of prismatic shape which were too heavy to be moved by tides and currents. This seaward wall was built on a wavecut bench.

Encouraged by the results, six trenches were sunk into the seabed and by adopting an airlift technique pottery, shell objects and other antiquities were recovered. In one of the trenches dug four hundred metres seaward, a unique seal made from shell and engraved with a three headed animal reminiscent of Indus seals was recovered. Further north in the central sector, designated as site BDK VIII, a fort wall of medium sized building blocks was exposed at lowest low tide. This forms an irregular hexagon with a perimeter of five hundred metres. Nine courses of masonry 1.5 metres high are intact though the original full height is not known. This must have been a pier or an enclosure wall for a very important group of buildings built on the wavecut bench. A twin rock-cut slipway to the south of BDK VIII clearly indicates that boats were launched here. Traces of a Late Harappan settlement are evident at Balapur Bay near the northern sector of the east coast. One kilometre seaward of the iron pillar on the shore there are remains of what must have been a massive stone wall. It lies mostly submerged except in low tide. In the mud flats in the Bay extending more than 1.5 kilometres seaward, pottery from the protohistoric period was found but the presence of currents and hard clayey sediment made excavation extremely difficult. The submerged structural remains identified in BDK I, II, VI and VIII point to the existence of a large port-city, at least four kilometres in length and 0.5 to 1 kilometre broad The *Mahabharata* has rightly designated ancient Dvaraka as a *nagari*, city, which it was, even by modern standards. An important find from the intertidal zone is a jar inscribed with the Late Harappan script.

The marine archaeological expedition's main problem was to identify the station for underwater search in the Arabian Sea. In Gujarat it is customary for sailors to make offerings to the Sea God, Varuna, also known as Daria Lal, in Gujarat. The Sea Goddess, Vanuvatimata, is worshipped even today at the Harappan port of Lothal although no boat visits it. Since there is a temple, Samudranarayana, dedicated to the Sea God, located on the shore we assumed that the ancient port town may not be too far away. This assumption proved correct. From seven expeditions at Dwarka five yielded extremely significant archaeological evidence and confirmed the tradition that a well fortified city existed, built on both the banks of the Gomati river, the submerged channel of which has been traced over a length of 1.75 kilometres from the Samudranarayana temple.

Two building periods have been recognized on the basis of ceramic and stratigraphic evidence from eighteen trenches sunk into the banks and the centre of the submerged channel of the Gomati. The river in ancient times cut through the rocks over a width of three to four hundred metres and its bed dips from four to seventeen metres in depth. A majority of the buildings traced are on the right bank while a few greatly disturbed ones stand on the left bank. Among the major buildings protohistoric Period I at six to eight metres below Mean Sea Level of Okha, are stone jetty and the inner and outer fortification walls with gateways flanked by circular bastions, parts of which are in situ. Several stone anchors and some stray finds such as the perforated bases of flag posts were also discovered. A stone pillar and a crescent shaped architectural element resembling the moonstone, *candrasila,* were laid bare. The most significant finds of Period I are three-holed triangular anchors made of limestone and sandstone weighing fifty to a hundred and fifty kilograms, and resembling in all its details the Late Bronze Age anchors from Syria and Cyprus used between the fourteenth to twelfth century BC. Honor Frost, an expert in the study of anchors, has identified the triangular anchors of Dwaraka as belonging to the Late Bronze Age.

A distinct ceramic ware were found with these anchors in the Black and Red ware and wave-rolled shreds of small Lustrous Red Ware bowls, dating to the fifteenth century BC. Some large, prismatic shaped sandstone anchors were found in the water, six to eight metres deep. They weigh a hundred to two hundred and fifty kilograms and might have been introduced at this period. Besides pottery, shell artifacts and a couple of stone bronze objects have also been found in the seabed. The horseshoe shaped perforated arches and the supporting frames and nails found here may be part of a bronze chariot. A bronze bell, a stone saddle quern similar to those from chalcolithic sites in the neighbourhood of Dwarka and a marble figure with only the feet intact were found nearby. They could belong to Period II though the possibility of an earlier date is not ruled out, as bronze carts were produced in Harappan times and the solid-cast wheeled animal figures of Daimabad indicate the

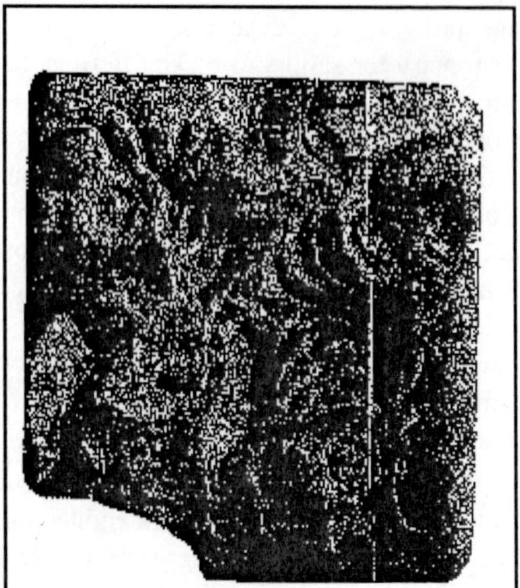

Conch shell seal engraved with a thriee-headed animal representing a bull, unicorn and goat.

religious affiliation of bronze figures in Late Harappan times. The maximum water depth at high tide where the Period I structure were found in situ is ten to eleven metres. After the submergence of Dwaraka in 1500 BC there was no occupation for almost a thousand years. This is also confirmed at Bet Dwaraka.

In Period II the harbour was closer to the Samudranarayana temple where iron rings embedded in the rock and stone pillars for tying boats have been discovered. The buildings constructed with smaller fraction blocks of miliolities were destroyed by currents and waves. A few walls were found at a 2.84 to 3 metre depth below Mean Sea Level of Okha. The maximum water depth at high tide is 6 to 7 metres. Among the important antiquities of this period recovered from seabed excavations are iron anchors and large prismatic shaped perforated stone anchors which are an improvement on the perforated triangular anchors. A wooden hull of a boat found in the gully is of a much later date. Two mutilated sculptures of deities, one of marble and the other of black stone, were also recovered form the seabed. The former appears to represent Vishnu.

The most important find from seabed excavations at BDK I-II is a small conch shell seal, with a perforated button on the back to hold a ring. A composite animal motif representing the short-horned bull, unicorn and goat is engraved on the front. The motif is of Indus origin but the art style suggests the influence of Bahrainian art, as is indicated by the exaggerated eyes and cursory treatment of the body. Composite animals symbolise the integration of different social or religious groups who worshipped animal deities. In the *Rigveda,* Indra is compared to a bull, Agni to a horse and goat. The Bet Dwarka seal testifies to the use of seals by the citizens of Dwarka, referred to in the *Harivamsa.*

The inscription on the shoulder of an earthern vessel found in the intertidal zone of BDK I-II is highly significant from the point of view of the chronology of the site and the evolution of the Indus script. Six letters in the inscription are identical with those in the Late Harappan script, 1900-1700 BC, and the Semitic script, 1600-1300 BC. The phonetic value of these letters is determined on the basis of the value of analogous signs in the deciphered Semitic and Late Harappan scripts. The inscription reads *mahhagacha* (*mahakaccha*) *shah-pa* in archaic Sanskrit and conveys the sense 'Sea Lord (*mahakaccha-shah*) protect (pa)'. The person offering something in the inscribed pot seems to have sought the protection of the Sea God. Only the last three signs resemble Brahmi letters, not the first four. On palaeographical grounds the inscription dates to the fifteenth-fourteenth century BC. A sixteenth-fifteenth century

BC amphora is another important find. A narrow mouthed, grazed bottle found in Bet Dwarka suggests that attempts were made to glaze vessels. The coppersmith's stone mould in which spearheads could be cast, and the iron stakes, the use of which is referred to in the *Harivamsa,* indicate copper and iron technology.

The thermoluminescence date of the Bet Dwarka pottery is 3520 years Before Present. This is further corroborated by the fourteenth-fifteenth century BC triangular anchors as well as the Lustrous Red Ware which is identical with that of Prabhasa, another site of the *Mahabharata* tradition. The palaeography of the evolved Late Harappan script on the Bet Dwarka inscription is of the fifteenth century BC. The Bet Dwarka seal also belongs to fifteenth century BC. It is therefore clear beyond doubt that Dwarka was a flourishing port in 1500-1400 BC. AD Pusalkar (*Studies in the Epics and Puranas of India in Vedic Age,* 1955; page 56) suggested the date 1424 BC for the *Mahabharata* war on reliable astronomical and literary evidence. The alternate dates, 950 BC recommended by Pargiter and 3102 BC calculated on the basis of the inscription at Aihole in Karnataka, do not stand the test of reliable astronomical evidence as mentioned in the various *Puranas.*

Subsequently, BB Lal excavated Hastinapura and on the evidence of a particular pottery, namely the Painted Grey Ware (PGW) concluded that it represented the culture of the *Mahabharata* period which he dated 1000-900 BC. This ware is found in the Ganga, Yamuna and Saraswati valleys. Had he taken into account the earliest culture of Hastinapura as represented by the Ochre Coloured Pottery (OCP) the date of the settlement would have been pushed back at least by five or six centuries or more. The OCP is nothing but waterlogged Late Harappan pottery found in eight sites of the *Mahabharata* tradition in northern and western India including Dwarka and Somnath. The excavations at Somnath (Prabhasa) have yielded evidence of the overlap of chalcolithic and iron age cultures. The Black and Red Ware and Lustrous Red Ware both of which occur in Dwarka and Bet Dwarka continue for some time at Somnath after 1500 BC.

Iron weapons are said to have been used for the first time in the *Mahabharata* battle, and since the date of the iron as known at Hastinapura was 900 BC, Lal dated the *Mahabharata* war to 1000-900 BC. The date of iron in India has now been pushed back to the thirteenth century BC, on the basis of the thermoluminescence date of pottery, associated with iron objects found at Gufrol in Kashmir and Tadasanahalli in Karnataka. Iron stakes and nails fabricated through primitive methods are found in Bet Dwarka along with an inscribed potsherd. The PGW culture, although associated with iron, reflects only the agro-pastoral economy of rural folk which stands in sharp contrast to the urban life of the *Mahabharata* period. The PGW culture cannot therefore be deemed to reflect the culture of the *Mahabharata* aristocracy. On the other hand, the great urban centre of Dvaraka does reflect the *Mahabharata* culture and it has been firmly dated to 1500 BC by the thermoluminescence dating of the pottery from Bet Dwarka, also found in the excavations at Dwarka. The traditional date, 3102 BC, based on the Aihole inscription and the testimony of Aryabhata is incorrect as pointed by SB Roy (*Date of the Mahabharata Battle,* Academic Press, Gurgaon, 1976). He has critically examined all the five approaches by scholars for dating the war and has supported Pusalkar's date.

The most important criterion in identifying the excavated buildings and artifacts at Dwarka and Bet Dwarka as Krishna's Dvaraka, has been the convincing evidence that the three thousand five hundred year old city of Dwarka lies submerged in the sea. All the ancient text including the *Mahabharata, Harivamsa, Vishnu, Matsya and Skanda Puranas* unanimously agree that Dvaraka was submerged. Secondly, the plan and architectural features revealed by the extant buildings reflect the description of Dvaraka nagari given in the *Harivamsa.* According to the text the city was eight yojanas wide and shaped like an *ashtapada.* The description of Patliputra given by Megasthenes, and the depiction of the Gateway of Sravasti on the north torana of Sanchi bring to memory the gateways of Dvaraka. In Bet Dwarka, however, there were enclosures within the fort. The *Harivamsa* mentions the moats of Dvaraka which were studded with iron stakes to keep the enemy away and an iron stake has been found in Bet Dwarka.

Fortifications of the city with gates laid bare in the sea, the remains of a temple and other buildings give a glimpse of the architecture of the times. There is also a reference in the *Harivamsa* to the reclamation of a strip of land measuring twelve *yojanas* from the sea. This is also substantiated by boulders dumped into the sea for a dry masonry foundation when the sea level was lower than at present. Bastions are built on them. The engineers of Lothal built a dock in 2300 BC and at the Harappan town of Dholavira in Kutch there is a huge anti-erosion wall along the banks of a now dry creek or water channel. Thus, it is no wonder if such walls and jetties were built at Dvaraka.

The *Mahabharata* refers to Arjuna storming the prosperous town of the Nivatakavachas, which was situated on the offshore island of a great sea—perhaps the Persian Gulf. Ships loaded with a variety of goods which berthed at Dvaraka are also referred to in ancient texts. The slipways of Bet Dwaraka are also referred to in ancient texts. The slipways of Bet Dwaraka and the jetty off Dwarka attest to hectic navigational activity. The prosperity of Dwarka can be attributed to overseas trade, pearl fishing, shell craft and boatbuilding. The use of a seal, *mudra,* as a passport for the citizens of Dwarka in the face of enemy attack referred to in the *Harivamsa* is confirmed by the conch shell seal found in the Bet Dwarka waters.

Every citizen should carry a mudra (seal) as a mark of identity and the guards had to make sure that this instruction was followed. Thus, there can be no doubt this was Krishna's Dwarka referred to in ancient texts. Within the fortification in Dwarka waters a segment of a large hall or palace has been traced. The wall of the building is ten metres long with considerably damaged cross walls. The fifteen to thirty five metre high wooded hills, on the eastern shore might represent the Raivataka Hill of the *Mahabharata*. Alternately the six to thirty meter high pinnacles in the Gulf of Kutch reported by the NIO scientists, may represent Raivataka Hill. The reference to Darukavana or Dwarka in the *Mahabharata* must be to the city state of Dwarka which included the present Okhamandal (Kusadvipa), extending from Shankhodhara in the north to Okhamadhi in the south and from Dwarka in the west to Pindaraka in the east. There were satellite port-towns at Arambhadvara (Aramda), Negeswar and Pindaraka. As the sea level was ten to twelve metres lower in 1500 BC, as indicated by the in *situ* structures in the Arabian Sea off Dwarka, the seven islands referred to in the *Periplus of the Erythrean Sea* in 50 AD must have been connected by land. Subsequently the sea level rose and submerged Dwarka and inundated the river channels.

Another contributory factor may be the subsidence of the shore. It is interesting to find similar evidence of the low stand of the sea and the subsequent transgression submerging Kassite sites also reported in Bahrain.

One of the objections raised is that unless evidence of writing from the *Mahabharata* age is found in Dwarka it cannot be considered as Krishna's Dwarka. This objection is ruled out since the Bet Dwarka inscription on the votive earthen vessel is written in the evolved late Indus script linked with Brahmi which has been hailed as a unique discovery (VS Pathak's *Presidential Address of the Epigraphical Society of India: Annual Session Jabalpur,* also *Marine Archaeology of the Indian Ocean Countries,* 1988). The language is Sanskrit and the word *mahagacha* (*mahakaccha of Mahabharata*) stand for Sea/Sea Lord.

Another objection is that merely because a township has been found in the sea it cannot be considered as Krishna's Dwarka. The criteria for identifying the submerged buildings as those of legendary Dvaraka are based on the date of the structures. The architectural features corresponding to the main features as described in the *Mahabharata* barring hyperbolic expressions and finally, the urban character of the city and its port. All the small buildings are levelled out except the fort, bastions and the two large buildings in which massive stones are used to give a glimpse of the city. The huge stone anchors confirm that large ships visited the port. The date 1500 BC is determined by the TL dating method and the age of similar triangular anchors used in Cyprus and Syria. Pottery is another criterion. A third objection is that the reclamation of the sea referred to in the *Harivamsa* should be traced. This has already been done and photographs of the bastion and other structures built on a foundation of dry masonry in the sea, published. According to ocean engineering experts this is a good evidence of reclamation.

27

Geological Foundations of Vedic Civilization

S.R.N. Murthy*

Indian Civilization, which is one of the oldest, if not the oldest, is beset with many difficulties in tracing its origin and evolution. Many problems of Indology have assumed great complications due to geological changes during its evolution through several millennia. Problems of Aryan origin, the development of riverine culture on the banks of the now extinct, river Saraswati, submergence of the Dwarka island, the geological significance of various pilgrimage centers, study of the earth in the *Vedic* and later cultures, origin and evolution of Indian architecture and sculpture and the influence of geological phenomena on the spiritual evolution of India are some of the most important problems which require the application of modern geology of India to Indology. Without the application of geological concepts these and other similar problems are difficult to solve. Now we may digress to discussing one of the above problems leading to origin of the Aryans in India.

The River Saraswati

Krishnan (1956) observed that:

> The Saraswati rises in the Siwalik hills of Sirmur on the borders of the Ambala district in the region of the junction of the talus fans of the Yamuna on the east and Sutlej on the west, and enters the plains at Abdhadri. It disappears in the sands after passing by Bhawanipur and Balachhappar but reappears after a short distance, flowing through Karnal. The Ghaggar which also rises in the same region joins it at Rasula in Patiala after a course of 110 miles. Further on, the river is called Hakra or Sotar whose dry bed is of considerable size and must have once contained a large river. It is lost in the sands near Hanumangarh in Bikaner. When the Saraswati was a live river, it must have irrigated an area of perhaps over 7000 sq. miles of what is now practically a desert.

* Eminent Geologist, Retired as Director, Geological Survey of India, presently based at Bangalore.

Recent studies about the paleochannels of the river Saraswati as seen from Landsat imageries and by regular traverses along the valley, by Agarwal (1984) and Balashankar (1988) have brought much data. According to Agarwal (1984):

> On the main Saraswati, both pre-Harappan and Harappan (like Kalibangan about 4500-3700 BC) settlements abound, but not settlements of later period. The Drshadvati (the Chautang) has a large number of late Harappan sites. Kalibangan on the Saraswati has been extensively excavated by the Archaeological Survey and Rakhigarhi, Mitathal, etc. on the Drshadvati have been excavated by the Kurukshetra University. Explorations on the Hakra in Pakistan by Rafique Mughal, on the Saraswati and Drshadvati area by A. Gosh, Surajbhan, K.N. Dikshit, R.S. Bisht, K.T. Dalal and others from the Archaeological Survey of India have provided a fund of information about the settlements on these river banks.

He further commented that:

> It is obvious that human settlements were affected by the vagaries of these vagrant rivers which may have been affected by tectonic factors. On the other hand, palaeoclimatic data based on pollen and geochemical measurements from the saltlakes show that, roughly, between 6000-4000 BC this area was much wetter than today. Besides a semiarid ecology cannot stand the pressure of large sedentary populations for very long. The large urbanised Harappan settlements could thrive only when the climate was wet and when the Saraswati carried a lot of water. They withered away in adverse ecological conditions.

According to Balashankar (1988):

> Recent geological investigations have revealed the diverse courses of the Saraswati under the sands of the Rajasthan desert. A study of the landsat picture conducted at the Space Application Centre of the Physical Research Laboratory, Ahmedabad, showed that the Sutlej once flowed into the Ghaggar (Saraswati) as did the Yamuna. The dry bed of the Ghaggar is thus considered to be part of the Saraswati. This study also showed that the Saraswati was in existence during the pre-Harappan era (2200-1700 BC) and that during the last 5000 years the rivers of the area have changed their course several times.

The Saraswati Research Team has concluded that the river existed. It has based its findings on the excavations at Kalibangan in the Thar Desert. It found evidence of earth quakes and abandoned settlements. The team's surmise that the chain of tectonic events which diverted the Sutlej westward and the Palaeo-Yamuna south-eastward were perhaps responsible for the subsidence near Marot and Bariwala into which the Saraswati seems to have vanished.

These observations of the Saraswati Research Team of 20 led by Dr. V.S. Wakankar have challenged Sir Mortimer Wheeler's theories that the

Aryans immigrated into India from the Caucasian region of Central Asia and that the Harappan civilization was destroyed by them.

The Problem of Aryan Origin

The theories are put forward to the effect that the Aryans immigrated into India from parts of Central Asia or the Arctic region. The discoveries of temples of Varuna and other deities in the Bogas Koi region of Central Asia was the basis for the theory that Aryans originated in Central Asia region and migrated from there into mid-east and south-east in branches and the early Aryans settled in India in the present area of Punjab and adjoining places. Later, Tilak (1925) in a theory proposed that the Arctic region was the home of *Vedic* Aryans and they have migrated in batches to other regions from time to time. The controversy is unsettled; perhaps geological evidences may be required to solve problems.

The first application of geological evidence to prove that the Arctic region was the home of the *Vedic* Aryans was made by Tilak (1925). According to Balashashtri Hardas (1967) the following geological evidences helped Tilak to propound his theory. They are:

1. The latest investigations in the geological conditions advance a theory, that about ten thousand years have elapsed since the close of the glacial age and the commencement of the post-glacial epoch. This estimate of the post-glacial epoch has been mainly arrived at from the freshness of the fossil deposits of the skeletons of animals recovered in the Siberian region.

2. Man is not merely post-glacial as he was believed to be some years ago. There is conclusive geological evidence to prove his widespread existence in the Quaternary, if not also in the Tertiary era.

3. There were at least two glacial and one inter-glacial periods; the territorial distribution of land and water on the earth during the inter-glacial period was quite different from what it is at present.

4. There took place great changes in the climatic conditions in the Pleistocene period; it being cold and inclement during the glacial, and mild and temperate in the Inter-Glacial periods, even as far as the Polar regions.

5. The arctic region both in Asia and Europe, was characterised in the inter-glacial period by cool summers and warm winters, making as if a perpetual spring. There is evidence to show that places like Spitsberge, where the sun remains below the horizon from November to March had once the luxuriant vegetation that grows at present only in the temperate or tropical zones. The descent of glacial age disturbed this congenial climate rendering the regions unsuited for the habitation of tropical plants and animals.

The theory of *Arctic home in the Vedas* presented by Tilak based on the above geological evidences have been contradicted by Lele, Pavgi, Aprabuddha and Das according to Hardas (1967). Hardas stated that:

> In his learned contribution '*The Rig-Vedic India*', Dr. Das controverts the entire Arctic theory propounded by Tilak. On the evidence supplied by the latest geological researches he has tried to prove that the region called the 'Sapta-Sindhu' was the original home of the *Vedic* people.

Palaeontological Record

The above inferences are based on *Vedic* evidence without considering the Palaeontological Record that is available in the Siwalik foothills of the Himalayas. The Siwalik hills in Punjab, Himachal Pradesh and Jammu and Kashmir point to the origin of man in this region. According to Pascoe (1973):

> At Haritalyangar, which is near the Kangra boundary, remains of vertebrates have been found by Pilgrim and Vinayak Rao throughout a vertical secession of some 600 ft. of strata in the Siwalik Himalayas. In the Nagri stage of the Haritalyangar fossils are plenty in the upper 2000 ft. of the total 3500 ft. thick sediments. Primates, as many as ten species, have been listed to occur in this stage.

Many of these fossils have been found to be synonymous and recent studies by Prasad (1975) have indicated that the primates of significance which have a bearing on the evolution of Hominoidea in the Siwalik region are five in number. They are: 1. *Sivapithecus indicus,* 2. *Sivapithecus sivalensis*, 3. *Sivapithecus chinjiensis.,* 4. *Ramapithecus brevirostris* and 5. *Ramapithecus punjabiens.*

The above fossils are found from Haritalayangar and Ramnagar areas. Pilgrims also (1915; 1927) discussed several species of primates from the Patwar plateau in Pakistan, Himachal Pradesh and Jammu.

Pinjore, a type area for Upper Siwaliks, is located to the south of Kalka near the eastern edge of Pinjore dune between the rivers Sutlej and Ghaggar. According to Pascoe (1973):

> About 1000 ft. above the basal beds of the section near the village Moginand and not far from Ghaggar river is the famous fossil locality from which Baker and Durand in 1936 excavated large numbers of the specimens which were subsequently described and figured by themselves, Falconer or others.

From the Pinjore range the first Siwalik fossils were collected by Falconer, Cautley and others. Most of the Siwaliks hills specimens were collected by Prasad and others in recent past.

Along with these primate fossils many fossils of rodentia, Laporiadea, Carnivora, Proboscidae, Perissodactyla, Artoidactyla etc. of mammals and others have been unearthed. According to Pascoe (1973):

> *There is no other part of the world in which the anthropoid apes are represented in such numbers and variety as in India, and the inference follows that the original centre of distribution of the group could not have been far from northern India.* The Nagri Stage of the Middle Siwalik, and in particular that portion of the stage exposed at the locality of Haritalyangar in the Simla hills has yielded them in great profusion. The Indian forms originally referred to the European genus Dryopithecus, which must have been near the starting point of the three modern genera of the gorilla, chimpanzee and orangoutang, have been distributed by Lewis amongst the four genera Sivapithecus, Sugrivapithecus, Bramapithecus and Ramapithecus.

However, Lewis' classification has been revised in recent years.

The Siwalik Hills which are dated about 20 million years contain well preserved mammalian remains of prehistoric animals including early man-like apes and hominids like *Ramapithecus.* The miocene formations in Himachal Pradesh near Haritalyangar and Ramnagar near Udhampur and Jammu, have yielded undoubted evidences of hominid remains in association with artefacts of early period. Pilgrim (1915, 192), Vinayak Rao and Iyenger made bold attempts to discover some of the rare fossil finds of *Sivapithecus* of the Dryopithecus group as well as hominids like *Ramapithecus.* Subsequently, Prasad (1975, 1989) made valuable collections of Hominid remains from Himachal Pradesh and suggested the possibility of radiation of higher apes including hominids in the Siwalik region. Several dental remains including well preserved mandibular and maxillary teeth collected from Haritalyangar, gave evidence, that the origin man-like apes and hominids like *Ramapithecus,* did take place in the Siwalik hills region.

Discussion

Considerable researches have been carried out by modern anthropologists and palaeontologists to decipher the origin of early man since the discovery of Neanderthal man in a cave in Germany over a century ago. The gorilla, the chimpanzee and the orangoutang at one time were considered to be man's ancestors. Yet others considered the Tarsius of Borneo to be man's ancestor, but the enigma continues. All these concepts have been totally changed. According to Wecker (1957) the Neanderthal man developed in the Central and eastern Asia while Sapiens evolved in Europe, Africa, Asia Minor and India. Further, he said that the Neanderthal man disappeared in the 4th Ice age and Homosapiens (human forms) evolved and began to live in caves, hunted big games, used fire, buried their dead, made special tools, clothed himself and produced religious art.

The above data goes to show that possibly one class of the Homosapiens based on *Ramapithecus,* a hominid evolved in the Siwalik region including Potwar Plateau gave rise to the *Vedic* Aryans (essentially belonging to the Europoidal race) most probably in the beginning of the present i.e. the fifth Inter-Glacial period. Just like the Aryan expansion in India, many batches might have migrated from India outside to Central Asia and Europe in later ages. The geological data however, points out that the Aryans originated from the Siwalik region.

Conclusion

From the foregoing it is assumed that there is sufficient evidence within India for tracing the origin of the Aryans. The scientific data permit further research on the origin of Aryans in India and Pakistan. There is need for fresh appraisal by Anthropologists, Archaeologists, Palaeontologists and Indologists in this direction.

Acknowledgement : This paper has received much improvement by Dr. K.N. Prasad formerly Director, G.S.I. to whom I am most grateful.

Notes and References

D.P. Agarwal, 1984, "Whatever happened to the River Saraswati", *Science Age,* February 1984, pp. 18-24.

R. Balashankar, 1988, "Quest for a River", *The Week,* May 29-June 4, pp. 8-11.

Balashastry Hardas, 1967, *Glimpses of the Vedic Nation,* Kamakoti Publishing House, Madras, p. 83-123.

M.S. Krishnan, 1956, *Geology of India and Burma,* Higginbothems. Madras.

E.H. Pascoe, 1973, *A Manual of the Geology of India and Burma,* III Edn.

G.E. Pilgrim, 1915, "New Siwalik Primates and Their Bearing on Questions of Evolution of Man with the Anthropoidea" Rec. *Geological Survey Of India,* 45 (I)

G.E. Pilgrim, 1927, "A Sivapithecus Palate and other Fossils from India", *Pal Ind.* 14. p. 1-24.

K.N. Prasad, 1989, *Some Observations on Hominid Evolution, Perspectives in Human Evolution*, pp. 93-110. Renaissance Publishing House, Delhi.

K.N. Prasad, 1975, "Review of Miocene Anthropoidea from India and Adjacent Countries", *Jour. Pal. Soc. Ind.* XX, pp. 382-390.

B.G. Tilak, 1125, *The Arctic Home in the Vedas,* Pune.

J.E. Wecker, 1957, "Neanderthal Man" *Scientific American,* V, 197 pp. 89-96.

28

Remote Sensing of the 'Lost' Saraswati River

Yash Pal, Baldev Sahai, R.K. Sood and D.P. Agrawal*

The area lying between the rivers Indus and Ganga has been the cradle of many important civilizations. The availability or lack of waters in the rivers flowing in this region determined the growth or decay of these civilizations. The river Saraswati is said to have been a mightier river than even the Indus in the *Vedic* and pre-*Vedic* times. Stein (1942) refers to the fact that in at least three passages in the *Rigveda,* the oldest surviving record in any Indo-language, a river course has been mentioned which corresponds to the present Sarsuti (Saraswati) and Ghaggar. *Nadistuti,* the famous hymn describes the Saraswati as flowing between the Yamuna in the east and the *Satudri* (Satluj) in the west. Since none of the present rivers obviously fits in with these descriptions, the appellations 'lost' Saraswati has often been applied to this once mighty historical river.

There is considerable literature on the subject trying to identify the Saraswati and to explain the desiccation of this region. A variety of hypotheses, often conflicting, have been put forth by various scholars like Oldham (1874), Krishnan (1952), Wadia (1975), Singh (1952), Stein (1942) and Indras (1967). Inadequacy of data has obviously lent itself to a variety of interpretations. To have a fresh look a the problem, Landsat imagery has been used for delineating the palaeo-channels of the Satluj, the Yamuna and the Saraswati so as to unravel the mystery of the 'lost' Saraswati. We find that the Landsat imagery with its synoptic views provides quite clear evidence for the delineation of the palaeo-channels and hence the course of the Saraswati.

---

* Physicists working at the Physical Research Laboratory, Ahmedabad with D.P., Agrawal, who is considered an authority on radio-carbon dating in Indian archaeology.

Techniques

The present study is essentially based on visual interpretation of the Landsat Imagery pertaining to the period 1972-77, in a variety of forms and formats. The Imagery used here comprises multispectral scanner (MSS) data in four spectral bands (0.5-0.6, 0.6-0.7, 0.7-0.8, and 0.8-1.1 um). In the interpretation of this imagery the enhancement techniques comprising enlargements, colour comprises prepared by colour additive viewer and the Diazo technique, density slicing, grey scale conversion, contrast stretching, band ratioing, using both the diapositives as well as the negatives, have been used (Sood *et al* 1978).

Apart from black-and-white paper prints and their mosaics, the negatives and diapositives in 70 -mm and 23-cm format were enlarged to 1:250,000 scale topographical maps supplied by the Survey of India.

The palaeo-channels, in most of the cases, stand out clearly because of the vegetation patterns on their beds. In other cases, the enhancement techniques help in delineating such channels.

Since the Landsat images any scene on the earth's surface every 18 days, a comparison of multidate imagery helped in making use of the seasonal effects also in demarcating these palaeo-channels.

River Systems

The present rive systems of the Satluj-Yamuna Divide which have a bearing on the subjects are the Satluj, the Ghaggar, the Saraswati, the Markanda, the Chautang, the Yamuna and their tributaries.

The rivers Satluj and Yamuna are perennial rivers, rising from the Himalayas and fed by glaciers. The rivers Ghaggar, Saraswati, Markanda and Chautang all rise from the Siwalik Hills and are non-perennial. They flow mainly during the monsoon. At present none of them reaches the sea or joins any major river as a tributary.

These river systems can be grouped into two main systems : (i) The Satluj System, and (ii) The Ghaggar System.

The Satluj System

Rising in the Himalayas, the present Satluj River takes a sharp, almost right-angled, turn to the west near Ropar. It continues to flow westward for more than 150 km and is then joined by the Beas, which comes from the northeast, near Harike. Only after this confluence the Satluj turns southwest (Fig. 1)

The study of Landsat imagery brings out the following:

(i) The sharp westward right-angled bend (Fig.2) in the course of the Satluj is suggestive of its diversion in the past, as at the point of

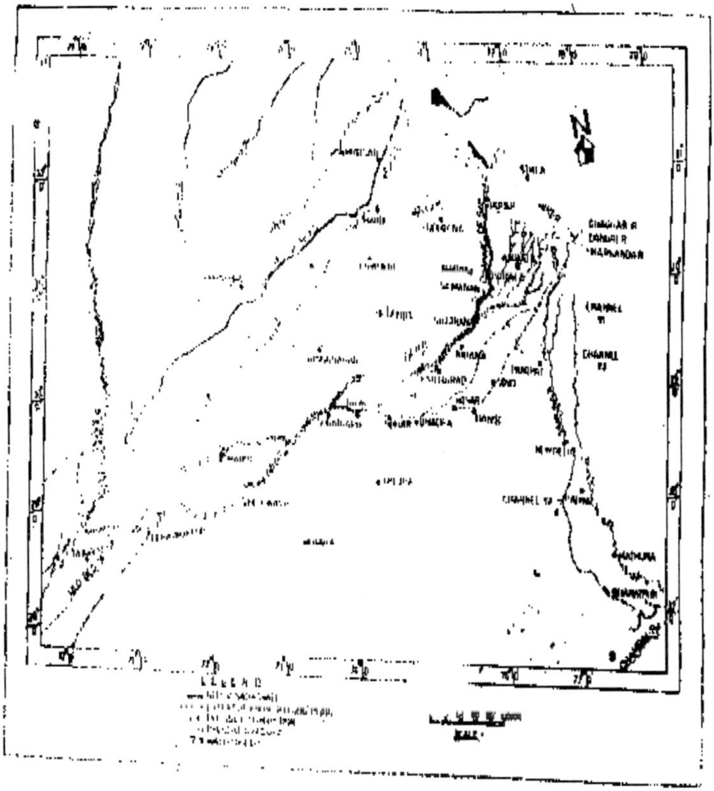

Fig. 1. *Northwestern Indian subcontinent with its present river system and the major palaeo-channels as deciphered from the Landsat imagery*

river capture or stream diversion similar elbows develop. No physical obstruction has been reported which could be responsible for this diversion.

(ii) There is sudden widening of the Ghaggar Valley about 25 km south of Patiala which is obviously a misfit if we take into account the considerably narrow bed of the Ghaggar upstream. This sudden widening can be explained only if a major tributary was joining the Ghaggar at this place. The satellite imagery does show a major palaeo-channel joining the Ghaggar here (Fig. 3).

Thus we see that both the sudden diversion of the Satluj westward and the abrupt widening of the Ghaggar bed south of Patiala can be explained only if we assume that the Satluj was coming through the palaeo-channel into the Ghaggar system at some point of time in the past. Our observations are supported by the field data of Singh (1952)

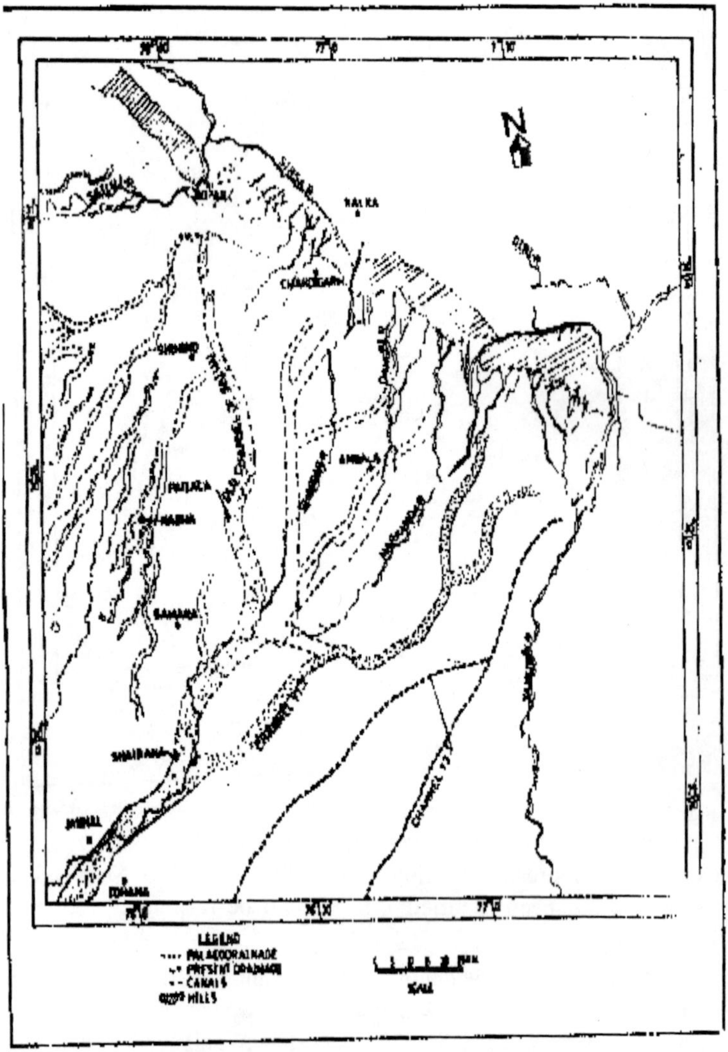

Fig. 2 *A detailed delineation of the present river and the palaeo-channels of the Sutlej and the Yamuna joining the old bed of the Saraswati.*

who mentions a channel starting near Ropar and leading towards Tohana (29.3-5N, 75.5-5E).

The area along this old course of the Satluj is called 'dhaia' meaning an upland or a high band (Singh 1952).

For the diversion of the Satluj three main causes could be responsible.

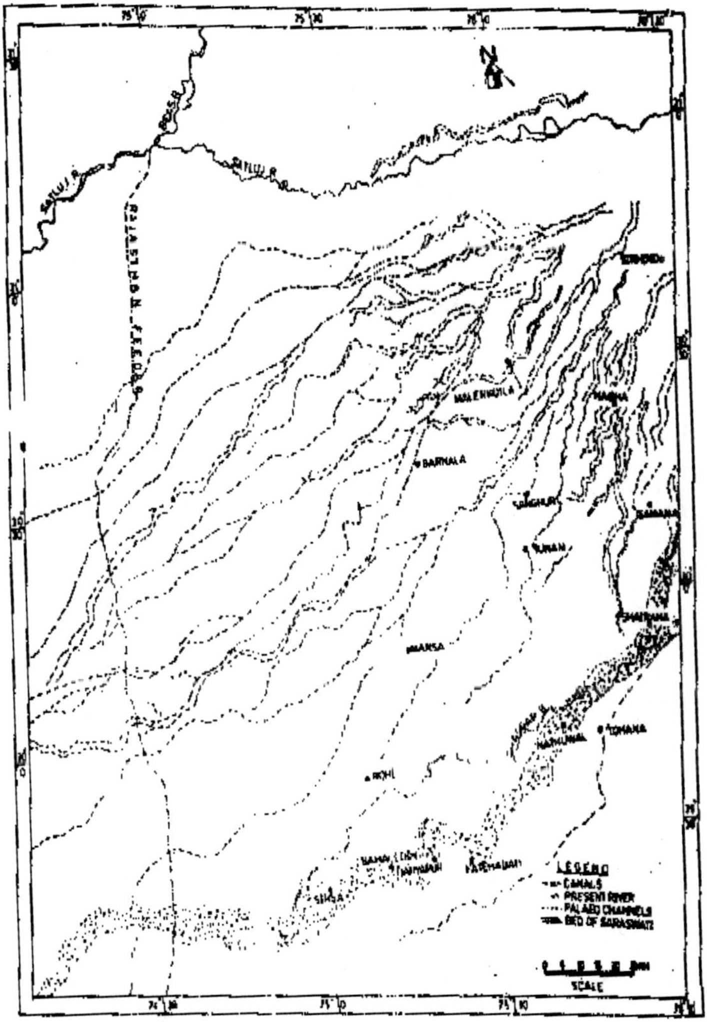

Fig. 3. Braided palaeo-channels of the Satluj lying between the present Satluj and the old Saraswati bed. The present Ghaggar can also be seen in the figure.

(i) Tectonic uplift which forced the Satluj to abandon its channel and to start flowing westward.

(ii) Capture of the Satluj by a tributary of the river Beas through headward erosion; and

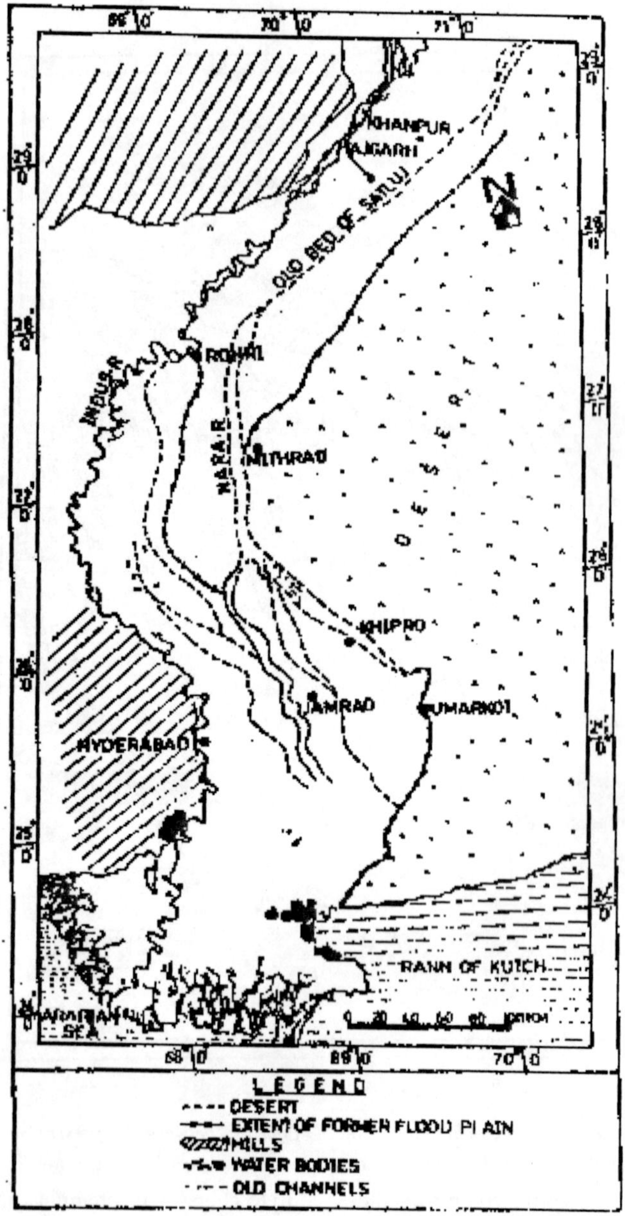

Fig. 4 Mapping of the Saraswati-Nara-Rann of Kutch connection from the satellite imagery. The Map shows that the Saraswati debouched into the Rann of Kutch through Nara.

(iii) Existence of a fault through which the Satluj diverted.

The physiography of the region shows that there is a depression westward (elevation less that 230 m) of the old Satluj bed and a corresponding uplift eastward (elevation more than 250 m). This may have gradually forced the Satluj to flow through its present channel. It is amply demonstrated by the multitude of small channels (Fig. 4) into which the Satluj braided till it found its present channel (Figs. 3 and 4). If one examines the old bed of the Ghaggar (Saraswati) it shows a peculiar feature: it tends to flow along straight lines joined together at sharp angles (Figs. 1 and 3). Obviously, this reflects a structural control as old Ghaggar seems to have flowed into an unstable channel controlled by the lineaments, probably enechelon faults. It might have required only a little tectonic movement to disturb its previous course and force it into its present channel.

Our studies thus show that the Satluj was the main tributary of the Ghaggar and that subsequently the tectonic movements may have forced the Satluj westward and the Ghaggar dried.

Whilhelmy (1969) considered the second alternative, i.e., river capture. The Satudri might have been a tributary of the Vipasa (Beas) and through headward erosion captured the waters of the river coming down the Himalayas near Ropar. Tectonic movements may have aided the river capture.

The braiding of the Satluj seems to have been echoed in a legend related in the *Mahabharata* which says that when Vasishtha threw himself into the Satluj to commit suicide, the river broke up into a hundred channels (Oldham 1874).

We have also examined the Landsat imagery of the Indus system and it appears that the confluence of the Satluj with the Indus may not be an ancient feature. The palaeo-channel of the river Beas, which is quite conspicuous in Landsat Imagery, joined the Indus independent of the Satluj (Fig. 1). There is a distinct palaeo channel which seems to suggest that the Satluj flowed through the Nara directly into the Rann of Kutch (Figs. 3 and 4.)

The Ghaggar System

We summarise below our observations on the Ghaggar system from the analysis of Landsat imagery.

(i) The ancient bed of the Ghaggar has a constant width of about 6 to 8 km from Shatrana in Punjab to Marot in Pakistan (Figs. 1 and 2). The bed stands out very clearly having a dark tone in the black-and-white imagery and reddish one in false colour composites.

(ii) There is a clear palaeo-channel southeast of the river Markanda which joins the ancient bed of the Ghaggar near Shatrana Channel Y1 (1 and 2). The present Saraswati mostly flows through this channel.

(iii) Another channel, Y2, which corresponds to the present Chautang seems to join the Ghaggar near Suratgarh (Fig. 1).

(iv) Near Anupgarh the ancient Ghaggar bed bifurcates and both the palaeo-channels come to an abrupt end; the upper one terminates near Marot and the lower one near Beriwala (Figs. 1 and 2)

These two terminal channels of the Ghaggar seem to disappear in a depression which is suggested by salt encrustation and the physiography of the area.

There is no indication of any palaeo-channel connecting the ancient Ghaggar with the Indus or the Luni.

Discussion

The vast expanse (6-8 km wide) of the Ghaggar bed can be explained only by assuming that some major tributaries were flowing into it in the past. It was mentioned earlier that at some point of time the Satluj was also flowing through it. The other major river system contributing waters to the Ghaggar may have been some prior-channel of the Yamuna. The evidence regarding the palaeo-channels of the Satluj-Yamuna Divide can be interpreted in the following manner. The three palaeo-channels Y1, Y2 and Y3 shown in Fig. 1. represent courses of some sizable ancient river which flowed south-east of the river Markanda and into the Ghaggar or into the Chambal during different periods. Channel Y1 joined the ancient bed of Ghaggar, Channel Y2 flowed into Chautang (Drishadvati) and Channel Y3 flowed through the present course of the Yamuna down to Delhi and then connected the small lakes south-eastward, past Bharatpur, and finally joined, probably, the Chambal. One could give this vagrant river the name of Palaeo-Yamuna. It would, therefore, mean that the Palaeo-Yamuna changed its course three times before assuming the present one. In the first instance it flowed through Channel Y1 into the ancient Ghaggar. Later on, it flowed through Channel Y2, which includes the present Chautang, and met the Ghaggar near Suratgarh. The third time it went southward and passed through the Channel Y3, joining the Ganga through the Chambal.

We are working with the archaeologists to date these episodes in the life of the Palaeo-Yamuna. The available data shows that the Channel Y3 of the palaeo-Yamuna was alive during the Painted Grey Ware (PGW) period (c. 800-400 BC) as indicated by the distribution of the PGW sites on its bank (Gupta *et al* 1977). Both the Chautang and the Ghaggar beds have archaeological mounds on their banks (Pande 1977; Dikshit 1977).

The Ghaggar continued to be a living river during the pre-Harappan (c. 2500-200 BC) and the Harappan times (c. 2200-1700 BC) radiocarbon dates). Even during the PGW times, there is some indication of habitation along the palaeo-channel, though the PGW mounds follow a very narrow river bed, perhaps indicating a dwindling water supply. The archaeological evidence for dating the Chautang is not very definite yet, though the late Harappan mounds along it appear to be a clear indication that it was a living river during at least the late Harappan time (c. 1700-1000 BC). Thus we see that during the last 5000 yeas or so the rivers of this area have changed their courses several times.

The history of these palaeo-channels seems to be fairly clear now, but there are still some lacunae in our knowledge as to the final date of the ancient Ghaggar. The satellite imagery seems to show as if it debouched into sea or a lake near Marot or Beriwala (Fig. 1). But to bring the sea so far inland in the mid-Holocene times looks quite improbable. The work of Agrawal and Guzder (1972) and S.K. Gupta (1972) on the western coast shows that the magnitude of the mid-Holocene marine transgression was only of the order about +5 metres from the present mean sea-level. Therefore we have to look for some other interpretation.

A profile of the land elevation shows that the Ghaggar ends in a depression: both westward and north-eastward the land elevation rises. For miles and miles around Marot one finds numerous place names with a suffix *toba*, which in the local language means a *playa*. This area may have been turned into a large lake in the first instance but desiccation led to the formation of *playas*. It is obviously improbable for such a mighty river to vanish into a shallow depression in its heyday. There is, therefore, a good possibility that the Ghaggar flowed into the Nara and further into the Rann of Kutch without joining the Indus.

The chain of tectonic events which diverted the Satluj westward and the Palaeo-Yamuna south-eastward was perhaps also responsible for the subsidence near Marot and Beriwala into which the Ghaggar seems to have vanished. This alone can explain the 'death' of such a mighty river into a lake because its main feeders, the Satluj and the Palaeo-Yamuna, were weaned away from it by the Indus and the Ganga, respectively.

Raikes published a paper in *Antiquity* in 1968 on the vagrancy of the Yamuna. He explained the vagrancy of the Yamuna under the influence of *Coriolis* force. He tabulated six shifts of the Yamuna during the period 2500 BC-AD 500 giving exact dates. It is difficult to understand as to why Coriolis force should affect the river Yamuna only and not other rivers around the world and why only during particular periods. We, however, feel the necessity of pointing out that the whole of the north-western India has to be taken into consideration to understand the vagrancy of practically all the rivers in this region. The causes for this vagrancy lie in neotectonism shown by the enechelon nature of the structural control along the main river systems in this area. The evidence for neotectonism is very clear in the rock-cut terraces on the upper reaches of the Markanda, as pointed by Rajaguru (1977). We have further evidence of earthquakes and abandonment of the site from the Kalibangan excavations (Lal 1979). The *Mahabharata* episode of Vashishtha mentioned earlier appears to be an echo of the same tectonism.

The short paper by Gose *et al* (1980) about the fluvial sedimentation in the Rajasthan desert covers palaeo-channel configurations, their chronology and their relationship with the palaeoclimatic changes. Our detailed study of the satellite imagery, employing all the available techniques, has however not shown any palaeo-channel which could join the river Luni with the old Ghaggar bed. We have therefore given the original Landsat imagery mosaic (Fig.2) so that our maps can be tallied with the observational data.

Conclusions

Palaeo-environmental changes in the north-western subcontinent have been caused by climatic, tectonic and anthropogenic factors. Tectonic factors assumed such overwhelming importance only because the major channels like those of the Saraswati were structurally controlled by enechelon faults. It was because of this reason that even relatively minor tectonic movements caused considerable changes in the configuration of the palaeo-channels. The distribution of the archaeological sites was also determined by the vagrancy of these rivers.

As discussed above, during the period 4-5 millennia BC north-western Rajasthan was a much greener place with the Saraswati flowing through it. Some of the present rivers joined to make the Saraswati a mighty river which probably discharged into the sea (Rann of Kutch) through the Nara, without joining the Indus.

We have thus shown that the Satluj flowed into the Ghaggar once. Some ancient version of the Yamuna (we termed it Palaeo-Yamuna) changed its course, at least three times, before joining the Ganga through its present course.

Notes & References

Agarwal, D.P. and Guzder, S. 1972. *Palaeobotanist* Vol.21, 216.

Dikshit, K.N. 1977, *Ecology and Archaeology of Western India,* eds. D.P. Agarwal and B.M. Pande (New Delhi: Concept Pub.) 61.

Ghose, B. Amal Kar and Zahid Husain 1980: *Man and Environment* Vol. 4, 8.

Ghosh, A. 1952. *Bull. Natl. Inst. Sct. India,* Vol. 1, 37.

Gupta, S.K. 1972, *J. Goel* Vol. 80, 357.

Gupta S.P., Shashi Asthana and Amarendra Nath 1977. *Ecology and Archaeology of Western India,* eds. D.P. Agarwal and B.M. Pande (New Delhi: Concept Pub. 79)

Indras 1967, *Lost Saraswati* (Vallabh Vidyanagar Sardar Patel University)

Krishnan, M.S. 1952. *Bull. Nati. Inst. Sct. India,* Vol. 1, 19.

Lal, B.B. 1979, *Essays in Indian Protohistory,* eds. D.P. Agarwal and D.K. Chakrabarti (New Delhi, Concept Pub.) 65.

Oldham, C.F. 1874, *Calcutta review,* Vol. 59, 1.

Pande, B.M. 1977, *Ecology and Archaeology of Western India,* eds. D.P. Agarwal and B.M. Pande (New Delhi, Concept Pub.) 55.

Raikes, R.L. 1968, *Antiquity,* Vol. 42, 286.

Rajaguru, S.N. 1977, *Ecology and Archaeology of Western India,* eds. D.P. Agarwal and B.M. Pande (New Delhi, Concept Pub.) 70.

Schumm, S.A. 1971. *River Mechanics,* ed. H.W. Shen (Fort Collins: H.W. Shen) Vol. 1, 4-1.

Singh, Gurdev 1952. *The Geography,* Vol. 5, 27.

Singh, S. and Ghose, B. 1977. *Ecology and Archaeology of Western India,* eds. D.P. Agarwal and B.M. Pande (New Delhi, Concept Pub.) 135.

Sood, R.K. Baldev Sahai and Subramanyam V. 1978, *Proceedings of Symposium on Morphology and Evolution of Landforms* (Delhi: Department of Geology, University of Delhi) 131.

Stein, A. 1942 *Geographical Journal,* Vol. 99, 173.

Wadia, D.N. 1976. *Geology of India* (New Delhi, Tata McGraw Hill) 52.

Whilhelmy, H. 1969, *Z. Geomorphol. Suppl.* Vol. 8, 76.

29

The Puzzle of Origins

New Researches in History of Mathematics and Ancient Ecology

Navaratna S. Rajaram*

On virtually no evidence at all, Frederick Max Muller, a great Sanskrit scholar but extraordinarily ignorant of science, propounded a chronology that placed the invasion shortly after 1500 BC, and assigned the composition of the *Rig Veda* to 1200 BC. Max Muller's formulation was severely criticised by several scholars including such luminaries as William Whitney and Horace Heyman Wilson as being entirely conjectural and baseless. Goldstucker in particular noted that Max Muller was guided in his chronology by his Biblical belief that the world was created on October 23, 4004 BC. It is helpful to note that such outstanding scholars as Hermann Jacobi and Moritz Winternitz refused to subscribe to the Aryan invasion theory. But due to a combination of factors, notably an absence of serious debate and Max Muller's growing prestige and influence, his theory and chronology became enshrined as 'official' history. This is still the case not only in Indian history books, but also in such supposedly authoritative sources as the *Encyclopaedia Britannica.*

In Max Muller's defence it must be noted that he himself later repudiated his chronology, in particular acknowledging: "*Whether the Vdic hymns were composed 1000 or 1500, 2000 or 3000 BC, no power on earth will ever determine.*" Further, he and his contemporaries were working without the aid of the profuse archaeological, satellite and other scientific data and methods that we now take for granted. No less a factor was Max Muller's own delicate political position in England as a

---

* Dr. Navaratna S. Rajaram, Scientist; over the past twenty years held faculty and research positions in several American Universities and high technology companies; worked extensively in the fields of Artificial Intelligence and Robaries; had been an advisor to the NASA, (U.S.A). Presently engaged in research on the history of Mathematics, Sciences as well as *Vedic* Literature.

former German nationalist employed by the British, a situation that was aggravated following German unification in 1871 when Germany began to be perceived as a major threat to British colonial ambitions. Regrettably, even so great a scholar as Max Muller had to be cautions in dealing with his British sponsors and their sensibilities vis a vis Indian polity and native aspirations. Academic freedom is a relatively modern luxury.[1]

Returning to Max Muller's chronology, we must note that this has had an important but largely unappreciated consequence. All subsequent discoveries have been *interpreted* in terms of the Aryan invasion theory, taking this theory to be a proven fact. The most striking of these has been the interpretation of the now famous Harappan ruins of the Indus Valley to be the result of the Aryan invasion and the Aryan-Dravidian conflicts. In this the Aryan invasion was treated as a historical fact, and the ruins of Harappa and Mohenjo-Daro were interpreted as the result of the Aryan-Dravidian wars. This interpretation was itself later offered as proof of the invasion.

Harappans were *Vedic* People

This is not the place to go into the various controversies that are now mainly of historical interest. More systematic examination of the archaeological remains has shown that the Harappans were part of the *Vedic* culture. Preconceived notions about the Aryan invasion and poor familiarity with the Hindu tradition and practices had led early excavators, notably, John Marshall and Mortimer Wheeler, to seriously misinterpret their archaeological finds. S.R. Rao, one of the world's leading authorities on Harappan archaeology observed:

> The negative evidence in the form of absence of the horse and rice in the Indus Civilization which was taken as evidence of its Dravidian origin is no more tenable in view of the occurrence of horse bones and rice at Lothal, Kalibangan, Surkotada and Ropar in India and Mohenjo-Daro in Pakistan. On the other hand, there is enough positive evidence in support of the religious rites of the Harappans being similar to those of the *Vedic* Aryans. Their religious motifs, deities and sacrificial altars bespeak of Aryan faith. (Talageri 1993, p. vii).

There is now further evidence showing connections between the late *Vedic Sutra* literature and archaeological remains, particularly the existence of fire altars and sacrificial altars at various Harappan sites from the borders of Iran all across northern India. These altars and the rites pertaining to them have been described in great detail in such later *Vedic* literature as the *Brahmanas* and the *Sutras*. All these bear testimony to the fact that the inhabitants of the Harappan world were culturally part of the *Vedic* Aryan fold. But most significantly, the famous mathematical texts known as the *Sulbasutras* were created explicitly to serve as manuals in the design and construction of such altars.

Thus the Aryan invasion theory would have us believe that the construction of *Vedic* altars was the work of the Harappan natives, while the *instructions* for building them were brought in by the invading Aryans. This is too preposterous a conclusion to be taken seriously. As a consequence of such absurdities, the Aryan invasion theory is no longer taken seriously by scholars today, except for a few diehard fanatics and others completely ignorant of modern research. It is only a matter of time before its true believers find themselves occupying the fringes.

Two puzzles of the Ancient World

Once we recognize the Harappans to have been part of the same continuous cultural spectrum of which the *Vedas* were part, the whole perspective shifts to the rise, decline and fall of the *Vedic* Harappan society. There is now sufficient evidence to assign the greater part of the Harappan civilization to the *Vedic Sutra* period.[2] A particularly intriguing consequence of recent research—the same research that has discredited the Aryan invasion model of history—has been to lend substance to traditional Indian accounts of their own history, at least in broad terms. In light of the fiasco with the Aryan invasion model of history, it would be extremely unwise, if not intellectually irresponsible to disregard all tradition and start a new model out of thin air. Such adventurism should be resisted at all costs. Scientific finds can only be the bare bones; it can never be the skeleton, let alone the whole body. With this perspective in hand, we can begin to address these two ancient puzzles.

The first puzzle as I noted is the collapse of the Harappan world around 2000 BC. At first its end was placed around 1500 BC, but this was merely a concession to the views of linguists and their date of 1500 BC for their postulated Aryan invasion. Subsequent scientific analysis of various sites found it to be too late. Even so staunch an invasionist as Mortimer Wheeler could not find support for a date later than 1700 BC. On the basis of additional data and tests in the years since, a date not later than about 1900 BC for the collapse of the 'mature' Harappan culture is now widely accepted. This may now have to be pushed back by at least a century on the basis of what has just come to light about the collapse of the neighbouring Akkadian empire of Sumeria and other ancient societies. The basic unanswered question is: what could have caused the simultaneous decline and end of nearly all the great centers of the farflung Harappan empire spread over an area exceeding a million and a half square kilometers. We now know that this was part of a global phenomenon, from India to Egypt and beyond. The society most severely affected seems to have been Akkadia, the name given to the Sumerian empire founded by Saragon of Akkad. What could have caused the near simultaneous collapse of civilizations over such a vast belt?

Seidenberg's Researches in the History of Mathematics

The second puzzle relates to the origin and spread of ancient mathematics. We must first note that the account of ancient Indian mathematics found in most history books is no longer tenable in view of Seidenberg's epoch-making research into the origins of mathematics, as well as fresh and more rational interpretations of Indus archaeology. Most history books still trace the origins of Indian mathematics to Greece following Alexander's invasion in 326 BC. As S.R. Rao's account makes clear (Rao 1991, P 2-3), the Harappan civilization c. 3000-2000 BC was the greatest urban civilization of antiquity. Neither Egypt nor Mesopotamia show any signs of urban planning that are even remotely comparable to the Harappan. The very existence of elaborately planned cities and harbours like Harappa, Mohenjo-Daro, Lothal and several others is evidence of no small facility with mathematics. The world had to wait more than two thousand years, until the rise of the Roman empire, before town planning and sanitation could attain the same levels as in the Harappan cities. It is inconceivable that such a great urban civilization could have been built and sustained for many centuries over a vast region without knowledge of mathematics. Those who claim otherwise are only exhibiting their ignorance of the sciences. A great civilization like the Harappan is impossible without supporting infrastructure in science and technology. And mathematics is the most basic of all the sciences.

As far as the mathematical basis of the Harappan civilization is concerned, there should be no mystery at all. While we do find statements of a mathematical nature in *the Rig Veda* itself, there is nothing in them to suggest the degree of sophistication necessary to sustain a great civilization like the Harappan. The *Brāhmanās,* notably the *Satapatha* and the *Taittiriya,* are more explicit, but we encounter systematic mathematical treatises for the first time in the *Sutra* literature that came soon after. These are the celebrated *Sulbasutras,* or the *Sulbas*, that were composed to serve as technical adjuncts to the *Srauta* part of the *Kalpasutras.* The *Sulbas* contain technical instructions for the design and construction of various altars; many examples of such altars have indeed been found among the Harappan ruins from the borders of Iran to Lothal in Gujarat. The architectural achievements of the great Harappan civilization were therefore secular manifestations of the 'ritual mathematics' of the *Sulbas* to use Seidenberg's interesting phrase. Thus there can be hardly any doubt at all that the mathematics of the *Sulbas* must already have bene in existence by the time the great Harappan settlements began to be planned. This means that the earliest layer of the *Sulba*, such as the *Sulba* of Baudhayana must have come to being not much later than 3000 BC. This date for the early *Sutra* literature is supported also by astronomy.[3]

Mathematics in *Sulba Sutras*

Until quite recently, the mathematics of the *Sulbas* failed to receive the attention it merits. To begin with they were dated absurdly late by scientifically ignorant scholars like Weber and Keith who wanted to trace everything to Greece. Second, no one seemed to raise the very basic question of the Harappan indebtedness to the mathematics of the *Sulbas*, not even Seidenberg, even though he established that the *Sulbas* are the source of all ancient mathematics—from Egypt to Mesopotamia to Pythagorean Greece. More than a century ago, Thibaut and Cantor had noted connections between the mathematics of India, Egypt and Greece but refrained from expressing the obvious conclusion. In fact Cantor went so far as to admit that he did not like the idea that in geometry, the Greeks were pupils of the Indians. It ran directly counter to the idea of the 'Greek miracle', a favourite fantasy of nineteenth century European romantic imagination. But those of us unromantic souls who do not believe in miracles are forced to look elsewhere for explanations.

It was left to B.B. Datta in 1934 to clearly express probably for the first time that Greek geometry was a derivative of the *Sulba*. But Datta was ahead of his time, and his chronology also ran against the then current orthodox view that held 1200 BC as the date of the *Rig Veda*. In addition, his work took no notice of Egyptian or Baylonian mathematics and was therefore somewhat limited in scope. Finally, it was an American mathematician, the late A. Seidenberg, who established the *Sulbassutras* to be the source of all known ancient mathematics—from India to Babylonia to Egypt to Pythagorean Greece.

In view of the epochal significance of Seidenberg's work, it is useful to briefly summarize the findings expressed in his two great papers. A monumental research program stretching over two decades enabled Seidenberg (1978) to reach the following momentous conclusions:

1. A common source for the Pythagorean and *Vedic* mathematics (i.e., the *Sulbasutras*) is to be sought either in the *Vedic* mathematics[4] or in an older mathematics very much like it.

2. The view that *Vedic* mathematics is a derivative of Old-Babylonia having been rejected, a common source for these mathematics, different from old-Babylonia of 1700 BC was indicated.

3. Thus what are regarded as the two main sources of Western mathematics, namely Pythagorean mathematics and Old-Babylonian mathematics, both flow from a still older source.

Babylonia and Greece Learnt from India

A question then naturally arises: what was this older common source like? Seidenberg himself provided the answer:

> ...its mathematics was very much like what we see in the *sulbasutras.* In the first place, it was associated with ritual. Second there was no dichotomy between number and magnitude:...
>
> In geometry it knew the Theorem of Pythagoras and how to convert a rectangle into a square. It knew the isosceles trapezoid and how to compute its area. It had a facility with whole numbers and knew some number theory centered on the existence of Pythagorean triples. It had a canonical solution for the circulature of the square; and in its attempts to square the circle, it learned to compute a square root.

This is none other than the *Sulba.* The source therefore is the *Sulba* itself, or what Seidenberg calls '*Vedic* mathematics'. But his most remarkable findings for ancient history and history of mathematics, though he himself seemed to have missed their full import, were the following.

> The arithmetical tendencies here encountered [in the *Sulbas*] were expanded, and in connection with the observations on the rectangle led to Babylonian mathematics.
>
> A contrary tendency, namely, a concern for exactness of thought (or the myth of its importance), together with a recognition that arithmetic methods are not exact, led to Pythagorean mathematics.

My own study, still somewhat preliminary, suggests that the Old-Babylonians did not receive the essentials of their mathematics from Egypt, but via a different route, possibly Sumeria or even the post-Harappan India.[5] I have also shown elsewhere (Rajaram 1994) that the use of pyramids as funerary edifices in early Egypt is traceable to the *Baudhayana Sulba,* in particular, to the pyramid shaped altar known as the *Samasāna-cit* described therein.

I have found it worthwhile to quote in *extensio* from Seidenberg's great paper. Though recognized among mathematicians and historians of science as a major contribution, his work, not to speak of its momentous implications, remains largely unknown among Indian historians, and in fact, among historians in general. Part of it is doubtlessly attributable to the technical nature of Seidenberg's papers; they are written for fellow mathematicians. (In the present paper I have left out the technical parts and have made, or at least tried to make my explanations accessible to the general reader). At the same time, his findings, or at least the implications of it, met with immediate resistance from a few Sanskrit scholars he seems to have consulted. Seidenberg himself complained:

> Sanskrit scholars do not give me a date so far back as 1700 BC (for the *Sulbasūtras*). Therefore I *postulate* a pre-Old-Babylonian source for the kind of geometric rituals we see preserved in the *Sulbasutras*, or at least for the mathematics involved in these rituals. (Original emphasis).

Clues from Egyptian Mathematics

It creates an even bigger problem when we consider Egyptian mathematics which forces one to place the *Sulbas* firmly before 2100 BC. Seidenberg found himself on the horns of a dilemma. As a mathematician he saw that his study left him no other conclusion possible. At the same time, not being a Sanskrit scholar he felt himself in no position to challenge the entrenched dogma of the Aryan invasion and the 1200 BC date for the *Rig Veda.* So he was forced to make such a statement as a compromise. But mathematics allows no compromises: it is at once the most exact and the most exacting of the exact sciences. Apparently he did not realize, or was reluctant to assert, that he had right before him a dramatic mathematical refutation of the Sanskrit scholars' claims and chronology! And yet he felt strongly enough about his own sense of mathematics to believe that he had shown the Sulbas to be the source of both the Old-Babylonian and the Pythagorean (Greek) mathematics to press his claim despite the objection of Sanskrit scholars. Reluctant though he was to overrule Sanskrit scholars, Seidenberg was even less willing to accommodate mathematical contradictions in his own work. As he himself had earlier noted, his work led to the following unequivocal conclusions:

> Hence we do not hesitate to place the *Vedic* altar rituals, or more exactly, rituals exactly like them, far back of 1700 BC.
>
> To summarize the argument: the elements of ancient geometry found in Egypt and Babylonia stem from a ritual system of the kind observed in the *Sulbasutras*. (Seidenberg 1962)

Who Borrowed from Whom?

The Egypt he refers to is of the Middle Kingdom of c. 2050-1800 BC. It was in fact my study of Seidenberg's work that led me to conclude that the Harappan civilization must presuppose knowledge of the mathematics of the *Baudhayana Sulba*, and therefore corresponds to the *Sutra* period. Even without the evidence of the *Vedic* altars, the indebtedness of the Egyptian Middle Kingdom to the *Sulbas* places the latter firmly before 2100 BC. One is saddened by the thought that at the time of his untimely death, Seidenberg was not aware of the details of Harappan archaeology. Had he known of it, his alert mind would surely have made the connection between the Harappan civilization and the mathematics of the *Sulbas*. It is also interesting to note that working from a completely different angle, K.D. Sethna made the Harappan-Sutra connection a decade before I found evidence for it on the basis of the mathematics of the *Sulbas*. *As a result of all these, the Harappan-Sutra-Sumeria equations should now be seen as beyond all doubt.* This now gives us a true sheet anchor for ancient history and chronology.

But this is not the end of difficulties for old theories. The conventional view had been that the origins of Greek mathematics are to be found in Babylonian mathematics. This view was based on the fact that a few numbers making up the so-called Pythagorean triples are found among Babylonian records. But a more detailed examination shows that the Greeks could not have derived their brand of geometry—technically known as geometric algebra—from these stray formulas from Babylonia or Egypt. (We can forget the 'Greek miracle'; there are no miracles in real life.)

The simple mathematical fact is: it is impossible to derive Pythagorean Greek geometry from the entirely computational arithmetic of Old-Babylonia. Thus the roots of Greek geometry are nowhere to be found in Babylonia. Then there is the problem of time—a vast gap of some 1400 years—after the Old-Babylonia of 1700 BC when we have no mathematical records at all from Babylonia, until we start picking up the threads again during the Seleucid period around 300 BC. The problem however is not primarily one of time, but of content and spirit. Greek and Old-Baylonian mathematics are as fundamentally mutually incommensurable as the circle and the square. But the picture changes at once if we include the *Sulba*. As Seidenberg notes:

> ...if one includes the *Vedic* mathematics, one will get quite a different perspective on ancient mathematics.
>
> The main issue is the origin of geometric algebra. The Sulbasutras have geometric algebra... Greece and India have a common heritage that cannot have derived from Old-Babylonia, i.e., Old-Babylonia of about 1700 BC.

This at once changes the whole perspective on ancient mathematics. Far from being a borrowing from Greece or Babylonia, Indian mathematics (*Sulbas*) must have been the source of both. This now stands revealed by the immutable logic of mathematics. A century of scholars have tried in vain to obscure the real facts by creating a mythical Aryan invasion and manipulating ancient chronologies. But now, thanks to archaeology and mathematics, and above all Seidenberg's monumental research, we know the *Sulbas* must have been the source.

But the mystery is only beginning. It is easy enough to understand that the highly practical-minded Egyptians and Babylonians chose only those parts of the *Sulbas* that were of practical interest to them. But why is there such a precipitous decline in quality as we go from the *Sulbas* to the Egyptian Middle Kingdom c. 2050 BC? Had the mighty *Sulba* tradition been irrevocably lost by the time the Eygptians found traces of it? And yet, how did the much later Pythagorean Greeks manage to get their hands on the philosophic part—the soul of the *Sulba*, so to speak—and build their own magnificent mathematical edifice upon it?

So here is the puzzle: what was it that made the flow of mathematics of the *Sulbas* take such circuitous route from India to Egypt and to Babylonia and suffer a severe degradation in quality in the process? And then, more than a thousand years later, how did it re-emerge in a near pristine form in Pythagorean Greece—much closer in content and spirit to the original *Sulbas* than what we find in Egypt and Old-Babylonia more than a thousand years earlier?

The cause of the first I think we know; for the second, the mysterious Greek-*Sulba* connection, I am afraid it is not really germane to the subject of the present article which is the fate of the ancient world.

Ancient Ecology

I: Decline and Fall of the Ancient World

As I noted earlier, one of thc mysteries of ancient civilizations is the cause of the sudden decline and disintegration of Harappan settlements spread over a vast area, over a relatively short period. At first it was attributed to the invading Aryans led by their leader (or God) Indra. At Mohenjo-Daro, Mortimer Wheeler picked up a piece of pottery and solemnly proclaimed: "Indra stands accused." His youthful subordinates were impressed, but it can now be seen for what it was—inexpensive theater. Also Wheeler who had just come back to archaeology from fighting in the Second World War was inclined to see battles and destruction at every site. We must however look elsewhere for the causes.

It is now clear that the collapse of the Harappan empire was part of a global phenomenon that affected the greater part of the ancient world in a belt from India to Egypt and beyond. The fact that the Saraswati was a dry river by 1900 BC has been used to place that date as the marker for the ending of the Harappan age. This is an inference in the right direction for we now know that it was loss of water that brought not only the Harappan, but also the neighbouring Akkadian empire to a close. The ecological picture however is far more complex, and the drying up of the Saraswati was part of a long process of increasing aridity that began more than a thousand years earlier (Street-Perrott and Perrott 1990). The *Vedic* Age and the Harappan civilization that followed upon it were apart of an enormously long 'boom-and-bust' hydrological cycle whose beginnings can be traced to the ending of the last Ice Age, c. 8000 BC. This now is indicated by two important recently completed studies.

The recent report of the French-American exploration in northern Mesopotamia has determined that the Akkadian empire ended in 2200 BC, the result of a prolonged drought that began at that date and persisted for nearly 300 years (Weiss, et. al. 1993). As they note in their study which is of obvious significance to ancient history:

> At approximately 2200 BC, occupants of Tell Leilan and Tell Brak (in northern Mesopotamia) were suddenly abandoned. . . At Tell Leilan, an occupational hiatus extending until reoccupation, historically dated at the beginning of period (1900 to 1728 BC), has been documented...
>
> (Weiss, et. al. 1993, p. 999).

There was thus a three hundred year hiatus until conditions turned benign again after this killing drought. By then the Amorites (of Hammurabi fame) had been firmly established in Mesopotamia, only to be themselves overthrown by the Kassites of India, in all probability displaced by the same catastrophe that ended the Akkadian empire. That this was part of an extensive climatic disaster that affected neighbouring societies also is clear from their momentous study. As the authors note:

> At 2200 BC, a marked increase in aridity and wind circulation, subsequent to a volcanic eruption, induced considerable degradation in land-use conditions. ....this abrupt climatic change evidently caused abandonment of Tell Leilan, regional desertion, and collapse of the Akkadian empire based in southern Mesopotamia. *Synchronous collapse in adjacent regions suggests that the impact of abrupt climatic change was extensive.* (Emphasis added: p. 995).

The Great Drought in 2200 B.C.

Whether a volcanic eruption was sufficient to trigger a drought so destructive is open to doubt; but whatever the cause of the drought, its effect now seems established beyond all doubt. The authors summarize their findings as follows:

> The abrupt climatic change that generated Habur hiatus I and the associated Akkadian-Gutti-Ur III collapse are synchronous with climate change and collapse phenomenon documented in the Aegean, Egypt, Palestine, and the Indus. The reoccupation of the Habur plains [in northern Mesopotamia] in the 19th century B.C., and the sudden emergence of centralized Amorite control...was evidently facilitated by the amelioration of climatic conditions...(p. 1002)

This should now help settle all arguments relating to the 'Aryan invasion' as the cause of the loss of Harappan sites. The scenario at Tell Leilan and Tell Brak with water starved populations deserting their sites leading to collapse being repeated in the Harappan society is all too easy to imagine. In fact, as S.R. Rao has noted:

> in Circa 1900 B.C. most of the mature Harappan sites were wiped out forcing the inhabitants to seek new lands for settlement. They seem to have left in great hurry and in small groups, seeking shelter initially on the eastern flank of the Satluj and the Ghaggar and gradually moving towards the Yamuna. The refugees from Mohenjo-Daro and southern sites in Sind fled to Saurashtra and later occupied the interior of the Peninsula. (Rao 1991, p.27)

This was the situation for three centuries following the Great Drought that began about 2200 BC. The 1900 BC date for the collapse of the mature Harappan phase may now have to be moved up by at least a century. But the important fact to note is the relatively rapid collapse of the far-flung Harappan empire. After this three century hiatus the empires began to breathe again in Egypt, Old-Babylonia and India. In India, the focus had long since shifted well to the East—to Magadha and other parts—less at the mercy of the killing drought.

This also explains the extremely antique look of the *Sulba*-based mathematics found in the Egyptian Middle Kingdom and Old-Babylonia that was so much a puzzle to Seidenberg and other historians of mathematics. We now know the answer: *the world that produced the Sulbasutras had long since vanished;* what remained in Egypt and Old-Babylonia were the scant remnants of the Age that produced such masterworks as the *Baudhayana Sulba.* So there was a cultural deterioration following the calamity. The great Harappan empire that had served as the bridge between India and the West had disappeared, the victim of this great natural calamity.

Sutra-Harappa-Sumerian World

As far as the principal chronological markers are concerned the picture now is as clear as it can be. The great Harappan empire—the *Mlecchadesha* of *Baudhayana* and the *Satapatha Brahmana,* the *Melukha* of the Akkadians—was no more than a shadow of itself by 2000 BC; the Akkadians and their neighbours the *Melukha* had fallen victim to the same calamity. This means that the Sutra-Harappa-Sumerian world ended before this epoch. In this, surely we have the answer to the cultural deterioration evident in the deterioration of mathematics and architectural sciences as we proceed from Harappan India to the Egyptian Middle Kingdom, and subsequently in Old-Babylonia also.

But the *Sulba* tradition remained in India, at least in those parts of India not affected by the killing drought, in the east, first in the Kuru-Pancala region and then moving further east to Kosala and Magadha. The cryptic *Sutra* style that produced at the hands of *Pānini*, *Patanjali* and *Baudhāyana* such masterpieces as the *Ashtadhyayi, Yogasūtra* and the *Sulbasūtra* was no longer in vogue and commentaries were being written to explain their contents. Even in Buddhistic times, the *Kalpasūstras* were known and taught to schoolboys as *Ketubha*.[6] The commentaries were no doubt needed to teach what by then were texts that were already becoming obscure and unintellegible.

Contacts however were beginning to be established between the Greeks and the Indians even before Alexander. The Pythagorean school, mainly religious and mystical with an interest in mathematics, found these commentaries a fertile source in their speculations. Here was a meeting of kindred spirits. There are indications that Indian priests practising exotic geometric rituals were resident in Greece at the time of the comic playwright Aristophenes (Rajaram 1994; Seidenberg 1978). *But until Indian scholars familiar with the ancient mystical traditions undertake serious study of the original Greek sources, the Indian-Greek connection will remain a closed book.* In all probability, Pagan Greece has been no less seriously misinterpreted by scholars of Christian Europe than India itself. Mathematics does offer a clue, but this can only be the tip of the iceberg. It is to be hoped that Indian scholars who still retain something of their ancient mystical traditions will undertake a serious study of the Greek sources in the original. The Pythagorean school, like the *Sulba of Baudhayana* combined religion and mathematics. They cannot properly be understood by looking at them solely as works of rational philosophy. That would be imposing a very modern perspective on a totally different world. Unfortunately, we have to leave this fascinating avenue unexplored at the present time.

While Egyptian and Old-Babylonian mathematical texts—mere fragment compared to the great *Sulbas*—allow us to establish some chronological markers, the unfolding ecological picture provides us the key to understanding the uniqueness of the *Vedic* Age.

Ancient Ecology

II: Ice Age as the Prelude to the *Vedic* Age?

As we just saw, the breakup of the Harappan civilization was part of a global ecological phenomenon over a vast belt from India to the Aegean. This we know was the *Sutra* period, c. 3000-2000 BC. We can conveniently take 2000 BC as marking the end of this age, at least as far as India is concerned. It is of course widely recognized that the Saraswati river went completely dry around 1900 BC. This has been used as a marker for the *Vedic* Age, in fact to 'prove' that the *Rig Veda* and the Aryans in India must have been in existence no later than that date. But as already noted, it is now clear that the drying up of the Saraswati was part of a far more complex desiccation process that culminated in the Great Drought of 2200-1900 BC. We now have evidence that the *Vedic* Saraswati that flowed from the "mountain to the sea" (as described in the *Rig Veda*) belongs to a much earlier epoch. A combination of data from the French SPOT satellite, and the Indo-French field study lets us know:

> ...we now know, thanks to the fieldwork of the Indo-French expedition, that when the protohistoric peoples (Harappans c. 3000 BC) settled in this area no large perennial river had flowed there for a long time. (Francfort 1992, p.91).

Why did Saraswati Disappear?

How are we then to reconcile this with the statements in the *Rig Veda*—there are more than fifty—that praise the mighty Saraswati as the greatest of rivers? There is a whole hymn devoted to the river. Vasishta (of the seventh *Mandala*) describes her as flowing from the "mountain to the sea". This can only mean that the *Rig Veda* belongs to an earlier age when the Saraswati was a great perennial river, long before the Proto-Harappan of c. 3000 BC. *The Rig Veda therefore describes the geography of North India as it was long before 3000 BC.* The fact that the Harappan sites came under the spell of encroaching aridity is supported also by this Indo-French satellite study (in addition to the French-American discussed in the previous section). What they found was not just a river valley civilization, but one with abundant *natural* supply of water.

> ...genuine, *natural,* hydrographic fossil systems, which are much smaller than the great Ghaggar (i.e., Saraswati), and almost invisible on the surface...can be examined by means of trial-pits. The canals are slightly carbonated depressions about 1 m deep and 300-500 m wide. *They mark the course of ancient waterways which were used, and in some places rerouted by man. These traces of small river channels, which were unknown until now, appear to have reached all of the archaeological sites...* Not only did they supply them with water but at the same time made-the surrounding area more fertile.... (Francfort 1992, pp. 98-99; my emphasis).

This then was the situation for many centuries before the Great Drought and global climatic change brought about the end of the Harappan and the Akkadian worlds. A civilization such as this one, nourished by generous natural water supply, and no doubt heavily populated would have been especially vulnerable to such an extended drought.

So the *Rig Veda* belongs to an age not only of abundant water when many areas now arid were fertile, but also of the perennial Saraswati that flowed from the "mountain to the sea". The Saraswati was fed by its two main tributaries—the Yamuna and the Sutlej, and also by numerous streams flowing into it. But these streams had also begun to run dry. In summary, the hydrology of the region was radically different from what it is today. As Farncfort notes:

> Archaeological sites are located not only on the banks of former natural waterways, but also at a distance from them, sometimes far away, and even in the middle of supposed large river beds. A good example of the latter case is seen in the Proto-Harappan site 114, which is situated on a dune in the middle of the Chautang river bed (one of the branches of the immense Ghaggar system), proving that it was established after a dry period of certain time... (Francfort 1992, p.95)

The 'immense Ghaggar system' was of course the *Vedic* Saraswati. All this fits neatly into a picture showing that the drought that struck in 2200 BC was the culmination of a long drying trend that began more than a thousand years earlier. One possible explanation is that it was the result of the depletion of ice caps that had accumulated to the north towards the end of the last Ice Age. The last Ice age ended c. 8000 BC, and for several millennia that followed there was a generous supply of water from the melting of its accumulated ice caps. As we shall soon see, there are several references to the cracking of melting ice caps in the *Rig Veda*. In fact the legend of Vrtra and his killing by the solar god Indra in all probability originated with this phenomenon.

New Light on Ancient Chronology

A digression: here is something else of interest of ancient chronology. The Chautang was the ancient Drishadvati channel through which the Yamuna used to flow into the Saraswati before changing its course and becoming a tributary of the Ganga. The Indo-French study shows that the Saraswati had already lost the Yamuna well before 3000 BC. That means the Saraswati was no longer the mighty river it used to be in *Rig Vedic* times. The *Mahabharata* describes the Saraswati as disappearing into the desert some forty-two days on horseback from its source. The Saraswati later lost the Sutlej also, resulting in its going completely dry by 1900 BC, possibly earlier. The *Mahabharata* therefore in all probability describes the Saraswati during the transition phase when it had lost the Yamuna but not yet the Sutlej. This again supports the traditional date for the *Mahabharata* War rather than the now popular c. 1400 BC. (See also Note 7).

Returning to the *Vedic* Age, the picture that one obtains, to the ending of the Harappan Civilization, is one of abundant water supply fed by the melting of glaciers that had accumulated during the last Ice Age. The fact that the *Rig Veda* seems to describe the discharge of waters by the melting of ice caps has of course been long recognized. In fact, even the rains are said to be caused by clouds 'breaking up', an obvious reference to the analogy suggested by the breaking and melting of ice caps. Yāska observes:

> Water is produced by cutting clouds into pieces.
>
> (*Nirukta*, 2.21)

Indra-Vrtra Conflict

An extraordinary explanation that can only be the result of observing water being released by the breaking of ice sheets. Of course, the periodic slaying of *Vrtra*—the 'coverer'—by the solar god Indra to release the water can be seen as a reference to the periodic melting of ice cover. This visible phenomenon was later applied to the rain-causing clouds. It is therefore not surprising that the word '*Vrtra*' was also extended to mean cloud. But this is not the only analogy to be found. The word *parvata* which is normally applied to a mountain, can also mean a cloud in the *Rig Veda*. This again suggests the analogy of ice being applied to clouds. Here are two remarkable verses attributed to seer Hiranyastūpa Angirasa, a very ancient sage:

> The body lay in the midst of waters that are neither still nor flowing. The waters press against the secret opening of the Vrtra (the coverer) who lay in deep darkness whose enemy is Indra.
>
> Mastered by the enemy, the waters held back like cattle restrained by a trader. Indra crushed the Vrtra and broke open the withholding outlet of the river.
>
> (*Rig Veda*, I.32.10-11)

It is difficult to give it any physical interpretation other than the release of the rivers by the cracking of the enveloping ice caps. There are many such images to be found throughout the *Rig Veda*. Note that though the Indra-Vrtra conflict was later mythologized in the *Brahmanas* and the *Puranic* literature, the *Rig Veda* refers to the periodic slaying of Vrtra. We now have archaeological and satellite data that lends support to this hoary literary account. I believe this constitutes overwhelming evidence that during the *Rig Vedic* times, the melting of the accumulated ice stock released abundant waters into the plains that later continued with gradually diminishing supply, almost to the end of the Harappan Age.

How about the connection between the *Vedic* Age and the Harappan civilization?—in particular the transition from the mainly spiritual *Vedic* society to the great material civilization of the Harappans. Here I believe a key is offered by the Vajasaneya-Taittiriya split immediately following the *Mahābhārata* War. We have already seen that the traditional date of 3102 BC for the *Mahabharata* War has the best empirical support.[7] The Age of Kali (coming at the end of the *Mahabharata* War) saw the destruction of ancient ruling houses, the split in the *Yajurvedic* tradition and the transition from the spiritual age of the *Vedas* to the intellectual age of the *Sutras* that included the Harappan civilization. It was truly the end of an epoch. The *Sutras* of *Panini* and *Baudhayana* are supreme monuments of the human intellect. Even *Patanjali's* great *Yogasūtra* is primarily an intellectual work that gives a rational explanation for the goals and results of the practice of *Yoga*.[8]

Rigvedic Age

Let me next try and reconstruct the scene as it was before the ending of the Harappan world. In this we see not only the emergence of the Harappan civilization, but also the seeds of the so-called Western civilization.

Let us begin with the situation as it was in the centuries following the *Mahabharata* War. It was the *Sutra* period, with two schools flourishing—the Eastern and the Western. In the Kuru-Pāncala country in the north but gradually gravitating towards the east was the Vājasneya school whose foremost exponent was Yajnavalkya followed by Āswalāyana and their successors. In the southwest was the great Taittiriya school whose foremost exponent was Yajnavalkya followed by Āswalāyana and their successors. In the southwest was the great Taittiriya school with *Baudhāyana* the leading figure. The northern school cultivated philosophy, while the Taittriya consolidated the natural sciences, especially mathematics. This mathematics, rooted though it was in the design of *Vedic* altars and religious ritual, was, as Seidenberg has clearly shown in his epoch making research, the seed from which sprang all ancient mathematics. This 'ritual mathematics', to use Seidenberg's expressive phrase, later gave rise to secular applications like architecture and town planning. It is therefore not surprising that millennium or so following the *Mahabharata* War should have been one of the great ages of urban architecture in the history of the world. It was the mathematics of the *Sulbas*—of *Baudhāyana*, *Āpastambha* and a host of others now lost—that made possible the great cities of the Harappan civilization, and the massive harbours like Lothal and other great engineering marvels. Without this scientific base there would have been no flowering of the Harappan civilization.

Without fairly sophisticated mathematics, especially without geometry of the kind found in the *Sulbas*, urban engineering feats of the kind achieved in design and construction of the Harappan cities are beyond conception. One does not get a great school of surgeons without knowledge of anatomy. A scientifically literate person hardly needs any further proof that the mathematics of the *Sulbasutras* must have existed before the great cities of the Harappan civilization were planned. These were not haphazard collections of dwellings, but carefully planned cities with water supply, drainage and streets laid out in regular geometric patterns. In the face of all this it is incredible that a century of scholars, not the least of whom have been present day Indian historians, should have believed that there was no geometrical knowledge in India before the advent of the Greeks under Alexander! It has to be wondered if there has been another instance of scientific ignorance to compare with this. It is like saying there were great surgeons who knew no anatomy.

This mathematics made its way to Egypt and Old-Babylonia as we have already seen. But compared to the scope and power to the geometric algebra of the *Sulbas*, the mathematics of Egypt and Babylonia are but fragments, little more than technical manuals of stray formulas and rules of thumb. They have lost also their religious roots, hardly surprising considering how far removed they are from the source in space and time. So by the time of the Egyptian Middle Kingdom (c. 2050 BC), there was little left of the vitality that made the *Sulba* of *Baudhayana* one of the great mathematical achievements in history. What then happened to bring this mighty *Sutra* tradition into eclipse? We now have the answer: the Harappan world ended with the great drought beginning in 2200 BC. This brings us to the end of the *Sūtra*-Harappa-Sumerian world, face-to-face with the ecological calamity that ended it.

Vajasaneya-Taittiriya Split

The *Rig Vedic* Age began auspiciously enough with nearly the whole of North India being fed by the melting of ice caps that had accumulated over millennia during the last Ice Age. Nothing however lasts for ever, and the accumulated deposits of ice began to be depleted. The great Ghaggar system—the mighty Saraswati—changed its course several times and eventually dried up. Already by the time of the *Mahābhārata* War, it was a shadow of itself, a sacred and nostalgic memory. The civilization then split into the Eastern and the Western, with the Kuru-Pāncāla and eventually Magadha becoming the center of orthodoxy. The Western people now produced the great works of rational thought—the great *sulbasutras* of *Baudhayana* and his school, the grammar of *Pānini* and school, but all deriving from a single mightly source—the *Rig Veda.*

This East-West split is also reflected I believe in the *Taittiriya-Vājasaneya*, or the so-called 'black' and 'white' schism found in the *Yajurveda* tradition. The many non-orthodox elements found in the *Taittiriya* can be accounted for by the Western non-Aryan influences. Tradition records that *Yajnavalkya*, the great master of philosophy extracted the '*Shukla*'—the white or the pure—portion from the impure *Taittiriya Samhita* by cleansing it of its non-orthodox elements. Here lies probably the root cause of Yājnavalkya's defection from his uncle Vaishampāyana and his teacher Vyāsa. The Eastern branch may have been more orthodox and 'pure', but it was also devoid of much of the free thinking vigor that is characteristic of the *Rig Veda.*

With this eastward and westward drift accompanied by the rational-spiritual split, the mighty *Vedic* tradition lost much of its former vitality. The expanding desert brought about by depleting water resources worsened the gulf between the two, and the western people were increasingly drawn into the orbit of the Middle Eastern Sumeria. This also resulted in the hardening of the orthodoxy in the East, giving rise to the rigidity found in the *Manusmriti* and other later works. It is then no accident that nearly all attempts at reform—like Buddhism and Jainism—should have originated in the East. (Zoroastrianism was earlier).

Ancient Chronology Reconstructed

The *Vedic* Age, and more particularly the *Rig Vedic* Age, was the beneficiary of this early age of water-abundance. North India then must indeed have been a veritable Garden of Eden. This gives us a first approximation for the chronology of the *Vedic* Age based on science. The date of early fourth millennium BC for the closing of the *Rig Veda* is seen to be largely in agreement with latest archaeological and satellite data. As the Indo-French study has shown, the perennial Saraswati that flowed "from the mountain to the sea" as described by Seer Vasishta of the seventh mandala had not flown for a long time when the so-called Proto-Harappans settled down in the area. This lends further support to the c. 3750 BC date for the ending of the *Rig Vedic* Age suggested by Hicks and Anderson (1990), derived also in Rajaram (1994) and Rajaram and Frawley (1994). We are now in a position to formulate the following *chronology*.

8000 BC	Ending of the last Ice Age
3750 BC	Ending of the *Rig Vedic* Age
3100 BC	Ending of the *Vedic* Age; the *Mahabharata* War; The *Taittiriya-Vajasaneya* split in the *Yajurveda* tradition

3000 BC	Beginning of the Harappa-*Sutra* period
2800-2200 BC	High Harappan-Sumerian civilization
2200 BC	Drought begins; the beginning of the end of the Harappan and the Akkadian civilizations
2200-1900 BC	End of the ancient world
1900 BC	Complete drying up of the Saraswati

Final Summary

In summary, the *Vedic Age*, more particularly the *Rig Vedic* Age, was a gift of nature's bounty, the beneficiary of a unique age of abundance brought about by the unique climatic conditions prevailing in the millennia that followed upon the ending of the last Ice Age.[9] The end of this idyllic Golden Age was also brought about by nature in the form of a gradual desiccation and global climatic change that climaxed in a severe drought in 2200 BC that lasted some three centuries. And this helps account for two historic puzzles: the simultaneous collapse of ancient civilizations over a vast belt from India to Egypt, and the precipitous decline in the quality of science as Indian mathematics made its way to Egypt and Old-Babylonia.

In addition, the latest data from archaeology and satellite photography led to the following conclusion: the *Rig Veda* belongs to a world before the rise of the civilizations of Egypt, Sumeria and the Indus Valley. It was a world before the dawn.

Acknowledgements : I am very grateful to Sri Mittal Ji for his invaluable help in locating several valuable sources of research. Professor Subhash Kak brought the important Indo-French Satellite cum field study to my attention for which also I am thankful. I have greatly benefitted from discussions with Dr. S.R. Rao who offered me insights into Indus archaeology from his unequalled storehouse of first-hand knowledge. At the same time it is fair to point out that Rao and Kak do not necessarily agree with all the details of my chronology though they too find no scientific or literary support for any invasion. Above all I am grateful to Professor K.D. Prithipaul for bringing to my attention the momentous implications of the French-American study in northern Mesopotamia. This article is dedicated to him.

Notes & References

1. This side of the history and evolution of the Aryan invasion theory, i.e. the role of German nationalism, British colonialism and Max Muller's personal ambition which led him to make certain 'bargains with the devil' is not widely known. Nor is it widely known (or is conveniently ignored) that he later repudiated his own theories. When I brought a few of these facts to public view in several popular articles and lectures, they were denounced by some Indian scholars as unnecessary and motivated by malice. By a strange twist of fate, the Aryan invasion theory, originally racial in origin, has now become a favourite of Indian Marxists who in the past forty years have erected an elaborate historical theory on the assumption that the Aryans and the *Vedas* are foreign to India. These were in the forefront of critics who attacked my efforts at historical revision. None of this can in any way alter the fact that science has now thoroughly discredited the theory. These are discussed in some detail in *Vedic Aryans and the Origins of Civilization* by Rajaram and Frawley, World Heritage Press, Ottawa and New Delhi.
2. On the basis of several such connections it is now all but certain that the Harappan civilization corresponds to the *Sutra* period. This was also the conclusion of K.D. Sethna on the basis of technical evidence, notably the presence of cotton found at Harappan sites. I was not aware of Sethna's pioneering work when I reached the same conclusion based on a comparison of the mathematics of the *Sulbas* and those of the Egyptian Middle Kingdom and Pre-Kassite Babylonia. (Following Seidenberg, I have also used the term 'Old-Babylonia' for the Pre-Kassite state ruled by the Amorites, c.1900-1750 BC).
3. This does not mean that the *Sutra* texts ascribed to the early figures like *Āswalāyana* and *Baudhāyana* have come down to us literally in the form in which they were composed. Unlike the *Vedas* which were sacred chants to be preserved in their pristine form, these were practical manuals that were revised and edited to reflect changes in language, usage, stellar positions (due to precession) and other factors. (The same incidentally is true of Shakespeare's plays. Even a superficial glance at the *Quatros* will convince any reader that they have been extensively edited.) Nevertheless, there is enough evidence in the early *Sutra* works like those of *Baudhāyana* and *Āswalāyana* that enables us to place them at the very beginning of the Harappan civilization, c. 3000 BC. This is also the date ascribed to them by tradition. (See Rajaram and Frawely 1994). Astronomically speaking, the Harappan civilization belongs to the Krittika period. S.R.Rao has identified at least one Harappan seal that suggests observations of the Krittika vernal equinox. Astronomical data in the *Sutra* literature admit no other conclusion.
4. To avoid any confusion it must be noted what Seidenberg (and I) have called '*Vedic* mathematics' has nothing to do with the famous monograph *Vedic Mathematics,* attributed to Sri Bharati Krishna Tirtha, the late

Sankaracharya of Puri, which is a posthumous work. The Swamiji's book is interesting, but a modern work not really germane to the history discussed in the present article. The '*Vedic* mathematics' referred to by Seidenberg is the mathematics of the *Sulbas*. For this reason I prefer the term 'mathematics of the *Sulbas*', but the other term is unfortunately too commonly used.

5. This may be inferred from the fact that the formulas used for the volume of the pyramid by the Egyptians and the Babylonians are different, while they both use the same approximation for $\sqrt{2}$. This approximation is derived by *Baudhāyana* in his *Sulba*. He also gives a formulas for the volume of the pyramid which is approximate but adequate for small pyramids. This suggests that the Babylonians did not derive their mathematics from the Egyptians as commonly thought, but directly from the Indians to the east, possibly via the Sumerians.

6. This raises some question about the currently accepted date of Buddha, 563-483 BC or alternatively, 623-543 BC. These are based on very questionable arguments to make them conform to some preconceived theories like the date of the Aryan invasion of India. (Later these dates so derived were used to derive the date of the invasion!) In light of the fiasco with the date of *Rig Veda,* the date of the Buddha must be treated as highly suspect and quite possibly wrong. 'All bets are off as regards the chronology of ancient India.'

7. Once we recognize the Harappan civilization to be of the *Sutra* period, it becomes impossible to support the popular c. 1400 BC date for the *Mahābhārata* War. *Sutra* authors like *Āswalāyana*, and *Yajnavalkya* of the *Satapatha Brahmana* show knowledge of the characters of the *Mahabharata*. Both of them (and *Baudhayana* also) must now be dated to c. 3000-2800 BC on the basis of mathematics, archaeology and astronomy. Astronomy of course overwhelmingly supports the traditional date of 3102 BC. This may also be taken as marking the date of the final reduction of the four *Vedas* by Vyasa and the approximate period of the transition to the *Sutra* period. The *Sutras* are intellectual works *par excellence.* The *Sutra* period, i.e., the Harappan era can now be seen to have been an age of great intellectual flowering.

8. Most readers will probably be surprised to see the *Sūtra* authors, especially *Panini* and *Patanjali* dated so early. Haven't Max Muller and others told us that *Panini* belonged to 400 BC and *Patanjali* came around 150 BC? But the same people also told us that the *Rig Veda* was composed around 1200 BC, a date which we now know is too late by some 2500 to 3500 years! *Sutra* works must be placed in the Harappan era. Further, nearly all authorities confuse *Patanjali* of the *Yogasutra* with the grammarian who wrote the *Mahābhāsya.* The latter is not a *Sutra* work. I have assumed that the whole chronology propounded by Western scholars and their Indian followers over the past century has been overthrown following the *Sūtra*-Harappan-Sumerian equation, and the chronology of the *Vedic*

Saraswati. The famous find known as Vasishtha's Head points to the same conclusion. Therefore, the dates given here have far greater empirical and scientific support, though they are by no means final or definitive.

9. This I believe makes it necessary to place the *Rig Vedic* period *before* the Harappan and not later as several including S.R. Rao have done. The centuries following the Harappan civilization must have experienced severe water shortages when the kind of society found described in the *Rig Veda* is hard to imagine. While I do concur with Rao's decipherment and also his conclusion that the language of the Harappan seals is related to Sanskrit, I find it impossible to accept that it is pre-*Vedic*. I find myself in agreement with S.S. Misra's analysis of the Indus script language showing it to be a much later Middle Indo-Aryan. This I believe confirms Rao's decipherment to be correct in essentials. S.S. Misra's *identification of the language as different from what Rao thought it to be ruled out the possibility that Rao has imposed his own preconceptions onto the seals.* He has avoided the trap that Father Heras fell into in the 1930's when he tried to read the language as some form of proto-Tamil. This is of major historical significance. I take Rao's reading of the Indus script to be a basic advance in our understanding of ancient India. I however, believe the language to be closer to Middle Indo-Aryan, related to the so-called 'Buddhist Hybrid Sanskrit', which, as Misra has pointed out is not a hybrid at all but a traditional Middle Indo-Aryan. This raises some interesting questions about the date of Buddhism. (See also Note 6 above.)

Bibliography

Sanskrit works cited

Rig Veda Samhitā

Nirukta (of Yaska)

Mahabharata, The

Taittiriya Samhitā (of the Yajurveda)

Vajasaneya Samhitā (of the Yajurveda)

Sulbasutra (of Baudhāyana)

References cited

Francfort, Paul-Henri (1992)

Evidence for Harappan irrigation system in Haryana and Rajasthan, Eastern *Anthropologist,* Vol.45

Hicks, H.H. and R.N. Anderson, 1990.

Analysis of an Indo-European *Vedic* Aryan Head—4th millennium B.C. *Journal of Indo-European Studies,* 18, 425-446.

Rajaram, N.S., 1994.

Language, mathematics and astronomy: a chronological synthesis for the *Vedic* Age. *International Journal of Indian Studies,* Vol.1 (January-June), 1994.

Rajaram, N.S. and David Frawley, 1994 (to appear).

Vedic Aryans and the origins of civilization: a literary and scientific perspective. World Heritage Press, Ottawa and New Delhi.

Rao. S.R. 1991.

Dawn and devolution of the Indus Civilization. Aditya Prakashan, New Delhi.

Seidenberg, A. 1962. The ritual origin of geometry, *Archive for History of Exact Sciences,* Vol. 1.

Seidenberg, A. 1978.

The Origin of mathematics, *Archive for history of exact sciences,* Vol. 18.

Sethna, K.D. 1981.

KARPĀSA in Prehistoric India; a chronological and cultural clue. Biblia Impex, New Delhi.

Stret-Perrott, F.A. and R.A. Perrott, 1990.

Reported in *Nature*, Vol.343.

Talageri, S. 1993.

Aryan invasion theory, a reappraisal. Aditya Prakashan, New Delhi.

Weiss, H.M.,A. Courty, W. Wetterstrom, F. Guichard, L. Senior. R. Meadow and A. Curnow. 1993.

The genesis and collapse of third millennium North Mesopotamian civilization. *Science,* Vol. 261. (August 20, 1993)

30

"Arya" in Sanskrit Literature

Dr. N.R. Waradpande*

Max Muller on an unlucky day used the word 'Aryan Race'. Thus arose truly, out of talk alone, an imaginary creature: *'Aryan Man'*.

— Dunn and Dobzansky, *Heredity, Race and Society*

Originally Max Muller used the words *'Aryan Race'* indicating that genetically the Aryans were a race with certain common genetic characteristics. He later changed this view and said that he does not regard the 'Aryans' a race in the genetic sense, but in the linguistic sense. The Aryans who invaded India spoke a language, from which Sanskrit is derived. He did not want to make any assertions about the genetic physical characteristics of the Aryans.

But Max Muller's subsequent amendment did not click. The word 'Aryan' continued to be used in the racial sense and the Aryan-invasionists generally assert that the invading Aryans were white, sharp-nosed and blond.

Meaning of "Arya"

This would not have mattered but for the fact that Max Muller used a word current in Sanskrit literature and gave it a meaning which it never had. This enabled him to create an impression that his Aryan man is not a creature of imagination but is widely referred to in ancient literature. This is by no means the case. That the "Arya" occurring in *Vedic* literature is altogether different from Max Muller's Aryan will be shown later. Not only in the *Vedic* literature, but also in classical Sanskrit, the word Arya is not used even in a single place to refer to a group of people, whether linguistic or racial. All through it is used as an adjective. *Amara Kosh* gives the following synonyms for "Arya": 1) of high family 2) a gentleman 3) good natured 4) righteous. The first meaning 'of high family' does not refer to race.

---

* A polymath, M.A. in Sanskrit & Philosophy, Ph. D. in Philosophy studied at Oxford, Served Government of India and retired as Chief Psychologist and Director of Psychological Research, A Portion from his "Aryan Invasion - A Myth" (Nagpur 1989) is reproduced.

The other meanings: 1) gentleman 2) good-natured 3) righteous etc. are clearly adjectives of an individual. No body would describe any society as a whole as gentle, good natured or righteous.

The *Sahitya-Darpana* gives the following rules about the use of the word Arya: 1) the actress and the manager in the play should address each other as Arya. 2) the elder, a *Brahmin*, and a minister should be addressed as 'Arya'.

Some readers may feel that the custom of addressing a *Brahmin* as Arya indicates that the word Arya refers to the *Brahmins* race. But it is absurd to suppose that a race can consist entirely of priests. The rule of addressing a *Brahmin* as Arya has to be interpreted in the light of other rules. The rules are about addressing individuals of certain categories. They do not show that Arya was a caste name.

The following verse is current as a definition of Arya:

> Arya is one who does what should be done, and never does what should not be done, and one who is never perverse.

Arya is often used like 'Sir' before the name of a person, and never after, e.g.. Arya Chanakya etc. I do not think anybody would be heroic enough to suggest that the word Sir is the name of a race.

The Aryan Invasion: A Myth

It may be argued that Max Muller may have been wrong in using an ancient word for signifying a linguistic or a racial group, but this by itself does not prove that there was no such group, i.e. the group may be called by some other name.

There certainly was a group of people, which spoke Sanskrit or its earlier form, the *Vedic* language, and this group could be called Arya, by stretching the ancient use of the term. But this does not suffice for Max Mullers's theory. According to his theory the Aryans spoke, not Sanskrit, but a language much more ancient than Sanskrit, a language from which Sanskrit and a host of other languages called Indo European are derived. It will be shown that this original Indo-European language is a figment of the imagination. Max Muller's use of Arya as a linguistic group is therefore not justifiable.

How far is this True?

It is frequently asserted that the *Rigveda* contains abundant references to the Aryan-non-Aryan conflict.

In order to answer this question, it is necessary to inquire what the word Arya occurring in the *Rigveda* means.

This word occurs in the *Rigveda* 36 times. Very often it is used as an adjective. In the places where it can be taken as a noun, it can not be shown to refer to any group of people.

In the following places it is used as an adjective-

> These white and Aryan Somas, by their stream of order, rts, shower wealth in the form of cows.(9/63/4)

Sayana takes *Aryah* which is nominative as *Aryanam* i.e. possessive and *Yajamananam* or of the sacrificer as understood. But this imposes too many changes in the text. There is nothing to prevent *Arya* being nominative as it stands as an adjective of Soma.

> Indra befriended Rjishva and plunged his chariot in the sky. Indra, the Arya, found an equal to the *Dasa*. He dispersed the *puras* of the deceptive aura Pipru (10/138/3/).

Here arya is an adjective of god Indra:

> Arya vows are bountiful. They spread in the world, elevate the sun, in the sky and create cow, land, horses, vegetation, mountains and water.(10/65/11)

Here arya is an adjective of vows:

In some cases the adjectives *Arya* is applied to the gods.

> Fire, wind and sun sprinkle semen in the three worlds. From that three Arya progenies came forth, the first being light. All three unite with the dawn. The Vasisthas know them all. (7/33/7)

Here one of the Arya progenies is light or Aditya according to Sayana.

The Meaning of *Varna*

Let us now consider the word used as a noun. Those who maintain that the Aryan race is mentioned in the *Rigveda* bank on the following hymn:

> Indra slayed the *dasyus* and protected the arya *varna*. He then gave horses, the sun, cows which are the sources of money, other enjoyments and land. (3/34/9)

Here the word *Varna* is translated as race, and the verse construed as referring to a victory of the Aryans over non-Aryans. But this construction is rendered absurd by the clear statement that the release of the sun was one of the results of this conflict. Is the sun a tennis-ball which the non-Aryans could steal and conceal in their pocket?

The word *Varna* occurs in other places also and since the word usually means colour, it makes the western scholars shout eureka. They take the word to refer to the colour of the skin and see a whiteblack conflict in the *Rigveda*. It is therefore necessary to discuss the meaning of the word in detail.

Sayana derives it from the root vr 'to choose' with the suffix n according to the Unadi rule 290. Similar formations are Karna from kr 'to do', 'jarna' for 'an old man' or 'an age-worn tree' from jr to 'age, sena i.e. 'army' from si 'to tie', drona i.e. container from dru 'to flow' 'panna' i.e. praise from pan 'to praise', anna i.e. 'food' from an 'to breathe' or that which enables one to breathe, and svapna i.e. 'dream' from svapa 'to sleep'.

In many of these formations, the suffix 'in' indicates agent. According to Sayana, in the world *varna*, it indicates causal agent. So the word *varna* comes to mean that which causes to choose. In the hymn 1/104/2 the word is used as an adjective of Indra, because Indra causes others to choose him by his remarkable qualities.

So *varna* means "distinguisher", a quality that marks out. The *Brahmana varna*, the *kshatriya varna*, therefore mean castes with distinct functions. So *arya varna* means the group of people performing the distinct functions like sacrifice etc. According to Max Muller the word Arya is derived from the root ar 'to til the soil'. In the *Rigveda* the people in general are called *Krishteeh* i.e. farmers. So the word *arya* seems to refer to the people whose means of livelihood was agriculture. The *Arya Varna* therefore means those whose occupation and distinguishing mark is agriculture.

The Colour of the *Dasas*

Though the word *Varna* does not mean race, it does mean colour and on this basis the western scholars render the phrase *Arya Varna* as Arya colour i.e., 'white colour' and thus bring back the idea that the Aryans were a white race. But no ancient literature states that the men to whom the word Arya is applied as an adjective were white in complexion. Escape is found from this difficulty in the colour of the *Dasas* which in some places is described as black and by implication, taking the colour of the Aryas to be white.

The following hymns are quoted in support of the view that the *dasas*, were black men.

> Indra protects the Arya sacrificer in battles *Svarmeedha*. For the sake of the humans, he punishes those who do not abide by *Vratas*. He flays the black skin. He kills all the killers. (1/130/8)

Here the word *Svarmeedha* is important. *Meedha* means 'sprinkled'. *Svarmeedha* battles are therefore battles which are sprinkled in heaven. So these battles are fought in heaven, not on this earth. Sayana suggests the meaning sprinklers of heaven i.e. heaven giving. But *Meedha* is a past participle, and rendering it as a noun signifying agent is a circumlocution. One could render the phrase as sprinkled for the sake of heaven. But even this involves some stretching. Battles are fought for winning, not for going to heaven. No doubt, it was supposed that those who are killed in battle go to heaven. But only the losers will describe their battles as heaven-going, not the victors. The composers of this hymn are victors, and not losers.

That *Svarmeedha Aji* means 'battle fought in heaven' is also clear from the immediately following statement that the *Avratas* were punished for the benefit of the entire mankind *'Manave'*, and not for the benefit of thc white alone, and that Indra burns all, not only the non Aryans.

That Indra killed the black *Asura* does not indicate that Krishna was a black non-Aryan. The following statement marks this clear:

> Krishna took refuge along with the 10000 in the Amshumati, the resplendent. The manly Indra seized the breathing one, and made him unstuck. (8/96/13)

Two facts are crucial; (1) Krishna was breathing inside water and (2) he was called Drapsa or drops a la Sayana. The 10000 others who took refuge with him were also obviously drops. Thus Krishna is clearly *not* a human being, and the hymn does not refer to any incident in human history.

The phenomenon referred to becomes obvious, if we bear in mind the role of Indra as god of rain, and that the phenomenon has taken place in heaven. The Krishna concealed in the Amshumati i.e. possessor of rays is the cloud with a silver lining. He had blocked thousands of drapsas i.e. drops to prevent rain. Indra snapped these bonds and bought rain.

Not a Human Skin

That black skin in the *Rigveda* refers quite often to the colour of the cloud or the night and not of human beings can be seen by various examples.

> The rays of the moon, burning the ritualless, pure in lustre, fill heaven and earth like a note and peel the black skin of the night. (9/73/5).

Here the peeler of the black skin is not an Aryan man, nor is the peeled a non Aryan. The peeling of the black skin refers to the dispelling of the darkness.

> These lustrous somas dispel the black skin, speedily like cows or speech. (9/41/1)

This is the description of *soma*, and this by itself makes unlikely any reference to the black skin of the non-Aryans and a conflict with them. Sayana renders the black skin here as the bark of the *soma* shoot. But no clear indication is available anywhere that the *soma* shoot was black.

Besides, *soma*-juice, which falls drop by drop, can hardly be described as flowing like cows or sheep.

The meaning becomes unmistakable, if we construe *soma* as moon and not as the *soma* plant, *Gavah* means 'rays' and not 'cow'. "Moonlight, fast like sound with its rays is destroying the black skin i.e. darkness of the night," is then what the hymn wants to convey. The phrase *Tvachmstknim* skin of the night in 9/73/5 corroborates this interpretation.

The Black India and the Black Aryans

A further corroboration is found in the description of Indra himself, the Aryan par excellence, as black in 4/17/14. This knocks the bottom of the whole black-non-back conflict. Sayana describes the allusion thus:

> There was a king called *Svashva.* He invoked the sun for getting a son. As a result the sun itself took birth as a son of Svashva. Late this son of Svashva was involved in hostilities against the sage Etash. Etash then prayed to Indra for protection. Thereupon Indra saved Etash.

Sayana construes the meaning of the hymn thus:

> Indra actuated the wheel-weapon of the sun. He restrained Etash who rushed for battle. The black cloud moving in serpentine ways protected Indra in the abode of water.

This interpretation is incongruous with the allusion given by Sayana himself. Indra who is said to have answered the prayer of Etash has restrained him instead of leading him to victory. After restraining Etash, from whom did the cloud protect Indra? It is strange that the almighty Indra, to whom the hymn-makers look for protection, was himself protected by the cloud, when there was no calamity befalling him. Moreover, no cloud is mentioned in the hymn. Wherefrom has Sayana brought it? Sayana's interpretation therefore cannot be accepted.

The hymn makes the following straightforward sense-

> This Indra actuated the wheel of the sun. He restrained the let loose Etash, this black one, moving in the skinbase which is the birth place of this region, brings rains.

The word *Tvak* 'skin' in this hymn is important. Sayana translates it as light, without quoting any basis. *Budhna* means base, Rajas stands for region i.e. heaven, earth etc. *Yoni* is source. So the skin-base is the source of the region(s). The skin, which is the source of the heaven and earth, can only be space. The *Krishna* is the Indra in the form of the cloud who controlled the intractable horse of the sun and brought rain. The reference is clearly to the black clouds, which engulf the sun.

Indra was a god and therefore he is credited with activating the wheel of the sun. He restrained the horse of the sun, means that he restrained the growing heat of the summer sun and brought rain. This is the description of the advent of the rainy season.

The Black Aryans

The word *Krishna* is used in a laudatory sense in the *Rigveda* in other places also:

> This auspicious fire has come with the auspicious dawn. The brother is following the sister or the lover is following his beloved dawn. He presents himself with clear and lustrous colours to the *Abhirama.* (10/3/3)

According to Sayana, *Abhirama* refers to the dark colour of the night. *Rama* means pleasing. This is reminiscent of the taste of the *Ramayana* and the *Mahabharata* describing Rama, Krishna and Draupadi as emblems of black beauty. This is diametrically opposite to the hatred of the black race, which western scholars try to foist on the *Rigveda.*

Some may charge Sayana of inserting the word black, when the text, as it stands, only uses *Abhirama* which does not mean black. But this charge does not stand. The last verse describes fire as peripateting between the two ladies: the sky and the earth. This can only refer to the sun. "The sun came with the auspicious dawn and by and by dispelled the darkness" is what the hymn is saying. If the word *Abhirama* is not translated as darkness, the hymn makes no sense.

That the hymn-makers were not haters of the black race is proved by the fact that many of them were themselves black. 1/17/7 states that the *Ashvins* restored the son of Krishna named Vishvaka. So the propitiators of the *Vedic* deities were fathered by the blacks.

In 10/31/11 Kanva is called the son of *Nrshada*:

> He, the dark *Shyama,* obtained wealth from the fire. The fire bestowed the lustrous *RTA* on the black *Kanva.*

Here the word *Shyam* i.e. 'dark' and the word *Krishna* i.e. black are used for *Kanva* in a laudatory sense.

There is one Krishna Angiras among the hymn-makers. 8/85/87 and 10/42/43 are composed by him. If Krishnasura is inferred to be black from his name, Krishna Angirasa also should be taken to be black. *Aitareya Brahmana* 3/34 states that the Angirasas were born of coal.

The *Vasisthas* are described as white. If all they hymn-makers were white, there was no point in signalling out *Vasistha* as white. This description makes it clear that the hymn-makers were of a mixed complexion, like the present day Indians.

Not only were the hymn-makers not white; the white complexion held no fascination for them. "With the blessings of Tvashtru let our offspring be tawny" says 2/3/9. The word *PISHANGA* is translated as tawny in English. Tawny is yellowish brown like wheat or reddish brown like snuff. The Meheshvari on the *Amarakosha* gives the meaning 'red mixed with black', which is the same as reddish brown. In any case *PISHANGA* is brown, the complexion of the majority of Indians today. The reason for praying for this complexion is that many of the *Vedics* like *Vashistha* were white and others like *Kanva* were black, without a tinge of red. These types were not sought after.

31

The Myth of the Aryan Invasion of India

David Frawley*

One of the main ideas used to interpret and generally devalue—the ancient history of India is the theory of the Aryan Invasion. According to this account, India was invaded and conquered by nomadic light-skinned Indo-European tribes from Central Asia around 1500-1000 BC, who overthrew an earlier and more advanced dark-skinned Dravidian civilization from which they took most of what later became Hindu culture. This so-called pre-Aryan civilization is said to be evidenced by the large urban ruins of what has been called the "Indus Valley culture" (as most of its initial sites were on the Indus river). The war between the powers of light and darkness, a prevalent idea in the ancient Aryan *Vedic* scriptures, was thus interpreted to refer to this war between light and dark-skinned peoples. The Aryan invasion theory thus turned the *Vedas*, the original scriptures of ancient India and the Indo-Aryans, into little more than primitive poems of uncivilized plunderers.

This idea—totally foreign to the history of India, whether north or south, has become almost an unquestioned truth in the interpretation of ancient history. Today, after nearly all the reasons for its supposed validity have been refuted, even major Western scholars are at last beginning to call it into question.

Pre-Vedic Indus Civilization

The Indus Valley culture was pronounced pre-Aryan for several reasons that were largely part of the cultural milieu of nineteenth century European thinking. As scholars following Max Muller had decided that the Aryans came into India around 1500 BC, since the Indus Valley culture was earlier than this, they concluded that it had to be pre-Aryan. Yet the rationale behind the late date for the *Vedic* culture given by Muller was totally speculative. Max Muller, like many of the Christian

---

* Young American researcher in Indian spiritual and literary tradition; recognised as *Vedacharya*; author of many books on *Vedic* knowledge and history.

scholars of his era, believed in Biblical chronology. This placed the beginning of the world at 400 BC and the flood around 2500 BC. Assuming those two dates, it became difficult to get the Aryans in India before 1500 BC.

Muller therefore assumed that the five layers of the four *Vedas* and *Upanishads* were each composed in two hundred year periods before the Buddha at 500 BC. However, there are more changes of language in *Vedic* Sanskrit itself than there are in classical Sanskrit since *Panini*, also regarded as a figure of around 500 BC, or a period of 2500 years. Hence it is clear that each of these periods could have existed for any number of centuries and that the two hundred year figure is totally arbitrary and is likely too short a figure.

Christian-missionary Bias

It was assumed by these scholars, many of whom were also Christian missionaries unsympathetic to the *Vedas*, that the *Vedic* culture was that of primitive nomads from Central Asia. Hence they could not have founded any urban culture like that of the Indus Valley. The only basis for this was a rather questionable interpretation of the *Rig Veda* that they made, ignoring the sophisticated nature of the culture presented within it.

Meanwhile, it was also pointed out that in the middle of the second millennium BC, a number of Indo-European invasions apparently occurred in the Middle East, wherein Indo-European peoples—the Hittites, Mittani and Kassites—conquered and ruled Mesopotamia for some centuries. An Aryan invasion of India would have been another version of this same movement of Indo-European peoples. On top of this, excavators of the Indus Valley culture, like Wheeler, thought they found evidence of destruction of the culture by an outside invasion confirming this.

The *Vedic* culture was thus said to be that of primitive nomads who came out of Central Asia with their horse-drawn chariots and iron weapons and overthrew the cities of the more advanced Indus Valley culture, with their superior battle tactics. It was pointed out that no horses, chariots or iron were discovered in Indus Valley sites.

This was how the Aryan invasion theory formed and has remained since then. Though little has been discovered that confirms this theory, there has been much hesitancy to question it, much less to give it up.

Further excavations discovered horses not only in the Indus Valley sites but also in pre-Indus sites. The use of the horse has thus been proven for the whole range of ancient Indian history. Evidence of the wheel, and an Indus seal showing a spoked wheel as used in chariots, has also been found, suggesting the usage of chariots.

Moreover, the whole idea of nomads with chariots has been challenged. Chariots are not the vehicles of nomads. Their usage occurred only in ancient urban cultures with much flat land, of which the river plain of north India was the most suitable. Chariots are totally unsuitable for crossing mountains and deserts, as the so-called Aryan invasion required.

Rigvedic Evidence

That the *Vedic* culture used iron and must hence date later than the introduction of iron around 1500 BC revolves around the meaning of the *Vedic* term '*ayas*" interpreted as iron. *Ayas* in other Indo-European languages like Latin or German usually means copper, bronze ore generally, not specifically iron. There is no reason to insist that in such earlier *Vedic* times, *ayas* meant iron, particularly since other metals are not mentioned in the *Rig Veda* (except gold that is much more commonly referred to than ayas). Moreover, the *Atharva Veda* and *Yajur Veda* speak of different colours of *ayas* (such as red and black), showing that it was a generic term. Hence it is clear that *ayas* generally meant metal and not specifically iron.

Moreover, the enemies of the *Vedic* people in the *Rig Veda* also use *ayas,* even for making their cities, as do the *Vedic* people themselves. Hence there is nothing in *Vedic* literature to show that either the *Vedic* culture was an iron-based culture or that their enemies' was not.

The *Rig Veda* describes its gods as "destroyers of cities". This was used also to regard the *Vedic* as a primitive non-urban culture that destroys cities and urban civilization. However, there are also many verses in the *Rig Veda* that speak of the Aryans as having cities of their own and being protected by cities up to a hundred in number. Aryan Gods like Indra, Agni, Saraswati and the Adityas are praised as being like a city. Many ancient kings, including those of Egypt and Mesopotamia, had titles like destroyer or conqueror of cities. This does not turn them into nomads. Destruction of cities also happens in modern wars; this does not make those who do this nomads. Hence the idea of the *Vedic* culture as destroying but not building cities is based upon ignoring what *Vedas* actually say about their own cities.

Further excavation revealed that the Indus Valley culture was not destroyed by outside invasion, but according to internal causes and, most likely, floods. Most recently a new set of cities has been found in India (like the *Dwaraka* and *Bet Dwaraka* sites by S.R. Rao and the National Institute of Oceanography in India) which are intermediate between those of the Indus culture and later ancient India as visited by the Greeks. This may eliminate the so-called dark age following the presumed Aryan invasion and shows continuous urban occupation in India back to the beginning of the Indus culture.

The interpretation of the religion of the Indus Valley—made incidentally by scholars such as Wheeler who were not religious scholars much less students of Hinduism—was that its religion was different than the *Vedic* and more likely the later Shaivite religion. Hence it was thought by them to be a kind of early Dravidian Shaivite religion. However, further excavations—both in Indus Valley sites in Gujarat, like Lothal, and those in Rajasthan, like Kalibangan—show large number of fire altars like those used in the *Vedic* religion, along with bones of oxen, potsherds, shell jewelry and other items used in the rituals descried in the *Vedic Brahmanas.* Hence the Indus Valley culture evidences many *Vedic* practices that cannot be merely coincidental. That some of its practices appeared non-*Vedic* to its excavators may also be attributed to their misunderstanding or lack of knowledge of *Vedic* and Hindu culture generally, wherein *Vedism* and *Shaivism* are the same basic tradition.

We must remember that ruins do not necessarily have one interpretation. Nor does the ability to discover ruins necessarily give the ability to interpret them correctly.

Racial Theory

The *Vedic* people were thought to have been a fair-skinned race like the Europeans owing to the *Vedic* idea of a war between light and darkness, and the *Vedic* people being presented as children of the light or children of the sun. Yet this idea of a war between light and darkness exists in most ancient cultures, including the Persian and the Egyptian. Why don't we interpret their scripture as a war between light and dark-skinned people? It is purely a poetic metaphor, not a cultural statement. Moreover, no real traces of such a race are found in India. Anthropologists have observed that the present population of Gujarat is composed of more or less the same ethnic groups as are noticed at Lothal in 2000 BC. Similarly, the present population of the Punjab is said to be ethnically the same as the population of Harappa and Rupar four thousand years ago. Linguistically, the present-day population of Gujarat and Punjab belongs to the Indo-Aryan language-speaking group. The only inference that can be drawn from the anthropological and linguistic evidences adduced above is that the Harappan population in the Indus Valley and Gujarat in 2000 BC was composed of two or more groups, the more dominant among them having very close ethnic affinities with the present day Indo-Aryan speaking population of India.

In other words, there is no racial evidence of any such Indo-Aryan invasion of India but only of a continuity of the same group of people who traditionally considered themselves to be Aryans.

There are many points in fact that prove the *Vedic* nature of Indus Valley culture. Further excavation have shown that the great majority of the sites of the Indus Valley culture were east, not west of Indus. In fact, the largest concentration of sites appears in an area of Punjab and Rajasthan near the dry banks of the ancient Saraswati and Drishadvati rivers. The *Vedic* culture was said to have been founded by the sage Manu between the banks of the Saraswati and Drishadvati rivers. The Saraswati is lauded as the main river (naditama) in the *Rig Veda* and is the most frequently mentioned in the text. It is said to be a great flood and to be wide, even endless in size. Saraswati is said to be "pure in her course from the mountains to the sea". Hence the *Vedic* people were well-acquainted with this river and regarded it as their immemorial homeland.

The Saraswati, as modern land studies now reveal, was indeed one of the largest, if not the largest river in India. In early ancient and prehistoric times, it once drained the Sutlej, Yamuna and the Ganges, whose course were much different than they are today. However, the Saraswati river went dry by the end of the Indus Valley culture and before the so-called Aryan invasion or before 1500 BC. In fact this may have caused the ending of the Indus culture. How could the *Vedic* Aryans know of this river and establish their culture on its banks if it dried up before they arrived? Indeed the Saraswati as described in the *Rig Veda* appears to more accurately show it as it was prior to the Indus Valley culture as in the Indus era it was already in decline.

Astronomical Data

Vedic and late *Vedic* texts also contain interesting astronomical lore. The *Vedic* calender was based upon astronomical sightings of the equinoxes and solstices. Such texts as *Vedanga Jyotish* speak of a time when the vernal equinox was in the middle of the *Nakshatra* Aslesha (or about 23 degrees 20 minutes Cancer). This gives a date of 1300 BC. Many *Brahamanas,* and the *Yajur* and *Atharva Vedas* speak of the vernal equinox in the Krittikas (*Pleiades; early Taurus*) and the summer solstice (*ayana*) in *Magha* (*early Leo*). This gives a date of about 2400 BC. Yet earlier eras are mentioned but these two have numerous references to substantiate them. They prove that the *Vedic* culture existed at these periods and already had a sophisticated system of astronomy. Such references were merely ignored or pronounced unintelligible by Western scholars because they yielded too early a date for the *Vedas* than what they presumed, not because such references did not exist.

Vedic texts like *Shatapatha Brahmana* and *Aitereya Brahmana* of eleven *Vedic* kings, include a number of figures of the *Rig Veda,* said to have conquered the region of India from "sea to sea". Lands of the Aryans mentioned in them are from Gandhara (Afghanistan) in the west to Videha (Nepal) in the east, and south to Vidarbha (Maharashtra). Hence the *Vedic* people were in these regions by the Krittika equinox or before 2400 BC. These passages were also ignored by Western scholars, and it was said by them that the *Vedas* had no evidence of large empires in India in *Vedic* times. Hence a pattern of ignoring literary evidence or misinterpreting it to suit the Aryan invasion idea became prevalent, even to the point of changing the meaning of *Vedic* words to suit this theory.

Vedic Culture not Nomadic

According to this theory, the *Vedic* people were nomads in the Punjab, coming down from Central Asia. However, the *Rig Veda* itself has nearly a hundred references to ocean (samudra), as well as dozens of references to ships, and to rivers flowing into the sea. *Vedic* ancestors like Manu, Turvasha, Yadu and Bhujyu are flood figures, saved from across the sea. The *Vedic* God of the sea, Varuna, is the father of many *Vedic* seers and seer families like Vasistha, Agastya and the Bhrigu seers. To preserve the Aryan invasion idea it was assumed that the *Vedic* (and later Sanskrit) term for ocean, *samudra*, originally did not mean ocean but any large body of water, especially the Indus river in the Punjab. Here the clear meaning of a term in the *Rig Veda* and later times—verified by rivers like Saraswati mentioned by name as flowing into the sea—was altered to make the Aryan invasion theory fit. Yet if we look at the index to translation of the *Rig Veda* by Griffith, for example, who held to this idea that *samudra* did not really mean the ocean, we find over seventy references to ocean or sea. If *samudra* does not mean ocean why was it still translated as such? It is therefore without basis to locate *Vedic* kings in Central Asia far from any ocean or from the massive Saraswati river, which formed the background of their land and the symbolism of their hymns.

One of the latest archaeological ideas is that the *Vedic* culture is evidenced by Painted Grey Ware pottery in north India, which appears to date around 1000 BC and comes from the same region between the Ganges and Yamuna as later *Vedic* culture is related to. It is thought to be an inferior grade of pottery and to be associated with the use of iron that the *Vedas* are thought to mention. However, it is associated with a pig and rice culture, not the cow and barley culture or the *Vedas*. Moreover, it is now found to be an organic development of indigenous pottery, not an introduction of invaders.

Painted Grey Ware culture represents an indigenous cultural development and does not reflect any cultural intrusion from the west, that is, an Indo-Aryan invasion. Therefore, there is no archaeological evidence corroborating the fact of an Indo-Aryan invasion.

In addition, Aryans in the Middle East, most notably the Hittites, have now been found to have been in that region at least as early as 2200 BC, wherein they are already mentioned. Hence the idea of an Aryan invasion into the Middle East has been pushed back some centuries, though the evidence so far is that the people of the mountain regions of the Middle East were Indo-Europeans as far as recorded history can prove.

The Aryan Kassites of the ancient Middle East worshipped *Vedic* Gods like Surya and the Maruts, as well as one name Himalaya. The Aryan Hitties and Mittani signed a treaty with the name of the *Vedic* Gods Indra, Mitra, Varuna and Nasatyas around 1400 BC. the Hittites have a treatise on chariot-racing written in almost pure Sanskrit.

The Indo-Europeans of the ancient Middle East thus spoke Indo-Aryan, not Indo-Iranian languages and thereby show a *Vedic* culture in that region of the world as well.

The Indus Valley culture had a form of writing, as evidenced by numerous seals found in the ruins. It was also assumed to be non-*Vedic* and probably Dravidian, though this was never proved. Now it has been shown that the majority of the late Indus signs are identical with those of later Hindu Brahmi and that there is an organic development between the two scripts. Prevalent models now suggest an Indo-European base for that language.

Mehrgarh Excavations

It was also assumed that the Indus Valley culture derived its civilization from Middle East, probably Sumeria, as antecedents for it were not found in India. Recent French excavations at Mehrgarh have shown that all the antecedents of the Indus valley culture can be found within the subcontinent and going back before 6000 BC.

In short, some Western scholars are beginning to reject the Aryan invasion or any outside origin for Hindu civilization:

> Current archaeological data do not support the existence of an Indo-European invasion into south Asia at any time in the pre-or-protohistoric periods. Instead, it is possible to document archaeologically a series of cultural changes reflecting indigenous cultural development from prehistoric to historic periods. The early *Vedic* literature describes not a human invasion into area, but a fundamental restructuring of indigenous society. The Indo-Aryan invasion as an academic concept in eighteenth and nineteenth century Europe reflected the cultural millieu of the period. Linguistic data were used to validate the concept that in turn was used to interpret archaeological and anthropological data.

In other words *Vedic* literature was interpreted on the assumption that there was an Aryan invasion. Then archaeological evidence was interpreted by the same assumption. And both interpretations were then used to justify each other. It is nothing but a tautology, an exercise in circular thinking that only proves that if assuming something is true, it is found to be true!

Another modern Western scholar, Colin Renfrew, places the Indo-Europeans in Greece as early as 6000 BC. He also suggests such a possible early date for their entry into India:

As far as I can see there is nothing in the Hymns of the *Rig Veda* which demonstrates that the *Vedic*-speaking population were intrusive to the area: this comes rather from a historical assumption of the coming of the Indo-Europeans.

Mortimer Wheeler's Conjectures

When Wheeler speaks of the Aryan invasion of the Land of the Seven Rivers, the Punjab, he has no warranty at all, so far as I can see. If one checks the dozen references in the *Rig Veda* to the Seven Rivers, there is nothing in them that to me implies an invasion: the land of the Seven Rivers is the land of the *Rig Veda,* the scene of action. Nor is it implied that the inhabitants of the walled cities (including the *Dasyus*) were any more aboriginal than the Aryans themselves.

Despite Wheeler's comments, it is difficult to see what is particularly non-Aryan even prior to the Indus Valley civilization.

Hence Renfrew suggests that the Indus Valley civilization was in fact Indo-Aryan even prior to the Indus Valley era:

> This hypothesis that early Indo-European languages were spoken in north India with Pakistan and on the Iranian plateau at the sixth millennium BC has the merit of harmonizing symmetrically with the theory for the origin of the Indo-European languages in Europe. It also emphasizes the continuity in the Indus Valley and adjacent areas from the early neolithic through to the floruit of the Indus Valley civilization.

This is not to say that such scholars appreciate or understand the *Vedas*—their work leaves much to be desired in this respect-but it is clear that the whole edifice built around the Aryan invasion is beginning to tumble on all sides.

In addition, it does not mean that the *Rig Veda* dates from the Indus Valley era. The Indus Valley culture resembles that of the *Yajur Veda* and the *Brahmanas,* or the later *Vedic* era. If anything the *Rig Veda* appears to reflect the pre-Indus period in India, when the Saraswati river was more prominent.

The acceptance of such views would create a revolution in our view of history as shattering as that in science caused by Einstein's theory of relativity. It would make ancient India perhaps the oldest, largest and most central of ancient cultures. It would mean that the *Vedic* literary record—already the largest and oldest of the ancient world even at a 1500 BC date—would be the record of teachings some centuries or thousands of years before that. It would mean that the *Vedas* are our most authentic record of the ancient world. It would also tend to validate the *Vedic* view that the Indo-Europeans and other Aryan peoples were migrants from India, not that the Indo-Aryans were invaders into India. Moreover, it would affirm the Hindu tradition that the Dravidians were early offshoots of the *Vedic* people through the seer Agastya, and not un-aryan peoples.

Socio-political Implications of Aryan Theory

In closing, it is important to examine the social and political implications of the Aryan invasion idea:

First, it served to divide India into a northern Aryan and southern Dravidian culture which were made hostile to each other. This kept the Hindus divided and is still a source of social tension.

Second, it gave the British an excuse in their conquest of India. They could claim to be doing only what the Aryan ancestors of the Hindus had previously done millennia ago.

Third, it served to make *Vedic* culture later than and possibly derived from Middle Eastern cultures. With the proximity and relationship of the latter with the Bible and Christianity, this kept the Hindu religion as a sidelight to the development of religion and civilization in the west.

Fourth, it allowed the sciences of India to be given a Greek basis, as any *Vedic* basis was largely disqualified by the primitive nature of the *Vedic* culture.

This discredited not only the *Vedas* but the genealogies of the *Puranas* and their long lists of kings before the Buddha or Krishna were left without any historical basis. The *Mahabharata,* instead of a civil war in which all the main kings of India participated as it is described, became a local skirmish among petty princes that was later exaggerated by poets. In short, it discredited most of the Hindu tradition and almost all its ancient literature. It turned its scriptures and sages into fantasies and exaggerations.

This served the social, political and economic purpose of domination, proving the superiority of Western culture and religion. It made the Hindus feel that their culture was not the great thing that their sages and ancestors had said it was. It made Hindus feel ashamed of their culture—that its basis was neither historical nor scientific. It made them feel that the main line of civilization was developed first in the Middle East and then in Europe and that the culture of India was peripheral and secondary to the real development of world culture.

Such a view is not good scholarship or archaeology but merely cultural imperialism. The Western *Vedic* scholars did in the intellectual sphere what the British army did in the political realm—discredit, divide and conquer the Hindus.

In short, the compelling reasons for the Aryan invasion theory were neither literary or archaeological but political and religious—that is to say, not scholarship but prejudice. Such prejudice may not have been intentional but deep-seated political and religious views easily cloud and blur our thinking.

Time to Reject

It is unfortunate that this approach has not been questioned more, particularly by Hindus. Even though Indian *Vedic* scholars like Dayananda Saraswati, Tilak and Aurobindo rejected it, most Hindus today passively accept it. They allow Western, generally Christian, scholars to interpret their history for them and quite naturally Hinduism is kept in a reduced role. Many Hindus still accept, read or even honour the translations of the *Vedas* done by such Christian missionary scholars as Muller, Griffith, Monier-Williams and H.H. Wilson. Would modern Christians accept an interpretation of the Bible or Biblical history done by Hindus aimed at converting them to Hinduism? Universities in India also use the Western history books and Western *Vedic* translations that propound such views that denigrate their own culture and country.

The modern Western academic world is sensitive to criticisms of cultural and social biases. For scholars to take a stand against this biased interpretation of the *Vedas* would indeed cause a re-examination of many of these historical ideas that cannot stand objective scrutiny. But if Hindu scholars are silent or passively accept the misinterpretation of their culture, it will undoubtedly continue, but they will have no one to blame but themselves. It is not an issue to be taken lightly, because how a culture is defined historically creates the perspective from which it is viewed in the modern social and intellectual context. Tolerance is not in allowing a false view of one's own culture and religion to be propagated without question. That is merely self-betrayal.

The End